Kings as Judges

How did representative institutions become the central organs of governance in Western Europe? What enabled this distinctive form of political organization and collective action that has proved so durable and influential? The answer has typically been sought either in the realm of ideas, in the Western tradition of individual rights, or in material change, especially the complex interaction of war, taxes, and economic growth. Common to these strands is the belief that representation resulted from weak ruling powers needing to concede rights to powerful social groups. Boucoyannis argues instead that representative institutions were a product of state strength, specifically the capacity to deliver justice across social groups. Enduring and inclusive representative parliaments formed when rulers could exercise power over the most powerful actors in the land and compel them to serve and, especially, to tax them. The language of rights deemed distinctive to the West emerged in response to more effectively imposed collective obligations, especially on those with most power.

Deborah Boucoyannis teaches Comparative Politics at George Washington University. This book is based on a dissertation that received the American Political Science Association's Ernst Haas Best Dissertation Award in European Politics and the Seymour Martin Lipset Best Dissertation Award from the Society for Comparative Research. She has published in *Perspectives on Politics, Politics and Society*, and other journals.

Kings as Judges

Power, Justice, and the Origins of Parliaments

Deborah Boucoyannis

George Washington University

CAMBRIDGE
UNIVERSITY PRESS

CAMBRIDGE
UNIVERSITY PRESS

Shaftesbury Road, Cambridge CB2 8EA, United Kingdom

One Liberty Plaza, 20th Floor, New York, NY 10006, USA

477 Williamstown Road, Port Melbourne, VIC 3207, Australia

314–321, 3rd Floor, Plot 3, Splendor Forum, Jasola District Centre, New Delhi – 110025, India

103 Penang Road, #05–06/07, Visioncrest Commercial, Singapore 238467

Cambridge University Press is part of Cambridge University Press & Assessment, a department of the University of Cambridge.

We share the University's mission to contribute to society through the pursuit of education, learning and research at the highest international levels of excellence.

www.cambridge.org
Information on this title: www.cambridge.org/9781316614969

DOI: 10.1017/9781316678367

First published 2021
First paperback edition 2023

A catalogue record for this publication is available from the British Library

ISBN   978-1-107-16279-2   Hardback
ISBN   978-1-316-61496-9   Paperback

Cambridge University Press & Assessment has no responsibility for the persistence or accuracy of URLs for external or third-party internet websites referred to in this publication and does not guarantee that any content on such websites is, or will remain, accurate or appropriate.

Contents

Figures

Tables

Preface and Acknowledgments

This book grew out of a long-standing preoccupation with the problem of reconciling Western liberalism with cultures, such as that of (even) Greece where I grew up, that had markedly different historical traditions, political behaviors, and social organization. Most available answers invoked traits that the West developed but seemed absent elsewhere – especially the vaunted tradition of individual rights but also, within social science, more materialist theories involving primarily taxation. There were many puzzling elements to these answers, not least that demands for rights were hardly absent elsewhere and neither were the bargaining games so preoccupying social science; to the contrary. Even more puzzling, however, was why such traditions had emerged in the West and, especially, England in the first place. They were commonly taken as a natural given, part of its native intellectual flora so to speak, but this begged the question. Solving this puzzle led to a journey in history and political theory to understand the origins of liberalism and of constitutional practices, the products of which are encapsulated in this book.

Its main conclusion is that much of the conventional narrative about the West is predicated on some misleading premises. Many key arguments need not only to be revised but often reversed. In what I call the normative/empirical inversion, the West, and especially England, did not distinguish itself by having stronger conceptions of rights (contrasted with other cultures' seeming predilection for authoritarianism) nor by a more strident and assertive commercial class that somehow "naturally" demanded, hundreds of years ago, rights that we scarcely ever see their contemporary counterparts demanding. Nor was war itself somehow more consequential in the West. Rather, the West, and England especially, differed initially by having central authorities that could more effectively impose collective obligations particularly on the most powerful; demands for rights were the response. As the West has long imposed its understanding of the world on others and modeled development theory on it, it is important for that understanding to be soundly based in history. The book thus attempts to reduce the distance between the historical record and the social science that engages it. Further, at a time when authoritarian governance is spreading across regions, it is vital to differentiate the type of strong state capacity that can steer society to more equitable and productive outcomes.

This project has been long in the making and has accumulated a large number of intellectual debts. Foremost is the debt to historians: without their remarkable and often humbling generosity, it would literally have been impossible. Historians divide in how they treat comparative works with a broad theorizing bent (some consider such projects a fool's errand), and I was lucky to find a substantial number who were sympathetic, some even extending what amounted to private tutorials to answer my questions. I can only apologize that the final product merely scratches the surface of the historical complexity they tried to convey. Brief exchanges with Robert Bartlett, John Brewer, and John Maddicott early on suggested that my argument about the English Parliament had a sound historical basis. Maddicott's major statement on the English Parliament especially offered indispensable guidance. Then a series of scholars (none of whom are responsible for the generalizations and inevitable simplifications that any such work entails) gave priceless advice as I navigated the complex and often poorly documented histories of fifteen countries over multiple centuries. John Hudson, who read the manuscript twice, offered invaluable correctives as I trod the treacherous grounds of the common law, though I may not, since then, have escaped more pitfalls. Mark Ormrod offered unstintingly generous advice at crucial points over the years, while his work informed many aspects of the book. Equally generous exchanges with Mark Bailey transformed some key claims. Gwilym Dodd's careful comments on the English material greatly improved the argument's precision, whilst Phil Bradford, Paul Brand, Alex Brayson, Peter Coss, Anne Curry, Neil Jones, and Andrew Spencer answered often seemingly small but critical questions. Caroline Burt and Richard Partington took time to expand my understanding of English dynamics. Steven Gunn gave very helpful feedback on military and fiscal data. Especially important was Thomas Bisson's early and generous guidance on many aspects of the book, even if it does not meet the conceptual challenge he set with his work.

My argument acquired its final form by engaging with the Russian and Ottoman cases. The work and feedback of Russian historians Valerie Kivelson, Ann Kleimola, and Nancy Kollmann were catalytic, whilst Dan Kaiser kindly answered key questions. Equally so, the Ottomanist Colin Imber gave crucial and early generous advice to the critical argument in Chapter 11, whilst Linda Darling offered vital correctives to my claims. Atçıl Abdurrahman, Cornel Fleischer, Evgenia Kermeli, Timur

Kuran, and Kaya Şahin also either generously commented on the chapter or answered questions. Paul Freedman gave repeated feedback on Catalonia, as did Teo Ruiz on Castile, while Adam Kosto probed the historical logic and Phil Daileader commented. Martyn Rady's successive feedback and work were vital on Hungary, as was that of Jan Dumolyn and Jaco Zuijderduijn on the Low Countries. Edward Coleman and especially Michael Martoccio gave salutary clarifications and comments on Italy. Justine Firnhaber-Baker alerted me to a crucial source from France. Last but far from least, economic historians Mauricio Drelichman and Kıvanç Karaman gave truly indefatigable feedback and guidance on historical data, as did Bas van Leeuwen. Bruce Campbell and Mark Dincecco also offered important advice. Most of these scholars did not know me personally yet they offered a model of disinterested academic exchange and generosity. The usual caveats apply.

Among social scientists, the greatest debt is to David Stasavage, who remained steadfast in his support right through to publication, as did John Hall. Sheri Berman and Markus Kurtz offered vital feedback and support, especially at a book workshop funded by the University of Virginia. Carles Boix and Jacob Levy gave crucial support to the project in its dissertation stage, as did Lisa Wedeen's and Alex Wendt's sharp critical skills very early on. The argument was born in the comparative seminars of David Laitin and John Padgett, who also raised the methodological bar that "qualitative" work such as this had to meet. Amel Ahmed, Ana Arjona, Cathy Boone, David Ciepley, Tim Crawford, John Echeverri-Gent, Thomas Ertman, Robert Fannion, Venelin Ganev, Arthur Goldhammer, Phil Gorski, Anna Grzymala-Busse, Steve Hanson, Yoshiko Herrera, Jacques Hymans, Jeff Kopstein, Andrew Kydd, Daniel Lee, Allen Lynch, Kate McNamara, Luis Medina, Carol Mershon, Kimberly Morgan, Víctor Muniz-Fraticelli, John Owen, Pasquale Pasquino, Andrew Schrank, Jonah Schulhofer-Wohl, Herman Schwartz, Rudy Sil, Dan Slater, Ronald Suny, Kathy Thelen, Edgar Franco Vivanco, Denise Walsh, David Woodruff, and Daniel Ziblatt commented at different stages on various parts of the manuscript, as did the anonymous reviewers. Kevin Narizny gave detailed and incisive comments on multiple chapters and drafts. Matt Kocher's early challenge on the Ottoman Empire spurred, in my eyes, one of the most creative chapters in the book. Peter Hall commented and also offered invaluable help at critical points. Special gratitude is particularly due to Harris Mylonas for both help and support along the way.

The project, in its dissertation stage, was supported by the Olin Institute for Strategic Studies at Harvard University and its Director, Stephen Rosen, who gave me a home at a critical time as a predoctoral fellow, and by the Program on International Security Policy at the University of Chicago and its Director, John Mearsheimer, and in its book stage, from various grants from the University of Virginia. It received important feedback at presentations at the University of Chicago, Harvard, Yale, the Juan March Institute, the University of Pennsylvania, Duke, the University of Virginia, and George Washington University and I thank their participants. I thank the editors of *Politics & Society* for permission to re-use parts of my article in Chapter 4. I also have to thank the countless librarians who procured to me the innumerable items I requested over the years. Geng Chen, Sam Hurley, Yue Li, Rachel Makarowski, Ashley Mehra, Daniel Smith, Mary Stenson, and Lujin Zhao provided crucial research assistance. Jeanne Barker-Nunn greatly helped improve the presentation. Finally, my gratitude goes to my editor, John Haslam, whose preternatural patience gave the book time to reach completion.

Tina Sotiriadi, a model of a friend through thick and thin, and Ioannis Psarras, a constant fount of wisdom, offered vital moral support and deep insight in this long journey, as did my dear friends and cousin, Anita Moraitou, back home. Ruari offered unconditional love to the end. My nephews and nieces, Dimitri, George, Stratis, Christina, Katerina, and Stefanos kept asking me, "Where is the book, auntie?" Well, here it is.

It is dedicated to my (Greek) father, whose memory always spurred me on, and to that of my (English) mother, who let me think for myself.

Part I

The Origins of Representative Institutions:
Power, Land, and Courts

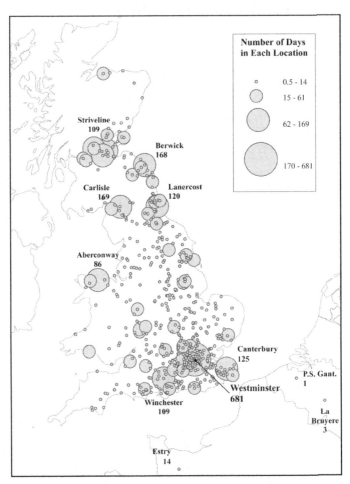

Frontispiece: Locations visited by Edward I in 17 years (1291–1307), weighted by cumulative days spent in each location.
Source: Hartshorne 1871.

1 Introduction: From Roving to Stationary Judges

"Common pleas shall not follow our court but shall be held in some certain place."[1] This was the seventeenth out of the sixty-three conditions that the barons imposed on the king of England in Magna Carta in 1215. Until then, barons seeking to settle disputes under royal jurisdiction, even disputes in which the king was not a party, often had to search for him around the realm.

Finding the king could be a wild chase: even after Parliament was fully formed in the 1290s, for instance, Edward I visited more than 1,300 English locations and several Continental ones over a seventeen-year period, spending fewer than four days on average in each (see frontispiece).[2] The image popularized by the economist Mancur Olson of the ruler as "roving bandit" extorting goods and services from the population[3] was not wrong: ruler visits were dreaded across Europe for the destruction they often caused.[4] English kings' retinues accidentally burned down houses; Edward I traveled with lions that killed working animals in Gascony, outraging the locals. Rulers and their retinues (which often numbered in the dozens or hundreds) forced local communities to subsidize these visits with foodstuffs and services. This practice, known as purveyance, was a heavy burden: over three weeks in the 1280s, the Flemish count required 10,600 herrings.[5]

But these "visits" were not lawless – Edward I paid compensation for the animals killed, for instance – nor was their purpose merely extractive.[6] Most importantly, these roving kings dispensed justice. In this book, I argue that this eager and often desperate demand for justice was fundamental for the development of the parliaments, or polity-wide institutions of representation, that emerged in medieval Europe. Moreover, this demand was tied to the king's status as "lord of all the tenants in the

---

[1] *English Constitutional Documents* 1894, 10.
[2] Hartshorne 1871; Bartlett 2000, 133–43. For the French king Philip Augustus' itinerations, see Baldwin 1986, 39–41.
[3] Olson 1993.   [4] As in Hungary; Myśliwski 2008, 273.
[5] Vale 2001, 142–43, 136n2, 147.   [6] Vale 2001, 136.

3

realm"; premodern land was held from rulers, as it technically does in Britain to this day.[7]

The role of justice in early institutions of governance has long been studied by historians, with three major accounts, Thomas Bisson's comparative study of the origins of European government, John Maddicott's account of the English Parliament, and Michel Hébert's overview of Western medieval parliaments, recently reviving interest.[8] Yet the topic has been generally neglected in social scientific accounts of the emergence of representative institutions and of state-building in general. With rare exceptions, such as the work of Timothy Besley and Francis Fukuyama,[9] law has been typically treated as a causally secondary public good.[10] Yet justice has strikingly emerged as a primary method of establishing rule in some of the most violent contemporary theaters of conflict: from Colombian rebels to the Islamic State in Syria, one of the primary tasks of some conquering groups has been to gain control of adjudication mechanisms, thereby strengthening their control over the population.[11] Although this fundamental insight – that control of justice means control of people – has been grasped by premodern rulers and violent modern warlords alike, it remains largely unexplored in the current literature.

Like the demands for justice, representation was pervasive in Western Europe since the medieval period at all levels. Misguidedly, a robust parliamentary tradition is today associated historically only with a small number of cases – England and the Netherlands especially – with most European cases developing some form of "absolutism," where rulers are deemed not to have been constrained by any institutions or even laws. Yet assemblies congregated in villages, towns, counties, or principalities throughout Europe.[12] They emerged in Italian city-states, the semi-autonomous cities of the Low Countries and the towns of France and Castile, in Russia, throughout the Holy Roman Empire, Poland, Sweden, and beyond. So, although classic narratives pit constitutional regimes against absolutist ones, *localized* representative practices survived even within absolutist regimes like France or Spain, where representation was eventually either suppressed or weakened by the eighteenth century.

---

[7] Simpson 1986, 47. See Chapters 3 and 11. This book will discuss mostly England, as Great Britain only became an entity after the 1707 union with Scotland.
[8] Bisson 2009; Maddicott 2010; Hébert 2014. The judicial perspective was first emphasized in seminal works by Frederic Maitland (1893) and later by Joseph Strayer (1970b). Justice is otherwise ubiquitous in premodern historical work, as seen throughout the book.
[9] Besley and Persson 2011; Fukuyama 2011a.
[10] Tilly 1990; Mann 1986, 422, cf. 511–12.
[11] See the fascinating work by Arjona 2016 and Revkin 2016.
[12] Lord 1930; McIlwain 1932, 682; Blickle 1997b; Blockmans 1978, 192; Marongiu 1968.

Only in some cases, however, did parliaments serve as the central organ of governance at the *polity* level.[13] This outcome was rare because it involved integrating extensive territories and diverse populations both inclusively and effectively under a stable center. England is the most representative case, with early Catalonia and Castile, Hungary, Poland, the Low Countries, and Sweden displaying variation in extent, robustness, and longevity, as we will see.[14] But England stands out by retaining the same parliamentary structure since the 1200s to the present day, with only an eleven-year interruption during the seventeenth century (1629–1640).

To explain such variation in representative practice, most scholarship has drawn on Cicero's observation that money, especially taxation, is the sinews of war.[15] In social science, taxation is typically related to representative origins through a balancing logic, especially since the pivotal works of economist Joseph Schumpeter and, more recently, political scientist Margaret Levi:[16] war-mongering rulers secured taxation from social groups endowed with new wealth and thus with greater bargaining power in exchange for rights. As Chapter 2 will discuss, this logic has been deployed across many works, from geopolitical accounts[17] to comparative history and sociology.[18] Historians too have emphasized the bargaining dynamic over taxes, as this dynamic is omnipresent in the sources.[19]

Few have thus challenged the centrality of money in state-building, despite Machiavelli's early doubts.[20] The concurrent rise of trade and representation after the 1100s has solidified this connection. However, the role of taxation in the emergence of representative institutions remains underspecified. For one thing, the hypothesis assumes that representative origins depend on rulers becoming constrained through the collective action of social actors. Attributing collective action simply to expected gains in rights, however, implies a functionalism that weakens the theory's explanatory power. The need to create institutions that serve group interests does not necessarily translate into an ability to do so.

[13] The polity level is assumed here to coincide with the area of nominal jurisdiction of a ruler. It is not a historically fixed concept. The maps by Nüssli 2008 offer reasonable approximations. I use "polity" to avoid the anachronistic term "national."
[14] Since the book focuses on the premodern period, England is treated as a separate unit.
[15] Cicero, *Philippic 5*.
[16] Schumpeter [1918] 1991; Levi 1988; Bates and Lien 1985; Blockmans 1978; van Zanden et al. 2012, 12.
[17] Hintze 1975b; Boix 2015.   [18] Downing 1992; Ertman 1997.
[19] Maddicott 2010. The word "judicial" includes activities beyond the simple application of the law, such as petitions, even administration. Adjudicatory is closer, but cumbersome.
[20] It "is not gold, as is acclaimed by common opinion, that constitutes the sinews of war, but good soldiers"; Machiavelli 1970, 2.10.

As we will see, views on which social group was critical varied, with most theories emphasizing urban ones. But all groups were composed of individuals typically divided by conflicts of interest or by tendencies to free-ride. War is often assumed to override such divisions, by mobilizing citizens around a "public good."[21] As economic historians Gennaioli and Voth noted, however, in the medieval period wars were actually a "sport of kings"[22] – usually they pursued the personal inheritance or interests of rulers.[23] Ironically, states involved in more defensive wars early on, such as France, developed weaker institutions. Further, scholars of the developing world, such as Miguel Centeno in his sociological analysis of Latin American state-building, have long noted that the posited connection between war and state-building has rarely been replicated outside the West.[24] This war-based logic also cannot explain why groups would request collective rights rather than individual ones or rents, as observed both historically and in the modern world.[25]

Some influential theories assume more specifically that rulers bargained with holders of mobile capital, who had the capacity to "exit" the state and remove their capital and could thus obtain concessions instead.[26] If so, however, how did regimes incorporate broader segments of the population, especially the countryside? This is a necessary trait for a regime to become inclusive – what I call territorial anchoring. As we will see, French and Castilian institutions did not include the countryside, only the towns. But in both cases, polity-wide representation faltered. This pattern, observed in further cases, has not been addressed.

Another key institutional feature remains unexplained in current theories: regularity.[27] It is not enough to discern the demand for consent; the question is why would subjects demand an institution to *regularize* their consent. Unlike in the modern period where taxation is constant, kings originally demanded taxation only irregularly – war taxes especially were "extraordinary." Though the time-hallowed motto of "no taxation without representation" would lead us to expect that their subjects would request representation in return, in fact communities across Europe, as elsewhere, originally only demanded assurances that taxes conceded would not become a precedent.[28] Communities or groups with strong

---

[21] Levi 1988, 96; Besley and Persson 2011.   [22] Gennaioli and Voth 2015, 1410.

[23] As noted in Harriss 1975, 34–35; Maddicott 2010, 170–71. No systematic assessment of war aims exists.

[24] Centeno 2002; Heydemann 2000.   [25] Haber et al. 2003; Slater 2010, 11.

[26] Bates and Lien 1985; Levi 1988.

[27] This also applies to theories emphasizing ruler succession as a cause for representative meetings; Blockmans 1976, 213–14; van Zanden et al. 2012, 11; Møller 2017.

[28] Harriss 1975, 427, 431; Prestwich 1990, 122; Mitchell 1951, 59; Paris 1852, 401–402; O'Callaghan 1989, 131.

bargaining powers avoided regularizing the impositions to increase the ruler's collection costs. The demand for regularity should only be expected when the burden was unavoidable (a predictable burden can be faced more efficiently) – but this would mean community bargaining powers were weaker.

Further concerns about the bargaining logic are raised when one looks beyond Western Europe. The regimes of premodern Russia, China, and the Ottoman Empire are commonly described as absolutist or even sultanic, so one might conclude that war-induced bargaining was not involved in state–society relations. Yet war was endemic: as economic historian Philip Hoffman noted, early modern China was at war as often as England and France, over 50 percent of the time.[29] Military technology was as developed in the Ottoman Empire and China before the 1600s as it was in the West, perhaps more so.[30] Nor was Western economic growth exceptional: some Chinese regions matched European ones before 1700.[31] As we will see, bargaining on taxes was equally common across regions. And councils even elected Mongol leaders from the thirteenth century.[32] Representative assemblies conveying local preferences to the political center are identified with the West, however.[33] Why that is so remains an important puzzle.

Understanding the preconditions of representative governance is not a remote historical concern. It remains a vital question today. Representative institutions shape our understanding of the state and the constitution of state power.[34] Moreover, since the work of economist Douglass North,[35] representative institutions underlie many accounts addressing both economic growth and the rise of democracy.[36] Representative practices often also exemplify the divergence of East and West.[37] Conventional understandings of Western political development have further informed policy prescriptions on emerging markets and democracies.[38] Yet democratic states and liberal orders are faltering in both developed and less-developed regions, as political scientists Levitsky and Ziblatt have argued, so a re-examination of the foundations of the liberal order remains important.[39]

---

[29] Hoffman 2015, 70.   [30] Ágoston 2005; Hoffman 2015, 13.
[31] Pomeranz 2011; Rosenthal and Wong 2011.   [32] Ostrowski 2004, 122–26.
[33] Marongiu 1968.
[34] Mann 1986; Ertman 1997; North et al. 2009; Fukuyama 2011a; Congleton 2011.
[35] North 1981; North and Weingast 1989.
[36] Acemoglu et al. 2005b; Stasavage 2003; 2011.
[37] Hall 1985a; Blaydes and Chaney 2013; van Zanden et al. 2012. Cf. Parthasarathi 2011; Kuran 2011.
[38] Moore 2008; Bräutigam et al. 2008.   [39] Levitsky and Ziblatt 2018.

Representative origins finally illuminate an enduring theoretical concern in social science: how to constrain power.[40] Political scientist Barry Weingast articulated the "fundamental political dilemma" as a conundrum: "A government strong enough to protect property rights and enforce contracts is also strong enough to confiscate the wealth of its citizens."[41] This dilemma afflicts both economics and politics and is resolved when actors solve their collective action problem to restrain the ruler. Variation in this capacity even explains why premodern growth rates diverged, according to economists Acemoglu and Robinson.[42] The paradigmatic case, especially since North and Weingast's work, has been England and the contractual equilibrium produced by the seventeenth-century Glorious Revolution,[43] though the logic has broad empirical relevance.[44]

But how social actors collectively constrained rulers remains unclear. For Olson, collective action was only possible when selective incentives or force were present, by rulers ("bandits") who became stationary and realized that encouraging growth would maximize their revenue, thus limiting "bandit" behavior.[45] However, this approach does not resolve Weingast's "political dilemma": if the bandit is powerful enough to encourage growth *and* extract from the population, he is still powerful enough to confiscate their wealth – this is the insight of the predatory theory of rule.[46] As political scientists Haber, Maurer, and Razo have argued, "the despot's commitment to protect property rights is purely volitional" and thus has no external constraint.[47]

To answer these concerns, this book makes some observations that depart from much of the conventional wisdom. First, it shows that justice was the critical factor shaping representative emergence. Taxation does not suffice to explain outcomes and neither does its proximate cause, war, as both were relatively irregular initially. Only when the irregular pressures of taxation were made to overlap *institutionally* with regular judicial incentives did representative institutions emerge as central organs of governance. Second, this regularity and overlap occurred not where rulers were weak or where they were balanced by powerful social groups, but where they were more powerful, in particular where they controlled most of the land in their territory and could grant it to subjects conditionally on the performance of obligations. Third, the most critical step for polity-wide institutions

---

[40] Power in this book is mostly understood as "a form of agenda control in which one actor denies the status quo to others in order to steer them into accepting alternatives more to his liking"; Moe 2005, 227.
[41] Weingast 1995, 1.   [42] Acemoglu et al. 2005b.
[43] North and Weingast 1989; Cox 2016.   [44] Gehlbach and Malesky 2014.
[45] Olson 2000.   [46] Levi 1988; Hough and Grier 2015, 63.   [47] Haber et al. 2003, 4.

was not the inclusion of urban, mercantile classes, as most accounts have it, but the compellence[48] of the nobility. It was when rulers could exercise power over the most powerful that they could effectively sustain polity-wide institutions. Fourth, the book argues that what distinguished the West and England in particular was not stronger individual, especially property, rights but, initially, the opposite: English rulers imposed the same collective obligations across communities and social orders throughout the polity and harnessed them to institutional structures at the center so effectively that demands for rights were the response. The empirical reality was one of conditionality and dependence on royal authority, which was endogenously transformed over time. This means, finally, that the historical record requires reconceptualizing representation as originally an obligation before it became a right.

Representative origins, in other words, invert the various logics widely assumed to explain representation. The following section examines some ways in which this occurs and which show that ruler strength was instead crucial. This revision clashes with the assumption that the prototypical constitutional state, England, was weak; I question this in the second section. A preview of the theory follows, and the chapter concludes by explaining the case selection and methodological approach.

1.1   The Inverse Logic of Representative Origins

Assumptions about origins invariably affect – and can distort – causal arguments about later stages of institutional development, so they remain vital. Despite theorists calling for more attention to institutional origins,[49] they remain overlooked. Perhaps the most basic intuition about representation is that it was, originally at least, a constraint on political authority by assertive social groups. Accordingly, the goal in building stronger representative regimes is to limit the powers of the state, an assumption that has had wide-ranging implications in various literatures and in development policy. For instance, it has suggested that to strengthen democracy (and develop economically), the power and scope of the state had to be limited, a perspective culminating in the Washington Consensus that prevailed until the 1990s.[50]

---

[48] The term "compellence" was coined as a noun for the verb "to compel" in deterrence theory; Schelling 1966, 72. Unlike coercion, it does not require force. Levi's notion of "quasi-voluntary compliance" (Levi 1988, 52–53) captures a part of the process, but focuses on the subject, not the ruler.

[49] Knight 1995; Capoccia and Ziblatt 2010.

[50] See the critique in Fukuyama 2004; Coffman 2017, 49–50.

A more general assumption is at play here, whereby the outcomes desired in modern liberal democratic representation – for instance limited executive authority, a separation of powers, and the protection of individual rights – were also conditions that enabled their emergence. So, explaining why some polities developed representative institutions whilst others did not involves searching for cases where social groups could already limit state power or secure stronger property rights; it meant looking in the past for early instances of the same condition that is desired today. The medieval historian Marc Bloch warned about this kind of endeavor. He called it the "idol of origins," the anachronistic fallacy of looking in the past for elements of the present.[51]

By contrast, this account suggests that original conditions were often *inversely* related to the outcomes of concern today. This gives rise to what I call the "normative/empirical inversion," whereby norms that are taken as constitutive of an institutional order are in fact inversely related to the empirical reality that generated them. I next examine three intuitive assumptions that shape our thinking about institutional and regime emergence whilst displaying this inversion: that representation limits the centralization of power, that it thus requires the separation of powers, and that it limits extraction by the state. More such reversals emerge throughout the analysis and are summarized in the conclusion.

1.1.1 The Inverse Logic of Emergence: Central Power and the Social Foundations of Political Institutions

Since liberal governance is broadly identified with limiting central executive power and protecting individual rights, it is natural that a central component of it, representative institutions, is assumed to serve those goals. This perception also permeates the historical state-building literature, which emphasizes patterns of "local government,"[52] and sociological studies that posit a balance of power between social actors, especially an "independent nobility."[53] Pluralism and political fragmentation thus undergird constitutional (and state-building) outcomes. This suggests a tension with the widely recognized, including now among economists, need for political centralization in both state-building and economic development.[54]

However, for an entire regime to be deemed representative, disparate preferences and practices need to be homogenized – outcomes need to be

---

[51] Bloch 1953, 29–34.   [52] Ertman 1997; Kivelson 1996, 151; Blockmans 1978, 192.
[53] Moore 1967, 417–18; Hechter and Brustein 1980; Hopcroft 1999; Zolberg 1980, 689.
[54] Osafo-Kwaako and Robinson 2013.

observed at the polity, not just the local, level. For a unit to be politically integrated, laws must emanate from an institution that incorporates all those affected. Even in federal states, some political centralization must be present if the state is to be viable, as the American founders discovered.[55] This reflects the conventional definition of state capacity as infrastructural power, following Michael Mann's classic definition: the capacity "to penetrate civil society, and to implement logistically political decisions throughout the realm."[56] Power concentration, by contrast, is often perceived as a suboptimal form of political organization:[57] it generally implies coercion and the suppression of local preferences, dynamics that are deemed inimical to constitutional (or democratic) regimes. It is typically identified with absolutism and premodern and modern despotisms, which are assumed to be "strong" states, stereotypically contrasted with "weak" constitutional ones.[58]

But as economic historian Stephan Epstein noted, this is an "assumption refuted by decades of research on pre-modern political practices that has shown how 'absolutism' was a largely propagandistic device devoid of much practical substance."[59] The assumed monopoly of power in absolutist regimes was rather an aspiration of rulers who resorted to violence and arbitrariness to handle intractable social groups. Even if military pressures led to increased capacity, unless this intractability was overcome, the outcome was not sustainable over time. This was the case with France under Louis XIV after the mid-seventeenth century: weakness in government control ended the regime a century later. The old insight of theorist Hannah Arendt, that violence can be a sign of weakness, is acutely relevant to this paradox.[60] In some modern scholarship too, as political scientist Joel Migdal has pointed out, coercion is often misinterpreted as evidence of strength.[61]

Further, the term "absolutism" usually implies that the ruler was acting without consent from the people, i.e. arbitrarily – again, in tension with representative premises. Indeed, in France, no central representative institution existed. The Estates-General were last called in 1614 and were very intermittent prior to that – hence the label "absolutist." However, it is not as if France lacked any representative institutions. It still had at least twenty-five functioning local assemblies in 1789 that raised revenue and troops highly effectively.[62] Many other Continental

[55] Wood 1969, 463–68.   [56] Mann 1986, 113; Soifer and vom Hau 2008.
[57] Scott 1998; North 1990, 113–14. See the dissenting revisionism in Treisman 2007.
[58] Anderson 1974a; DeLong and Shleifer 1993; Ekelund and Tollison 1997, 227; Carruthers 1996, 14, 23; Acemoglu et al. 2005a, 454.
[59] Epstein 2000a, 13. See also Mettam 1988; Major and Holt 1991; Henshall 1992.
[60] Arendt 1970; Davies 1990, 6; Bates 2008.   [61] Migdal 1988, 36; Chaudhry 1993.
[62] See Chapter 5.

absolutist regimes like Castile or the Holy Roman Empire countries also had rich histories of local assemblies. However, as these assemblies were geographically and socially delimited, they did not define the regime as a whole.

The difference rather was that England had one *central* institution as the main organ of governance.[63] Accordingly, although in England consent is assumed to define the regime, this is only the optical effect produced when consent is negotiated centrally, in Parliament. Where consent was secured, coercion was latent, but control was higher.[64] Consent was not absent in the other "absolutist" countries, as we will see; instead, it was exercised (and often denied) in an infinite number of local contestations. Historians of non-Western, so-called "despotic" regimes, like Russia and the Ottoman Empire, have often come to understand state–society relations in similar terms.[65]

Explaining how representative institutions became effective organs of polity-level governance thus requires understanding why they became *central* institutions. This, I will argue, required strong and effective centralizing powers.[66] Central power was thus not only congruent with demands for consent; it was, I will argue, a necessary precondition for their effective institutionalization.

1.1.2   The Inverse Logic of Emergence: Separation of Powers and Institutional Fusion

The importance of centralization also emerges from another important aspect in the history of representative institutions. A hallowed principle of Western constitutionalism since at least the eighteenth century has been the separation of powers, drawing on sources from classical antiquity. It has served as a bulwark against abuse and the corruption of the liberal democratic order, especially in the American political tradition but extending far beyond it.[67] Yet the English political system ignored the principle since its inception.[68] The House of Lords was the highest court of the land as well as the upper legislative chamber from the thirteenth century. Rather than separating powers, it fused them. The original

---

[63] Runciman 1993, 51.

[64] The early modern Netherlands offer an important variation, explored in Chapter 7. See Gorski 2003, 35.

[65] This will be explored in Part IV.

[66] Dincecco 2011 makes this case effectively for a later period, as does Grafe for Spain; Grafe 2012, 211.

[67] Vile 1967.

[68] Other constitutional monarchies, such as Sweden and the Netherlands, established parliamentary supremacy in the modern period.

judicial power was that of the king, who headed Parliament as supreme judge over all subjects, especially as subjects held land "of the crown."

The English crown's adjudicatory role was not exceptional in the premodern period, however. Rulers western and eastern dispensed justice in their courts, as did lords with more local powers. As we will see, tsars in Russia just as much as sultans in the Ottoman Empire were formally bound to dispense justice to their subjects. In fact, the fusion of judicial and administrative functions has been seen as characteristic of "ancient oriental monarchies."[69] However, it was a universal trait. The difference lay in that, in some European cases, especially England, judicial powers became fused with executive and legislative ones in a representative structure. The implications of this dynamic have been overlooked. Although much of social science would treat rare occurrences as outliers of less significance for any general theory, a deeper understanding of influential cases remains necessary, as some social scientists have argued.[70] Explaining why the English Parliament displayed a fusion of functions whilst its French and most other Continental counterparts did not, offers valuable insights into institutional formation. For an account of origins, the English case poses a powerful challenge.[71]

This is not to suggest that fusing judicial and executive or legislative functions is desirable today. After all, even the United Kingdom has established greater separation of powers by creating a Supreme Court in 2005. But it does suggest that the role of judicial processes in spearheading political integration requires analysis, as studies of the European Union are also powerfully showing.[72]

1.1.3   The Inverse Logic of Emergence: Security of Property Rights and Levels of Extraction

Any account of parliamentary institutions also has to grapple with the pivotal contribution by North and Weingast on credible commitment, which linked the English Parliament to the provision of "secure property rights, protection of ... wealth, and the elimination of confiscatory government."[73] This argument has encapsulated the neo-institutional perspective, which revolutionized economics by focusing on secure property rights; these allowed social rates of return to approximate private ones. From this perspective, after Parliament became sovereign, it could

---

[69] Pipes 1974, 288.   [70] Rodrik 2003; Gerring 2004.
[71] Some scholars rightly reject Whiggish models of explanation and consider England a perfidious exception; Bates 1988; Spruyt 1994. I defend England's theoretical relevance, without, however, teleological or triumphalist overtones.
[72] Stone Sweet 2000; Kelemen 2016.   [73] North and Weingast 1989.

credibly commit not to default on debt, thus enabling the sharp rise in public borrowing that fueled Britain's economic growth and political expansion.

The assumption of more secure property rights has been challenged, however, by economic historians, who noted that rights did not change much after 1688.[74] Moreover, the capacity to raise public debt seems more directly tied to a greater state capacity to tax and raise long-term debt,[75] itself enabled by the role of Whig ideology,[76] ministerial accountability,[77] or a thriving commercial economy.[78] Further, neo-institutionalist scholarship originally focused on "confiscatory government" as the main threat to property rights. It posited a zero-sum game between the ruler and subjects, following the intuitive premise that "the property rights structure that will maximize rents to the ruler (or ruling class) is in conflict with that that would produce economic growth."[79] Accordingly, if economic growth was to be assured, institutions would protect property by reducing rents to the ruler. Secure property rights do not necessarily imply a less extractive or less powerful state, and North later acknowledged the centrality of state institutions in securing such rights, albeit not in the early stages of development.[80] However, the association of security with limits to extraction has persisted;[81] "confiscatory taxation" is deemed a form of expropriation. North ascribed Spanish decline to a combination of war and excessive taxes and regulation.[82] The logic is echoed in Acemoglu and Robinson's distinction between "inclusive" and "extractive" economic institutions and in Carles Boix's between "producers" and "looters."[83] Critically, it survives in current politics.[84]

Historical evidence shows the opposite to be the case. Economic historians in particular have argued that we need to move beyond "simplistic notions of predation and constitutional regimes."[85] For instance, Spain has been the classic exemplar of a predatory state in the neo-institutionalist literature, assumed to extract at levels that undercut economic growth.[86] Yet Spain was raising a similar percentage of GDP from taxes in the late 1500s to England after 1698, less than 10 percent (or about a third, depending on the estimate used), as Drelichman and Voth noted,[87] and a smaller percentage in the late eighteenth century, as shown

---

[74] Coffman et al. 2013.   [75] Brewer 1989, 88–134; Dickson 1967.
[76] Stasavage 2007b; Pincus and Robinson 2011.   [77] Cox 2016.
[78] Karaman and Pamuk 2013.   [79] North 1981, 28.
[80] Hough and Grier 2015, 30. See North 1990, 35, 54–60, 113–16 and North et al. 2009, 7.
[81] Brennan and Buchanan 1980; Acemoglu and Robinson 2005a.   [82] North 1990, 116.
[83] Acemoglu and Robinson 2012, 73–76; Boix 2015.   [84] Skocpol and Williamson 2016.
[85] Grafe 2012, 25.   [86] Ekelund and Tollison 1997.
[87] Drelichman and Voth 2014, 248.

by Regina Grafe. She has also emphasized that Spain was not "predating" on its colonies: "95 percent of taxes raised in the Spanish Americas were spent in the Spanish Americas."[88] That more "predatory" states generally extracted less is a pattern that applies across European cases and was noted long ago, especially by P. K. O'Brien and Philip Hoffman.[89] Recent econometric studies have confirmed the observation. Mark Dincecco found that centralized but "limited" government achieved around a 60 percent increase in per capita taxation compared to less constitutional regimes after 1660.[90]

None of these ground-breaking accounts, however, test whether this capacity might predate parliaments. Instead, they assume that high extraction was endogenous to representation. Revenue increased, they posit, because as "more political control accrues to elites, it becomes more likely that new tax funds will be spent on items that will benefit them (versus the ruler only)."[91] However, data by Karaman and Pamuk on Prussia provocatively suggest that, once cost of living is controlled for, agricultural Prussia showed a similarly remarkable increase in capacity without a parliament between 1650 and 1790.[92] High extraction may thus be independent of parliamentary structures.[93] If we are to understand the origins (and effects) of such institutions, we thus need to specify the levels of extraction before parliaments emerged as coordinating devices. We also need to understand the distributive politics in this process, especially who was burdened by taxation. After all, the real distinction in Acemoglu and Robinson's account is not between inclusive and extractive institutions, but inclusive and exclusive ones: as they note, colonial Spanish America did not lack secure property rights; it just restricted them to the colonists. It was the "mass of the people" who were subject to coercion and whose resources were expropriated.[94]

This book argues that regimes are often classified as extractive, coercive, or absolutist when they can only tax the weaker social groups, while power-holders remain beyond state control – what Hoffman and Rosenthal described as taxes being "disastrous at the margin."[95] Constitutional structures, by contrast, required strong state powers, as we will see. They were not more "limited"; their scope was typically broader while their strength was greater.[96] They were just more regulated

---

[88] Grafe 2012, 9, 21.
[89] Mathias and O'Brien 1976; O'Brien and Hunt 1993; Hoffman and Norberg 1994.
[90] Dincecco 2009, 74–75, 61.   [91] Dincecco and Wang 2018, 349.
[92] Karaman and Pamuk 2013.
[93] Some modern studies reach similar conclusions; Timmons 2010; Cheibub 1998.
[94] Acemoglu and Robinson 2012, 76, 81.   [95] Hoffman and Rosenthal 1997, 35.
[96] See the distinction in Fukuyama 2004.

and thus less arbitrary. The escalation of European wars after 1400, often seen as a cause, was predicated on this early institutional development.

1.2   England: Representative Emergence and the Myth of State Weakness

How can this argument about royal strength be reconciled with the widespread assumptions of representation emerging in weak states? England especially is habitually assumed to be weak before 1660 or even 1500, as were all European territorial states.[97] Moreover, if English rulers were instead powerful, why would they acquiesce to an institution that would eventually constrain them? Could they not foresee future limits to their power?

The assumption of English weakness has prevailed due to the importance of seventeenth-century developments for constitutional history. For the German historian Otto Hintze, for instance, England was able to preserve its constitutionalism because it was unburdened by heavy geopolitical pressures and had a commercial economy and a weak state.[98] The English seventeenth century was indeed a period of great turmoil and internal weakness. After all, it saw the decapitation of its king and a protracted civil war which gutted royal power. However, this proves rather uncharacteristic if a longer timeframe is adopted. The historian John Brewer showed in his pathbreaking work that England was far from a weak state after 1688.[99] The taxing advantage that historians have shown since 1700 is a powerful indicator of this strength and one that contemporaries understood well. Even Adam Smith noted approvingly that England taxed more than twice per capita than France did in the eighteenth century.[100]

This advantage is easily attributed to a newly sovereign Parliament. But as Brewer observed, it dated to the Anglo-Saxon period.[101] Medieval English fiscal prowess has long been noted by historians.[102] The connection of fiscal extraction to war was compellingly showed by Mann across the medieval period.[103] Yet English extraction in both taxation and troops raised for war exceeded that of France even before the period of Parliament's emergence and throughout its early formation, as I show in this book.[104] Only after 1500 did France indeed extract more than

---

[97] Gennaioli and Voth 2015, 1411; Karaman and Pamuk 2013.   [98] Hintze 1975c.
[99] Brewer 1989, 3–7.   [100] Smith [1776] 1981b, V.ii.k.78.   [101] Brewer 1989, 3–7.
[102] See Chapter 6.
[103] Mann 1988. Anderson 1974a, 113–18 also emphasizes English early strength.
[104] Systematic data for this early period are not available for other cases.

England for about 150 years, but this lead should not be projected to the period of origins.

This is not to say that English rulers were omnipotent; they routinely strained to raise resources,[105] whilst rulers who were fiscally autonomous dispensed with assemblies. Some princes, in Thuringia and Meissen for instance, avoided representation until the fourteenth century because of income from silver mines, as did the Teutonic Order due to its grain revenues (though such instances were rare).[106] English kings lacked such abundance. However, the balance of power with social groups was in their favor: English rulers' lack of autonomy was relative. This explains why they would acquiesce to parliaments – in fact, as we will see, premodern rulers generally preferred them. When already strong, rulers did not see their powers diminished. What is commonly assumed to be a parliamentary limitation to ruler power eventually often emerges, as this account will argue, as the regularization of their jurisdiction and increase of their revenue.

In fact, even after Parliament formed, in the early 1300s, it was still "widely accepted that the king had no superior in the kingdom and could not be sued." Though we assume that the ruler being above the law was distinctive to absolutist or sultanic regimes, it was the empirical reality against which English earls and barons were still strenuously fighting. Nobles could lawfully distrain the king if he infringed rights affirmed by Magna Carta, but such right looked too "antique in conception and unworkable in practice," not least because the king could now use the charge of treason against any challenger. This right to resort to force against the king ultimately developed on constitutional lines (unlike for instance in the Ottoman case) only because Parliament had already created a community on behalf of which these noble defenders could claim to speak.[107] How this came to be will preoccupy the first two parts of this book.

The key, however, was that Parliament itself was predicated on this strong royal power, allaying endogeneity concerns. These conclusions about the role of power will be further supported by assessing power balances across the cases examined in this account.

1.3   The Argument

This set of observations illuminates the three crucial puzzles identified earlier, which the bargaining hypothesis leaves unexplained: why

---

[105] Southern 1970, 152; Kaeuper 1988, 63.   [106] Blockmans 1998, 35.
[107] All quotes from Keen 2003, 69–71.

negotiations on taxation became regular and institutionalized when incentives are normally to avoid them, especially under conditions of low public goods provision; how different social groups solved their collective action problem and raised effective resistance to a ruler; and how exchanges with groups controlling most wealth (and status), typically assumed to be commercial, led to the incorporation of lower orders of society and especially the countryside, which alone allows us to term a regime inclusive and territorially anchored, i.e. representative.[108] I elaborate on these connections next.

Taxation was a top-down demand imposed, initially at least, on an irregular basis. Social actors had little incentive to support a central institution that only extracted from them without also meeting some systematic demand. That demand is widely associated with war pressures. But war was also intermittent and a top-down imposition. The demand for justice, on the other hand, was a bottom-up, pressing, daily concern across social orders. Crime and order, corruption of officials and local power-holders, and especially disputes about property rights in land were pervasive concerns throughout all cases, generating spontaneous demand for adjudication. The expression of grievance had a universal medium: the petition submitted to the ruler's court. This was non-routine justice, appealed to when regular channels failed. The practice dated to antiquity and occurred throughout the premodern world, from ancient Rome, to Western Europe, to the medieval and early modern Ottoman and Russian Empires, as well as the Far East.[109] In the twelfth and thirteenth centuries, Europe saw a remarkable trend of petition-making that transformed political interaction just as parliaments were forming. Petition-making seems typical of polities with low institutionalization; perhaps relatedly, petitions today are a re-emerging part of governance in a period of democratic crisis.[110]

Premodern rulers across regions were supreme judges in their realm and their court was also a court of law. When rulers could centralize judicial practice at their court, subjects had incentives to demand that meetings become regular. Conversely, rulers then had a ready forum in which to present tax demands. This overlap of the judicial and fiscal functions generated a process I describe through the historical institutionalist mechanism of institutional layering, which was crucial for the emergence of representative regimes that were polity-wide and inclusive.[111] The greater the ruler's capacity to enforce this structure,

---

[108] These terms are relative for this period.
[109] Millar 1992, 203–73; Kümin and Würgler 1997; Zaret 2000; Heerma van Voss 2001; Hung 2011; Keirstead 1990; Schneider 2006; Haboush 2009; Takeuchi 2014.
[110] Karpf 2016.   [111] See Chapter 2.

the more regular the representative institution. As political scientist Robert Bates has noted, coercion can be socially productive.[112]

Ruler power was also fundamental in solving the collective action problems of different social groups. The most effective institution-builders, as we will see, were rulers who controlled most land in their territory and thus the distribution of land rights. When subjects received land conditionally from the crown, they were burdened with common obligations, especially to provide military, judicial, and administrative service. Joint obligations created incentives to act in common, especially when taxes were imposed across all social orders with few immunities.

Crucially, attendance at the royal court and representation were also originally obligations, just as jury duty remains to this day.[113] This requires recalibrating a key assumption, since we deem representation to have been a hard-won right. Its obligatory character is clear in a very common practice: representatives throughout Europe often adopted the Roman legal form of plenipotentiary powers, the powers given to legal agents to represent litigants in court. This legal form was transposed to political practice, as explained in Chapter 4, so that local communities would be collectively bound by decisions of their representative; it was not, initially, a right demanded from below. This point has been lost in modern social science, even though, I argue, it was critical to the trajectory of representative institutions.

The capacity of premodern rulers to enforce these obligations varied widely. Justice was a universal demand, but ruler preponderance occurred only rarely, and institutional outcomes depended on the interaction of the two. Existing accounts, as seen above, have predicated such outcomes on mercantile wealth and debt. But this cannot explain how a regime became inclusive and anchored throughout the territory. Urban populations, where mercantile wealth is assumed to be concentrated, were limited – throughout Europe the average until 1800 ranged between 11 and 16 percent of total population and they only exceeded 30 percent in the Iberian peninsula, Belgium (briefly), and the Netherlands, whilst England formed its Parliament when urbanization was at 4 percent of the population.[114] To explain territorial anchoring beyond narrow urban pockets, compellence of the nobility was key.

This was so for two main reasons. On the one hand, without power over the nobility, rulers had limited access to the populations under noble jurisdiction. When nobles could be compelled, by contrast, as in

---

[112] Bates 2014.

[113] Post 1943a; Brown 1970. The obligatory character of representation was disputed by some English historians; these concerns are addressed especially in Chapter 4.

[114] Bairoch et al. 1988, 259.

England, rulers could summon representatives from across society, both rural and urban. Needing allies, the nobles themselves often included their dependent tenants. Contrary to most accounts, the step of including broader social groups is thus temporally and causally secondary; elite compellence comes first. When the high nobility could not be compelled, as in most Continental cases, it was often the king who incorporated lower social groups into assemblies as a counterbalance. Without including the countryside under noble jurisdiction, however, representation had limited political effects, as in France and Castile: urban groups dominated but representative institutions lacked the strength and inclusiveness to become effective instruments of governance of the whole polity. The result is identified with absolutism, even though, as discussed in Chapter 5, realities on the ground suggest weak, not absolute, power. In other cases, such as Hungary, Poland, even Russia, weak rulers challenged by powerful magnates created a new, lower and dependent nobility instead and generated representative activity with that group.[115] This resulted in what I call "second-best constitutionalism," which also proved less resilient over time.

Compellence of the most powerful was also necessary because these were the groups that were powerful enough to curtail the ruler.[116] Nobles were the hardest group to systematically involve in representative institutions, however. They hardly lacked joint interests that could have enabled collective action: they were linked by ties of kinship, patronage, marriage, fealty, ritual, and property, as sociologist Julia Adams has shown for the early modern Netherlands and many historians for France.[117] However, only rarely did they coordinate so as to produce enduring institutions, despite frequent rebellions. After all, Adams explains Dutch decline through elite failure at the polity level. Collective action was historically rare, I argue, because it mostly depended on a ruler capable of compelling nobles to attend the center.

Nobles typically had a collective interest in doing so when they faced inescapable common obligations, whether in state service or taxes. When nobles could gain exemptions from obligations (usually in exchange for military service), they lacked incentives to cooperate in countering the crown's demands. We will see that it was their absence – not the assumed royal "absolutism" – that made representative institutions founder, as in France and Castile. By contrast, English rulers ensured that nobles were

---

[115] As we will see, all rulers adopted this mechanism to a certain extent, but where the high nobility was not also compelled, institutions faltered.

[116] This does not mean that European monarchs were hostile and in permanent conflict with their nobilities; Asch 2003.

[117] Adams 2005, 137–63. For France, see indicatively Kettering 1989.

regular attendees at the crown's court, sessions of which eventually coagulated into Parliament – they also performed service in addition to their military duties and contributed to taxation. Also crucial was the role of fiscal ties, either through loans or debt, in cultivating the patterns of dependence this account posits as necessary for representative institutions.

Noble presence is what sustained Parliament after all during the critical period of its emergence: after 1258, nearly sixty out of seventy Parliaments contained no popular representatives.[118] As argued in Chapter 2, separate accounts are needed to explain the rise of the institution of Parliament as a regular forum (in which compellence of the nobility was key) on the one hand and representative practice itself (where inclusion of broader strata is the issue) on the other. But a key observation emerges from the account: no elite compellence, no enduring representative institutions.

The "fundamental political dilemma" is thus resolved when coercion is successfully channeled through institutions that conscript the most powerful challengers, who could then counteract the ruler. This solved both the collective action problem of the nobility and enabled the territorial anchoring of the regime. These dynamics, I argue, flowed from the effective distribution of land by rulers under conditional terms and from the relations of dependence generated by royal judicial powers (Figure 1.1).

This account, however, based as it is on collective obligation, conflicts with the conventional assumptions about the importance of Western individualism and private property rights for the Western trajectory, especially in England.[119] A recurrent finding of this book is that traits that appear unique to the West, and England in particular, can be found across cases with very different institutional outcomes, sometimes in more radical form. Chapter 11 for instance will show the striking similarities between English and Ottoman property rights in land, both of which

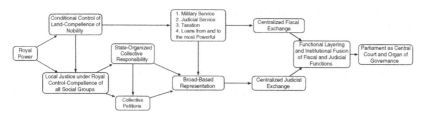

Figure 1.1 The English pathway to representative emergence

[118] Sayles 1974, 18.   [119] Macfarlane 1978; North 1990.

were conditional, contrary to stereotypes in the field that assume that Ottoman rulers arbitrarily suppressed such rights.

Moreover, rulers in all cases examined in this book strove to build effective judicial structures at the local and central level, typically drawing from a common pool of instruments. Petitions for instance inundated the court in London as much as in Moscow or Istanbul. Another major instrument deployed to impose order locally was collective responsibility, whereby a group was held responsible for the actions or obligations of a member. Where English outcomes differed was in the greater capacity of the English crown to impose such duties at the supra-local level and to summon all administrative units (the counties and towns) of the polity in a systematic way to the center. "Common petitions" in the English Parliament integrated local grievances into general political demands resulting in legislation: this is how the bill of legislation was born. Collective responsibility was foremost applied in representation itself, binding the whole community to the commitments of a representative.

Locally, the more such judicial instruments were under royal control, the easier it was to mobilize them on a systematic basis across the polity to serve ruler needs, whether to contribute to taxation or to perform service. If collective responsibility was not systematically aggregated at the center and if royal courts did not have binding power throughout the polity, a central system of representation could not be sustained.

By contrast, I show how in the Russian and Ottoman empires state weakness meant that social life was organized mainly at the local level, with weak mechanisms of aggregation: the state was unable to impose uniform organization at a supra-local level, with only some few exceptions (as in some episodes in Russian history). As a result, judicial interaction between center and periphery in those cases was highly atomized. Before we attribute this variation to cultural differences or conceptions of rights, to warfare pressures or economic conditions, as existing theories do, we must assess the differential capacity of rulers to achieve institutional change. As we will see, this capacity typically *preceded* the pressures of war and it shaped economic change.

In short, this argument predicts that, if we observe inclusive representative practices at the *polity* level, we should expect greater ruler power, conditional rights over land, and power over the most powerful (in most cases the nobility). These factors enable both the imposition of service and collective responsibility locally, but also, critically, the central summoning of localities that fused judicial and fiscal exchange. The cases studied range along different points on these continuums (Figure 1.2).

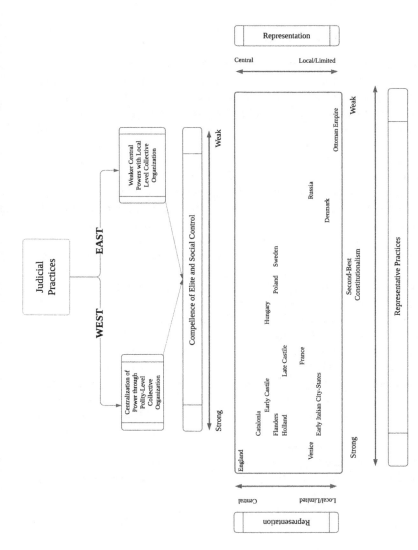

Figure 1.2 Variation of cases on key dimensions

This book is not claiming that polity-wide representation is, was, or should be the only form of governance. Multiple other forms have existed, many highly functional. Nor does it assume that other regions exhibited some "failure" in not developing representation. It simply takes the form that prevailed in Europe, for better or worse, and seeks to illuminate some of its necessary conditions.

1.4   Case Selection and Plan of the Book

The principle of organization of this book is mostly analytical. Masterful accounts on premodern regime formation, by Brian Downing, Thomas Ertman, and many eminent historians, already offer a chronological presentation of institutional development. This analysis aims to specify not a full causal model, but only some necessary conditions for the outcome, representative institutions as central organs of governance. As sociologist James Mahoney points out, analysis of necessary conditions is "important when evaluating certain outcomes of exceptional interest."[120]

A specification of necessary conditions omits factors that were historically important but causally secondary to the question. For instance, the Church is not treated separately here but as another landowner, though for many related questions its contribution was fundamental. Church strength seems to have varied inversely with that of the state; cases identified here as weak typically had strong Churches. This is historically important but not theoretically central. It does not alter the main claims advanced here; it supplements them.

The cases examined are England, France, Castile, Catalonia, Hungary, Flanders, Italy, the Ottoman Empire, and Russia, with brief consideration of additional cases (Holland, Poland, Sweden, Denmark, the Swiss Cantons, and the Holy Roman Empire). The concept of a case is problematic: temporal variation exists within cases (which is leveraged to increase confidence in the conclusions, as in Hungary) and some cases consist of multiple separate units (e.g. Flanders and Italy). However, the focus here is on polity-wide governance; further studies can test the hypotheses at the more micro level.

Cases were selected on two main criteria. The first is sufficiency in establishing necessary conditions; the second is availability of evidence on critical variables in the very early period, before the institution first appears. Some methodologists have argued that if about five cases with the outcome of interest display the posited factor, necessity can be

---

[120] Mahoney 2000b, 397.

affirmed with 95 percent confidence.[121] This study aims to show that strong central powers, especially over the most powerful social groups, are a precondition of representative institutions at least in the major cases typically examined in social science. For this, England is a "crucial test," since it generated most alternative hypotheses challenged in this account.[122]

This is then confirmed through the method of congruence in further cases, to assess whether the values of the necessary condition and outcome co-vary in the expected direction.[123] Early Castile, Catalonia, and Hungary offer confirmation, as do periods of Flemish and Dutch history, with indications on other cases. The logic is also observed in cases where ruler power was weaker and only sufficient to control a lower nobility, the pattern I call second-best constitutionalism.[124] This also explains historical "anomalies," such as the brief representative activity in seventeenth-century Russia, as well as periods of Hungarian and Polish history. The argument is strengthened by considering cases thought to prove the conventional logic: city-states, where participation appears to occur without strong rulers. I show how these are cases of omitted variable bias due to a truncated temporal frame.

Cases where ruler power was low and the outcome is not observed only indirectly support a claim about necessity.[125] Still, France and Spain had weak representative regimes and I show their kings were generally too weak to enforce conditionality. Moreover, variation in the degree and type of control across time shaped outcomes in the predicted direction: representative institutions were phased out at the central level in France, but not in Castile where original powers were higher. Ordinal comparison therefore increases confidence in the mechanism's plausibility.

The necessary condition of power preponderance is measured through different observable implications. The conventional measure is taxation.[126] It will be shown to be initially exogenous, as some taxing capacity precedes representation. Further indicators of this capacity – land control, the granting and enforcement of conditional rights to land, the creation of a uniform court system, the fusion of judicial with political and fiscal functions, the imposition of judicial service, especially on the most powerful groups, and of the obligation of representation – are

---

[121] Dion has shown this, using a simple Bayesian model of inference; Dion 1998, 135; see also Mahoney 2000b, 395–96; Goertz 2003, 54–55.
[122] Gerring 2007, 120–21.   [123] George and Bennett 2005, 181–204.
[124] Mahoney 2000b, 408–409 advises against combining ordinal and nominal comparisons but only because of the problems in affirming necessary and sufficient conditions jointly. Given the focus on necessary conditions, this analysis is less bound by this restriction.
[125] Braumoeller and Goertz 2000; Seawright 2002, 185.
[126] Besley and Persson 2009; Hendrix 2010.

examined through structured, focused comparisons across Western European cases, though data are highly unsystematic. Clearly separating cause and effect is hard, as many of the effects reinforce the cause (judicial centralization increases royal power) but some ruler capacity must be already present.

England is then set against two prototypical contrasts, Russia and the Ottoman Empire, which did not develop polity-wide representative institutions, even though their rulers are claimed to have controlled all the land, as English kings did. Unlike arguments on sufficiency, ones on necessary conditions are unaffected by cases that have the condition but not the outcome. Nonetheless, such cases help identify what distinguished the "West" from regions without a representative tradition. Although they appear to be very different cases compared to England, they are remarkably similar across many key dimensions.

Cases with some representative activity but limited evidence on the early period of origins cannot be assessed, since later periods often display inverse dynamics. England after the fourteenth century seemed like a case where "rights" led to "constraints" on royal authority, but this outcome cannot inform us about conditions of emergence. Accordingly, some well-known cases cannot be treated here and await more detailed information on the early period (Norway, Iceland, Norman Sicily, many small central European kingdoms, Portugal, Austria).[127] The early United States, by contrast, has rich records that promise an intriguing comparison. So do the negative cases of the Byzantine Empire, Japan, and China. The comparison with China, which has so many similarities with the West, holds the most promise to deliver a full theory; this I suspect will be predicated, again, on the importance of infrastructural power, coupled with that of ideational factors, such as the principle of representation and community, and structural factors, such as the prominence of clans.

The structure of the book is as follows. Part I explains how regularity was achieved through a layering of judicial and fiscal functions and institutional fusion by comparing the English and French *institutions* (Chapter 2). It shows how this fusion results from nobles being compelled to perform service, including attending the royal court, which solved their collective action problem. It thus shows how, when rulers effectively controlled nobles and local judicial structures, they could achieve "territorial anchoring" (Chapter 3).

Part II explains how representative *practice* was originally an obligation that was more effectively imposed where compellence powers were already higher, as in England (Chapter 4), further comparing with

---

[127] Marongiu 1968.

France and Castile (Chapter 5). The English extractive advantage is supported by comparing rates of military extraction and both micro- and aggregate-level data on taxation (Chapter 6).

Part III addresses a major alternative hypothesis ascribing representation to trade growth by examining Italian city-states and the Low Countries (Chapter 7) and Catalonia (Chapter 8). It also shows how the institutional effects of trade were endogenous to strong central authority by comparing two classic cases, the English and Spanish wool trades (Chapter 9).

Part IV examines the hypothesis posited, the role of land control and conditionality, in a comparative framework. It shows how faced with a strong nobility, rulers would often develop the second-best constitutionalism exhibited in the Hungarian, Polish, Swedish (Chapter 10), and Russian (Chapter 12) cases. That conditionality was not sufficient for representation to emerge, however, is shown by comparing English and Ottoman land law (Chapter 11).

Part V brings all these strands together to attribute the emergence of polity-wide representative regimes to the supra-local organization of collective responsibility by the state, by comparing the role of petitions and collective responsibility in England, Russia, and the Ottoman Empire (Chapter 13). The conclusion examines some implications of the argument, primarily on the intractable question of the origins of power.

2 A Theory of Institutional Emergence: Regularity, Functional Layering, and the Origins of Parliament

"Representation," the historian Wim Blockmans wrote, "appears whenever a government finds itself forced by the concentration of power in the hands of its subjects to share power with them through institutionalized consultation."[1] In this perspective, the main agent of progress was typically the "third estate." The assumption stems from liberal and Marxist historiography, drawing from Adam Smith to Augustin Thierry, Karl Marx, and others, who emphasized either the middle or the working classes.[2] Increasing prosperity, in such accounts, endowed these groups with greater material powers, thereby strengthening their bargaining position and capacity for collective action and leading them to demand greater political powers.[3] Only with the participation of the third estate will some scholars assert that we have a "fully developed parliament."[4] Constitutionalism failed where "overstrong" rulers suppressed rights and trade and engaged in confiscatory taxation.[5] While such changes did occur, the central question is whether they adequately explain representative *institutions*.

A central theme of this book is that the emergence and consolidation of regular institutions that structured governance inclusively cannot be deduced from material change alone. This is especially so because the process that generated a regular institution (the subject of Part I) must be distinguished from that which generated representative practices per se (the subject of Part II). The former depends on the most powerful social actors, as argued in this book, whereas the latter involve broader social groups. The two processes are routinely conflated. Distinguishing between them allows us to avoid the functionalism that besets many explanations. But it also allows us to highlight how much harder the process of representative emergence is. By not assuming that a single dynamic explains all aspects of institutional development, this analysis

---

[1] Blockmans 1978, 192.
[2] Smith [1776] 1981b; Guizot 1851; Thierry 1853; Marx 1981. In Moore 1967, the third estate was not an "agent" but only conditionally conducive to democracy.
[3] Boix 2015.　[4] van Zanden et al. 2012, 4.　[5] DeLong 2000.

reveals multiple dynamics that often do not co-evolve and can be in tension with each other.[6] Nonetheless, they all depend on the same necessary condition, as is shown in the next chapter: the crown's capacity to overpower its most powerful competitors in crucial ways and over time.

To analyze this complex process, this chapter first defines the key necessary condition of the argument, state power based on land, and the dependent variable, polity-wide representative institutions. It then explains how existing theoretical perspectives do not adequately account for the three main dynamics of the emergence of representative institutions outlined in the Introduction: how they became regular, how they solved the collective action problem of attending groups, and how they succeeded in including all social groups, not just the third estate or merchants. The chapter then explains the first of these dynamics, regularization, through a theory of functional layering and institutional fusion, before addressing the other two dynamics in Chapter 3.

2.1   Two Key Concepts

2.1.1   Some Key Necessary Conditions: State Power, Royal Control over Land, and Conditionality

How is state power defined? The major sociological treatment of social power remains that of Michael Mann, who identified four sources: ideological, economic, military, and political.[7] Here, the emphasis is on state control of land, which combines all four sources. Land was the most important economic resource in the period and is still relevant in the developing world today.[8]

State control of land in the premodern period is typically identified with patrimonialism, where state land was the personal estate of the ruler, fusing the notions of public and private.[9] This is often identified with non-Western regimes, such as "tsarist" Russia or the "sultanic" Ottoman Empire,[10] emblematic of their divergent paths and limited "freedoms."[11] Yet, state control of land was the default condition throughout the premodern world, in both East and West, especially in the prototypical constitutional state, England. Strangely enough, the literature has not noted that in England, as legal textbooks affirm to this day, "all land is owned by the Crown. A small part of that land is in the Crown's own occupation" (known as demesne land). The "rest is

---

[6] Pitkin 2004.   [7] Mann 1986.   [8] Boone 2014; Albertus 2015.
[9] The classic sociological exposition of the concept is in Weber 1978, 231–32.
[10] Anderson 1974a; Pipes 1974.   [11] Pipes 1999.

occupied by tenants holding either directly or indirectly from the Crown";
allodial land (land not subject to obligations to an overlord or ultimately
the king) "is unknown."[12]

This land regime dates to the Norman Conquest in 1066, though major
reforms occurred in 1660 and 1925.[13] Subjects did not "own" land in the
absolute sense understood in Roman law; even the highest lords were
"tenants-in-chief." Tenants had the obligation to offer military, judicial,
and administrative service, counsel on government affairs, and financial
aid; their inheritance was restricted and they could be dispossessed of
their land for wrongdoing. As we will see in Chapter 3, obligations on all
orders of English tenants were astonishingly broad.[14] Control of land
rights thus cannot distinguish between East and West; rather, I argue,
the difference lay in whether rulers could enforce such rights and in
whether they granted land conditionally or not. England was more effective on both counts.

Following the classic statement by Joseph Schumpeter, scholars have
often assumed that kings' de facto control over land was confined to the
royal demesne, thus attributing representation to the demesne's increasing inadequacy in meeting royal expenses.[15] This indeed occurred in
Continental cases; it also, however, greatly contributed to the precarious
trajectory of representation in that region, as this book argues. In
England, historians have noted that kings' demesne resources were
"insignificant" already from the earliest period of the Angevins
(1154–1216)[16] – their public powers as kings were, however, unrivaled.

Even before Parliament emerged, English kings controlled land far
more effectively than French and other Continental rulers, owing to two
advantages. They inherited a "ubiquitous" system of Anglo-Saxon counties and hundreds (itself the product of strong Danish kingships), whereas
its Carolingian equivalent in France was very weakly enforced.[17] This was
no mere path-dependent heritage, however: William I had exterminated
the Anglo-Saxon aristocracy that controlled most land and had brutally
suppressed rebellions after 1066.[18] He reversed the previous land distribution by appropriating directly 64 percent of land by area and more than

---

[12] Megarry and Wade 2012, 22. See also, Gray and Gray 2009, 56; Cooke 2006, 13–17;
Pollock and Maitland 1898, 232–33; Bloch 1965, 171–72, 188.
[13] Simpson 1986, 23–24.
[14] Poole 1946; White 1933. Not all obligations were land-based.
[15] Schumpeter [1918] 1991; Martin et al. 2009a; Gennaioli and Voth 2015, 1412.
[16] Wolffe 1971, 22. Wolffe argues that the discourse on the king's demesne developed later
and was turned into a "myth" by Blackstone and Stubbs; Wolffe 1971, 40–50. This does
not mean that income from the demesne did not decline; Barratt 1999a, 76.
[17] Cam 1935, 196, 199; Ertman 1997, 38–59, 158–66.
[18] Crouch 2002, 87–166; Huscroft 2009, 115–72.

a fifth of the land by value directly and a quarter of its income. The key was that he granted about half the kingdom to Norman nobles conditionally, none of whom held individually more than about 10 percent. The Church held about a quarter of the land.[19]

Crown tenants-in-chief were the main political actors in the early stages of institution-building. Kings controlled them through "the blunt instrument of confiscation and disinheritance," though they also resorted to the "destruction of castles and the payment of ransom."[20] Royal conflicts with the barons are vividly traced by historians, creating an image of royal weakness.[21] However, overall, the top ranks depended on the crown more intensely than on the Continent. Though scholars focus on the increased security of property rights in England,[22] it is the rights of lower tenants at the expense of lords that were being fortified in royal courts through the common law, as we will see. The lords did not acquire more secure tenure in the twelfth century. Instead, even earls saw their tenures frequently disrupted by the king;[23] this was "a key element" in royal power.[24]

Similar (though not identical) terms of land control are found across the cases in this book. Conditional land grants to nobles were widely observed, but conditionality varied across cases. It was also relatively high in Catalonia, twelfth-century Castile, the Low Countries, in declining intensity and consistency. Conditionality also underlay the French king's power. Yet his de facto jurisdiction was confined to the royal domain, the Île-de-France.[25] Faced with vassals who often controlled forces rivaling his own, the French king lacked analogous compelling powers. In order to pacify the land, French kings needed the Church's cooperation and invoked the Peace of God; the English king imposed the King's Peace.[26]

In fact, conditionality was often weakly imposed across cases. It was confined to the lower social orders in Hungary, Poland, Sweden, and Russia and limited as far as the upper nobility was concerned. Where higher orders had allodial rights, we will find that representation was undermined. However, whether conditionality was successfully enforced was not a function of representative institutions, since it often long preceded them, as in England. It was instead tied to overall state capacity, which, in turn, was originally independent of economic wealth or its usual proxy, urbanization. Rights were more conditional in England than

---

[19] Fleming 1991, 227–28; Ormrod 1999, 22; Warren 1987, 55; Corbett 1957, 505–16.
[20] Holt 1972, 38; Kosto 2012.   [21] Bartlett 2000, 4–11; Maddicott 2010, 106–276.
[22] North et al. 2009.
[23] McFarlane 1965, 147–48; Holt 1972, 30–36; Spencer 2014, 66–68.
[24] Hudson 1994, 59, 15; Waugh 1986, 812.
[25] Lot and Fawtier 1958, 99–182; Lot 1904; Soule 1968, 14.
[26] Maddicott 2010, 434; Firnhaber-Baker 2006.

Castile, though England was poorer around 1300. English GDP per capita is estimated between 50 and 70 percent that of Spain around 1300, as calculated by economic historians Álvarez-Nogal and Prados de La Escosura,[27] while English urbanization was a paltry 4 percent to the Iberian peninsula's 30 percent, with the largest cities being in Castilian territory.[28] Yet English kings enforced conditionality more effectively.

Why some regimes adopted mostly conditional rather than allodial rights is not easily explained but it was also independent of parliamentary structures – conditionality is found in the Ottoman Empire as well, as Chapter 11 shows, and throughout the premodern world.

The historical term often employed for these conditional grants of land is "feudalism."[29] The term is both controversial and multivalent.[30] It also involves concepts like vassalage and homage that specify the relation between the lord and his dependents. These concepts undergird the assumption of a feudal "contract" between lord and vassal that scholars have posited as a crucial medieval legacy for modern democracy.[31] But the analysis of the Ottoman case in Chapter 11 will show that it is misguided to assume contracts per se were unique to the West.[32] The perspective taken in this argument, by focusing on the general principle of conditionality rather than the specific forms it could take, is not affected by these controversies, so I have avoided using feudalism as a term.

[27] Though the data only permit what they call an "eclectic exercise," the authors give PPP-adjusted current price estimates; Álvarez-Nogal and Prados de La Escosura 2012, 23. Broadberry et al. 2015, 375 have the most informed estimates for England.

[28] Bairoch et al. 1988, 259.   [29] Bloch 1965, 163–75.

[30] The concept of feudalism was challenged as anachronistic by two historians, Elizabeth Brown (1974) and Susan Reynolds (1994) (though major medievalists have defended the term, carefully defined; Bisson 1978; 1994; Bartlett 2000; Magnou-Nortier 1996). Their important challenge does not apply to England or this argument. Reynolds states that "England contributes much the best evidence of a connection between fiefs and military service and of the hierarchy of property rights – indeed the only evidence of either that fits the model without heavy interpretation." The only point where England "fits the model very badly" is in having "an exceptionally strong and bureaucratic central government" – a central claim in my argument; Reynolds 1994, 480, 323–95. Moreover, her claims about France refer to the period preceding the one covered here, and she does not deal with Spain.

Others see feudalism as a system of political decentralization and fragmentation; Spruyt 1994; Blaydes and Paik 2016, 552. However, political fragmentation only emerged when the apex of the feudal pyramid, the king, was too weak to enforce his claims on his subjects, as in France or Germany; Ganshof 1964, 160–67. Finally, feudalism is distinct from manorialism, where unfree peasants and free tenants were dependent on their lord for land tenure and the administration of local justice; Holton 1985; Anderson 1974a; Barzel and Kiser 2002.

[31] Moore 1967, 415.

[32] Further studies, however, could re-examine these concepts that pose interesting comparisons with cases like Japan; Ravina 1999.

2.1.2 Dependent Variable: Polity-Wide Representative Institutions

The dependent variable in this book is how *polity-wide* representative institutions emerged as central organs of governance, namely as institutions that generated the rules applying to and integrating most citizens.[33] This is the institutional foundation and precedent for what is commonly called constitutionalism, namely the principle that government should be delimited by laws.[34] What matters for this analysis is that this process integrates not only urban dwellers, merchants, or communes but landholders and peasants as well, i.e. a diversified society over an extended territory.[35] *Local* assemblies were actually so widespread throughout Europe, in villages, cities, city-leagues, and principalities, that their emergence is not the hardest puzzle. Accordingly, the aim is not to explain the practice of representation per se; this is non-controversially traced to classical and Church precedents that revived throughout Southern Europe after the eleventh century, as well as to Northern European traditions.[36]

As we will see, localized assemblies did not naturally scale up to representative governance at the polity level. The bigger polities that mainly included representatives from towns rather than the broader countryside, like France and Castile, became absolutist. Most city-states were replaced by principalities. Yet city-state and territorial assemblies are typically treated as instances of the same phenomenon.[37] Representation in city-states responded to different incentives than in more extensive territories, however, as I argue in Chapter 7. They also failed to integrate non-urban populations. The conditions for effective statehood – fiscal centralization that allows the state to exercise distributive politics and influential groups being incentivized to enforce them[38] – are better exemplified by England.[39] Republics never solved the fundamental political problem of including extensive and diverse populations under unified rule. The two federations

[33] Integration is not the same as voting power, which came centuries later for some.
[34] The term "constitutionalism" is not entirely anachronistic. In Fortescue [c. 1470] 1997, ch. 13, "political government" denotes law-delimited rule and institutions.
[35] Whereas the term "representative" is today identified with elections, a body representing the whole electorate, and an executive that is accountable to the people, these restrictions did not fuse until after the early modern period. The medieval conceptions of representation, in contrast, could be either descriptive (when similar individuals stood in for each other) or symbolic (when the most prestigious part of society embodied the lesser), or they denoted authorization or delegation; Tierney 1983.
[36] Edwards 1934; Post 1943a; Møller 2018.   [37] Stasavage 2010; Dincecco 2011.
[38] Dincecco 2017, 24.
[39] This argument may sound like it is advocating English exceptionalism; the original intention was the opposite. This is an analytical conclusion challenging another dominant misconception, the optimality of decentralized rule.

that did, Switzerland and the Netherlands, displayed, as we will see, some critical similarities with England.

The literature typically selects criteria that proved crucial for the modern history of effective representation: inclusion of the third estate, voting, collection and administration of taxation, veto power, frequency of meetings, election of the executive.[40] On all these counts, city-states were often far ahead compared to territorial states. Yet, later chapters will show that the more advanced an institution was along many of these radical dimensions early in its development, the less long-lived and/or inclusive it was – these features therefore do not correlate with the consolidation of the institution over time. This is a key paradox of representative dynamics: what is important for modern outcomes was often inhibiting in the early stages of emergence.

Take, for instance, frequency.[41] A parliament that meets twice a year does not necessarily constrain a ruler's power more than one that meets once every two years – especially given, as this book argues, that parliaments often reflected the will of the ruler rather than of the people. Fewer meetings may indicate inconclusiveness or greater societal capacity to resist.[42] Moreover, frequency has to be weighted by duration. English parliaments could last from 17 days to 190.[43] Whereas long duration could mean an excess of business, it could also occur because parliament would not grant taxation, in which case extended sessions became "open forms of coercion of a reluctant assembly" by the ruler.[44] When frequency was halved in England in the 1400s, it was counterbalanced by longer length.[45] Without a link to ultimate outcomes, frequency cannot inform us about assembly strength.

Another common indicator is inclusion of the third estate.[46] Blockmans, for instance, showed how even "emancipated communes of free peasants gradually developed representative systems from the bottom up" and often princes were not necessary.[47] However, areas where this occurred (as in the rich agricultural regions of north-central Europe) are not where polity-wide representative institutions prevailed (with the aforementioned Swiss and Dutch qualified exceptions discussed in Chapter 7). Rather, they prevailed where the *nobility* was more effectively compelled by the ruler. From the perspective of this analysis, therefore,

---

[40] Herb 2003; Stasavage 2010; van Zanden et al. 2012.
[41] van Zanden et al. 2012; Stasavage 2010.   [42] Burkhardt 2015, 168.
[43] Under Edward I and in 1445–46 respectively; Maddicott 2010, 339; Ormrod 1995, 36. Also, Blockmans 1976, 224.
[44] Lewis 1962, 14.   [45] Roskell 1956, 155–56.
[46] See the nuanced and rich corrective in Hébert 2014, 175–98.
[47] Blockmans 1998, 34.

distinguishing between pre-parliaments including nobles and "full" versions that included urban representatives would be misleading.[48] Both councils and meetings designated as parliaments are relevant, since "contemporaries were far less concerned than modern scholarship" about these distinctions.[49]

A more consequential variation, I argue, was between communities that sent their representatives with full powers to commit them to the king's requests (*plena potestas*) or with strict instructions, i.e. an *imperative mandate*, that stripped them of the authority to bind the community to a central decision.[50] Although the latter format appears more democratic, it undermined effective governance and encouraged fragmentation. Where central decisions became binding across the polity instead, parliament became a more effective central organ of governance. Otherwise it was just a bargaining device with groups that were socially and geographically separate, as was widely observed not just in European polities that turned absolutist, but in non-western regions as well.

Rejecting a sharp break like inclusion of urban groups as definitive, however, fuses the logic of emergence with that of consolidation over time. Ultimately, as we shall see, the issue is not simply a *historical* account of origins that ends at some conventional date but a *theoretically* informed specification of the core ingredients of a formula that proved resilient over time. Without assuming any teleology, the English Parliament became robust enough to survive even under the "absolutist" threats of the sixteenth and seventeenth centuries or the conflicts of the fifteenth. For an institution to become path-dependent, its key features had to achieve "lock-in." Path-dependence, according to Mahoney's concise definition, involves "historical sequences in which contingent events set into motion institutional patterns or event chains that have deterministic properties." These patterns or event chains made change very costly, which is how the institution "locked-in."[51] In England, this process stretched into the fourteenth century, as we will see. Parliamentary emergence was a process, not an event. Accordingly, this account will treat emergence and early consolidation as intertwined.

Survival into the modern period is analytically separate, however. As Blockmans wrote, "it was not the privilege of one particular type of institution: until the end of the *ancien regime*, federations of towns and

---

[48] Similar views are expressed in Lousse 1935, 699–703. Future studies will benefit from more fine-grained distinctions; see already Møller 2017.

[49] Dodd 2007, 70n58; Bradford 2007, 59–60. The term "parliament" "was applied to a purely baronial assembly as late as 1325"; Tait 1914, 752.

[50] See the overview in Hébert 2014, 219–40 and Part II.

[51] Mahoney 2000a, 507, 515. See also, Pierson 2000, 252.

villages, as well as regional and general estates and parliaments, *Landtage* and *Reichstage*, with two, three or four chambers continued to function."[52] Nonetheless, by 1800, polity-wide institutions that integrated different social groups, that actually legislated and governed with (some) popular participation, and that mainly required expanding the electorate to become fully democratic, instead of regime change, even revolution, were rare; England stands out.[53]

It is also important to distinguish this account from much contemporary scholarship that does not explain representative institutions or practices per se, but related concepts that are easily conflated with them. Schumpeter's classic article explained "the tax state," Tilly explained state emergence, Levi national revenue systems and policies, North, Wallis, and Weingast explained open social orders.[54] Representative emergence also differs from determining tax-and-spend equilibria in advanced democracies.[55] Finally, representation is also a separate dependent variable from democracy, as scholars emphasize,[56] though empirically the two concepts are indeed fused in the post-war period. Representative institutions predated the universal franchise by centuries. The Frankfurt Parliament of 1848 introduced free and almost universal suffrage, but it was preceded by the Confederate Diet (the *Bundestag*), which drew on the Imperial Diet (the *Reichstag*), itself dating to the medieval Holy Roman Empire.

Yet bargaining over taxation appears intuitively important,[57] especially given powerful mottos like "no taxation without representation," and the frequent conflation of representation with democracy has increased its apparent plausibility as a key mechanism. It is important to note, therefore, that suffrage increases have only rarely been linked to taxation – most strikingly via the women's vote.[58] Where the bargaining logic has illuminated the process of democratization – how institutions expanded to include broader social groups or how they extended more rights to included groups – it has typically been through war[59] and the fear of revolution[60] not taxation of empowered groups. Taxation per se is instead usually a dependent variable in the literature.[61] Tilly, in a brief statement, linked democracy to "intervention-resistance-repression-bargaining cycles," exemplified by absolutist France. But these led not to democracy

---

[52] Blockmans 1998, 61.
[53] England had had its revolution already of course and had pervasive corruption and inequality to combat, but the point stands as far as its institutions are concerned.
[54] Schumpeter [1918] 1991; Tilly 1990; Levi 1988, 4; North et al. 2009.
[55] Timmons 2005, 532.   [56] Dahl 1971; Pitkin 2004.   [57] Martin et al. 2009a, 22–26.
[58] Lott and Kenny 1999; Teele 2014.   [59] Skocpol 1992; Scheve and Stasavage 2012.
[60] Przeworski 2009.   [61] Boix 2003; Acemoglu and Robinson 2005.

but to revolution, terror, monarchy, and two empires, before becoming democratic.[62] Historical origins suggest the disconnect is not accidental. In any case, universal suffrage is analytically distinct from whether a central institution exists that local actors have incentives to support or attend.

2.2   The Theoretical Landscape: Alternative Theories and their Limitations

As discussed in the Introduction, the bargaining logic that permeates most current explanations of representative institutions fails to explain the three major puzzles posed by representative emergence: institutional regularity, the collective action problem of different social orders, and the territorial anchoring of representative regimes. In this section, I examine some key theoretical works in greater detail to establish this point and thus illuminate the contribution of my argument, whilst raising some additional empirical concerns. I first discuss geopolitical and bellicist arguments and then consider historical institutionalist accounts.

2.2.1   Bargaining in Geopolitical and Bellicist Arguments

Perhaps the classic form of the geopolitical argument was articulated by Otto Hintze, who challenged economic and class-based theories, especially of Marxist origin, by focusing on war intensity.[63] According to him, "England, with her insular security, was not directly exposed to the danger of [Continental] wars. She needed no standing army ... of Continental proportions, but only a navy ... In consequence she developed no absolutism. Absolutism and militarism go together on the Continent just as do self-government and militia in England."[64]

One could question the premise of insularity, as England was frequently invaded until 1066, by Romans, Danes, and others. If being separated by water provided security, England would not have been able to invade France repeatedly; its "insularity" after 1066 was due to its effective internal organization, which made invasion costly. Even if we accept Hintze's premise of insularity, however, his logical conclusions do not follow, and regularity and collective action remain unexplained. Absent an external enemy and coercive state capacity, why would social

---

[62] Tilly 2009.

[63] Hintze 1975a; 1975c; 1975d. The argument dates to seventeenth-century parliamentarians; Brewer 1989, 10.

[64] Hintze 1975c, 199. I address Hintze's work on medieval estates, which was more complex, in the next section.

actors collectively attend a central institution (parliament) and agree to taxation? When state coercion is weak, incentives are to free-ride and shirk even in modern, public-goods-providing states, making consent to taxation and representation even harder to explain in a premodern context. Accordingly, collective action and constitutional structures should wane when war pressures and state coercive powers are weak, contrary to Hintze's predictions.

Similar concerns affect theories explicitly predicated on this geopolitical logic, for instance Charles Tilly's pivotal formulation on state formation, that "war made the state and the state made war."[65] Within this logic, representative institutions are not a dependent variable, but emerge incidentally through either a balance of power with social actors or a weak bargaining position of the ruler. For Tilly, "Kings of England did not *want* a Parliament to form and assume ever-greater power; they conceded to barons, and then to clergy, gentry, and bourgeois, in the course of persuading them to raise the money for warfare."[66] For Levi, it was "the relatively weaker bargaining position of English monarchs vis-à-vis their constituents [that] led to concessions that French monarchs did not have to make."[67] These foundational statements thus introduced a social contract to explain institutions as concessions flowing from royal weakness, challenging elitist theories predicated on coercion.[68] The bargaining logic is also widely invoked by historians, who see English kings making "humiliating concessions" to obtain direct taxation.[69] However, both bargaining parity and royal weakness suggest social actors would *resist* an institution becoming regular. They also can't explain how actors coordinated to demand concessions in common.

To address such concerns, many scholars point to the Military Revolution. This was a "process whereby small, decentralized, self-equipped feudal hosts were replaced by increasingly large, centrally financed and supplied armies" that required increasingly "sophisticated and expensive weaponry."[70] It therefore increased the fiscal needs of rulers and also displaced cavalry, thus undermining the nobility. However, similar changes occurred in Qin China (after 356 BCE): it was as immersed in war and saw cavalry replaced by infantry, as political scientist Victoria Hui has noted, without developing representation.[71]

---

[65] Tilly 1975, 42.   [66] Tilly 1990, 64, 30.

[67] Levi 1988, 97, 112; North and Thomas 1973, 83–84; Barzel and Kiser 2002. Levi notes, however, that the original weakness she posited led to Parliament, which enhanced taxing capacity; she calls this a "paradox"; Levi 1988, 97, 120.

[68] Levi 1988; Martin et al. 2009a, 18.

[69] Dodd 2007, 139. Also, Maddicott 2010, 173–75, 300–10; Burt 2013, 153–54.

[70] Downing 1992, 10; Roberts 1956.   [71] Hui 2005, 80, 152.

Some explanation is therefore needed why Western elites had collective bargaining capacity to demand representation whilst their Chinese counterparts did not.

For some scholars, this collective action problem is solved by Europe's "rampant" political fragmentation: elites could trade taxes for representation when threats were external and multidirectional and "exit" was easy.[72] But this fragmentation remains unexplained, raising endogeneity concerns. It was not a natural given. It resulted from the political development that occurred in the centuries preceding the earliest starting point of most econometric studies, the fifteenth century. "Fragmentation" is the optical effect of multiple units achieving comparable internal organization and cohesion, allowing them to withstand the attacks of neighbors. This organization, as we will see, was since the eleventh century typically predicated on assemblies and forms of governance that varied mainly in how they aggregated activities at the supra-local level; they were products not of trade but of Roman or other law and collective organization – the topics of this book. They ensured that power was centralized in each unit effectively enough.

Conversely, ancient China would not be described as highly centralized[73] if all units had had the administrative efficiency of the Qin, for instance, that was impressively described by Hui.[74] Moreover, Chinese centralization was more apparent than real in later eras: the Ming regime (1368–1644) suffered from "under-taxation" since its formative stage.[75] Chinese bureaucracy was also highly fragmented and localized, even "impotent" at this time – suggesting that the characterization of China as centralized is misguided, as Hall emphasized long ago;[76] instead, it echoes the normative/empirical inversion identified in this book. In the 1780s, Chinese per capita extraction was less than a twentieth of Britain's.[77]

Another type of geopolitical explanation addresses the problem of collective action by focusing on the transaction costs produced by distance and geographic scale.[78] Political scientist David Stasavage has shown in his cross-country study of European territorial states and city-republics between 1250 and 1750 that negotiation was simpler and representation more likely when all could assemble "around the bell of

---

[72] Dincecco and Wang 2018, 341; also Hoffman 2015, 104; Gennaioli and Voth 2015.
[73] Dincecco and Wang 2018.   [74] Hui 2005.
[75] Huang 1998, 107, 111, 113, 148–71; Fairbank and Goldman 1998, 132–33.
[76] Fairbank and Goldman 1998, 133; Hall 1985a, 33–57.
[77] Dincecco and Wang 2018, 349. Size mattered of course, but as I point out elsewhere, it did not preclude some core area developing strong infrastructure and ruling other regions "imperially." This is what England did after all.
[78] Fawtier 1953; Guenée 1968; Blockmans 1978; 1998.

a church,"[79] as republican theory emphasized.[80] Indeed, England never integrated the conquered territories of Scotland, Ireland, or even Wales. French rulers acknowledged the drawbacks of the "grande distance" in establishing institutions[81] while the logistics of large assemblies were daunting.[82]

However, the effects of geography are underestimated in small territories and overestimated in large ones. First, France's overall size cannot explain why institutions were not formed over some sub-region. Brittany and Flanders were not further from Paris than the North or Cornwall were from London. Moreover, size problems could be mitigated through committee systems.[83] Conversely, even the smallest units, city-republics, failed to retain participatory government over time or to extend beyond their borders, as Chapter 7 argues. The variation in how collective action was inhibited by similar distances in some cases but not in others remains unexplained.

Moreover, attendance was high even in large polities when actors found it in their interest. Cities were sending so many delegations to Paris on business (*pro negociis ville*) that an ordinance in 1262 limited their numbers.[84] Further, French nobles were present in Paris. Many powerful bishops and magnates had residences, *hôtels*, there. The Duke of Berry in the early 1400s had at least six.[85] "Paris served as a magnet for the Flemish court" centered at the count's *hôtel*.[86] Though they would avoid meetings where concessions or work were demanded of them, a visit to the royal court on major religious feasts was highly coveted. The *Parlement* gave ceremonious access to the king and cultivated patronage networks. Lords, and especially the twelve peers of France, were tried in Paris at least until 1300.[87] Logistical problems may have been more serious than in England, therefore, but they were not insurmountable.

Further, smaller distances could still impede attendance. Travel was burdensome enough to require proctorial representation for English nobles and especially clergy.[88] True, the "poor safety of the roads from the multitudes of armed men … throughout the kingdom" exacerbated French conditions.[89] But conditions were also dangerous in England in times of crisis, as in the 1310s and 1340s, when the king had to offer safe conduct to parliamentarians.[90] Had these conditions been constant, the

[79] Stasavage 2010, 628; 2011. See also, Dincecco 2011.   [80] Madison et al. 1987.
[81] Du Mège 1844, 206.   [82] Bisson 1972, 555–56.
[83] As for 1356 and 1484; Lewis 1962, 10.   [84] Bisson 1969, 360, 362.
[85] Favier 1974, 108, 93–113.   [86] Vale 2001, 147.
[87] Desportes 1989; Sautel-Boulet 1955; Lemarignier 1970, 326.
[88] Roskell 1956, 156–57, 172–74.   [89] Du Mège 1844, 206.
[90] Ormrod 1990b, 106; Bradford 2007, 99. For the continent, see Hébert 2014, 278–93.

institution may never have consolidated. Moreover, the cost of sending representatives was high: stunningly, it was double the wage for military campaigns for knights, 4 shillings daily, and 2 shillings for burgesses.[91] Such cost caused bitter debates within communities.[92] Yet parliament still formed.

While geopolitical, bellicist, and distance-based accounts address the problem of collective action, they don't resolve it. By taking the fiscal bargaining logic as sufficient, they also don't broach the problem of regularity and territorial anchoring.

2.2.2   Historical Institutionalist Explanations

Historical institutionalist approaches avoid the perils of functionalism, as they draw on factors such as historical legacies and timing, as well as the pressures of war and geopolitics and the extent of commercial development. They are typically based on path-dependence and explicitly theorize temporality and sequencing. They integrate history and highlight the long-term effects of small or contingent events.[93] The two major accounts, by Brian Downing and Thomas Ertman, however, have a broader dependent variable than this study, namely regime type.[94] Accordingly, parliamentary institutions are either exogenous or not fully explained in these accounts.

In Downing's account, parliaments were taken as given: where medieval representative institutions existed and escaped the pressures of the sixteenth-century Military Revolution and where rulers could raise financial support externally through loans, rather than internally through coercion, constitutional regimes survived. Ertman described the variation in representative institutions through Otto Hintze's classic distinction between bicameral and tricurial assemblies.[95] He explained this variation by arguing that bicameral assemblies emerged where local, territorial ties were strong and estate divisions weak, as in England, Poland, and Hungary.[96] Where the Carolingian legacy had created fragmentation, as in Latin Europe, the nobility, the clergy, and the burghers had deep divisions and weak territorial ties, so the tricurial system prevailed.[97]

---

[91] Maddicott 1981, 78–80; Cam 1963, 237.   [92] Cam 1963, 239–47.

[93] Pierson 2000; 2004; Mahoney 2000a.

[94] Downing 1992; Ertman 1997. Ertman's theory also explains the variation between bureaucratic and patrimonial regimes.

[95] Hintze 1970; Ertman 1997, 20–21.

[96] Sayles 1988, 56 suggests bicameralism reflects the judicial specialization of the two orders, with lords judging cases. But this applied to tricurial systems too.

[97] Whether these developments happened before or after the onset of geopolitical competition in 1450 further determined whether the regime became patrimonial or bureaucratic, although this variation is not central to my analysis; Ertman 1997, 21–34.

Did territorial ties generate bicameralism? And were they the historical legacy of the Anglo-Saxon period? Can these ties thus explain the crucial feature of the English Parliament Ertman also notes, that "members of the different orders were mixed together in both chambers"?[98] In fact, nobles did not actually have strong territorial ties in the early period, especially as the crown ensured landed estates were typically spread across counties.[99] Some historians even argue that the gentry's ties were not territorial, to the county, but to the lords.[100] Accordingly, I argue, boundaries between social orders were weak due to greater royal power.[101] The "legal dividing line in English society [was set] between the free and the villeins, and not between noble and non-noble" by Henry I.[102] Further, all tenants-in-chief had common fiscal burdens which created "the union of the prelacy and barony," as the nineteenth-century historian William Stubbs noted.[103] In any case, territorial ties would not explain why localities were integrated into a central Parliament, how the crown achieved territorial anchoring. The stronger the localities, the weaker their integration in the center should be.

In France, by contrast, social orders were defined by legal privilege, by "private" laws and customs.[104] The French (and German) nobility was "a nobility of the blood," unlike the English one.[105] Moreover, local, territorial governance structures were not weak in France – they were just weakly subordinated to the center. From the 1300s, the three orders were summoned by bailiwick ("par bailliages et sénéchaussées") and elected in local assemblies.[106] Territorial attachments were strong across all orders in the medieval period, just as in the sixteenth century,[107] though perhaps somewhat less for the Church.[108] The third estate, as we will see, had only urban not rural representation, and was endowed with great independence.[109] This made French particularism a daunting obstacle to state expansion; local assemblies proliferated, even deciding on taxation, thus undercutting the Estates-General, as we will see in Chapter 5.

Accordingly, the bicameral structure of the English Parliament cannot be linked to territorial ties or to the mixture of orders per se. Bicameralism

---

[98] Ertman 1997, 21.   [99] Bartlett 2000, 219; Prestwich 1990, 60; Maddicott 2010, 393.
[100] Prestwich 1990, 60–63; Maddicott 2010, 435–36.
[101] Ertman repeatedly noted England's strong central government, though he adopts a collaborative model where social groups worked together with the crown; Ertman 1997, 159, 163–64, 24. This account focuses on effective compellence by the crown.
[102] Maddicott 2010, 435–36.
[103] Stubbs 1880, 185. The Polish clergy was also summoned to the Senate; Bardach 1977, 293.
[104] Contamine 1997, 21, 21–45.   [105] Stubbs 1880, 192–94.   [106] Luchaire 1892, 503.
[107] Major 1951, 73–75; Hébert 2014, 165–69; Lewis 1962, 9.   [108] Bisson 1972, 562.
[109] Lemarignier 1970, 300–301.

also cannot help us explain the origins of the institution, as the chambers separated late in England, in 1341, almost half a century after the institution was fully fledged[110] (similarly in Poland it was instituted in 1504, more than a century after assemblies begun).[111] Furthermore, the English *system* was not technically bicameral – the clergy were convoked separately by the archbishops after the 1330s.[112] Separate convocation reflects church–state relations and state strength more than territorial ties. Though originally it reflected greater clergy independence,[113] it eventually weakened the Church. Church complaints from "1280 were still being presented twenty, thirty and forty years later ... And always the royal response is guarded, evasive, or an uncompromising refusal."[114] Illustrating a common pattern observed in this book, "the side which rejected the union for the sake of independence fell into a state of subjection": the more independent a social group originally, the more it was weakened eventually.[115] Accordingly, the parochial clergy was, like the towns, more heavily taxed than the counties and the barons (at least 10 versus 6.6 percent), suggesting greater subjection to the crown.[116]

Existing historical institutionalist accounts thus take either representative institutions themselves or their territorial integration as given. As they are predicated on war, moreover, they also do not explain the regularity of institutions or how groups achieved collective action. Next I address the problem of regularity, by tying it to royal power.

2.3 Solutions to the Problem of Regularity: Functional Layering and Institutional Fusion

Polity-wide representative institutions became regular when they needed to involve functions that had greater inherent regularity and bottom-up demand. Justice, not taxation, fulfilled that role. The result was a layering of functions, which echoes a form of emergence in historical institutionalist literature, institutional layering.[117] In institutional layering, change occurs when new institutions are superimposed over pre-existing structures, combining new arrangements on pre-existing structures. It is a form of path-dependent institutional change that typically does not rely on increasing returns.[118] Instead, it generally emerges when actors seek to subvert the status quo because they are not strong enough to

---

[110] Powell and Wallis 1968, 328–29.   [111] Miller 1983, 73.
[112] Denton 1981, 100; Finer 1997, 1040.
[113] Denton 1981, 107; Clarke 1936, 126–40.   [114] Bradford 2007, 163.
[115] Pollard 1920, 194.   [116] Stubbs 1878, 339, 335–41. Tax rates later changed.
[117] Thelen 2003, 225–28.   [118] Thelen 2003, 226; Pierson 2000, 259.

radically change it. This often results in antagonistic relations between institutional layers.[119]

A slightly different logic and terminology is displayed in this account, which distinguishes between the institution and its functions. When an institution dispenses functions that generate weak incentives towards regularization (e.g. the top-down demand for taxation), other functions (e.g. the bottom-up demand for regular dispensation of justice) may compensate, enabling the institution to combine different functions and become regular. Functional layering generated institutional fusion. When rulers dispensed justice centrally and were able to enforce attendance and service across the most powerful social group, as in England, they had a regular forum available to make fiscal and political demands. As Chapter 3 will show, strong royal powers were necessary for such fusion to occur.

The insight remains relevant because in conditions of low political development, institutional autonomy may impede growth rather than secure it. This is one more case of the normative/empirical inversion identified throughout the book. Norms that appear fundamental for a political order may be directly contrary to the conditions of its emergence. In the following section, I present the empirical context in more detail.

2.3.1   The Regularization of the English and French Parlements: Paths of Functional Layering and Institutional Fusion

Though the Paris *Parlement* is known as a judicial institution, the English Parliament was also England's "High Court of Parliament" (remaining so until 2005).[120] In fact, both institutions are connected to the judicial functions of the king's court, the *curia regis*, known as the King's Council, which included a small group of magnates and officials that helped the king govern.[121] Both institutions initially had political, i.e. consultative, administrative, and fiscal functions.[122] Decisions on war and peace were taken at the court, where powerful subjects were obliged to give "counsel and aid" due to their "dependent tenure."[123] The *Parlement* even issued incessant diplomatic missions to European crowns and mediated disputes between French kings and feudal vassals or foreign

---

[119] Schickler 2001, 15–16; Thelen 2003, 226–28; Mahoney and Thelen 2010, 25–26, 29.
[120] The term is first recorded after the 1380s; McIlwain 1910.
[121] Shennan 1998, 14; Ducoudray 1902, 22–46; Langlois 1890; Doucet 1948, 167. For the royal Council, see Lot and Fawtier 1958, 75–82; Lapsley [1914] 1925, 8; Tout 1920, 146–55.
[122] Bisson 1969; Maddicott 2010; Shennan 1998, 151–87.
[123] Maddicott 2010, 443, 188; Harding 2002, 171, 203–10; Langmuir 1961; Villers 1984, 96; Rigaudière 1994, 167. Counsel and council are distinguished in Spencer 2014, 51–64.

rulers.[124] The "parallels between the development of [the English Parliament] and the growth of the French king's *parlement* are unmistakable."[125]

Yet, the two institutions diverged. To explain why, first I present the empirical evidence on regularity of judicial functions, showing how fiscal functions were separated from judicial ones in the French case, whereas they overlapped in the English institution. Then I show that nobles had common incentives to attend Parliament in both cases, flowing from the administration of legislation and justice delivered by the crown. But as Chapter 3 will show, it was English nobles that were present at higher rates, because the crown was able to compel them, thus endowing the institution with greater regularity.

2.3.2   Regularity and Taxation?

The bellicist logic assumes that war pressures necessitated taxes, forcing rulers to grant parliaments. If so, taxation should account for institutional regularity early on. Despite its prevalence, the assumption has not been empirically tested. Doing so shows taxation to be very irregular. Parliament is considered to have its fully-fledged form in 1295, including all three orders. Yet only about 24 percent of the sessions of the English Parliament dealt with taxation between 1216 and 1300 and about 5 percent additional sessions on war matters without taxes considered.[126] The period that saw the introduction of the third estate, between 1260 and 1290, had the lowest rate of tax-related parliaments, 15 percent (Figure 2.1). In the earlier period between 1235 and 1257, dominated by the nobility alone, 31 percent (17) dealt with taxation.[127]

Similarly, the French Estates-General, which lacked a judicial function, had very low frequency.[128] In fact, purely fiscal meetings were even fewer: only 12 out of its 22 meetings over a full century (1300–1399) raised taxes – the rest dealt with domestic policy (Figure 2.2). The Estates-General were suppressed between 1484 and 1560 and also from 1614 until the French Revolution, making the regime absolutist. If the English Parliament had had a primarily fiscal purpose, its frequency would likely have been similar to that of the Estates-General. As we will see, in none of the cases in this book was taxation a regular feature of early

---

[124] Ducoudray 1902, 319–20; Aubert [1890] 1977, 187–226; Bisson 1969.
[125] Harding 2002, 170; Fawtier 1953, 275.
[126] Complete tallies will require further consultation with primary sources.
[127] Maddicott 2010, 288, 455–72.
[128] Many meetings on taxation were held at the sub-national level in France. I consider these in Chapter 5.

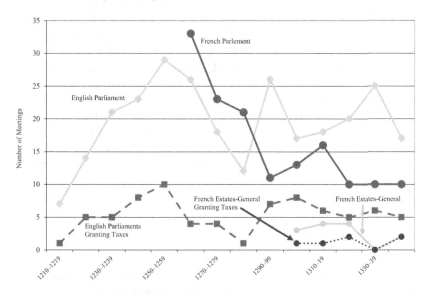

Figure 2.1 Meeting frequency per decade of the English Parliament, English Parliament sessions granting taxation, French Estates-General, and Paris *Parlement*
Sources: Fryde 1996; Maddicott 1994; Bradford 2007, 133; *Actes du Parlement de Paris* 1863; Furgeot 1920; Soule 1968; Hervieu 1879; Desjardins 1871. Fryde 1996 was supplemented by Matthew Paris 1853 for tax grants, though further primary sources should improve this assessment.

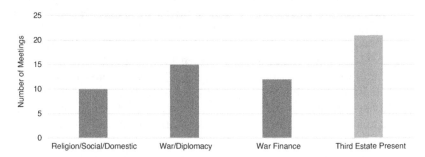

Figure 2.2 Number of French Estates-General by purpose, 1302–1399 (total meetings: 22).
Sources: Hervieu 1879; Desjardins 1871; Taylor 1954; Bisson 1972; Strayer and Taylor 1939.

representation. The *Parlement*'s frequency, however, rivaled that of the English Parliament.

This is not to say that taxation was inconsequential; its role in the expansion of representation will be examined in Part II. But it was not regular enough to produce a regular institution. Accordingly, in the remaining sections I examine the constant, overwhelming, and universal need for law, justice, and peace, first among the nobility, then in the broader population. This judicial interaction was regularized where nobles were more systematically compelled to serve in different capacities.

2.3.3   Royal Legislation: Incentives to Attend

Nobles had great incentives to seek out the king's court since legislation was passed there. The legislative role of Parliament could be easily over-looked, as ever since the seventeenth century English common law is widely conceived as the product of custom and judge-made precedent. As Hayek stated, it was not "the product of anyone's will but rather as a barrier to all power, including that of the king."[129] Ironically, more evidence exists of deliberate polity-wide rule and law creation by English kings (writs, assizes, statutes, or charters), some of which continue to shape English law, than by their French counterparts in this period.[130] This was the case with the major reforms under Henry II (1154–89),[131] "when it first becomes possible to recognize the existence of an English 'common law.'"[132] Common law was mostly land law originally,[133] which was "common" because it could be applied only in royal courts.

Social scientists North, Wallis, and Weingast projected a contractual logic on this process. In their account, English land law spread because "the dominant coalition" within the elite "manipulate[d] the economy to provide the incentives for powerful individuals not to use violence."[134] But the emerging land law of the king did not (just) provide *incentives* for powerful individuals; it sharply restricted their powers.

Nobles indeed were affected by royal legislation because Henry II asserted jurisdiction over all serious crimes and most land disputes held

---

[129] Hayek 1973, 85.

[130] See the list of statutes in Baker 2002, pp. xiii–xix and chapter 12. Also, Harding 2002, 186–90; Hudson 2012, 258–60, 498–500.

[131] All dates refer to ruling years.

[132] Brand 2007, 215; Hudson 1996a, 22–23. Historians disagree about whether common law was the product of deliberate action or an unintended consequence of Henry's drive to rule; Milsom 1981; 1985. The judicious conclusion is that he was the driving force of reforms, even if not their direct origin, building on reforms by Henry I (1100–35); Hudson 1994; 2012, 528–30. See also, van Caenegem 1988; Brand 1997.

[133] The definitive account now is by John Hudson 2012.   [134] North et al. 2009, 77.

by free tenure (through the Assizes of Clarendon in 1166 and Northampton in 1176).[135] But this meant that cases were removed from local courts where noble lords were too powerful for tenants to accuse. Two immensely popular legal forms of action on property, *novel disseisin* and *mort d'ancestor*, could only be tried with a royal writ in a royal court.[136] They protected the rights of weak tenant heirs by enabling them to act against powerful lords, a "remarkable fact."[137] When royal justice was made available to all free men, it effectively undermined honorial lordship.[138] It gave free sub-tenants far more security than tenants-in-chief,[139] whilst subjecting the nobility often to more onerous impositions.[140] Indeed, at least after the 1150s tenure was more commonly disrupted at the top of society.[141] The institution that regulated these relations was the king's court originally and eventually Parliament.

Did war/fiscal pressures motivate royal legislation? As Besley and Persson point out, fiscal and legal capacity were complementary.[142] But precise links are more precarious. According to political scientists Blaydes and Paik, mobilization for the Crusades between 1092 and 1272 spearheaded institutional development. Though the Crusades strongly impacted society before 1150, no institution emerged then. The Saladin Tithe was indeed raised for a Crusade in 1188 and was polity-wide,[143] but its success depended on Henry II's major legislative reforms – the latter, moreover, occurred during relative peace and no Crusades. War encouraged royal judicial expansion thereafter at points, as in the 1240s[144] or around the Crusade of 1271–72. But such war pressures afflicted French rulers equally, as well as many of their European counterparts; they translated into wide, public taxation only in England however, as historian Mark Ormrod pointed out.[145]

Magnates benefited from some new rules. They could now bequeath land across generations by using entails, through the Statute of Westminster II (1285).[146] They also improved their position, as Max Weber noted,[147] when a royal statute barred their tenants from creating sub-tenants, a practice called subinfeudation (*Quia Emptores* in 1290).[148] However, this also reduced the number of intermediate tenants of the

---

[135] Hudson 2012, 498–99, 514–19. An assize was a session of a court of justice, or a piece of legislation, as in these uses of the word, or a form of action.

[136] Hudson 2012, 604–606, 609–14. See next chapter.

[137] Milsom 1981, 139; Hudson 2012, 856.

[138] Milsom 1976, 149–51; Hudson 2012, 849. Honors were "assemblages of estates held by military tenure"; Bartlett 2000, 219.

[139] Hudson 1994, 280; 1996b, 212–18, 219; 2012, 848; Harding 2002, 132.

[140] See Chapters 2–4, 6, 11.   [141] Holt 1972, 30–36; 1982, 207–10; Hudson 1994, 59.

[142] Besley and Persson 2011, 15.   [143] Blaydes and Paik 2016, 558–60.

[144] Burt 2013, 29.   [145] Ormrod and Barta 1995, 69.

[146] The Statutes of the Realm 1810, 71–95.   [147] Weber 1978, 258.

[148] Baker 2002, 260–61; Raban 2000, 124.

crown, strengthening royal control. The same year, all lords had to confirm with what warrant (*Quo Warranto*) they held their lands and jurisdictional rights – such country-wide royal inquests were pursued by rulers across Europe,[149] but English kings could better implement them.

Incentives for broader social strata to attend also increased under Edward I, when common law greatly expanded. Many civil, criminal, and administrative matters, from debt to slander, extortion, murder, rape, and the timing of assizes, were regulated through the Statute of Westminster I in 1275. Attendance was unusually high, maybe even eight hundred county and borough representatives may have been present, who then disseminated the information locally through the county courts.[150] The Statute "marked the growing importance of [Parliament] as a focal point for reform and contact between king and subjects."[151] However, law itself generally "was the work of assemblies to which the commons were not summoned," as Stubbs noted.[152] Only after the 1320s were the Commons integral to this process.[153]

French legislation, by contrast, was hampered by relative royal weakness. When law on property was passed, as on the succession of fiefs, it was limited to the royal domain. Legislation was not a royal monopoly; the king "could not place the ban in the land of a baron without his consent," as attested in the *Établissements* of Saint Louis, a legal compilation of 1272–73.[154] In England, by contrast, the Assize of Northampton in 1176 was enforced in thirty-four out of thirty-seven counties.[155] The French nobility legislated in their own domains instead.[156] Royal legislation typically affirmed local customs.[157] This meant that the *Parlement*'s activities incentivized the French nobility much less than its English counterpart. Regional boundaries were only occasionally transcended, as with the ordinances on Jews; records suggest no more than twenty-six barons as witnesses.[158] Towns, however, accepted royal legislation, for instance on town government corruption and incompetence – some resisted, but the crown helped towns counteract the nobility.[159] This jurisdictional variation eventually shaped representation in the Estates, as we will see. The nobility

[149] Pécout 2010.   [150] Maddicott 2010, 292, 448.   [151] Coss 1989, 47.
[152] Stubbs 1880, 268.   [153] Bradford 2007, 170–71.
[154] Rigaudière 1994, 127; Lot and Fawtier 1958, 290–300.
[155] Maddicott 2010, 400. Some franchises existed (e.g. the Palatinates of Durham, Lancaster, and Chester), as well as some private courts, and the powerful Marcher lordships; Holdsworth 1922, 109–32. But common law procedure penetrated even there; Hudson 2012, 855.
[156] Rigaudière 1994, 162–63.   [157] Shennan 1998, 50–53.
[158] Lot and Fawtier 1958, 291. Caution is required with the French evidence, as records are scant; Decoster 2002.
[159] Bisson 1969, 360; Spruyt 1994.

was not effectively integrated, and the third estate only involved towns: the "enormous mass" of peasants had no representation.[160]

Jurisdictional weakness probably also encouraged the French crown to assert absolute rights of legislation, challenging the imperial prerogative. This trend forged the notion of the state and legitimized its extractive claims: edictal power underlay the power to tax. The canonist rediscovery of Roman law was instrumental in this, as was the Aristotelian idea of the common good or *pourfit* (profit), which royal legislation had to serve.[161] Although by the 1280s the legist Beaumanoir could declare that legislation also required deliberation "par très grant conseil,"[162] these developments were not institutionalized through the *Parlement*. Instead, the *Parlement*'s legislative role consisted of registering royal letters and ordinances, eventually developing the right of remonstrance: a royal act was only valid when registered through the *Parlement*.[163] These powers obliged the king to respond if the *Parlement* refused registration, but they were limited.[164] With less power to impose legislation on matters directly affecting the nobility, the crown's capacity to incentivize it via legislation was constrained.

2.3.4   Demands for Justice: Incentives to Attend

The definitive function of medieval kings, however, was judging.[165] Both rulers and subjects had incentives to interact over justice; kings established control over populations, whilst subjects had common grievances, typically concerning titles to land, official corruption, and crime. Judging was also more regular than legislation, which was occasional.[166]

The English royal court was so popular as an adjudication center after Henry II extended it beyond the "great men" that "suitors paid money to the king to have their cases tried there," in fact large amounts "for writs, for pleas, for trials, for judgment, for expedition, or for delay."[167] By the

---

[160] Rigaudière 1994, 167–68.

[161] Rigaudière 1988, 212 and passim; Hilaire 2011, 237–50.

[162] Beaumanoir 1900, 1499–1516.   [163] Rigaudière 1994, 215–17.

[164] Shennan 1998, 159–61. Deadlocks were resolved through a parliamentary session in the king's presence, the *lit de justice*; Hanley 1983; Holt 1988.

[165] Bartlett 2000, 178; Lot and Fawtier 1958, 289–300; Rigaudière 1988, 205.

[166] In English historiography, the judicial function was for long controversial. It was championed as "the essence" of Parliament by two staunchly conservative historians, who dismissed the political function as overrated and anachronistic in Whiggish accounts; Richardson and Sayles 1981. Ironically, the arch-conservatives focused on justice as a major *popular* demand, while their progressive critics, by focusing on taxation instead, chose the perspective of the *king* who resented the judicial functions. Today, even critics concede justice is important, though, as here, not sufficient (as discussed in Boucoyannis 2015a).

[167] Holdsworth 1922, 48.

late 1100s, eligible cases in England were already diverted from local courts to the king's courts, the King's Bench and the Court of Common Pleas.[168]

Parliament initially consisted of sessions of the royal court where kings dispensed extraordinary justice "on a very large scale."[169] They heard cases on land leases, fines, disputes between nobles, bishops, and laity, city franchises, reprisals against foreign enemies, corruption of judges and royal officials and more.[170] The cases heard concerned magnates or the king himself or they involved "grave questions of public law" or the king's equity.[171] By 1290, Parliament's role was acknowledged in legal literature: "doubts are determined there regarding judgment, new remedies are devised for wrongs newly brought to light, and there also justice is dispensed to everyone according to his deserts."[172]

As Stubbs noted, judicial functions also excluded the Commons initially; only nobles, lay and clerical, participated.[173] Nobles attended court because major property disputes were decided there and they were personally tried there,[174] especially after the law of treason expanded from the mid-fourteenth century.[175] The Parliament that tried the last native Prince of Wales, in 1283, attracted the highest number of nobles known to have been summoned, 110.[176] The next chapter shows how high these numbers were compared to France.

Yet, the French king's essential role was also that of "grand justicier," widely attested in contemporary sources[177] and already extensive under Philip Augustus (1180–1223).[178] Louis IX (1226–70) judging under the oak tree at Vincennes is a classic image from the chronicles.[179] His reign was instrumental in consolidating the *Parlement* as an institution: the term was applied to the judicial sessions of his court's meetings after it ceased to be itinerant in 1248.[180] The Paris *Parlement* also focused on conditional landholding. From the 1250s, many of the *Parlement*'s judgments were "enforcements of the king's rights to homage and jurisdiction in the fiefs of his tenants-in-chief; or the punishment of unlicensed alienations of

---

[168] Hudson 2012, 537–42, 569–73; Turner 1977.
[169] Maitland 1893, lxxxii; Musson and Ormrod 1999, 26–28.
[170] See Sayles 1988, 21–22, for a list of such cases under Henry III (1216–72); Harriss 1981, 44–45, 49–52.
[171] Holdsworth 1922, 354; Plucknett 1940, 109–13.
[172] See the common law treatise *Fleta* (Sayles and Richardson 1955), from shortly after 1290.
[173] Stubbs 1880, 271.
[174] Holdsworth 1922, 40; Powell and Wallis 1968, 406; Musson and Ormrod 1999, 27.
[175] Bellamy 1970.   [176] Maddicott 2010, 287, 293.   [177] Rigaudière 1994, 188.
[178] Baldwin 1986, 37–44.   [179] Joinville 1821–27, 184–85; Shennan 1998, 13–14.
[180] Hallam and Everard 2001, 314; Ducoudray 1902, 22–45; Fayard 1876, 4–10; Langlois 1890, 78; Shennan 1998, 10ff.

royal fiefs, especially into the 'dead hand' of the Church (churches never died, so their fiefs never escheated to the king),"[181] just as in England. When royal judgments affected broad groups of tenants, decisions amounted to legislation.[182] Broader demand for *Parlement* intervention was so high that eligibility to be heard was regulated: for instance, actions to recover land seized (the same act of *novel disseisin* that helped spread the common law in English royal courts) were sent to the local tribunals of the *baillis* and *sénéchaux* instead (the bailiffs of north and south, respectively).

All groups were affected by the *Parlement*'s jurisdictional expansion, but to varying degrees, according to their power. Nobles could be tried in the royal Court, including the dukes of Normandy, Burgundy, Aquitaine, as well as the counts of Flanders or Champagne or the king of England. But these were vassals who competed with the French king in strength and holdings – an internal power balance English kings never faced. Edward I forfeited Gascony by not appearing in the *Parlement*, for instance, triggering the Anglo-French wars between 1294 and 1303.[183] Noble resistance was strong, especially as the crown sought to abolish the privilege of judicial duel.[184] Yet nobles, whether counts or dukes, sometimes brought their own disputes to court. The *Parlement* was also where the peers (*Pairs de France*) were judged by the king.[185] But seigneurial conflict remained rampant locally, suggesting the limits of royal jurisdiction.[186]

The communes, however, pursued justice at the royal court.[187] The towns' alliance with the crown was the lynchpin of political scientist Hendrik Spruyt's account of state emergence.[188] It was through their courts that towns "were fitted into the scheme of royal government."[189] They needed royal support of their own growing jurisdiction vis-à-vis the lords, especially regarding markets. The *Parlement* adjudicated in conflicts, often splitting jurisdiction across litigants.[190] Ecclesiastics also complained of noble incursions, and the king had a duty to protect them.[191] The increasing calls for justice even under "weak kings," from Louis VII (1137–80) to Charles VI (1380–1422), demonstrates that the *demand* for justice itself was genuinely bottom-up, not one predicated on the crown's organizational powers.[192]

Since nobles were not obligated to attend, the *Parlement* never became an effective body for the king to raise tax demands and different bodies needed

---

[181] Harding 2002, 208; Ducoudray 1902, 302; Le Mené 2000.   [182] Harding 2002, 123.
[183] Harding 2002, 168.
[184] Lot and Fawtier 1958, 317–23, 419–30, 296–99; Harding 2002, 124, 162.
[185] Ducoudray 1902, 307–12; Langlois 1890, 84–85; Lemarignier 1970, 326.
[186] Firnhaber-Baker 2012.   [187] This went back to the 1140s; Harding 2002, 157.
[188] Spruyt 1994.   [189] Harding 2002, 116, 115.
[190] Hilaire 2011, 287–324; Bisson 1969, 366–68.   [191] Harding 2002, 62.
[192] Lot and Fawtier 1958, 298, 350.

to be called, either locally or at the polity-level. Tax concerns, however, were raised there; judicial courts, including the *Parlement* after especially 1270, often negotiated taxation. "Parliamentary investigations of right [on taxation issues] became, in effect ... negotiations for payments." For instance, the *Parlement* of 1271 rejected the pleas of three cities and imposed assessments on them, but others succeeded.[193] As we will also see in the Ottoman Empire, judicial processes handled some functions of representative institutions. A lack of the latter did not mean arbitrary government.

2.3.5   Petitions: Bottom-Up Incentives to Attend

One specific form of adjudication was to play a central role in both institutions: petitions. It is these that allowed the people to contribute to government, since counsel and consent were confined to the magnates, as Stubbs noted for England.[194] Rulers had a duty to address petitions,[195] one that echoed the practice of the Pope, to whom tens of thousands of petitions survive from this period.[196]

A slow trickle in England in the twelfth century became an unstoppable flood in the late thirteenth due to a "momentous innovation," in Maddicott's words:[197] "for the first time the voice of the aggrieved and of the socially insignificant could be heard at the centre of government," as petitions became accessible across social orders from the 1270s.[198] Originally complaints required purchasing a writ from Chancery in London, which was expensive and remote.[199] However, expanding on precedents from the 1250s, oral complaints were accepted locally ("in eyre") and transcribed into written "bills" that were sent to the center, thus institutionally connecting local grievance to governmental response.[200] The language was even changed from Latin to the more common French.[201]

Parliament became the focal point for submitting petitions from the 1270s to the 1290s, when the institution congealed (Figure 2.3).[202] Similar developments occurred in France, as well as throughout Europe, from Spain, to Germany, Flanders, and later Poland, Russia,

[193] Bisson 1969, 368–71.   [194] Stubbs 1880, 270.
[195] For different types across Europe, see the comprehensive review in Hébert 2014, 476–502.
[196] Millet 2003.
[197] Maddicott 1981, 62. See also Harding 2002, 147–86; Brand 2004; Dodd 2007; Ormrod et al. 2009.
[198] Maddicott 1981, 62. The innovation lay in its political use, as petitions (*gravamina*) had been presented by clergy to the king long before; Jones 1966; Dodd and McHardy 2010.
[199] Baker 2002, 53–69.
[200] Musson 2001, 162–63; Musson and Ormrod 1999, 44; Harding 2002, 178–86.
[201] Brand 2004, 25.
[202] They were presented to the king and his Council, not Parliament per se, some to queens; Dodd 2007, 52; Plucknett 1940, 113–14; Maddicott 2010, 295–96.

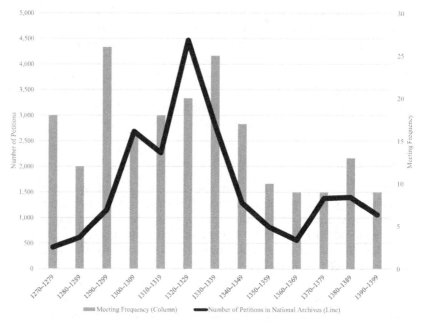

Figure 2.3 Surviving petitions and parliamentary frequency, England, 1270–1399
Sources: Ancient Petitions (SC8), National Archives. These are simply surviving petitions (Ormrod 2009, 5). The more complete records for 1305 suggest more than 360 petitions, so these figures probably underestimate totals; Brand 2004; Maitland 1893. Historians Dodd and Ormrod have now digitized this massive corpus, sparking extensive scholarship on the topic; Ormrod et al. 2017, 1.

and elsewhere, as we will see. However, the level of organization varied across cases, as did the institutional effects of this demand.[203] Although war surely enhanced the ruler's incentives to call Parliament, especially in times of crisis like the 1290s, it cannot explain bottom-up demand for *regularization*; such requests for justice can. And maybe war would not have been embarked upon, if resources could not be effectively tapped.

The Paris *Parlement* was even less propelled by war, but its regularity was similar to that of the English Parliament. War (with England) had ended in 1243, when the French crown ushered its own "bill revolution" with the great inquest (*enquête*) of 1247. Until then, "only aggrieved churches and substantial landowners" could access the king.[204] After

---

[203] Harding 2002, 160–90. See Dumolyn 2015; Hébert 2014, 465–96.
[204] Harding 2002, 161.

that, oral complaints against the king and his officers could be accepted from across the population, as they were submitted to the local clergy who could transcribe them.

Petitioning was pervasive in both cases: in England, "in the late Middle Ages assiduous petitioners sought out the king in all manner of locations and occasions, and by the seventeenth century it was necessary to provide the monarch with a special bodyguard on state days specifically to prevent unwanted (and unwashed) supplicants from thrusting petitions into his hand."[205] French kings had clerks (*juges de la porte*) following them around the country to handle petitions submitted to them personally.[206]

What kinds of concerns were transmitted to the center? Were petitioners asking for rights? The term "rights" invokes an abstract tradition of high-minded principle, of the sort claimed to place Europe apart. However, the tradition stemmed from mundane concerns, which differed little from cases beyond Europe. Claims only gained abstractness, as we will see, by eventually being framed in general terms – a process that would have been impossible absent the institutional organization described here which depended on royal strength (the advanced learning of the law, especially in the Church, was of course also crucial).

Petitions were typically extra-judicial, i.e. they were used where regular law offered no remedy or where court decisions conflicted; they appealed to royal grace.[207] In England, nobles would press claims to lands, franchises, and money. County and borough communities would petition to challenge the crown's fiscal claims or to make "requests for keeping roads and bridges in repair and complaints of the abuse of tolls, the privileges of the stannaries, or the inconvenient situation of a county gaol."[208] The gentry would seek redress from intimidation or other miscarriage of justice. Free tenants and villeins would petition against the exercise of lordship, as did communities or "estates of men, for instance, the tin-miners in Cornwall or the king's clerks in chancery."[209] Very common and serious were grievances about abuses and corruption of royal officials (about a third of a county total in the early period),[210] uncompensated purveyance (levies of war supplies imposed by the king),[211] but also rampant crime and wrongdoing.[212]

Complaints were no different in France: they often targeted the crown's local representatives wielding judicial, military, fiscal, and

[205] Ormrod 2009, 7.   [206] Rigaudière 1994, 150–51.   [207] Dodd 2007, 323.
[208] Lapsley 1951b, 141.   [209] Haskins 1938, 7; Harriss 1981, 49; Brand 2009.
[210] Maddicott 1981, 64.   [211] Harriss 1981, 50.
[212] Harding 2002, 128–46. Whether fluctuations in judicial measures reflect variation in the levels of violence or administrative capacity remains a contested topic, as evidence is poor; Bellamy 1973; Clanchy 1974; Kaeuper 1988, 134–83.

administrative powers, the *baillis*, the *sénéchaux*, and others. They could range from a *bailli* favoring the rich over the poor or extorting money from a prisoner, to the king not heating the banal-oven in a village (as obligated qua feudal lord).[213] Crime was also pervasive, as were claims against other subjects. Such petitions, especially by the Church, spread royal justice.[214]

All kings had incentives to encourage petitioning. Just as in communist China today,[215] authorities learned about provincial conditions and official corruption this way. Kings would also seek information through formal inquests or informal requests.[216] Petitions also allowed rulers to enforce their jurisdiction, including in outlying territories such as Gascony, which had no direct representation, and Scotland, and to "reinforce military conquest."[217]

Petitions had a profound impact: they increasingly generated legislation.[218] They were the basis of legislative bills; the earliest entry for "bill" in the *OED* defines it as "a written petition." "As Stubbs said long ago, nearly all the legislation of the fourteenth century is based upon parliamentary petitions."[219] This is, after all, the definitional function of parliament: popularly-based legislation. No account of representative origins can be complete if it does not explain how local grievances transformed into governmental action.

This process was more encompassing in England. Petitions were originally mostly private,[220] but they increasingly aggregated demands at a supra-local level, leading to the "common petition."[221] This was a gradual process, however, as petitions claiming to represent the "community of England" were initially presented by the barons. Knights and burgesses, eventually termed the Commons, lacked a "collective voice."[222] Only after the 1310s did the "public and frequent complaint of middling people"[223] secure legislation in response to demands, for instance against lords subverting justice.[224] By the 1320s, the Commons even had an "agenda for legislation."[225] After this time,

---

[213] Ducoudray 1902, 302.

[214] In France, the term *petitio* was connected to ordinary, not extra-ordinary, justice, contrary to English practice; Hilaire 2011, 152–60, 217–30.

[215] Takeuchi 2014, 22.   [216] Harding 2002, 109–28; Hoyt 1961, 15.

[217] Maitland 1893, lx; Dodd 2007, 40–46.   [218] Musson and Ormrod 1999, 151–57.

[219] Cam 1970a, 182. See also, Hébert 2014, 503–506, 487–90; Harding 2002, 187–88.

[220] Harding 2002, 179; Brand 2004.

[221] As with proctorial representation, Church precedent was important: *gravamina* were corporate petitions submitted since the 1230s; Jones 1966. The time lag with secular petitions shows why Church precedent did not suffice.

[222] Dodd 2007, 128–29; Harding 2002, 188; Haskins 1938; Sayles 1974, 102.

[223] *Rotuli Parliamentorum* 1783, 117.   [224] Dodd 2007, 130–31; Ormrod 1995, 30–37.

[225] Ormrod 1990a.

common petitions aggregated demands from both counties and boroughs, i.e. both rural and urban populations, into generalizable requests.[226] By the 1340s, the Commons were the conduit for popularly supplied legislation in Parliament.[227] By 1377, the full Parliament had to assent to statutes.[228] By 1450, the Commons were not only presenting the issues via petitions; they were proposing the remedy that became legislation.[229] Petitions were thus the mechanism that generated representative, inclusive governance.

Grievances also led to legislation in France, as with the "*établissement général*" of Louis the Pious in 1254.[230] The reforming ordinances of the fourteenth and fifteenth centuries responded to public petitions, for instance the provincial charters of 1315.[231] More well known from later history are the *cahiers de doléances* (lists of grievances), associated with the Estates-General or delivered to the king,[232] which were similar in purpose. The French trajectory splintered their submission process, however, between the Royal Council, the *Parlement*, and the Estates-General, weakening the institutional mechanisms of centralization. Nor do we see the supra-local organization observable in England in common petitions.

This difference is also reflected in the king's presence. This was soon considered central to the English Parliament. "It was widely accepted that the king had a responsibility to provide answers to all petitions before a parliament closed."[233] Edward I thus had to request, in 1280 and 1293, that the "flooding" of petitions reaching perhaps hundreds per session be regulated because they distracted him from the "great business of his realm."[234] When petition hearing declined, public reaction was sharp. The anonymous *Mirror of Justices*, from the early 1300s, protested that "it is an abuse that whereas parliaments ought to be held for the salvation of the souls of trespassers, twice a year and in London, they are now held but rarely and at the king's will for the purpose of obtaining aids and collection of treasure."[235] Moreover, Parliament could not normally be convoked without the king (except by his representatives). Strikingly, between 1275 and 1399, English kings were absent from perhaps 12

---

[226] Dodd 2001, 133–42; 2007, 256–57; Ormrod 1995, 35; Harriss 1963b; Rayner 1941a; 1941b. Individual petitions continued; Dodd 2001.

[227] Ormrod 1995, 33; Musson and Ormrod 1999, 146–57.   [228] Harriss 1981, 45.

[229] Ormrod 1995, 37.

[230] Harding 2002, 149–52. French historians are now also turning to petitions; Bubenicek Forthcoming was unavailable.

[231] Rigaudière 1994, 183–85.

[232] Rigaudière 1994, 176; Langlois 1909; Contamine 1976.

[233] Ormrod 2009, 7; Harding 2002, 180.

[234] Maddicott 2010, 442; Dodd 2007, 50–51.

[235] The Mirror of Justices 1895, 155; Dodd 2007, 72.

out of 154 parliaments,[236] although they could occasionally go rowing whilst appointing nobles to supervise the hearing of petitions.[237] In France, by contrast, the king's presence was "extraordinary" in the *Parlement* by 1290;[238] he would attend only for high-stakes cases (called *lits de justice*).[239] The next chapter explores why that came to be.

*

In this chapter, after more precisely defining the main necessary conditions and the dependent variable of this account, I showed how existing theoretical perspectives either suffer from empirical problems or fail to explain how regularity, collective action, and territorial anchoring are achieved. I then explained the first feature, institutional regularity, through the constant polity-wide demand for royal justice or grace. This was common to the two cases (as it was throughout Europe and beyond, as later chapters show). Rulers in both cases were asking for taxation, sometimes under pressure from war, and subjects were uniformly asking for redress of wrongs. Yet only England displayed the functional layering and institutional fusion that was critical for a polity-wide representative institution. What follows probes the comparison with France to show how power differentials explain much of this variation.

---

[236] Prestwich 1988, 442; Bradford 2011, 6.   [237] Prestwich 2003, 103.
[238] Lot and Fawtier 1958, 335, 365; Shennan 1998, 24.
[239] Hanley 1983; Hilaire 2011, 158.

3   Explaining Functional Layering and
      Institutional Fusion: The Role of Power

Why did functional layering occur in the English Parliament but not the French *Parlement*? And how was it turned into a productive mechanism enabling institutional consolidation rather than dysfunction? Liberal tradition has emphasized the need for separation of powers, a classical principle that shaped Western constitutional development, whereby judicial powers must be distinct from legislative ones.[1] By contrast, the English common law had no "fear of judicial lawmaking."[2] The trajectory of the English Parliament and the French *Parlement* traces this divergence to its roots and shows how functional layering had constitutional effects. It also shows the importance of state capacity.

As the previous chapters showed, where judicial and fiscal concerns were integrated, parliaments became regular. The same conditions solved the nobility's collective action problem and integrated local structures into central governance, creating territorial anchoring. All these dimensions, I argue, are ultimately traceable (though not reducible) to ruler capacity to compel the nobility and broader social groups to perform services. This capacity was relative, not absolute, as English rulers also struggled to enforce their powers. Nevertheless, institutional practice was more integrated and encompassing in England than on the European Continent. Explaining this requires also moving beyond the micro level, where power failures loom large, to a more aggregate picture, where distributional patterns become apparent.

The question – how differential state capacity causes institutional outcomes to diverge – has implications for social theory too. Power was neglected in institutional analysis, as the rational choice emphasis on cooperation and equilibrium[3] often assumed that change was exogenous,[4] as did much sociological theory.[5] Change was thus effectively unexplained, a challenge only gradually addressed in neo-institutionalist

---

[1] Vile 1967; Montesquieu [1748] 1989.   [2] Merryman and Pérez-Perdomo 2007, 17.
[3] As noted in Moe 2005.   [4] Shepsle 1989; Calvert 1995.
[5] DiMaggio and Powell 1983; Fligstein 1996; cf. Padgett and Powell 2012.

economics.[6] Some institutional accounts, especially those predicated on path-dependency and critical junctures, also assume exogeneity:[7] once in equilibrium or stable conditions, internal modes of change are weakened.

Power and distributional conflict were re-introduced as themes by Jack Knight,[8] while historical institutionalists Thelen and Mahoney used both to explain institutional change as endogenous.[9] In their cases, institutions are typically already formed and binding, providing incentives to "change agents" seeking to appropriate resources. These are usually weaker actors seeking change, confronted with institutional power-holders, and their strategies mostly reflect their cognitive limits and pre-existing rules.[10]

Institutional origins allow us to further probe the mechanisms of endogeneity and exogeneity. Periods of origins cannot assume pre-existing structures;[11] actor power is critical. Power resources shape rule choice itself, even before distributional outcomes can be considered. They do so, however, in a counterintuitive way in this context. Parliaments are typically expected to form where rulers are weak and bureaucratic roles separated and to fail where rulers concentrate different functions. Instead, weak rulers often compensated by selecting rational (in the Weberian sense), proto-bureaucratic procedures, such as separation of powers, as in France, or clear bureaucratic roles, as in the Ottoman Empire – yet in those cases parliaments either failed or never emerged.[12] Strong rulers, by contrast, often concentrated different functions, as in England, generating more patrimonial yet more integrated institutions – and strong parliaments.[13] Weber noted the paradox of England also being "the first and most highly developed capitalist country" despite a patrimonial structure. Conversely, he tied a bureaucratic structure to political decentralization. But these correlations are typically missed.[14] Bureaucratic structures are today's desideratum, but constitutionalism sometimes initially consolidated better through patrimonial ones. Institutional fusion is one such instance.

Next I show why alternative explanations of variation in institutional fusion are incomplete. The subsequent three sections present the proposed explanation, based on ruler power over the most powerful, by examining its observable implications. At the micro level, greater English royal power implies higher noble attendance at Parliament and

---

[6] Ménard and Shirley 2014.   [7] As noted in Capoccia and Kelemen 2007.
[8] Knight 1992; see also Moe 2005.
[9] Thelen 2003; Mahoney and Thelen 2010. See also Greif and Laitin 2004.
[10] Mahoney and Thelen 2010, 12–13, 27.   [11] Slater and Simmons 2010.
[12] The last section argues France was originally bureaucratic, before patrimonialism spread.
[13] As we will see, this did not preclude also using bureaucratic practices selectively.
[14] Weber 1978, 977. Rudolph and Rudolph 1979, however, insightfully noted this.

involvement in petitioning and judicial functions than in France – although we also need to determine if this reflected a crown too weak to resist demands for participation or strong enough to enforce it. At the macro level, strong powers predict greater capacity to impose legal uniformity. This variation is confirmed by the long-standing literature on the evolution of the two legal systems, common law and civil law, that of Legal Origins. Finally, the explanation is supported by empirical evidence on the precocious mobilization of all subjects for judicial and other duties in England, in the final section. This challenges stereotypes of a "small" English state and establishes the preconditions for the territorial anchoring of Parliament in local structures of governance.

3.1   Social Causes of Institutional Variation: Power over the Most Powerful

Why Parliament fused judicial and fiscal functions whilst the *Parlement* became primarily a judicial court is not extensively treated by historians. Brief explanations focus on differential patterns of timing and specialization. For instance, it could be that the *Parlement* specialized because no alternative judicial bodies existed when it formed, unlike in England.[15] The *Parlement* emerged around 1250, about four decades before the French central courts took clear shape,[16] so it was the main venue for judicial concerns, requiring more lay professionals to handle them than in England.[17] Had the *Parlement* been preceded by specialized courts, maybe its main chamber, the *Grand'Chambre*, could have diversified along English lines instead; it already handled some "high politics" functions, as seen.

But the logic is not airtight. English royal courts may have operated already from the 1190s,[18] but this did not reduce pressures on Parliament itself, especially since court and parliamentary functions were not identical. The crown was as overwhelmed by petitions as in France, yet fusion still occurred.[19] In any case, the prior existence of central royal courts in England and their delay in France were themselves endogenous to the

---

[15] Langlois 1890; Harding 2002, 185.

[16] The Chamber of Pleas (*Chambre des Requêtes*) and the Chamber of Inquests (*Chambre des Enquêtes*); Lot and Fawtier 1958, 339–50; Ducoudray 1902, 73–84; Shennan 1998, 14–23.

[17] Langlois 1890.

[18] Hudson 2012, 537–42, 569–73; Turner 1977. The Courts of King's Bench and of Common Pleas were different sessions of the royal court, so the distinctions were fluid early on.

[19] Only after the 1400s was Parliament's judicial role eclipsed by its political and legislative functions; Autrand and Contamine 1979, 148.

master variable proposed here, ruler strength. England formed central courts earlier because the crown already had jurisdictional near-monopoly, as argued in the next sections.

Instead, I argue, judicial and fiscal functions were fused where nobles attended representative institutions (or the king's court initially) at higher rates, including for judicial purposes. Attendance was higher when the ruler could compel the nobility. Once compelled to attend a central forum whilst subject to similar obligations, nobles were better able to solve their collective action problem: they had incentives to cooperate in their inter-actions with the king. Their inescapable frame of obligations, moreover, made English nobles increasingly invested in co-opting parliamentary activities, especially petitioning, as we will see. Their regular involvement with Parliament thus made it the obvious forum in which the king demanded taxation. French nobles, by contrast, lacking such incentives, were increasingly displaced by officials within the *Parlement*, making it less relevant for tax-raising purposes. These trends help explain why the two institutions diverged.

3.1.1   The Micro Level: Noble Attendance at Representative Institutions – Solving the Collective Action Problem

First, however, we need to show, as far as the limited records permit, that English nobles had higher levels of attendance than their French counter-parts. All such comparisons are precarious, as they are mainly inferred from lists of summonses, since English nobles were not paid for attending, while parliamentary rolls that recorded those present are too inconsistent. Scant records survive in France. Moreover, the groups differed in structure. The English nobility was small, maybe amounting to 0.01 percent of a population reaching 4.7 million by 1300, when their immediate family is included.[20] The highest rung of the nobility were the earls, who num-bered usually about 12;[21] next, about 200 barons ("lords") were tenants-in-chief holding enough land to pay an entry fine (*relief*) of £100.[22] Below them were the gentry, viewed either as lesser landholders distinct from the nobility or as lesser nobility, with knights ("sirs") at the highest rung; they held land in exchange for military service[23] and numbered around 1,250.[24] The French nobility included powerful ranks such as dukes and counts; it was also larger and included the knightly class, bringing

---

[20] Ormrod 1990b, 96.
[21] Prestwich 1990, 29. Dukes appeared in 1337; Ormrod 1990b, 95.
[22] Powell and Wallis 1968, 223–25; Prestwich 1990, 30; Sanders 1960.
[23] Coss 1995, 39; 2003, 1–19.
[24] Prestwich 1990, 62. See the major study by Coss 2003.

the total up to about 2 percent of the population in the thirteenth century (about 200,000 members).[25] Yet fewer were present at the center, both in proportionate and absolute terms.

3.1.1.1 Noble Attendance at the English Parliament   Originally the king summoned mostly his tenants-in-chief, men holding directly of him, owing counsel and aid; this included high ecclesiastics.[26] Noble status only emerged from the king's summons to parliament itself after the fourteenth century – the summons was not an inherited legal privilege, as on the Continent.[27]

Noble presence in parliament is first assessed from lists of those summoned to Parliament.[28] Between 1283 and 1483, an average of 70 lay peers per session were summoned (Table 3.1) – about one third of the possibly 200 barons known.[29] Of those summoned, between about 40 and 80 percent actually attended in that period (we cannot infer a secular increase, as early attendance was also high).[30] Attendance can also be approximated through lists of nobles witnessing royal charters. These suggest that the average earl was present for at least 60 percent of the Parliaments of Edward I,[31] even though earls often fought abroad and Parliament was occasionally held far from London. So, when English historians note that "no more than" a third of those summoned attended,[32] as in 1307, this typically means absolute numbers (57) larger than the maximum recorded for the three times larger population of France, as we will see.

This evidence can be supplemented by biographical information provided in the *Oxford Dictionary of National Biography*, which allows us to cross-reference parliamentary attendance with other types of recorded service and obligations. The *ODNB* entries are culled from sources by historians; they don't specify the frequency of attendance for each person, only the

---

[25] Kibler and Zinn 1995, 666. Contamine 1997, 53 estimates about 350,000 nobles around 1300. Nobles were 30 percent in the Estates of 1468 and 1484; Bulst 1992, 346–47. Size does not directly inform us about power structures. Enlarging the nobility could be seen as a royal strategy to dilute its power, implying royal strength. However, as Chapter 5 argues, a large nobility is likely observed under conditions of royal weakness, as it also multiplies privileges that limit royal power. It can imply noble strength, but without collective organization nobles saw that strength reduced. Partible inheritance also increased the size of the nobility, in Poland and Russia, for instance; see Frost 2015, 63 and Chapter 13. Finally, a smaller number of nobles did not make it easier to compel them: it depended on how powerful those nobles were. If they had lands that rivaled the king's, compellence would still be hard.

[26] Maddicott 2010, 443; Prestwich 1988, 446–47.   [27] Stubbs 1880, 200–201.

[28] Palgrave 1827. Even summonses are not definitive; see the caution in Prestwich 1985.

[29] Prestwich 1990, 30.   [30] Numbers calculated from Roskell 1956, 160–79.

[31] Spencer 2014, 57.   [32] Prestwich 1988, 447.

Table 3.1 *Number of nobles in the English Parliament*

	Lay peers summoned to Parliament	Lay peers per 100,000 of population
1283	110	2.42
1295	64	1.35
1301	101	2.14
1304	103	2.18
1306	78	1.66
1307	99	2.10
1341	53	1.15
1377	60	2.40
1399	50	2.38
1413	38	1.85
1449	48	2.51
1453	56	2.92
1483	45	2.14
Average	70	2

Sources: Maddicott 2010, 286–87; Roskell 1956, 155. For population, Broadberry et al. 2010.

minimum of known practice, and not with any claim of completeness. They establish a rough baseline, to be qualified by more detailed studies.[33] A search in the *ODNB* for the period between 1200 and 1350 generated information for 317 earls and barons and 61 ecclesiastics.[34] This involves about 7 earls and 25 percent of estimated barons (49) active around the year 1250.[35] Forty-four percent of nobles before 1250 are recorded as attending the king's court, rising to almost 80 percent after 1250 (see Table 3.2).

3.1.1.2 Nobles and Petitions in the English Parliament   We have seen how bottom-up demand for justice especially via petitions explained why broad social groups supported a regular central institution. But the nobility's presence was critical in the early stages. Not only was their status crucial for the practice to take root but petitions in the name of the community of the realm also originated with them, as Chapter 2 noted. Popular

[33] Although for historians this information is too crude to be of use, for non-specialists it serves to confirm that when attendance is claimed to be obligatory, different sources can corroborate the claim, absent systematic data.

[34] The total number of entries generated was 756, of which 493 had relevant information including 199 knights and gentry. The search criteria were: "field of interest: (Royalty, rulers, and aristocracy) – active between 1200 and 1350," accessed 5/30/2015. Their new search engine produces a few additional results.

[35] By active I mean adults in 1250. The gentry is not generally considered nobility, so they are discussed separately in Chapter 4.

Table 3.2 *Recorded (i.e. minimum) noble attendance at the king's court or Parliament in the* ODNB

Nobles	Pre-1250		Post-1250	
	Total number recorded	Percentage present in Parliament	Total number recorded	Percentage present in Parliament
Lay	78	44	239	79
Ecclesiastical	16	69	45	76

Source: *Oxford Dictionary of National Biography.*

representatives claimed the petition-making process only after the 1310s–20s.[36] Early "community" petitions did not originate in the knights and burgesses (the Commons); rather, they simply claimed to refer to common rather than particularistic concerns, a point now emphasized by historians. Either the nobility channeled them, claiming to represent the community, or clerks designated them as common.[37]

Nobles also gradually became involved in judging petitions, part of their increasing involvement in administration.[38] They greatly outnumbered royal officials since the 1280s,[39] and appear as *triers* of petitions after the 1310s[40] (whilst churchmen, who were themselves both nobles and tenants of the crown, and officials dominated in the early period).[41] Their role is attested by complaints that proceedings were delayed for days until "grantz et autres" arrived, as some petitions could not be decided without the "common assent of the magnates."[42] By the 1340s, "earls were frequently being appointed auditors. Thus the judicial committees begun under Edward I had become larger and more distinguished by 1348, with the clergy and magnates outnumbering the officials."[43] By the late 1300s, almost fifty nobles could be trying petitions, though numbers of triers decreased again after that.[44]

Nobles were not keen to perform this service. Like their French counterparts, they had to be commanded to "sit in one place and hear the whole of the petition."[45] However, once forced to participate, petitions were important enough for them to seek control of the process, as they did

---

[36] Ormrod 1995, 34.
[37] Dodd 2007, 126–33; Rayner 1941b, 549–51; Bradford 2007, 164.
[38] See the important study by Spencer 2014, 60–64.   [39] Maddicott 2010, 286–87.
[40] Richardson and Sayles 1931, 542–49; Maitland 1893, lx–lxi.   [41] Dodd 2014.
[42] Musson 2001, 200; Roskell 1956, 163.
[43] Bradford 2007, 160; Plucknett 1940, 114–15; Richardson and Sayles 1932, 382.
[44] Pollard 1942, 208n2, 202.
[45] Richardson and Sayles 1932, 385n10, loose translation.

after 1311, displacing the royal bureaucracy of ministers.[46] Ironically, the sidelining of bureaucratic personnel helped Parliament remain an institution that included the most powerful actors and to thus sustain its centrality. The crown's original capacity to compel noble attendance and service thus incentivized nobles to capture the institution; collective action among them was channeled through a framework of obligation.[47]

3.1.1.3 Nobles and Petitions in the Paris Parlement   Whilst the role of English nobles in petition-hearing grew, France witnessed the opposite trend: in the *Parlement* nobles were less involved and eventually sidelined; it was the law professionals, such as justices and clerks, that became the key staff. Evidence is slim on French noble involvement in royal meetings.[48] However, general trends differed from English ones both at the micro and the macro level (examined in the next section).[49]

After the Paris *Parlement* regularized in the 1250s, the high nobility and clergy received individual summonses to the institution on the same basis as English peers: their tenurial status and social standing.[50] Unlike English nobles, however, French ones were paid to attend, so the crown restricted their numbers in 1345: fifteen nobles and fifteen prelates in the main pleading institution, the *Grand'Chambre* – though others could come unremunerated.[51] Historical estimates of noble presence vary from scarce ("We catch glimpses of great men in occasional attendance")[52] to "considerable."[53] Nonetheless, attendance was irregular and a function of the meeting's importance[54] – and absolute numbers seem a fraction of the English ones that averaged around seventy per session.

Attendance cannot be confirmed by lists of summonses to a *Parlement*;[55] it is known mostly from highly incomplete summaries.[56] It appears very limited: one record that names the nobles attending lists only seventeen, in 1331. But it included one king, two dukes, seven counts, and

---

[46] Sayles 1950, 459–60; Holdsworth 1922, 359.

[47] During crises, royal capacity to coerce nobles to attend declined, as in the early 1340s; Powell and Wallis 1968, 351–53; Roskell 1956, 166–67. This was a harbinger of political troubles ahead; however, the institutional machinery of Parliament was already entrenched.

[48] Bisson 1972, 544n15. The main sources are *Les Olim* 1842 and Ducoudray 1902. These list all surviving documents in the Archives; Hildesheimer and Morgat-Bonnet 2011.

[49] Shennan 1998, 14–15; Harding 2002, 163.

[50] Villers 1984, 96; Rigaudière 1994, 167.   [51] Lot and Fawtier 1958, 355–56.

[52] Bisson 1969, 355.   [53] Lot and Fawtier 1958, 356.

[54] Lot and Fawtier 1958, 337, 356.   [55] Lewis 1962, 11.

[56] Over the 60-year reigns of Louis IX and Philip III (1226–85), 36 lords are recorded, 32 lords over 30 years under Philip the Fair (1285–1314), and 82 in the five sessions under Louis X (1314–16); Ducoudray 1902, 106–10; Lot and Fawtier 1958, 334–35.

others.[57] Participation was high for judicial occasions, as this argument predicts: the *Parlement* was judging the Duke of Burgundy,[58] so attendance fulfilled an obligation to the crown.[59] Similarly, the count of Flanders' appeal in 1290 drew sixty persons, though how many were nobles seems unknown;[60] regardless, this is still lower than the English noble average. These (precarious) figures suggest 0.10–0.35 nobles attending per hundred thousand of population, compared to 2 in England.[61]

Does war predict noble attendance better than compellence, as dominant hypotheses imply? Some evidence appears strong. The French king summoned far higher numbers when faced with war: an average of 400 nobles were summoned in six baronial assemblies between 1315 and 1320.[62] This parallels English summoning patterns. However, no permanent central institution followed from these assemblies. As Bisson notes, they had no connection with *parlements*.[63] No comparable capacity to enlist nobles for judicial service and *regular* attendance thus existed, as we will see in Chapter 5. When war lapsed, so did the assemblies.

In the *Parlement* itself, the great lords increasingly gave pensions to procurators (*avocats*) to represent them, only appearing for "important affairs" as judges.[64] Procuration was far more widely allowed in France than in England, where it is not attested for nobles before 1307 but was frequent for ecclesiastics.[65] Eventually, noble "elimination from the *Parlement* happened softly, imperceptibly."[66] The highest ranks of temporal lords across all cases examined in this book still participated in *governance* in the Royal Council of course – they shared power that way.[67] It was service, whether judicial or administrative, that was more cumbersome and the barons and the bannerets were indifferent.[68] So although some judicial service was delegated to French knights until the 1360s,[69] after this, officials, often men of "humble origins," gradually replaced them. By the early fifteenth century, even knights only appeared exceptionally in the *Parlement*.[70]

Parlement procedures were thus institutionalized without reliance on nobles, unlike in England. We often associate the *Parlement* with

[57] Ducoudray 1902, 108.   [58] *Les Grandes Chroniques de France* 1837, 343–49.
[59] See also Shennan 1998, 157; Aubert [1890] 1977, 1–21, 44–49.
[60] Bisson 1969, 355.
[61] French population in the early fourteenth century is estimated at 17.7 million by McEvedy and Jones 1978.
[62] Calculated from Taylor 1954.   [63] Bisson 1969, 366.
[64] Ducoudray 1902, 320; Lot and Fawtier 1958, 356.
[65] Roskell 1956, 173, 163; Snow 1963, 334.
[66] Lot and Fawtier 1958, 356, 342; my translations.   [67] Lemarignier 1970, 32–59.
[68] Roskell 1956, 199; Lot and Fawtier 1958, 355–71.   [69] Lot and Fawtier 1958, 358.
[70] Shennan 1998, 110.

hereditary and venal office and the *new* nobility of the "robe," but this only developed later, after the period of war and crisis in the late 1300s.[71] Originally, the *Parlement* had a bureaucratic character, as discussed in the final section, which reflected noble distance from the institution, whilst English nobles were increasingly engaged.

3.1.1.4 Compellence or Weakness? Inferences about Power from Observed Attendance Patterns Noble attendance patterns don't directly inform about power dynamics, however. Noble presence could result from royal compulsion or from noble demand. Conversely, noble marginalization could result from royal weakness or from royal design. Although the answer will be fully developed in Part II, some initial insight on this conundrum follows below.

First, the summons used language of compulsion. To the lords, the English king wrote, "We command and require you, as you love us and our honour"; to the bishops, "we command you, strictly enjoining you in the fidelity and love in which you are bound to us"; and to the representatives of the shires (counties) and towns, "we strictly require you" to elect representatives "to have full and sufficient power for themselves and for the community ... for doing what shall then be ordained according to the common counsel in the premises, so that the aforesaid business shall not remain unfinished in any way for defect of this power."[72] This language was used throughout Europe. French kings also stated, "we require, order and command you ... to delegate three or four good men ... [with] full powers from you to agree, do and undertake all that shall be decided."[73] The formula was almost identical in Germany and similar in Ireland and elsewhere, having Roman law origins.[74]

Older scholarship derived the obligatory character of the early sessions of Parliament from an observed unwillingness to attend or from limited re-election,[75] but the evidence can be interpreted different ways.[76] Nonetheless, frequent re-elections of representatives, which perhaps suggest greater willingness to attend Parliament, mostly occur from the early fourteenth century,[77] when Parliament was established: incentives increased as parliamentary decisions bounded those absent.[78] As for barons, as Stubbs noted, they too were "glad to escape the burden of attendance ... to avoid the expenses by which their richer brethren

---

[71] See also, Shennan 1998, 111–48; Menes 2010; and page 83 below.
[72] *English Constitutional Documents* 1894, 30–31; Stubbs 1913, 477–82.
[73] From a summons of 1318; Taylor 1939, 113n12.
[74] Richardson and Sayles 1981, 172–73; Picot 1901, 1, 27; McIlwain 1932, 686.
[75] Pollard 1920; Richardson and Sayles 1981.   [76] Edwards 1925; 1926.
[77] Maddicott 2010, 313, 338, 370.   [78] Post 1946, 230.

maintained their high dignity."[79] It is only later that the "vassal's duty to give counsel" was transmuted "into the vassal's *right* to give counsel."[80] In any case, attendance rates do not offer independent evidence of preferences, if royal power to compel is the question.

However, a second observation is that those summoned needed some excuse to obtain a pardon for non-attendance,[81] as occurred with court jury duty.[82] Exemptions seem rare, although enforcement varied widely and is hard to document for the early period.[83] Moreover, elected knights guaranteed their attendance at Parliament by nominating other freeholders as surety (*mainpernors*).[84] Attendance still suffered, as we saw, since threats of forfeiture were not always credible.[85] Yet it was lower in France even in absolute terms, though "important nobles" were equally obligated to attend and had to be "hindered by legitimate impediment" in order to be excused.[86] The same held in subnational *parlements*, like Brittany's where absenteeism was less common,[87] and in the French Estates-General: representation by attorney required a valid reason, even a broken leg, but this had to be "known in the whole neighborhood."[88]

Finally, even restrictions on participation that appear to indicate royal suppression emerge differently on closer inspection. In France, prelates were marginalized only after the crown failed to reverse their irregular presence,[89] which undermined the institution.[90] The king was "aware of obstructing them from the government of their affairs," but he "wanted in his *Parlement* men who could attend continuously without departing, and who were not preoccupied with other great occupations," according to the edict of 1319.[91] So he finally exempted prelates from the obligation to attend and turned to professionals instead. An act suggesting autocratic tendencies resulted from weakness faced with mounting opposition. Further evidence on royal compulsion will be presented next and in Part II, on taxation.

3.1.2   The Macro Level: Compellence at the Local Level and the Divergence of Common and Civil Law

The preceding evidence has suggested the differential capacity of the two crowns to engage nobles in government routine at the center and thus

---

[79] Stubbs 1880, 219–20.   [80] Maddicott 2010, 77, 443.
[81] McIlwain 1932, 687; Picot 1901, 63–70; Aubert 1894, 39–41.
[82] Holdsworth 1923a, 103–104.
[83] Roskell 1956, 158–59. For jury duty, see similarly Waugh 1983, 962–66.
[84] Maddicott 1978a, 32; Illsley 1976, 25, 28–30.   [85] Roskell 1956, 162.
[86] Bisson 1961, 260.   [87] See the references in Lewis 1962, 23n108.
[88] McIlwain 1932, 688.   [89] Ducoudray 1902, 101.   [90] Lot and Fawtier 1958, 342–43.
[91] Floquet 1840, 42; my translation.

endow them with common interests; this capacity was critical for the institutional fusion I have argued was central to polity-level parliamentary emergence and consolidation. But the evidence examined, especially for France, is relatively weak. It receives additional support, however, from the pre-existing literature on probably the most important divergence in European premodern law: that between common and civil law. Historians have long ascribed this divergence to the English crown's greater strength in establishing centralized adjudication: the micro-evidence in the previous section is thus supported by the macro-scholarship on "Legal Origins."[92] I discuss this next.

3.1.2.1 Legal Origins: A Natural Experiment and the Hidden Hand of Government Compellence   The divergence between common and civil law in England and France with only a brief time lag is usually understood as the expression of deep-rooted differences in legal approach and philosophy. This prevalent view is expressed in Hayek.[93] Weber likewise argued that English justices and lawyer guilds resisted foreign ideas.[94] Ertman ascribed the legislative involvement of the Commons to strong local governance and to the lesser influence of Roman traditions. Common law was the "custom of the community, not ... a body of (manmade) rules promulgated by the emperor or king for the public good."[95] Chapter 2, however, noted the strong legislative role of the crown. France, conversely, in many ways exemplified the organic growth of customary law, as historians have noted.[96] Further, the two societies applied very similar legal mechanisms before the twelfth century for dispute adjudication, often emerging out of common traditions.[97] Their divergence is thus a much bigger puzzle.

Part of this variance can be examined through a natural experiment. The Pope abolished the judicial duel and ordeal for adjudicating guilt in Church proceedings at the Lateran Council of 1215, and reform swept through secular authorities. England acted in 1219 and France in 1258, but the two kingdoms diverged. England adopted the jury-based trial to adjudicate criminal cases; France adopted the canonist inquisition. Juries conscripted local men, whereas the inquisition applied Roman law concepts and relied on a judge directing an inquiry, collecting facts and secretly examining witnesses via increasing numbers of judicial officials and experts.[98]

---

[92] Dawson 1960; 1968; Bongert 1949; Berman 1983. Social scientific statements on legal origins move in different directions; Glaeser and Shleifer 2002; Porta et al. 2008.
[93] Hayek 1960, 131–249.   [94] Weber 1978, 976.   [95] Ertman 1997, 168.
[96] Cohen 1993, 28–39; Rigaudière 1994, 135–138.   [97] Berman 1983, 478.
[98] Dawson 1960, 39–93, 116–128, especially 47, 43–53; Holdsworth 1922, 312–332; Brown 2011, 204–5; Lot and Fawtier 1958, 388–89.

The French path differed in more ways, one of which is highlighted here. French rulers intervened in local justice by instituting the *Parlement* as a final court of appeal, which used Roman law to adjudicate between local customs. English kings, by contrast, just sidelined older local courts by extending new central courts that homogenized legal practice in part through the writ, a royal command. I show how all these variations depended on the greater powers of the English crown.

Jury vs. Inquest. Juries were a common European heritage of both the Anglo-Saxon and Frankish traditions.[99] In France, juries established valid custom (*enquête par turbe*) until the 1600s.[100] England did not turn to them due to isolation from Roman law, however.[101] Justices applied Roman-inspired canon law in ecclesiastical courts.[102] Even some of Magna Carta's clauses "represented a choice among competing rules of law," customary, canon, and Roman law.[103] A broad menu for choice thus existed, often described as the European *ius commune*.[104] Trial by witness, where the judge selected the most convincing testimony as in France, also "threatened to be a serious rival of trial by jury."[105] But it was abandoned. Juries were adopted instead, though they imposed a tremendous burden on local communities, as discussed later.[106] Why?

It could be that in 1219 not enough clerics with advanced education (*magistri*) were available to serve as judicial professionals. But *magistri* were already numerous by that time.[107] They reached a third to a half of canons by 1230 in some studied regions[108] and were increasingly present in administration by the 1250s,[109] when canonist procedure was fully developed.[110] It's not as if French judges were highly specialized; little formal qualification was needed to practice law in France until the fifteenth century and judges were not numerous.[111] Moreover, that the jury

---

[99] A Frankish/Norman origin is mostly admitted for England; van Caenegem 1988, 79; Pollock and Maitland 1898, 142–3; Haskins 1915, 110. For Anglo-Saxon precedents, see Turner 1968, 10.

[100] Dawson 1960, 46–47; Holdsworth 1922, 314–15.

[101] Roman law refers mainly to the *Corpus Iuris Civilis* of the sixth century; civil law begins in the eleventh century with the work of the Glossators commenting on the *Corpus*.

[102] Hudson 2012, 533.

[103] See the debate in Helmholz 1990, 1207–14; 1999; and Garnett and Hudson 2015, 15–25.

[104] Bellomo 1995; Ibbetson 2001.

[105] Pollock and Maitland 1899, 637–41; Holdsworth 1922, 303.

[106] Masschaele 2008, 10–11.

[107] Thomas 2014, 243 has identified 550 English *magistri* by 1216 and postulates a total of a thousand. "New men" also advanced in the ranks; Turner 1985.

[108] Thomas 2014, 112–13.

[109] Barrow 1989; Dodd 2014. Only by 1300 did the clergy get replaced by laymen in administration; Prestwich 1990, 76; Maddicott 1978b, 17–18.

[110] Dawson 1960, 47.   [111] Bubenicek and Partington 2015, 159.

was established did not mean it could not get replaced if superior alternatives emerged later. Deeply rooted practices could be transformed by royal intervention, as when subinfeudation was prohibited in 1290. Another hypothesis is that maybe English lords accepted juries because they could manipulate them.[112] This holds for the later period, when the nobility had organized collectively and was more unconstrained: by the fifteenth century, jury corruption consumed the Commons.[113]

However, by 1219, the jury was already widely popular in England because it was employed in the possessory assize. As Maitland noted, the assize jury "was associated with the protection of the weak against the strong." Moreover, what made its spread "possible was the subjection of the England of the Angevin time to a strong central government, the like of which was to be found in no other land."[114] As economists Glaeser and Shleifer also noted, the "generally accepted" view is that English rulers could restrict noble control of local justice, at least initially, making the jury possible.[115] Key to this was the removal of independent jurisdictional powers from noble elites.[116] By contrast, in "France the royal power was obliged to struggle for supremacy against great feudatories."[117] In other words, English rulers adopted the jury because they could: the crown could mobilize society en masse and this served them well.[118] But rulers also incentivized juries by allowing defendants to consent to them. As with much medieval consent, however, when it was not forthcoming, it was coerced: defendants refusing jury trial faced starvation or being crushed by heavy weights.[119]

Writs and Parallel Courts vs. Roman Law and the Court of Appeal. Royal strength was also important for the way in which the two crowns integrated the judicial system and addressed variation in customary rules. The *Parlement* became a court of appeals from seigniorial or provincial courts, using Roman law to decide which customary rules had precedence rather than establishing independent law.[120] The "French Crown had to develop an appellate jurisdiction precisely because so much jurisdictional initiative remained intact at a local level."[121] It lacked exclusive jurisdiction over serious crimes (felonies) or over serious civil offenses (trespasses).[122] Judicial business was mostly "being conducted in the courts of dukes, counts, viscounts, barons and seigneurs of all

---

[112] Brown 2011, 205–206.   [113] Carpenter 1983, 215.
[114] Pollock and Maitland 1899, 631–32.
[115] Glaeser and Shleifer 2002, 1200–1201. See also the evidence in Chapter 2. Legal historians of course develop far more nuanced arguments; Kamali and Green 2018.
[116] Cam 1935, 193.   [117] Holdsworth 1922, 315–16.   [118] Dawson 1960, 47–48.
[119] Masschaele 2008, 81, 79–82; Pollock and Maitland 1898, 149.
[120] Berman 1983, 469–73; Dawson 1940, 55, 766–68; Rigaudière 1988; 1994, 191–92.
[121] Hilaire 2011, 39–57; van Caenegem 1966; Small 1977.   [122] Berman 1983, 477.

sorts."[123] The *Parlement* became more in demand by improving its efficiency.[124] As the seventeenth-century jurist Charles Loyseau noted, it saved France from being "cantonized and dismembered as in Italy and Germany and maintained the kingdom as an entity."[125] But even this unity was weakened by the local *parlements* established over time.[126]

In England, the crown already monopolized both capital and most routine land cases, which were heard in the royal courts and by royal commissions.[127] The judicial system was homogenized by erecting parallel courts that sidelined local ones. These new royal institutions applied uniform procedure instead of Roman law: royal courts were increasingly accessed through royal writs, which were "royal commands, given by the chancellor, for the resolution of individual disputes."[128] Writs provided remedies for legal wrongs; otherwise "legal fictions" were used.[129] There were about 50 set forms of writs by 1258, about 900 by the early 1300s, reaching 2,500 in the 1500s until their abolition in 1832.[130]

These commands, however, implied a drastic intervention in local affairs. If lords did not render justice to their tenants, for instance, the writ of right allowed the sheriff to intervene.[131] Barons failed to stop their loss of jurisdiction (by the writ *præcipe*) with clause 34 of Magna Carta. They were further challenged when itinerant royal courts conscripted local tenants for service; this prevented locals from serving as judges ("suitors") in baronial courts and undercut baronial court revenues and patronage ties. "Suit of court became an issue of the first political importance"[132] in the 1200s, especially during the revolt of the 1250s and 1260s.[133] Yet suit of court declined.[134] The remedies available through royal writ proved more efficient than existing custom, such that by the 1250s thousands of writs were removing cases from local courts.[135] Consequently, the county court lost jurisdiction over most cases by the end of the 1200s to the royal courts, as discussed below. Procedure harmonized substantive legal practice, but only because the crown could impose it throughout the polity, overcoming noble resistance.[136]

---

[123] Cam 1935, 192.   [124] Rigaudière 1994, 189–97, 218.
[125] Loyseau 1678, 113, my translation.   [126] Rigaudière 1994, 205–17.
[127] Dodd 2007, 40–41.   [128] Glenn 2014, 228; Hudson 2012, 535; Musson 2001, 157.
[129] Baker 2002, 201–202, 255–56; Maine 1906, 20–42.
[130] Musson and Ormrod 1999, 118.
[131] Hudson 2012, 557–61; Pollock and Maitland 1899, 62ff.   [132] Carpenter 2000, 45.
[133] Spencer 2014, 122–23, 145; Brand 2003.   [134] Palmer 1982, 81, 56.
[135] Palmer 1982, 141–306; Milsom 1981, 125–30, 134–49.
[136] Milsom 1976 raised important qualifications about the early steps of this process, seeing them grounded more in feudal obligation, but they are compatible with the argument presented here.

Royal capacity is thus also reflected in the great divergence in legal systems, common law and civil law.

3.1.3 The Macro Level: Compellence at the Local Level and Territorial Anchoring

3.1.3.1 England: Territoriality or Unit Homogeneity? We have seen how, by compelling English nobles into service, the king inadvertently alleviated their collective action problem and ensured they were regularly present in a forum that he could also use for fiscal/political functions. This enabled functional layering and institutional fusion. The third condition for representative emergence identified in the Introduction remains crucial: how the centralized exchange of Parliament was territorially anchored throughout the polity, thus becoming an effective organ of governance. This is typically taken to depend on the "self-governing, self-taxing, participatory elite of England"[137] that is well attested from the later period. But how did this elite come to be? Why are English actors taken to be "self-governing" and engaged in a "collaborative venture" with the crown, whilst their French counterparts were "non-participatory?" For Ertman, the reason is that they were "[u]nencumbered by the legacies of dark age, neo-Roman state-building in general and opposition from old entrenched elites in particular"[138] – coercion was thus less necessary, cooperation easier.

In this account, by contrast, these outcomes were *due* to coercion. As noted in Chapter 2, old Anglo-Saxon elites were indeed not entrenched, but only because the Normans wiped them out. This predominance allowed Normans to deploy the same state-building blocks as the French and others only much more effectively: itinerant officials. It was not the organs of *local* government that made England more territorial and participatory, but a penetration of the royal institutions described above into the localities so effectively that they *sidelined* local institutions, especially the county court.[139] As part of this process, the crown also conscripted many subjects to staff the royal courts, as seen in the next section. Itinerant commissions were used across Europe but were more effective where rulers could penetrate outlying territories. In Germany, for instance, the emperor lacked such reach, as we will see in Chapter 10.[140] The French also attempted to penetrate the localities but failed relatively, precisely because, as Ertman notes, magnates were more

---

[137] Kivelson 1996, 152.   [138] Ertman 1997, 24.
[139] Manorial, merchant, franchise, and ecclesiastical courts also existed but had limited jurisdictions; Hudson 2012, 556–58; Holdsworth 1922, 64–193.
[140] Harding 2002, 160.

powerful.[141] The *baillis* and *sénéchaux* were originally also itinerant collegiate bodies sent from the center to dispense justice locally, modeled on Norman precedent, but they lagged in local integration.[142]

English territorial governance thus did not flow from a spontaneous predilection for cooperation fostered by propitious structural conditions onto unpaid amateurs; the state compelled its subjects.[143] Royal justice expanded by developing numerous offshoots of the king's court (the *curia regis*) (Figure 3.1). These were either central courts, such as King's Bench and Common Pleas,[144] or itinerant commissions dispatched to the counties as extensions of the central courts. These commissions exerted control over county and other local courts, eventually sidelining them, generating deep conflict with the barons, as noted.[145]

The most important English itineration was the general eyre of the king's court, which visited counties to hear pleas of the crown as well as criminal cases and civil pleas with juries of twelve to twenty-four members. "This provision apparently imposed from above was seized upon hungrily from below, and the system developed with a rapidity that now seems startling."[146] It was an extraordinary event, every seven years,[147] which engaged the entire county – almost two thousand could attend.[148] Other itinerant commissions also handled judicial business. Commissions of assize dealt with the possessory actions, such as *novel disseisin*, that allowed even lowly free tenants to protect their rights against their lords; they were so successful they could reach two to three thousand per year in the 1270s[149] and lasted until 1971. Gaol delivery, oyer et terminer, and trailbaston dealt with crimes.[150] Nobles sat on criminal commissions and supervised commissions of assize staffed by gentry.[151]

Commissions conscripted juries to obligatory service unless a legitimate excuse (*essoin*) could be presented, as with Parliament. The level of monitoring was astounding. Permissible excuses cover seventy printed pages of the standard edition of the thirteenth-century text of Bracton. Investigations determined whether the petitioner had "fallen into an accident willingly, when he would easily have avoided it."[152]

---

[141] Ertman 1997, 24, 55–57.   [142] Berman 1983, 465–67; Lemarignier 1970, 338–45.

[143] For a similar critique, though still retaining the emphasis on "semi- autonomous local jurisdictions," see Somers 1993, 600n17, 598.

[144] Central courts were also originally itinerant, as Magna Carta complained; the King's Bench continued into the fifteenth century.

[145] Holdsworth 1922, 64–75.   [146] Bubenicek and Partington 2015, 152.

[147] Milsom 1981, 27–31.   [148] Holdsworth 1922, 267, 265–76; Brown 1989, 117.

[149] Masschaele 2008, 72; Baker 2002, 20–22; Musson and Ormrod 1999, 116–19.

[150] Musson and Ormrod 1999, 44–49; Baker 2002, 17, 39.

[151] Musson and Ormrod 1999, 70–73; Putnam 1929, 26–35.

[152] Bracton 1977, 72, 71–146; Bartlett 2000, 699.

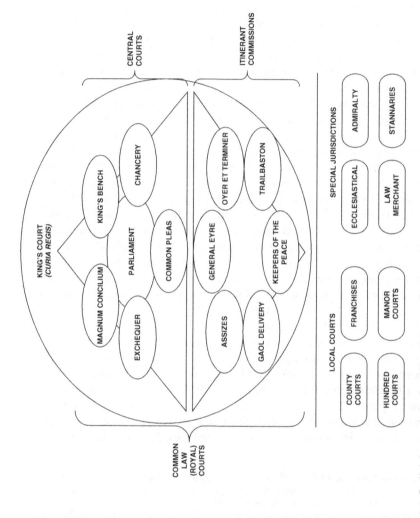

Figure 3.1 Judicial structure of medieval England

Note: Some local courts, e.g. of some hundreds, were under royal jurisdiction. This is not a complete list.

Penalties ranged from physical restraint (chains and imprisonment) to excommunication and distraint (the removal of goods or land until the subject complied). Eventually, fines were the chief mechanism of enforcement.[153] Penalties were predicated on royal power, especially the sheriff, a royal appointee serving "at the king's pleasure."[154]

In the next section we will see the remarkable level of conscription that juries involved. They performed broad judicial roles: in both criminal and civil cases, they asserted facts relating to the case, substituting not just for witnesses but also for the investigating officials that assisted French judges and delivered verdicts, under unanimity rule mostly (jury of trial and assize);[155] in criminal cases, they also presented persons suspected of crimes (jury of accusation), facing penalties if they did not or did so falsely.[156] Juries, which proliferated as Parliament grew, therefore implied far more extensive service than the older "suit of court" performed at local courts.[157] Suitors had served usually twice a year and assisted the judge in judging, mostly using majority rule.[158] They also bore collective responsibility for any "false judgment," which was punishable by fine, making service a burden.[159]

Obligation to serve in England did not end with suit of court and jury duty, moreover. Landholders were also charged with appointments to perform tasks both for local governance and royal service, at their own expense. This was "self-government at the King's command."[160] The list of tasks, flowing mostly from land tenure, was astonishing. Subjects investigated land rights and obligations, they measured and valued land, agricultural equipment, crops, and movables. They protected the royal forest and the king's hunting, purchased ships for him, conveyed provisions and equipment required for his travels (especially wine), and built and repaired his houses and castles, bridges, and roads.[161] Instead of paying for an extensive bureaucracy, the English crown compelled its subjects. As a result, by "the fourteenth century, the tradition that all work at the local level should be done at no cost to the king by the propertied men living in the counties and boroughs was firmly established."[162]

---

[153] Hudson 2012, 310–12, 588–600; Holdsworth 1923a, 104; 1922, 337–39.
[154] Bartlett 2000, 149.   [155] Pollock and Maitland 1899, 625–27.
[156] Berman 1983, 448–51.
[157] Service in local seigniorial courts is not included for both cases, as the aim is to compare state structures.
[158] Palmer 1982, 81; Pollock and Maitland 1898, 550, 552.
[159] Pollock and Maitland 1898, 536–38, 558, 617–18; Palmer 1982, 76; Capua 1983, 63–82.
[160] White 1933.   [161] White 1933, 76–130 on the early 1200s.
[162] Baker 1961, 50; Poole 1946.

Such service was not unique to England; it was found throughout Europe, from France[163] to Russia, as we will see. As Russian historian Valerie Kivelson noted regarding judicial service, "With minor alterations, [such] lists would describe local participation in Muscovite legal-administrative affairs."[164] Judicial service was prevalent throughout the premodern world – local courts could not operate without community participation.[165] In fact, echoing Susan Reynolds' thesis on parallels between communities across Europe,[166] many or even most regime-building blocks observed in England were common across cases as diverse as France, Russia, Germany, Hungary, and Spain among others: service was pervasive, land was an overriding concern, the ruler served as judge, county courts elected officials or representatives, accountability was institutionalized, and similar legal procedures were available not least through diffusion.[167]

England differed, first, in applying these obligations more effectively throughout the polity (as tax extraction data will also suggest). Judicial institutions were not "feudalized,"[168] that is, appropriated by local lords as in Germany, France, and elsewhere,[169] at least in the period of parliamentary emergence. Second, in England these obligations were systematically aggregated across all thirty-seven counties at the center, through Parliament. What appears as "territoriality" is the effect of homogeneous governance harnessed at the center, especially of the integration of county courts into parliamentary procedure. Perhaps the quintessential "organ of local governance," the county court remained critical to local life, despite the royal commissions eroding much of its jurisdiction. It bound all grades of landholders and imposed originally an onerous duty, meeting every twenty-eight days.[170] It has been described both as a "microcosm" of county society and as "a local parliament."[171] It incorporated the lay and ecclesiastical nobility, the shire knights and borough representatives, though not all attended. It executed laws, raised juries and troops, and assessed and collected taxes. It is also where royal laws and decisions were proclaimed, where information was shared to shape public

---

[163] Baldwin 1986, 225–30.   [164] Kivelson 2002, 477.
[165] See the overview in Padoa Schioppa 1997.   [166] Reynolds 1997.
[167] For instance, see Rigaudière 1994, 219; Kivelson 1994, 46–47, 231–34; Arnold 1991, 6, 186–210; Berman 1983, 505–10. For the purposes of this analysis, however, what matters is not whether specific features were indigenous or imported, but what conditions enabled them to take root.
[168] Cam 1935, 193, 198.   [169] Arnold 1991, 186–210.
[170] Hudson 2012, 48–50, 276–80, 550–54.
[171] Maddicott 1978a, 33; Stubbs 1896, 215.

opinion, and where petitions were often drafted to be presented in Parliament.[172]

The county court is likewise where representatives to Parliament and other officials were elected.[173] Just as for juries, the king directed the sheriff to organize elections in the county court through an assembly of knights and "honest men."[174] The "institution of electing representative knights for local purposes was [thus] in active operation for nearly eighty years before such representatives were summoned to parliament."[175] Here again, similar patterns occurred throughout Europe.[176] In France, Castile, Hungary, Poland, even Russia, local assemblies were also instrumental for representative practice, as we will see. England integrated these practices better at the center.

Did this mean greater participation in elections? The only available estimate comes from after the franchise was restricted through the Act of 1430 to those with an income over 40 shillings, positing about 15,000 freeholders (3 percent of adult males). But this responded to a Commons petition which complained of "excessive numbers of people" voting, "the majority [of whom had] little or no means."[177] No estimate of those numbers exist. Yet, in theory, all landowners, aristocratic and gentry, should have been eligible to participate before the Act, as well as the free substantial tenants and yardlanders, and some part of the urban professionals. A "hypothetical" estimate has been offered by Bruce Campbell for these groups in 1290.[178] Counties possibly comprised about 22,000 landowners, and 80,000 free substantial tenants and yardlanders,[179] who could conceivably be eligible to vote. Both groups amount to at least 9 percent of adult males, compared to about 12 percent eligible before the First Reform Act of 1832.[180] But some part of the 137,000 urban professionals must also have been eligible, so the total could have exceeded that (without probably reaching the 18 percent eligible after 1832). This highlights the precocity of the early period and the "backsliding" that later

---

[172] Maddicott 1978a, 33–34, 40. Even those doubting the centrality of county courts see them as organs of royal governance; see Carpenter 1994, 347–48, 375–78; Coss 2003, 211.

[173] Cam 1970b, 273–78; Morris 1926, 139–42. The same procedures applied to boroughs.

[174] Holt 1981, 16; Maddicott 1981, 72–73.

[175] Stubbs 1896, 237; Palmer 1982, 263, 291; Holdsworth 1922, 68–69.

[176] Picot 1874; Hébert 2014, 200–19. For borough elections, see McKisack 1962, 11–22.

[177] Payling 1999, 245; Maddicott 2016, 349.

[178] Campbell 2008, 940. Adult males for 1290s are calculated on the basis of Campbell's assumption of mean household size of 4.4.

[179] About half the tenants must have been villeins, i.e. unfree.

[180] O'Gorman 1993, 176.

occurred in constitutional practices, though, surely, as today, only a fraction would get to participate in elections.[181]

Finally, England appeared as more "territorial" compared to the non-participatory mode of Continental Europe because, unlike in most of the latter, the rural countryside had independent representation, through the county court. In France and Castile, as Chapter 5 explains, the countryside was under noble control, so only towns represented the third estate. To the degree that Hungary and Poland also originally had independent county representation, their representative character was initially more robust, and other cases vary in the same way. English administrative units were more homogeneously and effectively centralized due to strong royal powers – territorial anchoring and local participation followed as a result.

3.1.3.2 Estimating the Size of the English and French Judicial Apparatus The next step in demonstrating the English crown's greater capacity to shape the judicial structure of the realm – and thus to foster the territorial anchoring I have claimed was central to parliamentary consolidation – consists in tentatively quantifying the extent of popular mobilization throughout the English countryside, especially the counties.

The assumed small size of the royal English bureaucracy is usually contrasted to the large number of French officials. The 40 judges serving medieval Languedoc alone contrast with the 20 to 25 judges serving all English courts in an area almost four times bigger.[182] One paid *officier* existed for every 380 French people in the 1600s, but only one justice of the peace for every 1,639 English people.[183] Moreover, the English royal bureaucracy, which included sheriffs, escheators, keepers, coroners, and collectors of taxes at the county level, was small, though constables, bailiffs, and customs collectors for instance were more numerous.[184]

However, as Harold Berman notes, the reason twenty justices sufficed in England is because they relied on local jurors to obtain information, a task that in France was delegated to paid officials facing robust private jurisdictions.[185] Focusing on official judges ignores the functions covered

---

[181] Sources on actual elections seem almost entirely lacking. Some rare records suggest that only a tiny fraction of "the better and more discreet persons" actually voted in London in the 1290s, over 100 in a city of 35,000, though this was likely not "characteristic"; McKisack 1962, 14–16.

[182] Strayer 1970a, 48.

[183] Webb and Webb 1906, 319–21. See also Aylmer 1961, 440; Brewer 1989, 15, 79–85, 102–14.

[184] A search in the *ODNB* returns 312 records for officials of the crown in the period between 1250 and 1300; again, a bare minimum. For local administration, see Willard and Morris 1940; Willard et al. 1940; Chrimes 1966.

[185] Berman 1983, 449.

above: the judicial obligations of all free subjects. These extended beyond serving as witnesses: though jurors were not strictly officials, they performed part of state judicial business.[186] In England, instead of "an appropriation of public power by the private lord, the private lord had been appropriated as an agent by the public power."[187]

French numbers can be approximated through the *Gallia Regia*, a list of royal officials from 1328 to 1515.[188] Out of about 5,600 records on officials active between 1328 and 1399, 2,300 are judicial officials: 1,039 judges or prosecutors are recorded[189] and 1,284 *baillis, sénéchaux, prévôts* and their lieutenants, who, like the English sheriff, had supervisory duties over justice. Since the focus here is on royal justice, these numbers don't include the large numbers employed in local, customary courts.

No historical estimates exist of total numbers of English jurors nor did statutory rules exist; service was set by custom. Until a representative sample of counties is studied, baseline estimates can only be offered that underestimate totals. Juries were drawn "from the ranks of free men who owned property."[190] They consisted typically of 12 members (though occasionally this could rise to 18, 24, even 80) and were called for civil cases mostly related to property (juries of assize) or criminal ones, either presenting accusations or delivering a verdict (jury of presentment or of trial). An estimate exists only for juries of assize: surviving records from the 1270s suggest maybe between 8,000 and 24,000 jurors were called annually.[191] It is unclear how many times jurors were called for other judicial events, like the large general eyres that were held in each county every seven years, or how often commissions for criminal and other cases were called. We know, however, that at the hundred level jurors were called about every three weeks (with regional variation) and that the sheriff's tourn was also held at least once per year (later more often); 270 hundreds were under royal jurisdiction.[192] With some conservative assumptions, we can posit at least a minimum of jurors serving across the royal hundred courts, sheriff's tourn, and assizes alone (and excluding the general eyre and multiple other commissions): between 50,000 and

---

[186] See the cautionary notes on confusing office with service, however, in Coss 2003, 44, 64, 149, and passim.

[187] Hilton and Le Goff 1980, 44.

[188] The volumes claim to contain "the majority" of officials, though they exclude some central bodies; *Gallia Regia* 1942, viii–ix.

[189] I included all types of *juges, procureurs, viguiers, vicomtes* and their lieutenants.

[190] Masschaele 2008, 163, 158–67.

[191] Calculations draw on Masschaele 2008, 72, who estimated at least 2–3,000 commissions were issued annually, not all of which called on jurors; maybe a third to two thirds did, giving a low estimate of 666 and a high one of 2,000 commissions.

[192] Total hundreds were 628 in 1272, of which 358 were run by lords and excluded here; Cam 1930, 137; Masschaele 2008, 57.

66,000 jurors.[193] The total number of those nominally liable for jury duty might exceed 200,000.[194]

These numbers simply establish magnitudes and should not be confused with historical estimates of total jurors in England; they also don't capture the complexities involved, e.g. that some jurors were called to serve repeatedly, though compliance was high until the early 1300s.[195] Even these partial estimates, however, suggest that around 1270 more than 1.5 percent of English subjects might be at some point dispensing unpaid judicial functions entrusted to paid royal professionals in France.[196] This is 150 times more than the percentage of judicial officials suggested by the *Gallia* (0.01 percent of the population). Laypeople were of course also involved in court proceedings in France in supportive roles, as many were in England, but they did not dispense justice.[197]

3.1.3.3 Amateur English Officials and Paid French Bureaucrats   Officials in France thus had duties often dispensed by "unpaid amateurs" in England.[198] But even official members of the English royal bureaucracy were often unpaid. For some scholars, this is just another symptom of the crown's weakness in the thirteenth century.[199] According to the historian Fryde, "only landowners of independent means could find the office [of sheriff] worth holding because of the temporary power and prestige it conferred."[200]

But such service was an obligation like jury duty that could only be excused for a reason. "Like other medieval offices the person nominated [for sheriff] was and is compelled to serve, and to serve without payment."[201] The reason why only "landowners of independent means" would take on the position is because already from the mid-twelfth century the sheriff's office "could set a man on the road to ruin," precisely due to the obligations it entailed.[202] The same applied to other commissioned officers. Financial burdens led to

---

[193] In the opinion of one legal historian, these calculations lead to a "low figure" (private communication). A detailed explanation of assumptions can be found on online Appendix B (see Figure 4.1 for details on the appendices).

[194] This number draws from the same estimates as for parliamentary elections above, n178; Campbell 2008, 940.

[195] Musson 1997, 122–23, 131.

[196] English population in 1290 was 4.75 million; Broadberry et al. 2015. French population in the early 1300s was 16 million; McEvedy and Jones 1978.

[197] Dawson 1960. French figures cover the period 1328 to 1399.

[198] The term "amateur" was usually attached to the later justices of the peace drawn from the gentry; however, many had a legal background; Bubenicek and Partington 2015, 163–64.

[199] Fryde 1991, 245; Hopcroft 1999, 78, 86.   [200] Fryde 1991, 245.

[201] Holdsworth 1922, 67.   [202] Maddicott 1993, 673.

under-performance and corruption,[203] but corruption was no less with paid officials in France, especially after offices became hereditary.[204] Office independence was curtailed by the crown, which prevented the sheriff's office from becoming either hereditary or locally elected and thus subject to local pressures throughout the period of parliamentary emergence.[205]

Not all English service was unpaid, moreover. From the 1250s, justices in the central royal courts were paid a regular salary by the crown,[206] initially supplemented by fees from court procedures. Some English offices were also sold as freeholds, as in France. Nonetheless, the most powerful officials, the justices themselves, served at the pleasure of the crown and "for good behavior."[207] As with the nobility in general, the crown intervened most forcefully at the top echelons in the hierarchy. When Edward I faced popular complaints, he removed two out of three judges from the King's Bench and four out of five from Common Pleas, fining them heavily for crimes as serious as murder and fraud. Although such a purge remained extraordinary, royal control was strong, despite English justices having higher status than their French counterparts.[208]

The French system, by contrast, is considered exemplary of patrimonialism, where administrative office becomes private, inheritable property that can be sold.[209] However, originally the opposite held: judicial officials were either appointed by the crown in a bureaucratic manner, eventually from candidates proposed by other members of the *Parlement*, or elected by their peers. Offices became informally hereditary and alienable only gradually, under Francis I (1515–47),[210] due to ruler weakness. Only "after several abortive attempts at abolishing [office inheritance] the royal treasury began to share in the deal, from 1567 on, by receiving a fixed fee from the successor," a practice systematized later with the *paulette*.[211] Ironically, purchase of office lasted longer in England because of the "veneration of inherited rights"; commissions on merit were not installed until 1871, 200 years after France.[212] The early con-

---

[203] For the tendency of unpaid tax assessors to under-assess, see Morris and Strayer 1940, 36.
[204] Doyle 1996.
[205] Holdsworth 1922, 66. Conditions later changed, however, and the office weakened.
[206] Brand 1992, 144–48; Holdsworth 1922, 252–55.
[207] Holdsworth 1922, 252, 246–52.
[208] Holdsworth 1923a, 294–99; Brand 1992, 103–12.
[209] This is the estate type of patrimonialism; Weber 1978, 232–36.
[210] Shennan 1998, 112–19.   [211] Weber 1978, 1033; Shennan 1998, 118.
[212] Henshall 1992, 93.

trast of patrimonial England and bureaucratic France again reverses common assumptions.

*

This chapter first offered evidence of the superior power of the English crown to compel the nobility to regular judicial service – a systematic obligation that solved the nobility's collective action problem and endowed it with incentives to co-opt parliamentary procedures handling the rise in petition-making. This helped explain why the English Parliament fused judicial and fiscal functions whilst the French *Parlement* did not. French weakness meant the Paris institution was dominated by administrators, making it less relevant for tax-raising purposes. The long-standing literature on Legal Origins corroborated the claim of English royal capacity, as did the evidence on the remarkable mobilization of English subjects for compulsory service that in France was carried out by salaried officials. English "amateurs" had little choice but to serve. This further explained how a central institution became anchored into local governance, eliciting the labels "territorial" and "participatory" so common in the literature.

All this, however, aimed to buttress an account of *institutional* emergence, which is predicated on noble presence and ruler capacity; it does not explain how *broad-based participation in parliament* was achieved. In Part II, I explain how institutional emergence interacted with the growth of representative practice and taxation, both flowing from greater royal infrastructural power.

Part II

The Origins of Representative Practice:
Power, Obligation, and Taxation

4 Taxation and Representative Practice: Bargaining vs. Compellence

How does an institution expand to provide greater participation in central governance and decision-making to broader sections of the population, whilst still compelling the most powerful actors in the realm? Both these conditions are necessary for a regime to be governing an entire polity rather than wielding authority over subsections of it. As we have seen, the intuitive logic adopted by most social scientists, including many historians, is that the demands for taxation by a ruler who lacks autonomous resources trigger counter-demands for representation from those below. So much evidence seems to corroborate this view that it is rarely appreciated how precocious such a response would be, if it were spontaneous. The puzzling nature of this assumption becomes clearer when it is noted that men living in the 1200s seemingly had responses to fiscal demands (a preference for enhanced constitutionalism) that are rarely encountered in the modern world, even in democracies.[1] A brief foray into the present might illustrate this.

"Why should [we] pay taxes, when the roads are in such disastrous condition?" This question, asked by participants in a tax experiment in the Congo recently,[2] could be heard in any developing or low tax compliance country.[3] It displays a compelling logic: each new generation called to contribute to taxation invokes the state's poor service provision or corruption and concludes tax evasion is justified. If one points out that most developed countries have high tax burdens, the assumption is that this is because they are rich and they can afford it – wealth was amassed before heavy taxation was imposed. This folk contractarianism reflects the bargaining hypothesis, which, as we have seen, assumes that it is "citizens who control the tax base"[4] and that groups have enough power to "inhibit the government's operation" by withholding funds

---

[1] Ironically, some Russian oligarchs may be the exception to this rule; see Frye 2021.
[2] See the fascinating study by Weigel 2020, 44.   [3] Cannari and D'Alessio 2007.
[4] Bates and Lien 1985, 58.

but not enough coercive capabilities to control it.[5] So, at least in the first round of bargaining, the state needs to offer concessions, to strike a bargain *before* taxpayers release resources. In an iterated game, citizens will only continue to pay taxes if the state keeps its side of the bargain. Today, weak states typically do not, and citizens feel justified in withholding resources. The result is tax evasion and state weakness, not greater representation.

Similar questions about the mechanisms tying taxation to regime type have long been raised by scholars working on the "resource curse," the propensity of states to display authoritarian traits when their main revenue consists of rents from a natural resource. This is typically explained by noting that dispensing with taxation obviates the need to respond to citizen demands.[6] Though highly intuitive, scholars of the Middle East have noted that "[p]redatory taxation has produced revolts, especially in the countryside, but there has been no translation of tax burden into pressures for democratization."[7] The latest quantitative assessments of the theory also suggest that resources seem to be a curse only where prior institutions were already compromised.[8]

Rather than seeing citizens of modern developing states as deficiently inclined towards ruler accountability compared to a small group of Europeans eight centuries ago, it might be more profitable to ask if we fully understand operating conditions in medieval Europe.[9] Especially since, as we will see in subsequent chapters, these modern patterns are strikingly similar to the Continental cases where tax demands were resisted and constitutionalism failed.

Indeed, this chapter argues that a fundamental feature of medieval representation has been neglected: it was originally an obligation before it became a right. I first explain its links to the Roman law principle of plenipotentiary powers and how its successful application depended on strong ruler powers. I then show how strong capacity to impose obligation preceded even the first constitutional "moment" in English history, Magna Carta, typically conceived as a bargain between a strong baronage and a weak crown before Parliament emerged. Finally, I show how representation expanded to include non-noble groups by process-tracing developments between Magna Carta and the coagulation of

---

[5] Tilly 1990, 64. As discussed in Chapter 2, arguments about representation differ from those about democracy; Tilly 2009.

[6] Mahdavy 1970; Chaudhry 1997.

[7] Waterbury 1994, 29. Slater 2010 also challenges the logic with South-East Asian evidence.

[8] Dunning 2008; Haber and Menaldo 2011; Ross 2012.

[9] As also done by Herb 2003 to different conclusions.

Parliament by the early 1300s. The point is to demonstrate that the English Parliament consolidated precisely because the state was better able to override the common preference to hold tax payments hostage to a bargain than its Continental or some modern counterparts. Chapter 5 shows how both French and Castilian "absolutism" can be explained by weaker state capacity, while Chapter 6 offers a quantitative comparison of England and France that demonstrates the English advantage.

4.1   The Compellence Model of Representation and its Historical Foundations: Obligation before Right

Although the nobility originally claimed to represent the community as a whole, nobles received personal summonses, whilst representation applied to community members, whether urban or rural. Representatives were, as we saw in Chapter 3, called to attend Parliament through royal commands; representation was not originally a right. In England, these commands almost invariably demanded representatives have plenipotentiary powers to ensure that parliamentary decisions "shall not remain unfinished in any way for defect of this power."[10] Similar commands were issued by French kings, though as we shall see they were rarely able to secure this outcome. But the general principle reflected the Roman laws of agency and the proctor, the agent who is granted full powers to act as a representative in court and whose agreements are binding on the principal.[11]

Representation thus imposed an obligation that resembled jury duty, which typically flowed from land held from a lord or the king. It had procedural ties to law courts, as Chapter 3 also showed: parliamentary representatives were chosen through the same process as jurors in county courts and borough assemblies.[12] The county and borough were summoned by the sheriff through a single writ issued by the king, which is probably why they were linked by historians long before they sat together in Parliament as the Commons.[13] Instead of bargaining, popular representation is thus better explained historically through a "compellence" model: the state *compelled* social actors to attend Parliament and the institution thrived only where this compellence succeeded. Today we take the obligation that follows from any agreement struck by our representatives for granted. Yet it is that dimension that was most precarious in

---

[10] *English Constitutional Documents* 1894, 29–31.
[11] Edwards 1934; Post 1943a; Holdsworth 1922, 357; Powell and Wallis 1968, 219–31, 285; Maddicott 1981, 73–75.
[12] Morris 1926, 139–42.   [13] Holt 1981, 3; Palmer 1982, 293–94; Stubbs 1896, 175.

the early stages of state formation. England differed in enforcing compliance at higher rates than other cases.

But England was again no pioneer: plenipotentiary powers appeared earlier in Italy and Spain and spread widely, in France included.[14] The practice is first recorded within the Church, allowing high-ranking clerics to avoid attending papal or local synods, which were costly and risky.[15] Canonist thought was instrumental for their articulation into elaborate principles of practice.[16] Proctorial representation is attested in royal meetings in England by the 1220s.[17] It was first extended to royal borough representatives in 1268[18] – crucially, boroughs had lower status and greater dependence on the crown than knights, as we will see. After 1295, proctorial powers were a stereotypical request of English parliamentary summons for both counties and boroughs.[19]

Non-compliance plagued the French kings, who faced recalcitrant social groups that insisted on the imperative mandate: when Philip the Fair was collecting taxes for the war in Flanders in 1309, the representatives were unauthorized to commit their communities, so they needed to consult back.[20] This was a frequent pattern in Spanish cities as well.[21] As the thirteenth-century French jurist Philippe de Beaumanoir stated, "no power of attorney is worth anything, unless he who grants this power does pledge himself to uphold firmly and stably whatever shall be decided or said by his attorney."[22]

Plenipotentiary powers tried to address a key problem, therefore. Although scholars focus on setting limits to political authority, this assumes that authority is established and effective. The real problem in early state-building, however, as in the developing world today, was free-riding. Rulers had business to complete, but not everyone wished to contribute, so rulers had to compel dispersed subjects to do so – even for wars that were not "national" but defending royal patrimony. This problem was especially acute when communal consciousness and collective action were weak – again, typical features of the modern developing world as well.

---

[14] Post 1943a; 1943b; Brown 1970; Maddicott 2010, 289–90; Rigaudière 1994, 165–66.

[15] Snow 1963, 327. This does not mean that the origins of the institution are ecclesiastical, as in Møller 2018 – they are Roman/judicial. That the Church elaborated it is an important historical point, but since the concept is not theological, it does not alter the institutional argument here. Derivation from the Dominican order, as in Barker 1913, is rejected by historians; Marongiu 1968, 33–41.

[16] Tierney 1995.   [17] Maddicott 2010, 207–17.   [18] Edwards 1934, 142.

[19] Anglo-Saxon precedents may have been important; Cam 1935, 198–99. But the formula was Latin and remained unchanged into the nineteenth century.

[20] Brown 1972, 354; Henneman 1970; Taylor 1954, 443–44.   [21] Lovett 1987, 18.

[22] Marongiu 1968, 230.

Representation addressed the problem of free-riding through the binding and compelling character of consent. To understand consent in the medieval period, however, we need to suspend the prism of rights through which the literature conceives it both in social science and political theory.

The dynamic resembles more a case with multiple co-owners of a property (though medieval subjects were far from on an equal footing). Even co-owners faced with a mandatory expense (let alone subjects of a lord) often prefer to avoid it. The consent of all would be sought in this situation not because consent could be legitimately refused;[23] the expense is part of the property obligations. Rather, any co-owner who withheld consent would be assumed to be withholding payment. This can typically stall the expense, as the other owners would fear being burdened disproportionately. Even where obligation is clear, enforcing it may be cumbersome. Once consent is given, however, meeting the expense without coercion is more likely. Everyone thus would be equally incentivized to secure the consent of all.[24] Those withholding consent would, by contrast, be deemed recalcitrant.

Unsurprisingly, not appearing at the English king's court was the mark of a rebel from the eleventh century.[25] It was also "something of a triumph" for the weaker French king to persuade the urban deputies "to come with full powers" to the Estates in the fifteenth century.[26] Few "rights" are involved in this context, at least originally. Demands for rights become consequential once individuals have complied with the request. It is compliance, the acceptance of the burden, that creates some entitlement. Sending representatives was "at first [a] misfortune and later [a] right."[27] And compliance depended on the differential capacity of leaders to enforce it.

Another classic maxim can be reassessed in this light, the *quod omnes tangit* (QOT): what touches all must be approved by all.[28] QOT was a mainstay of medieval constitutionalism, but it seems little emphasized that the invocations of this "right" were in commands of higher-ups, kings or higher prelates, not subordinates standing their ground. Some scholars simply assume that the latter is the case: one account affirms "the right of the archdeacons to be consulted before the higher prelates of England could grant a subsidy to the king," whilst referencing the renowned

---

[23] Harriss 1975, 8, 20–23. See also below, at n31.

[24] The obligation is also similar to that stemming from judicial (procedural) consent; Post 1943a. Litigants who submit a case to judgment commit to accepting its decision, whether favorable or adverse (just as in democratic politics). Further, "judgment is imposed on everyone, present or absent"; Vallerani and Blanshei 2012, 19. See also Oakley 1983.

[25] Maddicott 2010, 77, 88.   [26] In 1421–39; Lewis 1962, 14.

[27] Pennington 1981, 191.   [28] Post 1946.

medievalist Gaines Post, but in Post it is the *bishops* who invoked the principle in refusing the subsidy before involving the archdeacons, who alone could confirm the value of the benefices to be taxed.[29]

The maxim enhanced the ruler's claim to make everyone liable, thus boosting compliance when royal powers were strong.[30] It is not as if the English Commons could, at least initially, actually *refuse* taxation to the crown when it invoked necessity – although "weapons of the weak" were always employed.[31] Only barons could reject demands and they only did so when royal policy was generally unreasonable.[32] Further, those who were not present to give consent were not exempt from the obligation.[33] Where delegates invoked QOT as a right of resistance, as in Germany in the late sixteenth century, representative institutions faltered.[34] Noncompliance was greater in cases where such binding mechanisms failed, as in France or Castile.

So, although the term "consent" is widely used in both historical and social scientific works, it differs critically from its modern understanding.[35] The Commons did not even acquire the right to agree to taxation until the statute of 1340, by which time Parliament was well entrenched, and they still deferred to the Lords and the crown on questions of war after that: in 1348 they declared themselves "too ignorant and stupid" to offer views on the French war.[36] Further, actual "redress *before* supply" does not occur in England before the seventeenth century; that is why medieval historians generally talk about "redress *against* supply" and why the redress of the same grievances kept being asked decade after decade.[37]

That consent implies obligation is also seen in the elective principle that underlies representation. We consider election a paragon of democratic practice, but as political theorist Bernard Manin has argued, it is an aristocratic and delegatory principle not a democratic and participatory or egalitarian one like lot.[38] Yet outside city-republics, lot disappeared entirely in modern democracies.[39] Conventional responses fail to explain why, since lot could still apply in local assemblies, so larger size was not dispositive.[40] Manin notes that unlike lot, election implied consent to representatives' decisions and therefore imposed the obligation to honor

---

[29] Monahan 1987, 100; Post 1946, 249.   [30] Decoster 2002.   [31] Scott 1985.

[32] Maddicott 2010, 176–77, 288–90, 305–306, 422. For the debate on necessity, see also Harriss 1975, 20–26, 32–39; Ormrod 1999, 31.

[33] Maddicott 2010, 425. This was not set early on, but it was by the fifteenth century; Roskell 1956, 156.

[34] von Oer 1983.   [35] Harriss 1975, 23, 19–48, 314–20; 1978, 722.

[36] Wilkinson 1977, 379–80; Miller 1970, 20–21.

[37] Maddicott 2010, 379, 305; Fawtier 1953, 282; Ormrod 1995, 37.

[38] Manin 1997, 79–93. The use of lot in communes is discussed in Waley 2010.

[39] See the provocative call in Landemore 2012.   [40] Manin 1997, 81–83.

those decisions even when private or short-term interest might go against them. In fact, as royal justices warned, election carried legal responsibilities for the electors if the elected defaulted on their obligations, causing communities to forgo demands for elections of sheriffs, for instance.[41]

Some historians, however, also questioned the obligatory character of representation, deriving it instead from bargaining around taxation.[42] The debate raged for decades, as some evidence was ambivalent, but mostly because arguments about obligation were championed by conservative scholars, despite the original case being made by the staunch liberal, Frederic Maitland.[43] The alternative bargaining, voluntarist view is the residue of a Whig, somewhat anachronistic perspective on English constitutional development.[44] As argued already, the obligatory character of representation is attested by enforcement devices such as penalties and royal pardons. By the early 1400s, representation was indeed a coveted right, so laws even prevented non-residents from getting elected, as magnates co-opted seats by promoting their followers.[45] This reflects the paradoxical contrast between conditions of emergence and maturity.

4.2   Obligation, Taxation, and Representation: The English Historical Record

The emphasis on obligation seems at odds with conventional narratives. Neo-institutional analyses[46] and other foundational studies[47] assume taxation provided a contractual basis to political progress in the remote European past. England offers the classic instances according to two prevalent narratives, drawing either on the seventeenth-century Civil War and Glorious Revolution or on Magna Carta in 1215: in the latter, rebels gained the right to be consulted over taxation from a king weakened by war; in the 1600s, exorbitant demands by the absolutist but cash-strapped Stuarts led to socio-political upheaval and bargaining that established Parliament as a sovereign body of government.

But these historical cases do not prove a causal mechanism tying taxation demands to representative emergence. The seventeenth-century narrative fails on timing, as the English Parliament was already meeting for 400 years. A revolution *did* occur in 1688, as rights were extended to broader social groups, especially under the impact of the

---

[41] Payling 1999, 239.   [42] Edwards 1934; Mitchell 1951; Prestwich 1990, 109, 127.
[43] I question this conservative association in Boucoyannis 2015a.   [44] Blaas 1978.
[45] Myers 1981, 163, 164–65.   [46] North and Thomas 1973, 83; North 1990, 113.
[47] Bates and Lien 1985; Levi 1988, 112; Tilly 1990, 154–55; Hoffman and Norberg 1994; Acemoglu et al. 2005a, 452–53; Acemoglu and Robinson 2012, 185–209.

increasingly important Whig merchant classes[48] and sovereignty shifted from crown to Parliament. Neither the institution nor the practice of representation, however, originated then. Focusing exclusively on the early modern period is thus misguided.[49]

Magna Carta, however, seems to connect taxation and first political rights. Although representation was not a demand in the charter (just the consent of the barons) nor was the institution of Parliament per se, the narrative captures well-entrenched intuitions about how these interrelate. Since Magna Carta precedes even the earliest references to Parliament after the 1220s,[50] it also allows us to address the concern about endogeneity of royal power. It shows that royal capacity precedes Parliament; though, indeed, once formed, Parliament increased such capacity exponentially, as Levi noted.[51]

4.2.1   Magna Carta as a Product of State Strength

The standard narrative on Magna Carta is that in 1215 English barons rebelled against John after he lost the war against the French. Desperate for funds, the king granted a charter of liberties – some of which established rights expanded in the seventeenth century and valid today, such as *habeas corpus*.[52] Magna Carta thus appears to suggest a bargain exchanging taxes with consent, due to war pressures, before Parliament emerged.

No taxation was exchanged in 1215, however – and the king just promised to engage in consultation, which his successor reneged on in 1225.[53] Magna Carta, moreover, only resulted in a long-lasting equilibrium because of conditions before and after the baronial rebellion, not bargaining per se. Bargaining was as common and often more radical on the Continent, as we will see, but it was in England that representation flourished on a systematic and inclusive basis. Why? First, John had *already* imposed on his subjects probably "the greatest level of exploitation seen in England since the Conquest."[54] Yet that burden fell disproportionately on the most powerful subjects holding land from the crown. Second, most articles demanded greater royal justice, not tax limits. Finally, the *real* changes that the charter instigated depended on subsequent royal strength.

John taxed the whole population, towns, church and countryside, as the crown's claims extended beyond a feudal basis to that of public authority defending the kingdom as a whole.[55] When overall tax collection under

---

[48] Brenner 1993; Pincus 2009.   [49] This emphasis is common; see Ross 2001, 332–33.
[50] Maddicott 2010, 157ff.   [51] See Chapter 6.   [52] Turner 2003; Halliday 2010.
[53] The reissue of 1225 did secure a tax grant; Maddicott 2010, 107.
[54] Barratt 1999b, 87.   [55] Harriss 1975, 8.

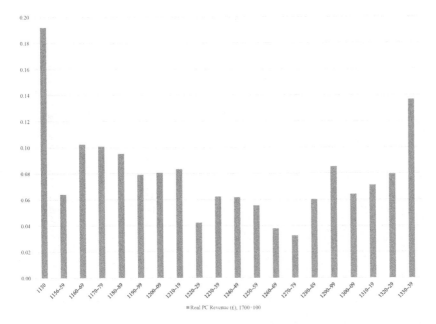

Figure 4.1 Real per capita taxation (£), 1700=100, average per decade, 1130–1339
Sources: The sources are extensively analyzed in online Appendix A (all online appendices can be found at dboucoyannis.weebly.com/ book_appendices). Briefly, for revenue: Ramsay 1925a with multiple adjustments from historians who have refined the estimates. For population and GDP deflator: Broadberry et al. 2015.

John is expressed in constant terms, however, per capita extraction does not appear as heavy as historians have assumed;[56] if anything, Henry II achieved slightly higher levels, which were not reached again until the Hundred Years War (1337–1453) (Figure 4.1). The exactions that had skyrocketed in real terms were mostly the feudal obligations that afflicted the king's tenants.[57] Scutage, for instance, was money paid instead of military service tied to land; John raised twice the rate per year than before.[58] The king's feudal rights also included wardship over infant heirs of feudal land and fines for consent of marriage for daughters or widows of feudal tenants. The sums collected from these duties reached unprecedented, even crippling, heights compared to his predecessor, sixteen times as much in total on average per year (Figure 4.2).

[56] Barratt 1999a, 63–67.   [57] Bean 1968, 12.   [58] Bartlett 2000, 164.

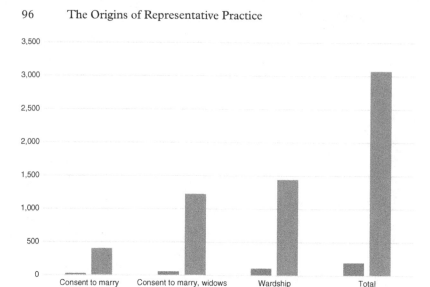

Figure 4.2 Average annual fines for wardships and consents to marry, from 1154-1216, adjusted for inflation, in pounds
Sources: Waugh 1988, 157–59 and the GDP deflator by Broadberry et al. 2015 extended to 1130 as described in online Appendix A.

Baronial demand for tax limits concerned these feudal land obligations. The key here is not the historically specific character of the obligation; it is that it applied to the most powerful social groups of the realm, who had ties of dependence on the center and were thus incentivized and able to act collectively. Nor is the claim here one of royal omnipotence; the crown was constantly struggling and repeatedly defeated. But even when it had to reduce knight quotas between 1190 and 1240,[59] it still did not reduce the tax burden.[60] The magnitude of the accomplishment will be seen in Chapter 6, by comparing with French revenues.

Moreover, as this argument predicts, taxation was not central to Magna Carta, as it appeared in only five out of its sixty-three articles (the main two, 12 and 14, were omitted from subsequent reissues of the charter, but remained important).[61] Instead, central to the document were land-based judicial concerns, especially on court hearings (44 percent of all articles – Figure 4.3). In fact, the barons were requesting the same security in their property rights that Henry II's reforms had provided to all free

[59] Prestwich 1996, 69–71.   [60] Maddicott 2010, 423.
[61] Maddicott 2010, 198; Hudson 2012, 844–64; Holt 2015, 314–34; Harriss 1975, 27.

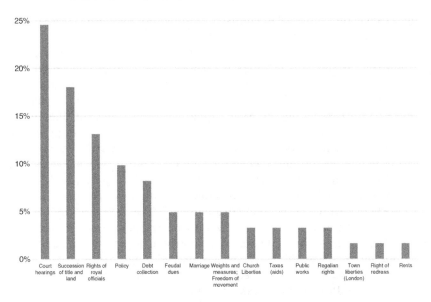

Figure 4.3 Distribution of article claims in Magna Carta
Source: Stubbs 1913.

men lower down the social scale discussed in Chapter 2.[62] Tenants-in-chief, holding directly from the crown, had no protection from the king's arbitrary will. The charter's reforms actually increased the scope of royal jurisdiction.[63] For instance, they increased protections of lesser tenants-in-chief and county knights, thus ensconcing the territorial anchoring of the regime.[64] The only election demanded was that of knights to assist county judges resolving property disputes (article 18).

Magna Carta did make the king less arbitrary,[65] but as we shall see it eventually made him more powerful. Moreover, "the problem of the lordless lord [the king] failing to provide justice remained."[66] The charter retained a central role in Parliament's later history, as a locus of contention between the king, the nobility, and the Commons throughout the 1200s and beyond. Indeed, almost every tax grant requested was tied to a reconfirmation of the charter in the 1200s. By the 1400s, Parliament had asked the king more than forty times to reconfirm it. This recurrent pattern has encouraged the narrative, even among the best historical scholarship, of a bargaining game that played out throughout the century

---

[62] Holt 2015, 124.   [63] Coss 1989, 42; Maddicott 1984.   [64] Maddicott 2010, 126–39.
[65] Carpenter 1996, 43.   [66] Garnett and Hudson 2015, 7.

and slowly built up Parliament itself – contemporaries also viewed many such instances as important royal concessions.[67]

However, bargaining was not what distinguished England from other countries, as the next chapters will show; it was more intense on the Continent, even in the non-Western cases. Moreover, in England it was asymmetric: that the king was repeatedly asked to reconfirm the charter meant that social gains vis-à-vis the crown were slow and that social groups were often not exchanging taxes for rights but taxes for promises that were repeatedly broken. The chronicler Matthew Paris gave a long list of bargaining promises when the king had "relentlessly made similar extortions from his faithful subjects." But on how Henry III would "fulfill his promises and agreements, in return for [the taxes he received], he alone knows who is not ignorant of anything."[68] Yet the taxes kept getting granted, eventually at per capita levels unsurpassed on the Continent.

Crucially, moreover, Magna Carta nowhere requested that a *regular institution* be created for "general consent" to be given, only that a summons be issued. The request for three parliaments per year was made in the Provisions of Oxford in 1258, indeed under conditions of royal weakness and social unrest – this was a radical demand. But radical demands were found all over Europe. England differed in that royal strength subsequently *grew*, especially after the 1270s, as we will see next, enabling those changes to materialize. Moreover, these demands stemmed from judicial concerns, not taxation. In 1311, the barons famously again demanded bi-annual parliaments not because they wanted to bargain on taxation more often but because, as they explicitly stated, redress of many wrongs could only be had there.[69]

The following section will trace this transition of Parliament from an "occasion" to an "institution" to assess the role of bargaining, especially under war pressures.[70] The analysis will show how the critical factor in retaining an institutional equilibrium over time was the relative power advantage of the crown.

4.3   Representative Practice Explained, 1227–1307: Taxes and the Commons

The English Parliament has no founding moment, but its institutional coagulation begins after Henry III's minority ended in 1227.[71] The term

---

[67] Maddicott 2010, 108, 148.   [68] Paris 1853, 17–18.
[69] "Ordinances of 1311" 1975, article 29.   [70] Myers 1981, 141.
[71] Maddicott 2010, 157–66 talks about the "emergence of an institution" from 1227. See also Fryde 1996, 533.

appears in meetings between the crown and magnates in the 1230s. By 1295, the so-called "Model Parliament" had acquired the core institutional and procedural form retained until 1918.[72] The role of bargaining should thus be reassessed before the 1230s.

In what follows I first examine some incidents that exemplify the bargaining dynamic so often invoked in the literature, in the early period after the 1220s, and once Parliament had acquired its established form, after the 1290s. Broader groups began to be incorporated in the intervening period, between the 1250s and 1280s, generating representative *practice*. The power balance between crown and barons will be examined for that period.

4.3.1 Bargaining Under Varying Ruler Power

Narratives emphasizing consent in parliamentary emergence often focus on the period between 1227 and 1258, when the barons opposed Henry III and his military campaigns.[73] The barons refused ten grants, exemplifying their bargaining powers. When taxes were later granted, the change is ascribed to baronial interest: the nobility deemed these later wars more "profitable."[74]

But focusing on the admittedly constant battle over consent in England is misleading. Not only was bargaining as or more intense on the Continent, as later chapters will argue, but English barons refused in the 1240s because they had been already forced to grant "countless sums of money," according to Matthew Paris. The feeling was that the king's extractions were "a scandal to the king and the kingdom," that he had "money untouched," that the money spent had brought "the least increase or advantage to the kingdom,"[75] since he was claiming his patrimonial lands in southern France. Ironically, in a pattern we will see repeated under the Stuarts, complaints became louder while real per capita taxation was comparatively low.[76]

Nor had these tax grants secured greater rights: the king flouted parts of Magna Carta to recurrent complaints and Parliament did not become more representative in the 1240s: no representatives were called. On closer inspection, the first period was not so much one of "bargaining" among near-equal actors[77] but rather of a period of royal weakness after prior excess, with little institutional payoff. Compared to French or

---

[72] Maddicott 2010, 289.
[73] Maddicott 2010, 175ff.; Barzel and Kiser 2002; Ertman 1997, 167.
[74] Barzel and Kiser 2002, 489.
[75] Paris 1852, 401, 399, 398–403; Maddicott 2010, 229, 174–75.   [76] See Chapter 6.
[77] Historians don't conceive of bargaining in near-equal terms.

Ottoman denials of taxation and non-cooperation, this was not exceptionally radical resistance.

Bargaining also looms large between 1290 and 1307, when the crown was much stronger. Apart from the charter, a major issue was Jewish lending.[78] In 1290, Parliament demanded that Jews be expelled in exchange for Edward I's demand for the greatest tax of his reign (£117,000;[79] notably, no war was being waged).[80] However, Jews were so weakened that their expulsion was not a costly concession. Jewish economic power had peaked in the 1240s: their wealth amounted to one third of the circulating coinage in the kingdom, making them the wealthiest per capita Jewish community in Europe.[81] By 1290, however, their power had withered. Over half of total Jewish capital had been transferred to the crown, including the queen, by 1258 and by 1270 Jewish lending was "overwhelmingly small scale, rural, and short term." By 1290, the community was "only an impoverished shadow of its former self."[82]

Accordingly, Jews were of little financial interest to the crown. They were expelled for the same mix of anti-Semitic and structural causes that other European rulers, unconstrained by parliaments, expelled their Jewish communities.[83] Its implementation within months contrasts sharply with the decades-long, but flouted, promises to uphold Magna Carta and other requests: unlike these, it cost the king little.

Bargaining again appears important in 1297, when the king was asked to reconfirm Magna Carta during highly adverse military conditions. Barons and especially the highest nobility, earls, were again the major protagonists. Some concessions were gained: the king did grant "the promise of 'common assent' to all future 'aids, mises and prises.'"[84] Representatives were henceforth summoned to all tax-granting parliaments. However, the promise of common assent was later broken again. After the king refused to abolish the wool tax, the maltolt, parliamentary bargaining shifted to mere "consent" over it into the 1370s: bargaining there was and concessions there were, but the king held the balance and only had to promise again to observe the charter[85] – but both the institution and extraction grew in strength. Most importantly, if the conflict had constitutional outcomes, it was because a "similarity of oppression" had brought lords and knights together to counter the

---

[78] Maddicott 2010, 293; Carpenter 1995, 356–57.   [79] Ormrod 1991, 153.
[80] This was a far harsher measure than the restraints on lending demanded in the 1270s; Maddicott 2010, 290.
[81] Stacey 1997, 93.   [82] Stacey 1995, 100; Stokes 1915, 167–68; Parsons 1994, 78–79.
[83] See Barkey and Katznelson 2011.
[84] Maddicott 2010, 303, 307 calls these "major concessions."
[85] Harriss' different interpretation still relies on royal capacity to deem abolition "unlawful"; Harriss 1975, 422, 420–49.

crown and to represent "the community," a point emphasized by Maddicott.[86] As the historian Caroline Burt noted, Edward I did not (generally) raise taxes arbitrarily like Henry III and John.[87] But he also collected amounts that reached levels not seen for almost a century.[88] Moreover, extraction increased even further in the century that followed, to levels only matched after 1640.

Conflict at the beginning and the end of the thirteenth century was therefore similar: baronial opposition articulated around Magna Carta and, despite temporary setbacks and relentless conflict, an increasing relative advantage of the crown.

4.3.2   Representative Advances under Baronial Advantage and Collaboration

Historical accounts accord much importance to the baronial reform movement of 1258–67, which forced the king to temporarily accept radical new forms of government, affirmed with the Provisions of Oxford of 1258 and Westminster a year later. To counterbalance the king, the barons summoned county knights in 1254, 1261, 1264, and 1265, extending societal representation.[89] This seems to confirm the logic of a weak king forced to concede rights to surging social groups.

However, these baronial conflicts did not differ much from the endless acts of contestation and resistance scattered throughout and beyond Europe, which produced charters and strident assertions of right, as seen in later chapters, yet no central parliament. The key difference, rather, was that it was the *barons* who called in the lower orders, due to their fear of an incipiently powerful crown.[90] In other cases, such as France, Castile, Hungary, Poland, even Russia, it was the *king* who turned to lower groups and gave them representation, because he faced a baronial class outside his control. As I will argue, this is to a great extent why representation faltered in those cases. Even when, as the historian Gerald Harriss pointed out, Edward I similarly incorporated the lower orders, he was responding to magnate *weakness*: magnates could not claim to represent underlying communities,[91] not least because the crown had undercut their power, as we have seen. Moreover, nobles were still compelled to contribute and lower orders were summoned with full powers, unlike in Continental cases.

[86] Maddicott 2010, 311, 302–11.   [87] Burt 2013, 7–8.   [88] See Chapter 6.
[89] Maddicott 2010, 255–61, 204; Prestwich 2005.
[90] The king had originally tried unsuccessfully to compete with the barons in appealing to lower groups; Maddicott 2010, 251–61.
[91] Harriss 1975, 42.

Moreover, the Commons had minimal social power in the early period. Elected knights were only present in 17 percent of the meetings and burgesses in 12 percent of meetings until 1307, the former rising to a third only after 1290 (Figure 4.4).[92] These were tax-granting meetings (except in 1283) – showing again the weak frequency and low representative impact of tax demands in the early period. The assent of the Commons was first required in the Statute of York in 1322, although it was not established practice until decades later.[93] Representatives were invariably present after 1327, but taxation was still not the main cause for summons: of about twenty-six parliaments in the next ten years, only five voted supplies.[94]

Although these episodes of community representation can be seen as a classic instance of English precocity, European equivalents were often earlier. Elected county representatives (knights of the shire) were called once in 1254 and then from the 1260s, but town representatives appeared only in 1265. Léon, however, first elected town representatives in 1188 and Castile saw thriving urban representation.[95] Nevertheless, the sequencing observed in England had beneficial institutional effects. Paradoxically, the crown's early strength made the early incorporation of towns less important, as the strongest actor, the nobility, could be compelled instead, including the rural countryside. Towns were incorporated early on the Continent because rulers were weaker and less able to tax the nobility directly. However, urban groups alone could not increase the inclusiveness of the institution; central institutions thus failed to become fully representative, as seen in the next chapter.

Focusing only on the period of the baronial revolt, finally, truncates the causal flow of the processes involved. The summons of representatives was predicated both on the pre-existing network of strong royal courts consolidated under Henry II and Henry III and on the judicial reforms that followed under Edward I, as described in Part I. Local courts were crucial for the system of petitions that enabled the institutional fusion described in Chapter 2 as well as the raising of taxes. If strong royal capacity had not preceded or followed, the baronial revolt would likely

[92] Similar calculations are in Sayles 1950, 456. If we follow Maddicott in including possible cases of lesser tenants summoned on a tenurial, not representative, basis, the Commons were still only present in 23 percent of all meetings until 1307.

[93] Maddicott 2010, 353–54; Lapsley 1951a.

[94] Sayles 1950, 460 (he admits only twenty-one parliaments). Similarly, Maddicott 2010, 336.

[95] Maddicott 2010, 379, 210–18; Kagay 1981, 42. That around 1295 the *Cortes* topped at 130 towns whilst England had about 160 called at some point, over similar populations, reflects, as seen in the next chapter, greater English royal powers; Plucknett 1940, 104–105. The average number in particular sessions was lower in both cases. In England it ranged from 75 to 85; McKisack 1962, 11, 27. Even in Castile, town participation only became regular after 1250; Procter 1959, 19.

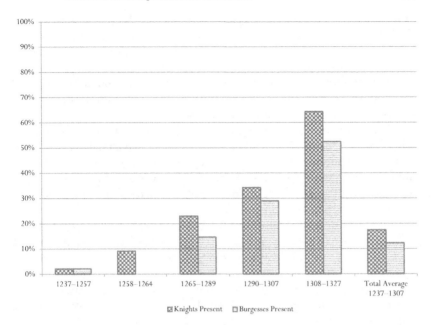

Figure 4.4 Number of English meetings with knights and burgesses present *Sources*: Fryde 1996; Maddicott 2010, 454–72. Both parliaments and consilia are included.

have been an abortive effort at premature constitutional reform, like many on the European Continent. Once grouped under a single institution and a common tax burden, opportunities for concerted action especially among the magnates and the county knights increased, thus strengthening their capacity to demand more from the crown.[96] Popular resistance grew in the fourteenth century, but only because initial conditions were originally inverted and had imposed uniform obligations.

4.4   Conclusion

This chapter has suggested we rethink the preconditions for the emergence of representative practices. In particular, it has questioned the widely accepted notion that bargaining over taxation with weak rulers was what distinguished effective representation. Rather, the key was treating representation as a legal obligation binding communities instead

---

[96] Maddicott 2010, 311–25. Urban representatives tended to have more local interests and petitioned less often; Maddicott 2010, 317–20; Dodd 2007, 266–68.

of a right. Tax bargaining happened throughout the premodern world. However, representative practice became inclusive and robust where royal capacity to compel all social actors, including to tax them heavily as we will further see in Chapter 6, was strong.

The notion of a bargain between state and society is an appealing one for modern liberals, but it should not be confused with an account of origins. The distinction matters greatly today. If citizens do not appreciate that government accountability requires that they pursue it assiduously – which they will typically do only if they have already contributed heftily to the public purse – the vicious cycle afflicting so many countries is unlikely to be escaped.[97] No representation without heavy or at least unavoidable taxation is a better descriptor of the dynamic that generated polity-wide participatory institutions.

Yet social science has displayed what may be called a "fiscal fixation," a conviction that taxation is "the skeleton of the state," usually traced back to Joseph Schumpeter's canonical 1918 essay, "The Crisis of the Tax State."[98] The claim has received compelling confirmation across a number of domains.[99] But Schumpeter drew on the experience of Germany and Austria, where, indeed, extreme fragmentation placed estates on a bargaining par with a weak emperor, as discussed in Chapter 10. However, although the Holy Roman Empire was rife with local assemblies, it did not produce polity-wide representative institutions, ones that genuinely governed, until the nineteenth century, if then, and after great turbulence. It is accordingly perhaps not the best model from which to derive a theory of representation, however useful it is for other domains. The next chapter examines two cases with stronger institutions, which, however, also did not succeed in generating a representative regime, France and Castile. The key variation was again in initial state capacity.

---

[97] Weigel's study 2020 corroborates this mechanism. That taxation must *precede* representation was also noted by Ross 2004, 238–39.
[98] Schumpeter [1918] 1991.   [99] Martin et al. 2009b.

5 Variations in Representative Practice: "Absolutist" France and Castile

"The division of classes was the crime of the old monarchy, and later became its excuse."[1] Tocqueville's analysis of the ancien régime has left an indelible imprint on our understanding of French political development and social theory more broadly.[2] Unfortunately, his explanation of the most crucial problem in his study – why ancien régime society was so divided and individualism undermined collective action – displayed a moralism that has imbued many subsequent studies and our understanding of representation.

Taking a voluntarist stance, he ascribed the steps generating French outcomes to purposive action: either a "crime" or an "art" practiced by "the majority of kings to divide the people, so that they can govern them more absolutely."[3] The critical event, in his account, that led England and France to irrevocably diverge despite similar origins was the levying of taxes without consent under Charles VII (1422–61). This ended the fourteenth-century tradition, he claimed, of "no taxation without consent." The reason for this was that the people were "tired of the interminable disorders" and the nobles were "cowardly enough to allow the Third Estate to be taxed provided that it remained exempt." He briefly admitted the crown was constrained by a powerful nobility. However, voluntarism also shaped his analysis of England: nobles were driven by "ambition" to engage with other social classes and retained their political liberty, preventing the divisions that led the French people into revolution.[4]

Though I will return to noble tax exemption in the next chapter, the book so far suggests that this diagnosis of a later period sidesteps the most critical factor: the power balance between the two main competitors, the crown and the nobility.[5] The English nobility did not intermingle with the "commoners" out of "ambition," at least not originally; it did so because it was compelled. And the French crown was not engaged in a crime or an

---

[1] Tocqueville 2011, 101.   [2] Elster 2009.   [3] Tocqueville 2011, 110.
[4] Tocqueville 2011, 94, 95, 93.   [5] But see Tocqueville 2011, 95.

art – it was compelled to choose the most feasible option given its disadvantageous position.

Although modern social science abjures moralism, similar assumptions of a crown suppressing representation in a "weak" society permeate major approaches. Much of the literature, despite great variation in explanatory models, sees France and other Continental countries through the prism of the later predisposition towards absolutism, which is identified with strong central power.[6] Downing viewed the Capetian and Valois kings as stronger than English ones, even while noting the strength of provincial institutions and the nobility.[7] Ertman often invoked English strength and the original Continental "fragmented political landscape" dating to the Carolingian collapse, which implies ruler weakness originally. However, he claimed that the "attempts of ambitious rulers to maximize their own power" favored "the creation first of a top-down, non-participatory pattern of local government and then of structurally weak, corporately organized representative assemblies which proved unable to stand up to" those rulers. The critical "switchmen,"[8] moreover, were the Roman imperial ideas that endowed rulers with "nearly limitless powers,"[9] an idea that was also central to Perry Anderson's account of the origins of the absolutist state.[10]

This view ties in more smoothly with later accounts, such as that of Barrington Moore, who predicated his classic account on a French nobility that was "a decorative appanage of the king" and was eventually destroyed – an outcome shaped by prerevolutionary developments.[11] Accordingly, the "French kings managed to establish 'absolutist' rule and govern without parliament" "by simply not convening it again, leading to the virtual impotence of the institution in the period between the 1570s and 1789."[12] The problem, therefore, was an overmighty ruler.[13] Ultimately, this echoes the "weak society, strong state" model that was incisively critiqued by Migdal.[14]

Historians, however, as we have seen, have long argued that absolutism emanated from royal weakness, not strength. In this chapter, I examine France and another classic case of European "absolutism," Castile, to show that rulers could not compel the nobility or the hinterland under its jurisdiction, preventing polity-wide inclusion in representative institutions. Accordingly, towns became the key actors in representative

[6] van Zanden et al. 2012, 17–18; Fryde 1991, 255; Acemoglu et al. 2005a, 454; Fukuyama 2011a, 332.
[7] Downing 1992, 113–15, 21.   [8] Weber 1946, 280.   [9] Ertman 1997, 36, 169.
[10] Anderson 1974a, 24–28, 420–22.
[11] Moore 1967, 40; Poggi 1978, 60–71; Badie and Birnbaum 1983, 107–15, 121–25.
[12] van Zanden et al. 2012, 6.   [13] Acemoglu et al. 2005a, 452–53.   [14] Migdal 1988.

practices, both in France and in Castile. Moreover, rulers could not impose plenipotentiary powers systematically on representatives, thus weakening effective governance. It was thus not Roman law that undermined representation; it was the weak enforcement of some Roman law, specifically of *plena potestas*, that did so. The Roman legacy was not monolithic; it contained both "absolutist" and "constitutional" elements and both were appropriated by medieval rulers. What determined the balance between them was the strength of the ruler – the less it was, the more the need for "absolutist" royal measures.

5.1   France

According to the Tocquevillian logic, representation lapsed in France because of deliberate royal policy over weak societal interests. This logic has a venerable pedigree, that of "divide et impera, the reprobated axiom of tyranny," as Madison called it.[15] It posits that division is a deliberate strategy of any tyrannical ruler who aims to weaken resistance by preventing collective action.

Such incentives are undoubtedly strong, and evidence can be found across cases where rulers chose to forgo assemblies, as this would concentrate social forces. Comparing the frequency of the English Parliament and the French Estates-General seems to reinforce this intuition (Figure 5.1). French frequency was zero for 21 out of 40 decades, but only in one in England.[16] Not calling parliament, however, I argue below, is the dominant strategy for rulers when they are faced with social forces that are capable of rejecting central demands.

5.1.1   Divide et Impera: "The Cunning Plan of the Romans" (Or the Strategy of Weak Rulers)

Assuming the king would prefer to enter into multiple negotiations and deal with his subjects separately is an intuitive prediction.[17] This Roman "cunning" was also noted by the thirteenth-century chronicler Matthew Paris.[18] But the reality, as Bates and Lien noted,[19] was generally different: in a memorandum from 1439, the king preferred central negotiations.[20] Otherwise, he would have to arrange multiple assemblies only for nobles (Philip V summoned seven in 1319).[21]

---

[15] Madison et al. 1987, Federalist 10; Machiavelli 1965, Book 6.
[16] As discussed, frequency does not directly express the strength of the institution; see Chapter 2.
[17] Elster 2006, 53–58 powerfully dissects Tocqueville's mechanisms.   [18] Paris 1853, 11.
[19] Bates and Lien 1985, 56.   [20] Jusselin 1912, 229–30.   [21] Taylor 1954, 443–44.

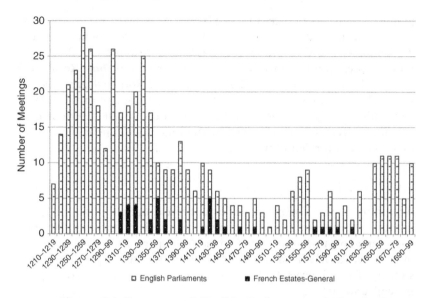

Figure 5.1 Frequency of English Parliament and French Estates-General per decade, 1210–1699
Sources: See Chapter 2 for England; for France: Hervieu 1879; Soule 1968.

The king acted more efficiently when he collected everyone at the center. There, nobles (or their representatives) faced many royal agents *and* the king, this semi-divine figure who cured the sick and was "anointed with the holy oil of Reims," "in all his glory and majesty."[22] One might think that, gathered in one place, the nobles could coordinate and present a common front against the king. In practice, however, they remained divided by regional particularisms. As we saw, English nobles acted collectively only after being compelled to serve the crown under common obligations, i.e. because the king was strong.

Conversely, when the king was weaker, he couldn't compel nobles to the center and the nobility's first preference, local negotiations, prevailed. He thus avoided the cost of summoning deputies to the assemblies. Even the nobility was compensated for attendance costs – unlike in England, where it attended as of duty. Representatives, moreover, were compensated more dearly in France than in England. Later comparative data, from the Estates of 1484, show that municipal officials and other third

---

[22] Fawtier 1953, 278, my translation; Major 1960b, 38.

estate representatives received 40–90 *livres tournois*, whilst in England burgesses and knights of the shire received 16 and 33 *livres tournois* respectively.[23]

Nobles therefore always preferred to defect and remain in the provinces, as the historian Fawtier also noted.[24] Locally, they just faced some royal commissioners who roamed the country to ensure compliance.[25] Divide and rule appears "cunning," but cunning is usually born of weakness. In the long term, however, the English case shows noble interests were better served when compliance at the center was originally effectively imposed, since it solved nobles' collective action problem.

As Tocqueville noted, division had self-reinforcing long-term effects. The more divided society is, the more effective rule is hampered. This was the predicament of the ancien régime: "It was no small undertaking to bring together citizens who have lived for centuries as strangers or enemies and teach them to take joint responsibility for their own affairs. It was easier to divide them than it is to unite them. We have provided the world with a memorable example . . . Indeed, their jealousies and hatreds survive to this day."[26]

5.1.2   Plena Potestas: *Where the Ruler's Dominant Strategy Failed*

The key problem in France, I argue, was that kings could not secure representatives with the power to commit their communities, as in England.[27] Moreover, taxation was only voted on by local assemblies.[28] Plenipotentiary powers were as known to the French as they were to the English. Procurations were particularly prominent in the municipalities of the south, where Roman law flourished,[29] such as Toulouse, which had advanced forms of self-government already from the 1190s.[30] Towns were major political actors, using representation for business matters. Proctorial powers were also granted for assemblies convoked for specific business, for instance coinage.[31]

But before 1322, the crown had only asked for representatives with plenipotentiary powers three times and they were either for moral support of a royal cause (the conflict with Boniface VIII) or not actually exercised.[32] Local communities were far more adept at withholding

---

[23] Major 1955, 226; Cam 1963, 237, using the exchange rates described in online Appendix A.
[24] Fawtier 1953, 277–78.   [25] Hervieu 1879, 229ff.; Major 1960b, 38.
[26] Tocqueville 2011, 101.
[27] The point is often neglected, though historians have drawn attention to it in the French context; Ulph 1951; Major 1960b, 29–30.
[28] Taylor 1939, 171–74.   [29] Brown 1972b, 359–64.   [30] Mundy 1954.
[31] Taylor 1938.   [32] Brown 1972b, 356–57; Rigaudière 1994, 166.

such powers, especially due to their experience with ecclesiastical negotiations. For instance, a papal legate exploited the powers granted to him by the diocese of Reims, in 1264, by tying the town to terms its citizens objected to. So, when the town was summoned to a royal assembly to approve taxation, it sent delegates with two mandates, one to hear and report back and one, as required by the king, to agree and commit, but only to a small loan.[33] By contrast, such limits on representative powers in England were the exception in a context of general compliance.[34] The French "government may have tried to enforce . . . a theory of procuration before 1314, but if so had given up the attempt" by 1321.[35]

After the defeat at Crécy in 1346, deputies did arrive at Paris with full powers, to support the eviction of the English from French territory.[36] Military pressures indeed encouraged subjects to cooperate. They did not, however, result in a regular institution. The Black Death further undercut royal efforts,[37] and compliance suffered into the fifteenth century. Persuading the urban deputies "to come with full powers" to the Estates was "a triumph" for the king.[38] Representatives repeatedly claimed they were unauthorized to approve the crown's demands and needed to consult with their communities.[39]

The fundamental difference was that in France (as we will also see in Poland), "large representative assemblies were used only to explain the need for a tax," whilst it was the provincial estates that "were the ultimate tax-granting institution"; only there could consent to taxation be given, reflecting the stronger *local* organization of the kingdom.[40]

5.1.3   Radical Demands and Institutional Proliferation

Demands for consent, therefore, were not unique to England. French communities asserted their local autonomy even more stridently. In fact, a paradox exists, where demands for consent were as or even more radical in absolutist cases; this will also be seen in Spain, Russia, and elsewhere. Despite strong demand, central representative institutions either failed to consolidate in a way that turned them into central organs of governance or never emerged in those cases.

French assemblies illustrate this. First of all, as community representatives arrived only with a "*mandat impératif,*" an imperative mandate to report back, they retained much stronger rights to "limit" the crown, thus

---

[33] Brown 1972b, 330–31; Decoster 2002, 27; Taylor 1954, 443–44.
[34] Sayles 1988, 55; Post 1943a, 402–403.
[35] Taylor 1968, 226n63. Also, Strayer and Taylor 1939, 141ff.; Bisson 1972, 551–53.
[36] Rigaudière 1994, 182.   [37] Major 1980, 14.   [38] In 1421–39; Lewis 1962, 14.
[39] Brown 1970, 18–26; Henneman 1970.   [40] Major 1951, 97; 1960b, 23.

undercutting the Estates-General, as historians have emphasized.[41] Urban communities also made additional demands. For instance, they demanded the right to judge whether war itself was necessary, initially attempted only by barons in England and only gradually by the Commons.[42] They also asked that tax collection cease once the cause for war ended – and the king obliged.[43] Occasionally, they demanded and obtained a refund if the threatened cause of war never materialized.[44] Cities of the Midi and North did not allow royal agents to interfere in their elections.[45] In 1355, facing military attack again, the Estates agreed to taxes but asked to participate in government, to collect and disburse tax proceeds, for estates to be held regularly, and for higher taxation on nobles than wealthy non-nobles. This was robust bargaining. But it failed to produce collective action or a regular institution.[46] So although the English Commons indeed placed constraints on royal power in the fourteenth century,[47] French demands were not weaker. They were often more radical. This did not make them less effective for subjects: the French initially conceded and paid much less, as the next chapter will show, despite central representative institutions being weak. When John Locke reported that in the 1670s the Estates of Languedoc "never do, and some say dare not, refuse whatever the king demands,"[48] he was expressing a dynamic that, if true, can't be projected back to the period of origins.

This radicalness characterized a popular movement that nineteenth-century historiography dubbed "democratic." Indeed, the mercantile bourgeoisie led by Étienne Marcel in the 1350s was remarkably assertive: they marched into the king's palace to kill dignitaries, which English merchants never did.[49] Far-reaching claims continued into the late fifteenth century: a member of the third estate advanced the proto-democratic claim that "the kings were originally created by the votes of the sovereign people" in 1484.[50] The Commons only made similar claims in Parliament two centuries later. A thirteenth-century text, *The Mirror of Justices*, had claimed that *earls* could judge royal actions, since they had elected the king to keep the peace; Edward I quickly stymied such claims.[51]

---

[41] Lord 1930, 138; Ulph 1951; Major 1960a, 6–9.
[42] Henneman 1989, 621. See Chapter 4, note 31.
[43] Brown 1972a; Artonne 1912, 166.
[44] Taxes were sometimes revoked in England though, as well; Bradford 2007, 133.
[45] Hervieu 1879, 34. Only some English privileged chartered cities enjoyed the same liberty; McKisack 1962, 12.
[46] Henneman 1983, 7; 1989, 622; Marongiu 1968, 100; Lemarignier 1970, 331–32.
[47] Bradford 2007, 138.   [48] Lough 1961, 238.   [49] Perrens 1860; 1873; Cazelles 1962.
[50] "[I]nitio domini rerum populi suffragio reges fuisse creatos"; Masselin 1835, 146, 140–57. Also, Lassalmonie 2000; Koenigsberger 1978, 192–93.
[51] Spencer 2014, 73–74, referring to *The Mirror of Justices* 1895, 6–7.

French demands were also not confined to merchants. The crown had to concede multiple charters to provinces around the country after many confrontations, especially around 1314. Many of these charters were permeated with the language of liberty and rights expressing aristocratic privilege. For some historians, the aristocratic nature of these leagues undermined collective action, as the people found little to support in their claims.[52] Nobles were simply not capable of collective action at a supra-local level.

Such local activism, however, had clear institutional imprints. The image of absolutism as eschewing institutionalized consultation altogether has been long contested, famously by Tocqueville, who pointed to many assemblies operating locally in the provinces known as *pays d'états*.[53] At least forty-nine such assemblies existed, of which twenty-five, in Brittany, Burgundy, Languedoc, and elsewhere, survived until the French Revolution.[54] They survived partly because, as path-breaking scholarship has argued, they generated important tax revenue for the crown throughout the ancien régime. Even at the local level, higher participation meant higher infrastructural control over local resources, including border military defense.[55] However, when at the Estates of 1588 "both clergy and nobility requested the transformation of all provinces into *pays d'états* so that taxes could not be raised anywhere without consent,"[56] they lacked the capacity for collective action that could secure this result.

The argument of this book predicts that the *pays d'états* should show early executive strength and some functional layering – such analysis at the level of constituent units is necessary for composite political units, as some comparativists have argued.[57] The early provincial evidence is too piecemeal to demonstrate this, but some key elements are there.[58] Languedoc was originally ruled by a count, and bishops wielded local authority based on land grants until the French king penetrated the region. Its *parlement* also considered petitions and was attended as of duty, like suit of court. Noble compellence was variable but is attested by the taxation of their urban property.[59] Brittany, Burgundy, and Normandy were early on ruled by semi-sovereign dukes, who dispensed justice in a *parlement* that assembled the nobility as well. Brittany seems to

---

[52] Lot and Fawtier 1958, 558–60.   [53] Tocqueville 2011, 187–95.
[54] For instance, Beik 1985; Collins 1994.
[55] Major 1994, 9; Potter and Rosenthal 1997; 2002; Kwass 2000; Blaufarb 2010.
[56] D. Parker 1996, 163.   [57] Naseemullah and Staniland 2016; Pepinsky 2017.
[58] A fuller consideration of the limited evidence on these cases can be found in online Appendix C.
[59] Bisson 1964, 109, 117, 131, 212, 265–88; Henneman 1983, 3–4.

be the one case with evidence of clear layering between judicial and political functions that assembled all social orders[60] – local histories described it as "the best regulated government in Europe."[61] Normandy fused judicial and fiscal powers in the Exchequer, the *Échiquier*; both nobles and clerics were liable for taxation early on.[62] Brittany and Normandy are also the two outliers in Stasavage's theory about the importance of distance: they met frequently despite their large size.[63] Institutional fusion helps explain the anomaly.

Although we typically think of France as a regime which suppressed consent, in fact consent and its denial were ubiquitous, often via local institutions and courts. If we record all meetings, including judicial ones, convoked by the crown with different social groups in different locations, we see that consultation frequency was actually higher in France than it was in England, except in the 1330s (Figure 5.2). The Estates-General, which required not only a polity-wide assembly, but also the presence of the third estate, emerges as very restrictive category. In Chapter 6, empirical data on tax extraction show that the French interaction type succeeded in imposing *greater* limits on royal capacity to extract, certainly until the sixteenth century, contrary to common assumptions in the field.

What has been presented as a contrast between regime types, even ruler preferences, was initially the optical effect produced by the location where exchange occurred. England appeared as involving more consent because we observe social actors coordinated at the center and engaging in the relevant discourse; exchange was thus centralized. France appeared as eschewing consent because we don't observe it at the center; it was dispersed in an infinite number of localities that actually succeeded better in limiting the monarch in his *fiscal* extractions. French exchange was decentralized – but political development was stymied. We have long labored under the (often misunderstood) Tocquevillian castigation of French "centralization" in the ancien régime and praise of English decentralization.[64] At the political level, however, conditions were inverted (as Tocqueville understood).

The fundamental condition leading to this outcome was the limited incorporation of the countryside. As we have seen, the most powerful social class, the nobility, was less under the crown's control than in England. As a result, "[s]trictly subjected to the jurisdiction of their lord, the peasants of the countryside, isolated in the frame of the seigneurie, found themselves essentially excluded from political

---

[60] Texier 1905, 87–88.   [61] de Carné 1875, 23ff.
[62] Neveux and Ruelle 2005, 88–91, 441; Floquet 1840, 13–15.
[63] Stasavage 2010, 640.   [64] Tocqueville 2011, book II.

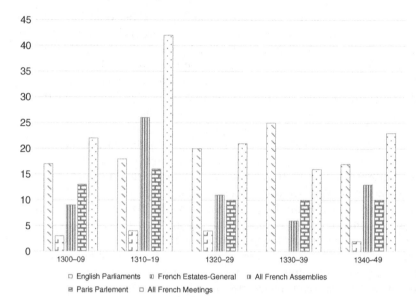

Figure 5.2 Frequency of English and French assemblies per decade, 1300–1349 *Sources*: Chapter 2 for England; for France, Figure 5.1 and Hervieu 1879. "All French assemblies" includes all Estates-General, as well as all assemblies that were regional or order-specific. "All French meetings" adds "All French assemblies" to *Parlement* meetings. Villers 1984 raised concerns about Hervieu 1879 as a source, but these are sidestepped by including all known assemblies. These figures do not include meetings with ecclesiastical representatives, so they under-report meeting frequency on both sides.

life."[65] This is why it was mostly the towns that were summoned to the assemblies by the king to represent the third estate, whether at the polity or the local level (until 1484).[66] These towns, as mentioned, were fundamental in furthering royal policy already from the twelfth century.[67] The assemblies would have been impossible without the system of representation of chartered towns, as there "was no regular machinery for summoning procurators from the semirural areas."[68]

[65] Rigaudière 1994, 163 (my translation), 167–68. Also, Hébert 2014, 184; Rigaudière 2003, 219. But see Cheyette 1962.
[66] Hébert 2014, 184.
[67] Harding 2002, 115–16; Rigaudière 1994, 178–80, 163, 167–68; Spruyt 1994; Lemarignier 1970, 302–305.
[68] Strayer 1980, 110–11.

Towns are central to many narratives of state emergence predicated on the political fragmentation of Europe, as we will see in Part III.[69] However, urban alliances with the crown did not secure institution-building at the polity level. Urban dominance in France meant the regime was not inclusive.[70] When the countryside was not integrated through a centralized system of courts and institutions, *polity-wide* inclusive representative regimes were stymied. By contrast in England, towns were "small islands set in the royal sea of the shires."[71] In Parliament, although more representatives were eventually summoned from boroughs (about 160) than counties (74), it was the county knights "who mattered most."[72] Broader inclusion happened where rulers controlled the nobility. No compellence of the elite, no inclusive representative institutions.

The same dominance of the urban sector and decentralization of exchange applies to the other major case of "absolutism" in Europe, Spain and its antecessor, Castile. Although typically examined as an example of royal suppression of consent, such outcomes followed from a fundamental central weakness.

5.2   Léon-Castile: From Feudal Centralization and Constitutionalism to Noble Immunity, Urban Dominance, and Absolutism

The Spanish monarchy in the early modern period was the "most powerful [mercantilist empire] in the world."[73] But it also long exemplified an absolutist ideology and intolerance to rights that suppressed growth.[74] This assessment is now qualified by historians, especially since the Castilian *Cortes* remained active at the height of "absolutism" in the seventeenth century.[75] Whether manifested in the control over "the administration of the *millones*, its attacks on the *Mesta* or the increasing compactualization of its relations with the Crown, the Castilian *Cortes* of the seventeenth century was far more important than before 1590."[76] The *Cortes* had the "ability to veto tax increases and limit the issues of long-term debt."[77] It was therefore more long-lasting and effective than the French Estates-General, a feature that has not been explained.

[69] Hechter and Brustein 1980; Hoffman 2015; van Zanden 2012.
[70] Only in 1484 was this redressed, but it was too late to shape institutional trajectories; Viollet 1866.
[71] Palliser 2000, 134.   [72] Plucknett 1940, 215.   [73] Mahoney 2010, 35.
[74] Anderson 1974a, 60; North 1990, 114; Acemoglu et al. 2005a, 453; DeLong 2000, 152–54; DeLong and Shleifer 1993.
[75] The literature is large; for a recent revisionist statement, see Grafe 2012.
[76] Thompson 1976, 275. See also, Jago 1981; 1992.
[77] Drelichman and Voth 2014, 41 and chapter 3 in the same volume.

Nonetheless, just as with the French provincial Estates, the Castilian *Cortes* did not shape the character of the regime, especially after the Spanish kingdoms were unified under the Catholic monarchs, Ferdinand and Isabella in 1479.[78] Scholars such as van Zanden, Buringh, and Bosker speak of the "Little Divergence," whereby countries in Southern Europe experienced constitutional decline, whilst the North (especially England and the Netherlands) saw an efflorescence that also allowed their economic takeoff. They attribute the decline to royal capacity to raise funds without consultation, which in Spain was further enabled by the discovery of American silver and the "resource curse" this entailed.[79] Historians have also affirmed Guicciardini's claim that Spanish monarchs had a dislike for "any manifestation of the representative spirit."[80]

That was not predetermined, however. The region had some of the earliest recorded instances of urban representation long before England, in the 1180s, as already noted.[81] The 1188 assembly at Léon summoned *elected* town representatives and is the first confirmed in Europe to do so.[82] The region pioneered the Church principle of plenipotentiary powers in the *Cortes*.[83] Towns were regularly summoned after 1250; in England, as seen, a general summons happened first in 1265, then sparingly until the 1290s and invariably only after 1327.[84] Castile further developed a thriving urban, commercial sector and regular parliaments.

The following sections show how these developments unfolded over three critical stages and how the factors identified in this account – distribution of land, taxation, fusion of judicial with fiscal functions via petition-making, collective organization, and degrees of territorial anchoring – explain the outcomes observed better than alternative theories. They all have a common denominator: variation in crown strength. The first stage saw the origins of representative institutions in the late twelfth century during a period of a strong crown engaged in military conquests that extended into the thirteenth. The next major stage occurred during the dynastic conflict of the fourteenth century, which reversed some key conditions from the period of emergence. The final stage came after the fifteenth century, when the Catholic monarchs unified the different Iberian

---

[78] The Spanish kingdoms included Castile, León, Navarre, Aragon, Catalonia, and Valencia.
[79] van Zanden et al. 2012, 17–18.   [80] Hillgarth 1978, 489.
[81] O'Callaghan 1989, 16. León and Castile unified first in 1037, then again in 1230; O'Callaghan 1975, 254.
[82] Kagay 1981, 42.
[83] Evidence is scant, but the earliest reference is from the 1270s; Procter 1980, 257–58; Post 1943b, 217–24.
[84] See Figure 4.4.

kingdoms with a weak base and the institutional framework of the kingdom took an "absolutist" direction. Royal capacity weakened at each step. I start by mapping out the corresponding patterns of representation.

5.2.1   Patterns of Representation

In bellicist logic, constitutionalism in Castile had an "intimate connection" to war.[85] Meetings increased after 1180, especially after 1200, when the Reconquest of the peninsula from the Muslims was indeed a major endeavor (Figure 5.3). However, towns were systematically incorporated only after 1250,[86] by which point most of the Reconquest was mostly complete (except for the southernmost area of Granada, with which peace was struck by 1273).[87] So, although, as van Zanden, Buringh, and Bosker point out, the *Reconquista* created military pressures to co-opt fighters and merchants, this itself did not increase the presence of the third estate, on which they focus.[88] The assembly spike after 1250 instead seems related more to successive crises that afflicted the kingdom, such as rampant inflation, corruption, and taxation that was already imposed.[89]

However, as we have seen, frequency alone can be misleading when the question is regime representativeness.[90] Towns represented the third estate and were the main taxpayers, already a sign of weak territorial anchoring of the regime. Town numbers moreover drastically declined over time, weakening the representative character of the *Cortes* by 1500 (Figure 5.4). Surviving lists suggest that towns rose from a maximum of 50 in 1188[91] to 130 by 1295,[92] then declined from 101 cities in 1315[93] to 49 in 1391[94] and just 18 by 1492,[95] the fixed number during the period of "absolutism."[96] Military pressures increased after the 1300s, as we will see, but representativeness decreased. In England, borough representation fluctuated until the 1330s from as high as 160 to about 70–90 in practice.[97] English levels thus remained far higher than in late Castile and increased under the Tudors,[98] despite overall similar populations – and

---

[85] Ertman 1997, 70; O'Callaghan 1975, 269–71.   [86] Procter 1980, 105–17.

[87] Procter 1980, 135, 118–51. Some historians end the Reconquest in the 1260s; Ladero Quesada 1984, 111; Rucquoi 1986, 60.

[88] van Zanden et al. 2012, 5.

[89] Ruiz 1982, 96, 99–100. Absent data on military expenditures and troop mobilization, all claims on these periods remain tentative of course.

[90] See Chapter 2.   [91] Procter 1980, 109.   [92] O'Callaghan 1989, 53.

[93] Ruiz 1982, 96–97.   [94] Merriman 1911, 480.   [95] Kamen 2014, 33.

[96] City numbers denote the maximum recorded, with some instances seeing fewer cities summoned (e.g. nine in 1272; Procter 1980, 134), whilst other meetings including different cities, bringing the total maximum to 180 between 1295 and 1315, for instance; O'Callaghan 1989, 54.

[97] Plucknett 1940, 104–105.   [98] Ball 1995.

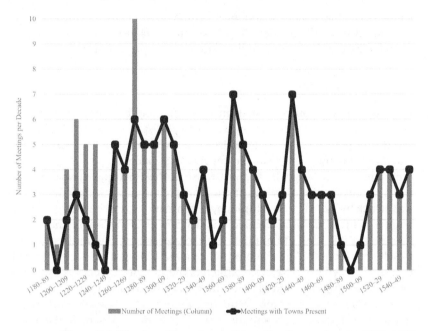

Figure 5.3 Number of meetings in Léon-Castile, per decade, 1180–1559
Sources: Cortes de Castilla 1861, supplemented with dates from
O'Callaghan 1989, 16 and amended by Procter 1980, 70–151.

towns were flanked by the county knights. The other Spanish kingdoms, reflecting relatively more stable representation, also retained higher numbers of towns proportionately in the assemblies: about twenty in Aragon and Navarre, eighteen in Catalonia, and about thirty in Valencia – despite a total population each of less than a tenth that of Castile.[99]

What accounts for that trend and how does it explain the trajectory of the *Cortes*? First, I examine how representative patterns reflected land distribution.

5.2.2   Land Distribution and Representative Scope in Castile

Both the rise and subsequent decline in representative scope in Castile depended on variation in royal strength. Castilian kings controlled the nobility less than their English counterparts. The land regime again shaped this variation. Until the 1230s, the period of early representative activity, kings distributed lands whilst retaining royal control. They

---

[99] O'Callaghan 1975, 585–86, 459–60.

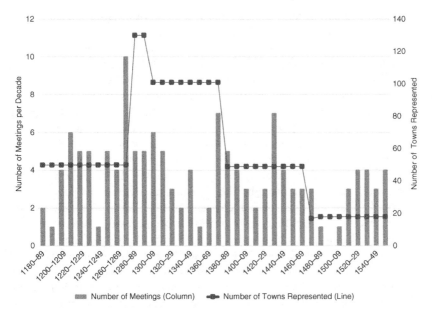

Figure 5.4 Meetings in Léon-Castile, per decade, and maximum towns represented 1180–1559
Sources: As for Figure 5.3 and footnote 96.

allocated estates to castellans (*alcaide*), who were "removable at the king's pleasure,"[100] as were all public officials.[101] They avoided the "disintegration of governmental authority" that is associated with the feudalism identified with Continental models. Administrative office was not turned into a benefice nor were noble benefices hereditary.[102] Consequently, administration was not too fragmented by entrenched territorial rights. The nobility was thus sufficiently incentivized to sustain royal institutions of governance, especially the Royal Council, the *curia regis*. The main representative institution, the *Cortes*, grew out of that Royal Council, as elsewhere in Europe.[103] Thus, when the *Cortes* frequency regularized after 1250 and royal cities summoned exceeded 100, royal strength was relatively high, as corroborated by other indicators below. However, Castilian kings were less able to compel key powerful subjects by the 1300s. The major power-holders escaped the extractive reach of the state, as they acquired jurisdictional immunities. With exempt territory increasing, the number of towns subject to taxation decreased, as did urban incentives to attend the *Cortes*.

[100] MacKay 1977, 97.   [101] O'Callaghan 1989, 10.   [102] MacKay 1977, 98, 97.
[103] Procter 1980, 1–2, 7–93.

Some crucial differences led Castile in a different direction than England. Nobles did not have as strong ties of dependence on the crown. Military service was not part of a conditional relationship (of homage) but a paid service.[104] This weakened the crown's relative control. By the 1300s, consequently, the military nobility and the Church appropriated large estates (*latifundia*) in the conquered territories, especially in the South.[105] So, although in the 1250s large estates could amount to only 12.4 percent of total area in Cordoba, by the 1350s, the large estates "accounted for 67 percent of the land surface."[106] This unleashed long-term centrifugal trends.

City representation sharply declined from the 1380s following the succession crisis that brought the Trastámara dynasty to power after 1369.[107] This led to a further concentration of land, as a few nobles were rewarded by the king with important privileges (*mercedes*) for their support. They appropriated judicial rights and collection of the sales tax, the *alcabala*, over territories that included large numbers of towns. Over the next three decades, about twenty families built large estates (*estados*) at the expense of the royal domain. Noble power had another major indicator, castles: 283 were built between 1400 and 1504, but only 12 belonged to the crown.[108]

Land was further "privatized" through a legal device that will be encountered again in the analysis of English and Ottoman land law: the *mayorazgo* or entail. It endowed the first-born with a continuous possession over land that was inalienable and exempt from inheritance taxation, establishing both primogeniture and fiscal immunity.[109] The *mayorazgo* thus removed land from royal jurisdiction, even though royal authorization was required until 1505.[110] Entailing was important especially between the reigns of Henry II and Isabella (1474–1504). After the 1480s, it was further extended to the middle and petty nobility.[111]

One hypothesis explaining the concentrations in land distribution is that they were endogenous to the high land-to-labor ratio that economists invoke to explain early economic prosperity in Spain.[112] By 1300, a territory about twice the size of England was populated by similar numbers, about 4 to 5 million.[113] But arguments from population density to institutional strength do not explain why political rule cannot

---

[104] Rucquoi 1993, 267; MacKay 1977, 97.   [105] Martín Martín 1984.
[106] Cabrera 1989, 469, 474.   [107] MacKay 1977, 134; Rucquoi 1993, 272–73.
[108] Rucquoi 1993, 272.   [109] Entails were not always tax-exempt.
[110] Gerbet 1984, 259–60.
[111] Over time, the *mayorazgo* was economically "disastrous" as it "froze" fortunes and tied noble income to land, the value of which declined drastically in the seventeenth century; Gerbet 1984, 261, 276.
[112] Álvarez-Nogal and Prados de La Escosura 2012.   [113] O'Callaghan 1975, 459.

consolidate in some compact region and expand further on an "imperial" or agglomerative basis. After all, England never secured effective control over Ireland, Scotland, or Wales, yet it still consolidated power in the south. Catalonia, as will be seen, developed robust institutions over a more limited area before becoming an empire. Low population density did not prevent the high regional institutionalization of the early United States either.[114] Moreover, the *Cortes* were inundated with suits showing land was still contested – the crown's role was crucial there.[115] Even if some lands were remote, a critical mass of conditional nobles could have been sustained in some sub-region but were not.

All these trends, however, increased the size of the nobility. It was disproportionately large compared to England and more similar to Poland. Ten percent of the population were noble, as all offspring retained noble status, unlike in England.[116] However, the truly powerful nobles, controlling most of the landed resources, were not more than 2 percent, as in France.[117]

By the 1470s, when the Catholic kings came to power, the nobility, together with the Church and the military orders, controlled practically all of the land by hereditary right, completely reversing the conditions that generated parliament in England: in some estimates, they "either owned 97 per cent of the land of Spain or possessed profitable rights of jurisdiction over it. Fifty-five per cent of the land in question belonged to the great noble houses, the rest to bishoprics, abbeys, the urban oligarchy, and lesser nobles."[118] Although Ferdinand and Isabella improved these conditions somewhat, their successors alienated extensive estates and towns to the military orders, especially from Church lands. By 1600, "about two-thirds of the 4,600 towns in Castile and one half of its 15,800 villages and hamlets were under private control (*señorío*)," with jurisdictional and tax immunities.[119] Regional studies confirm these patterns. In Salamanca, "over 60 per cent of the population fell under noble jurisdiction." In Valencia, "the king has only 73 large and small towns, and over 300 are seigneurial; in Aragon the crown in 1611 had

---

[114] Acemoglu et al. 2002 dismiss the connection after 1500 and Osafo-Kwaako and Robinson 2013 for Africa.

[115] Procter 1959.

[116] Gerbet 1992, 349; 1977–79. Drelichman 2007 showed that noble status was mostly sought for government office, not fiscal exemption.

[117] Sobroqués 1957, 418.

[118] Hillgarth 1978, 499; citing Vicens Vives 1969, 295 and Sobroqués 1957, 418–20. Note, however, Vassberg's 1984, 90–91 general reservations about the evidentiary basis of such claims.

[119] Kamen 2014, 231, 22–25, 143.

jurisdiction over only 498 of 1,183 centers of population, with nobles and the Church in roughly equal control of the remainder."[120]

The sharp decline in city representation is related to these trends, even though the frequency of the *Cortes* remained fairly robust, as the final section will further discuss. The connection of limited inclusion with weak control over land and the powerful actors holding it is thus observed in Castile as in France.

5.2.3   Taxation

Given the crown's weakness, the argument would predict that the nobility and clergy were exempt from direct taxation. Indeed, similarly to France, the nobility and clergy were exempt from direct taxation, as were the urban oligarchies that attended the *Cortes*.[121] Yet again, however, taxation was not central to the early meetings, confirming the pattern discerned by Wim Blockmans across European cases.[122] In Castile as well, "no evidence of any direct intervention of the curia in questions of taxation" exists before the 1250s, although records are scanty.[123] Yet representative activity was becoming regular.

Taxation begins to be a systematic concern of the *Cortes* only after the 1250s, i.e. after decades of representative activity and after the Reconquest pressures subsided. New taxes were raised: the direct *servicios* (either a capitation tax or a tax on movable property), customs duties on imports and exports, various aids, and the *alcabala* (fully from the 1340s).[124] These taxes mainly burdened the cities and the countryside they controlled, as their rising complaints towards the end of the thirteenth century attest.[125] The exempt nobility only occasionally consented to a direct levy on their vassals. The clergy mostly agreed to contribute, as its interests were originally closer to the crown.[126] The principle of consent was acknowledged on many occasions, but it did not imply the right to refuse taxation: "there was no specific instance during this period when a request for taxes was rejected."[127] However, the *Cortes* sometimes required redress of grievances before consenting to tax, though the evidence is only suggestive.[128] Castilian tax-farming, in most instances indicating weak extractive capacity, was extensive.[129] In later periods,

---

[120] Kamen 2014, 230.   [121] Kamen 2014, 83; Ladero Quesada 1999, 192–96.
[122] Blockmans 1978, 202; Møller 2017.   [123] Procter 1980, 81.
[124] Procter 1980, 186–202.   [125] Ruiz 1982, 99.
[126] Procter 1980, 190–91, 133–35, 201; O'Callaghan 1989, 132–33; Ladero Quesada 1984, 114.
[127] O'Callaghan 1989, 132, 130–36.
[128] O'Callaghan 1989, 75–76; Blockmans 1998, 60. Cf. Merriman 1911, 484.
[129] Procter 1980, 199–200.

Spanish monarchs also sold towns to raise revenue, which further depleted their demesne.[130]

Systematic comparative data on rates of extraction in England and Castile are not available before 1500. Indirect evidence for comparative English fiscal strength comes from monetary data.[131] Until the 1540s, the English crown never debased its coinage (with one minor exception), a sign of strong fiscal control under the centralized London Royal Mint since the 1270s.[132] In Castile, an extraordinary subsidy was paid every seven years by non-noble free men only to prevent debasement, the *moneda forera* (as in 1202),[133] similarly to France.[134]

More direct evidence on extraction, by Karaman and Pamuk, suggests that in 1500, Spain (including Aragon) was raising more than twice per capita what England was (as seen in Chapter 6, English extraction declined in this period).[135] One per capita estimate posits output in Spain to be 28 percent higher than in England in 1500.[136] If so, given the tax exemption of the nobility and their subjects, a far heavier tax burden was shouldered by the cities and their hinterlands and the Church[137] than in England, explaining the perception of inefficient, oppressive taxation.[138] This also suggests, once again, that capacity to extract determined which groups were included in institutions – the critical actor for polity-wide inclusiveness of the institution, however, was the nobility and in Castile it was eventually absent.

5.2.4   Functional Layering and Institutional Fusion at the Cortes: Towns, not Countryside   Castilian constitutionalism thus needs to be explained: if it preceded fiscal bargaining, why did the *Cortes* begin to assemble, with both nobles and eventually towns originally present? Another feature is puzzling: a regular *central* institution emerged in Castile, whereas it did not in France, when both nobilities were not taxed. The argument so far has suggested that central institutions became regular when judicial and fiscal functions were fused. Unlike France, Castile also displayed this institutional fusion. Judicial functions were key, and they involved not only the nobility but primarily the towns.

Despite lacking a pressing fiscal incentive, some nobles attended the *Cortes* up to the middle of the fourteenth century, in particular the magnates and the king's chief collaborators (*ricos hombres*). Numbers

---

[130] Nader 1990.   [131] Karaman et al. 2019.   [132] Mayhew 1992, 144–45, 117–37.
[133] O'Callaghan 1989, 133–35.   [134] Sussman 1992.   [135] Karaman and Pamuk 2013.
[136] Álvarez-Nogal and Prados de La Escosura 2012, 23.
[137] Ladero Quesada 1973, 192. Their less reliable Maddison estimate places Spain marginally below England.
[138] Ekelund and Tollison 1997, 129.

can only be loosely inferred from lists of witnesses of royal charters, which suggest comparatively far lower levels of attendance in the thirteenth century than in England, about 20 to 25 nobles[139] to England's average of 70 over a similar population (4–5 million).[140] This was the same probable number as in France, however, that had three to four times the population. Castile is therefore in an intermediary position.

The primary incentive for the nobility, as contemporaries stressed, was "the feudal obligation to give counsel as royal vassals."[141] Other business was also administered, for instance, witnessing donations to churches, monasteries, and individuals.[142] Nobles, as in England, attended originally out of obligation.[143] No right of attendance existed, only the de facto presence of the same families in the king's court.[144] The nobility's interest in the *Cortes* remained strong, however, because the royal court functioned as a judicial tribunal.[145] It is where nobles were tried for treason, crimes, or negligence in administration.[146] It is also where disputes among nobles, towns, and ecclesiastical institutions were presented, as well as appeals from judgments rendered by other courts in the kingdom (whilst the English royal court had extensive first-instance jurisdiction, as we have seen). Such judgments were often and upon request made by the king himself. The *Cortes* regularized further under Alfonso X (1252–84), who promised to hear suits three times a *week*, as did subsequent kings.

Another key concern for the nobility was, as in England and France, the legislation passed in the *Cortes*.[147] When Alfonso X passed new laws requested by the municipalities, the *Fuero real*, the nobles originally consented together with the prelates. But in the *Cortes* of 1272, the nobility demanded that their right to trial by peers be affirmed and that the king appoint two judges from their own order to hear their more routine pleas in accordance with their own *fueros* (customs) – a request that was granted.[148] The attempt to impose a highly Romanized law code, the *Espéculo*, and the great compilation, the *Siete Partidas*, also faltered due to this noble resistance.[149] That different rules and different judicial personnel applied to groups according to social or regional origin suggest the relative weakness of the Castilian crown to impose judicial and

---

[139] O'Callaghan 1989, 52, 47. The highest number of abbots attested was thirty-nine; O'Callaghan 1989, 48.
[140] O'Callaghan 1975, 459.
[141] O'Callaghan 1989, 51, 52; Sánchez-Albornoz 1991, 56–74.
[142] O'Callaghan 1989, 13; 1975, 584.   [143] Procter 1980, 1–2.
[144] O'Callaghan 1989, 51–52.
[145] The Curia remained the highest court only until the end of the fourteenth century; Procter 1980, 3.
[146] Procter 1980, 92.   [147] Procter 1980, 203–23.   [148] O'Callaghan 1989, 117–18.
[149] Procter 1980, 243, 249; O'Callaghan 1989, 117–20.

legislative uniformity throughout the kingdom – a critical difference from English conditions with long-term consequences.[150] Yet, the extent of organized noble contestation suggests that royal powers were higher than in France.

Petitions were equally central in Castilian developments. Royal willingness to respond to these petitions cannot be divorced from the rising fiscal pressures due to war. But the necessary condition for this need to translate into institutional growth was the servicing of popular judicial needs, which were centralized by the crown through conditional rights, especially tied to land. Although systematic evidence is lacking, the nobility's somewhat greater dependence on the crown than in France is attested by its petitions for exemptions; the nature and quantity of petitions could measure this relation.[151] This dependence helps explain the institutional fusion observed in Castile, as the *Cortes* served both judicial and fiscal functions, unlike the French Estates-General.

The towns, however, were the main drivers of institutional fusion. We have seen in Part I how the English crown's capacity to harness supra-local collective action across the nobility, boroughs, *and* counties was fundamental for Parliament's representative and inclusive character. Kings could impose collective responsibility across all social orders – presence in Parliament obligated local communities to abide by central decisions, enabling the crown's territorial anchoring across the countryside, not just towns. In Castile, this pattern was reproduced mainly with the towns, and "only those on royal demesne."[152] As the historian Teofilo Ruiz has argued, towns were the Crown's main allies, seeking royal protection against magnates.[153] Spanish urbanization was between double and quadruple that of England, generating a thriving commercial sector.[154] Urban municipal structures allowed considerable self-governance based on councils (*concejos*) and separate law codes (*fueros*), but under royal lordship. It was with this dependent group that the key ingredient of constitutionalism developed – an instance of the second-best constitutionalism we will observe in Hungary, Poland, Russia and elsewhere.

Judicial interaction, including by petitions, was here as well key in forging institutional relations between crown and society via representation. Royal towns pursued justice in the royal courts already from the

---

[150] O'Callaghan 1989, 158–61, 118; Procter 1980, 239.
[151] Hébert 2014, 466–68; O'Callaghan 1989, 74–75.
[152] Procter 1980, 161; Hébert 2014, 180.   [153] Ruiz 1982, 96.
[154] Urbanization estimates from 1500 (de Vries 1984, 37; Álvarez-Nogal and Prados de la Escosura 2007, 337) have halved Bairoch's (Bairoch et al. 1988, 259) numbers for Spain.

1180s, just as the *Cortes* was institutionalizing.[155] They were incentivized to attend, since royal courts resolved disputes relating to landholding and vassalage[156] and they had *corporate* representation from the 1220s.[157] So although they attended the central court rarely before 1250 for political purposes, the judicial prehistory offered a critical backbone to representative practice connecting "the representation of towns as suitors in cases tried before the king's court, and their representation in the cortes." By 1250, Castilian towns provided corporate powers (*cartas de personería*) to those representing them as suitors in the king's court and probably the *Cortes* too. A thirty-year precedent in judicial courts prepared for political representation.[158]

Petitions were again a vehicle for legislation. Towns protested taxation, economic problems, abuses by royal officials, and other mundane concerns, recorded in *cuadernos*.[159] Petitions could be presented to the itinerant king throughout the country, sometimes in oral form, but the *Cortes* became a major venue for their consideration. The king could disregard petitions submitted to him; nonetheless, he was sworn to uphold the *posturas*, understood as a "contractual agreement between the king and his people."[160] As in England, the demands resulted in *decreta, constitutiones*, and ordinances, though legislation also originated in royal initiative.[161] Collective petitions soon became here too an instrument for initiating legislation that was supra-local. Town representatives collectively attending the *Cortes* were exposed to similar concerns from different regions.[162] As a result, "collective petitions, presented by all the towns of the kingdom, or of a province, stood a better chance of a favourable consideration than one presented on behalf of a single town."[163]

Obligation was central to these patterns: penalties were imposed for non-attendance, reaching the large sum of 1,000 *maravedis* for great towns. Compensation, however, seems much lower than England's: in 1250, the towns paid representatives one half a *maravedí* a day for the

---

[155] Procter 1980, 105–17; 1959, 22; Ruiz 1982; Hébert 2014, 180.
[156] O'Callaghan 1989, 14, 18.   [157] Procter 1959, 18–19.
[158] Procter 1980, 164–65. But regular corporate representation of towns cannot be ascertained before 1305; Procter 1959, 14, 21. Ecclesiastical precedent was probably important here as well; Procter 1959, 14; Post 1943b.
[159] Procter 1980, 212–23; Ruiz 1982; O'Callaghan 1975, 588.
[160] O'Callaghan 1989, 122–23; MacKay 1977, 104–105.
[161] O'Callaghan 1989, 18; Procter 1980, 203–23.
[162] Petitions, however, were presented to the small curia and the *Cortes* developed from the great curia, but the processes were connected; Procter 1959, 17.
[163] Procter 1980, 207, 204–209.

journey to Toledo and one *maravedí* for Seville.[164] English burgesses were paid 2 shillings a day, which maybe equaled 3.7 *maravedí*.[165]

In fact, the Castilian institution had some major differences that placed it in an intermediary position between France and England. As in France, its corporate organization did not extend to the countryside, which was not separately represented. Most of it was under noble jurisdiction and not represented at all, some was under municipal jurisdiction.[166] In England, both (rural) counties and (urban) boroughs generated collective petitions that produced bills of legislation. Broad-based incorporation is evidently a necessary condition for parliament to become a central instrument of governance polity-wide; when lacking, the different estates were not united on a common platform.

Even the town associations formed from 1282 in Castile, the *hermandades*, which exercised power during minorities as "the vanguard in the *cortes*," lacked unity.[167] As a result, a "principal weakness of the *Cortes* was the failure of the estates to join together in presenting common proposals to the king": no sense of common interests existed.[168] Accordingly, "the Castilian assembly was unable to turn this right of petition into a right of legislation," nor did the common petitions develop into bills, as in England.[169] The implication of this account is that this disparity flowed from the weaker powers of the ruler and more limited involvement of the groups concerned, especially the nobility. Weaker royal powers are also reflected in the rarer imposition of plenipotentiary powers, which we saw were crucial for English outcomes. Mandates were typically limited, not plenipotentiary, leaving towns greater discretion, as in France.[170]

Yet in developing functional layering and institutional fusion, Castilian outcomes also differed from French ones, despite a similar crown–city alliance, and resembled English ones. Castilian capacity to do so must reflect, in this book's logic, greater relative royal power. Systematic early evidence is not available to definitively prove it, but the Karaman and Pamuk data between 1500 and 1600 (the earliest available) suggest that Spain extracted between double and three times per capita in taxes than France and equal to up to twice when adjusted for purchasing power, while output per capita is estimated as equal.[171] Moreover, extraction burdened the urban groups central to the fusion (which explains why the

---

[164] O'Callaghan 1989, 58.
[165] Maddicott 1981, 78–80. *Maravedis* fluctuated in value; the closest exchange rate is from 1291/1300; Spufford 1988, 292.
[166] O'Callaghan 1989, 14.   [167] Blockmans 1998, 55.   [168] O'Callaghan 1989, 128.
[169] Merriman 1911, 485; Procter 1980, 209.
[170] Procter 1980, 164; Holden 1930, 894–903.
[171] Karaman and Pamuk 2013; Álvarez-Nogal and Prados de La Escosura 2012, 23.

town-based *Cortes* were so robust). Alternative explanations of representative differences are even less plausible, as neither geographic size nor military pressures varied between France and Spain.

5.2.5   Royal Absolutism or Pathologies of Urban Dominance?

The urban constitutionalism just described was precocious and, at the micro level, quite similar to what was observed in England. But did the gradual restriction of urban participation result from royal weakness rather than, as some narratives hold, increasing royal autonomy, especially after the discovery of American silver?[172]

Silver revenues become significant after 1540, yet urban restriction had already occurred, so they cannot explain these patterns.[173] Key indicators of royal weakness, however, have been already mentioned: noble and clerical immunity, as well as limited jurisdiction and lack of common law across social orders and regions. But the question is also answered by examining the increased urban dominance, which developed predictable pathologies. Stasavage showed how urban autonomy can lead to capture of internal institutions by oligarchies that then restrict growth.[174] In Venice, it was powerful merchants seeking to secure political and economic advantage that were responsible for the closure of its political system.[175]

Castilian cities displayed this pattern too. They used to be seen as mercantile, progressive bulwarks against autocracy. This eighteenth-century narrative has not withstood historical scrutiny, however. As Ruiz has argued, town leaderships increasingly operated as narrow, closed oligarchies composed of non-noble knights, the *caballeros villanos*.[176] After the 1250s, the knights gained privileges from the crown, especially tax exemption, which helped them counter the non-urban nobility and other towns. It was this group that eventually controlled the *Cortes*, in which it negotiated not just judicial issues but also the taxes burdening mostly the *pecheros*, the tax-paying inhabitants.

Consequently, the *Cortes* were also transformed into an oligopoly, which indeed made participation a privilege to be jealously guarded. But this impeded broader representation due to resistance by the members of the *Cortes*, not the crown. By the early 1500s, the fiscal benefits from participating in the decisions in the *Cortes* were such that cities vigorously opposed other cities entering. For instance, in a petition to

---

[172] van Zanden et al. 2012, 17–18.   [173] Drelichman and Voth 2014, 265.
[174] Stasavage 2014.   [175] Puga and Trefler 2014.   [176] Ruiz 1977; 1982; Rucquoi 1987.

the king in the *Cortes* of Valladolid in 1506, the representatives of the towns said:

It is established through some laws, and by custom from time immemorial, that eighteen cities and towns of these kingdoms shall have a vote in the Cortes through their representatives, and no more; now some cities and towns are trying to obtain the right to be able to vote as well. Since this would bring great harm to those towns that already have a vote, and would cause great confusion, we supplicate your Majesties reject this petition, because all voting rights are already defined by the laws of these kingdoms.[177]

The towns' request was upheld. The crown, faced with powerful urban groups, could no longer dictate the terms on who was summoned nor did it have the power to enforce polity-wide representation, as originally in England.[178] The decline in number of towns charted above (Figure 5.4) reflects this power shift. Urban oligopolies prevailed because of the crown's weakened territorial control since the fourteenth century.

The increasing "absolutism" of the Castilian crown, consequently, cannot be reduced to an increasingly coercive strategy towards society as a whole. It resulted from an ever-decreasing domain over which the crown could exercise full jurisdiction – some towns were included, but the fiscal burden also burdened the poorest and weakest members of society, the satellite villages and areas of the towns. Poverty was widespread.[179] In the long run, the Spanish regime as a whole was defined by conditions in Castile: Aragon's population was about a tenth of Castile's around 1500. When most subjects were under private jurisdiction, the representative practices observed could not shape the whole polity. The dire picture painted by economic historians of Spain having "weak, incompetent, incoherent governance" after 1500[180] had medieval roots. This did not mean it did not have great conquering powers that enabled its imperial sprawl, but it may help explain the patterns of its colonial governing structures dissected in recent accounts.[181]

---

[177] *Cortes de Castilla* 1866, 233; Clemente Campos 1993, 359; Merriman [1918] 1962, 221.
[178] O'Callaghan 1975, 585–86; Kamen 2014, 143. To the degree that conditions changed in England, as after the sixteenth century, it approximated an absolutist regime.
[179] Kamen 2014, 220–24.   [180] Drelichman and Voth 2014, 253; Grafe 2012.
[181] Mahoney 2010.

6   No Taxation of Elites, No Representative Institutions

> Princes are more powerful and more dreaded by their enemies, when they undertake anything with the consent of their subjects.
>
> Philippe de Commines[1]

Rulers are often assumed to be predatory and to resist conceding rights to their subjects, but contemporaries understood well the dividends of consent.[2] The question, rather, was which rulers could secure this consent rather than face a fragmented polity. The key factor, I have argued, was relative power over the most powerful subjects, in most cases the nobility. It is widely assumed, however, that extraction in England was low in the early period;[3] even some historians assume that the nobility was lowly taxed. Major econometric studies have confirmed England's extractive advantage compared to France after 1660, but earlier ones begin around 1500 when English revenues were lower – thus supporting the intuition that its fiscal precocity was endogenous to the increasing powers of Parliament after the seventeenth century.

Another prominent mechanism invoked to explain the interaction of fiscal politics and representation involves debt. It echoes a story in Plutarch's *Lives*, that of Eumenes, a Macedonian general who neutralized his main enemies by borrowing money from them, forcing them to "forbear all violence to him for fear of losing their own money."[4] This logic illustrates a paradox: borrowing vests the lender in the survival of the debtor. This applies, for instance, to the seventeenth century, when English elites developed critical fiscal ties to the state, as analyzed by sociologist Bruce Carruthers.[5] Public debt is also the centerpiece of Stasavage's account of public institutions and policy change: when representative institutions included state creditors, as in both

---

[1] Cited in Hallam 1869, 125.   [2] These dividends are emphasized in Hall 1994.
[3] Englishmen were "very lightly taxed" for scholars such as Richard Pipes 1999, 133, for instance.
[4] Plutarch 1914.   [5] Carruthers 1996.

Italian city-states and early modern England, they were more likely to consolidate and enable economic growth.[6] But these accounts either focus on the period after 1688 or fail to account for the medieval English case. They therefore don't illuminate the question of parliamentary origins.

In this chapter I show that even before Parliament emerged, English extractive capacity far exceeded that of France, not just in fiscal but in military terms as well. I first show that the Eumenes paradox was operative in this early period, only it did not involve merchants but the nobility. It is not commercial wealth per se that mattered but extraction from the most powerful actors, those integrated in hierarchies of dependence throughout the polity.[7] Accordingly, I show the heavy burdens of the English nobility, by examining noble debt and loans to the crown, as well as other measures of noble fiscal ties to the crown. I then show how in France noble taxation was low; in fact, the ruler's capacity to extract from nobles co-varied with the frequency of the Estates-General. In the final section, I offer comparative data that, unlike previous estimates, trace England's military and fiscal extractive capacity to the period of institutional origins and control for its increasing wealth.

6.1   Taxation of the Rich, the Eumenes Paradox, and the Origins of Representative Government

Although merchants dominate later accounts, the most socially and economically relevant group in the medieval period, as sociologists Hechter and Brustein have also argued, was the nobility.[8] Noble compellence is critical in explaining the more extended territorial reach of the English Parliament, as we have seen. In fiscal matters as well, when the most powerful were bound to the crown, whether by debt or taxation, the population under noble lordship was better integrated into the polity-wide royal institutions; this was a real "trickle-down" effect.

The idea that the English crown had strong extractive capacity, especially over the most powerful, however, counters assumptions not only of social scientists, but of some specialists as well. Historical sources strikingly depict "English kings [who] strained every nerve but could never be

---

[6] Stasavage 2003; 2011.

[7] Tax is often distinguished from rent, on the assumption that taxes incentivize holding rulers accountable but rents do not. However, when economic coercion was intricately tied to political force, rent was not a purely economic factor. Feudal dues were rent payments, since they stemmed from personal grants of land, but the conditionality they expressed was deeply political in nature; Wood 2002.

[8] Hechter and Brustein 1980; they employ a different logic, however.

rich enough."[9] But this is not surprising: the English were competing with France, which had three times the population.[10] Rather, surprising was that they managed to match, even exceed, the French in per capita extraction, as shown in the final section.

Nonetheless, English rulers are also claimed to have been highly constrained in their capacity to tax magnates especially when Parliament consolidated, in the 1290s.[11] A classic study of English taxation, by James Willard, asserts that the "people who were not wealthy paid the taxes of England in the thirteenth and fourteenth centuries just as they do today."[12] This ties in well with common conceptions of the English crown as originally weak in extractive capacity.[13] Further, some historians point out that the tax burden of specific nobles was paltry. The Earl of Cornwall, who was probably the richest lay magnate in the 1290s and Edward I's cousin, had "an annual income amounting to several thousand pounds." Yet, his tax burden was trivial: in 1296, "he contributed about £10 to a tax on movables." Another highly ranked but undertaxed noble was Roger, Earl of Norfolk. His assessed direct taxes amounted to only 4.5 percent of his income on some of his properties between 1294 and 1298.[14] Such evidence appears dispositive – until it is contrasted with the loans and debts of some of these powerful actors to the crown, as done next. I then discuss the aggregate picture and further consider the mechanisms that link these observations.

6.1.1   Low Fiscal Burden for Nobles?

The Earl of Cornwall may have contributed only £10 in 1296, but he had lent the crown about £18,000, about 35 percent of the average annual tax raised by Edward I. Moreover, he was obliged to participate in battle *and* contribute troops. Further, he "was regularly summoned to parliament throughout the 1290s, served as a frequent witness to the king's charters, and continued to advance major loans to the king and his courtiers." When he died childless, his estate escheated to the crown. This most powerful magnate, therefore, was lightly taxed but delivered huge amounts to the crown without reimbursement.[15]

---

[9] Southern 1970, 152.
[10] The ratio remained about the same between 1200 and 1300, increasing to over five at some points before 1700; McEvedy and Jones 1978; Broadberry et al. 2015.
[11] Fryde 1991, 248–50.   [12] Willard 1934, 163.
[13] Levi 1988. As mentioned, Levi notes that this capacity increased after Parliament formed.
[14] Fryde 1991, 249.   [15] Vincent 2004a.

The Earl of Norfolk may have faced a similarly low rate on some of his income, but this amount also has to be set against extensive military service and financial debts, typically from commuted military obligations, to the crown. Roger participated in all the major Welsh and Scottish campaigns. Moreover, his incentives to be present and support Parliament were high: when he needed to negotiate his overdue debts that exceeded £2,000, he had to submit a petition in Parliament. He was also involved in royal adjudication, for instance "he was one of the magnates asked in 1292 to examine the pleadings" over who should succeed to the Scottish throne. Foremost, when he died, the crown took over his lands and office, "as had been agreed" when he was still alive.[16]

Drawing conclusions from tax obligations of a few highly placed nobles alone can therefore be misleading about the power relations involved. Though a systematic picture is lacking, other earls might even be paying up to 50 percent of their community's direct tax burden in the fourteenth century, as Ormrod has noted.[17] Next, I consider some aggregate evidence about the burdens on the nobility flowing from their tenurial position and the high capacity of the crown.

6.1.2   Low Fiscal Burden for Nobles? The Aggregate Evidence

Patterns of noble obligations to the crown can be reconstructed from prosopographic evidence in the *Oxford Dictionary of National Biography* introduced in Chapter 3, for the period from 1200 to 1350. As noted already, these data should not be confused with historical estimates; they simply offer a *minimum* that confirms what historians know but remains unquantified, namely that obligations did not exist just on paper but were enforced.

Before purely fiscal obligations are considered, a broader context of compellence must be noted that included military duties, penalties for not complying with duties, and of course the judicial obligations and parliamentary attendance discussed in Chapter 3, all of which had a fiscal dimension (Table 6.1). These obligations were almost universally enforced among the nobility – more than 93 percent are reported as serving militarily after 1250 in the *ODNB*,[18] whilst the lower number before that date (81 percent) draws on more limited records. Military obligation was tied to parliamentary summons: "the lists used for military summonses were used to identify those who should come to

---

[16] Prestwich 2004; Fryde 1992, 260.

[17] Ormrod 2008, 650. As Ormrod notes, some limited groups enjoyed immunities.

[18] Almost all nobles owed service, so this number may reflect exemptions as much as problems in the data.

Table 6.1 *Financial ties between crown and lay nobility*

	Lay nobles	
	Pre-1250	Post-1250
Military obligation	81%	93%
Attendance at Parliament	44%	79%
Judicial and other obligations	42%	35%
Estates forfeited or seized	44%	32%
Debts to crown	31%	23%
Parliamentary petitions related to debts/escheats etc.	35%	15%
Franchises investigated/reclaimed	22%	13%
Removal from office/other penalty	12%	13%
Loans to crown	1%	5%

Source: Oxford Dictionary of National Biography.

parliament";[19] both were mostly tied to land tenure. Those mentioned to have attended after 1250 reach almost 80 percent; they appear lower for the previous period, 44 percent, when records were scarcer, the crown weaker, and the institution less established. More than a third of nobles are mentioned as having performed high judicial service, as a justice or hearer of petitions, reflecting the dynamics examined in Chapter 3. When obligations were violated, the crown imposed penalties, for instance removal from office. At least 12–13 percent in the two periods met that fate.

The fiscal dependence of the nobility on the crown, on the other hand, is indicated primarily by five main measures: the seizure of estates by the crown as punishment for non-performance of obligations or wrongdoing, debts owed to the crown, parliamentary petitions for reduction of debt or other obligations, franchises (sets of privileges and exemptions) investigated or reclaimed by the crown, and loans to the crown.

Only about 5 percent of nobles are mentioned as having lent funds to the crown after 1250, again probably an underestimate.[20] However, nine out of thirteen lenders came from the top ranks, the earls. The small numbers were counterbalanced, therefore, by the disproportionate amounts involved – earls were, after all, the richest subjects. The social status of lenders also endowed these loans with disproportionate significance, as we will see in the next section. That the nobility lent to default-prone, unconstrained sovereigns defies the concerns about expropriation in the neo-institutionalist literature.[21] As Drelichman and Voth

[19] Prestwich 2005, 131.
[20] Historians have focused more on loans from external sources, for instance Italian bankers and merchants; Fryde 1955.
[21] North and Weingast 1989.

provocatively showed for the 1500s, even "lending to the borrower from hell," Philip II, could be profitable.[22] And nobles did not always lend to the crown for profit. Instead, obligation flowed from their tenurial status, creating an asymmetric exchange.

This asymmetric dynamic also underlies debt, which burdened "virtually all the magnates" especially under Edward I, but which also remains unquantified.[23] Thirty-one percent of nobles are recorded as being debtors before 1250 and 23 percent after, though these are again surely underestimates. The nobility mainly owed to the crown in the thirteenth century, with the crown owing more after the fourteenth.[24] Much debt originated in commuted military service (scutage), but also in various breaches. Clergy often paid in fines what they would have paid in taxes.[25] Or the king could pardon debts in exchange for military or other kind of service.[26] Edward I forced magnates to fight in Gascony by threatening to collect debts.[27] The exchange was not always quid pro quo bargaining; it was often done ex-post, as a reward.[28] Parliament in fact became an important locus for the submission of petitions related to debt, with at least 35 to 15 percent of nobles recorded as doing so in the two periods.

Finally, a major indicator of royal power over the nobility was the crown's capacity to either permanently "forfeit" or temporarily "seize" the land of royal tenants, if a breach had occurred. Greater security of property rights is widely assumed in England compared to Continental kingdoms, so it is striking to note that over 44 percent of nobles are mentioned as having their estates seized or forfeited before 1250, dropping to about 32 percent after that. These measures all attest the remarkable infrastructural capacity I have argued preceded *and enabled* the emergence of Parliament.

6.1.3   Political Effects of Fiscal Dependence? The Micro-Evidence

Fiscal dependence of the nobility on the crown shaped attitudes towards taxation in different ways. On the one hand, powerful lords habitually resisted royal penetration and extraction from their own tenants. For

---

[22] Drelichman and Voth 2014.   [23] Fryde 1992, 251.
[24] Fryde 1955; McFarlane 1947.   [25] Prestwich 1990, 76.
[26] Spencer 2008, 39–43; 2014, 91–92.   [27] Prestwich 1990, 42; 1972, 236.
[28] The evidence on clergy fiscal ties seems weaker, with fewer debts to the crown, possibly on account of their great wealth, but higher lending to the crown, at about 8 percent of the sample having loaned to the king, triggering the Eumenes effect. Evidence on merchants is also insufficient to draw conclusions (but see Chapter 7). About 42 high-status merchants, like mayors of London or aldermen, are recorded as active between 1200 and around 1350. About half lent money to the crown and about 40 percent were elected to Parliament – and about 45 percent had judicial or other obligations.

instance, earls' bailiffs could prevent royal tax collectors from entering the counties, as did Edmund of Almain in 1290 or the Earl of Lancaster in 1319.[29] However, noble "inability to claim exemption" from taxation[30] also meant they had incentives to spread the burden. The remarkable extractive powers of the English crown would not have materialized if resistance was greater than compliance.

For instance, nobles who lent extensively to the crown might be incentivized to be more open to royal authority penetrating the localities and taxing tenants across the polity separately, as taxation was needed to repay royal debt. Though few nobles lent so extensively early on, their preeminence in society meant that their preferences had wide societal effects. Support for representative practice of course was not a crude function of pecuniary goals of the uppermost nobility. Lending to the king was shaped by their prior relationship, which already aligned some of their interests (many were royal relatives). Nonetheless, it likely affected their stakes in this matter.

This hypothesis in fact explains at least some noble support for taxation other approaches leave unexplained or dismiss as a "representative pose."[31] For instance, Maddicott mentions that Richard of Cornwall, the king's brother, pressured knights and the clergy to accept a tax in the 1250s.[32] But Richard was also the "richest earl in England, and one of the richest men in Europe, [who] spent a large part of his fortune in supporting the regime of his feckless elder brother, Henry III." Before 1254, he had made "massive loans" to the king.[33] He was also closely involved with the king's military pursuits, and was given the mint to administer, which was a source of profit. Earls could also use their social prestige within their communities to legitimize taxation. When papal legates were raising a tax for the 1241 Crusade to the Holy Land, they invoked Earl Richard's sanction. Owing to "the favour in which [he] was held," Matthew Paris wryly observed, by "this method of draining the purses of the English, an immense sum of money was obtained."[34]

Another major lender to the crown was the leader of the baronial revolt in 1258, Simon de Montfort, the king's brother-in-law. The crown owed so much to him that the committee of twenty-four members who were entrusted with the government under the Provisions of Oxford also dealt with his debt.[35] Since the Parliaments of 1264 and

---

[29] Willard 1934, 172, 170–74.   [30] Maddicott 2010, 430.

[31] Maddicott 2010, 309. He suggests that the higher ranks "may have been less hostile" towards taxation without an explanation; Maddicott 2010, 221, 437.

[32] Maddicott 2010, 221. The Earl of Gloucester helped Richard, but the *ODNB* lists no loans from him.

[33] Vincent 2004b.   [34] Paris 1852, 359.   [35] Maddicott 2004; 1994.

1265, which Simon called, knights from the counties were somewhat more systematically summoned to serve as representatives, thus ensuring broader participation and engagement with the tax burden. Although we see such participation as an eagerly sought-after right, in practice it ensured that lower social orders were now actively involved in covering the king's obligations, as explained in Chapter 4. This is not to be taken as a motive, but as an enabling condition that altered typical conflicts of interest in such circumstances. Further, the nobility co-opted their own tenants by extending to them privileges from the crown as well.[36] Similar preferences might operate on debtors to the crown, on the margin: they might welcome taxation as reducing somewhat royal pressure to collect noble debts that were often handled through Parliament.[37]

Fiscal pressures on earls were not always in the same direction: excessive taxation affected their own incomes, which reverts to the traditional fiscal logic, of demanding limits on taxation when faced with high extraction. For instance, in 1297 the earls of Warwick and Arundel protested they were unable to contribute to the expedition in Flanders.[38] Earls could also defend others facing exorbitant royal demands, including the Church, as did the Earl of Cornwall.[39] And indebtedness was not deterministic: the Earl of Norfolk had large debts to the crown, but this led him to oppose the king in 1297.[40] However, although systematic evidence about all nobles who lent or owed to the crown and about their preferences on taxation is lacking, overlapping incentives towards the extension of representation can be discerned in some of the key actors in the formative thirteenth century.

If the nobility faced a fiscal burden, was the English system one that taxed the rich and spared the poor in the early stages of institutional formation? As late as 1327, the very poor were indeed exempt from taxation.[41] The poor were little taxed, though they generated much wealth that was taxed.[42] Unlike elsewhere in Europe, however, everyone else was taxed: from "the highest and the lowest of medieval fold, no one was free from the payment of taxes unless he had been granted the privilege of exemption," and these were few in the early 1300s.[43] Individual

---

[36] Maddicott 2010, 253, 251–61.

[37] For the role of compellence in royal loans in a later period, see Harriss 1963a; Fryde 1955.

[38] Prestwich 1980, 141–42. See also the opposition by the Earl of Gloucester in 1288 and 1294; Maddicott 2010, 289; Prestwich 1988, 404, 457.

[39] Paris 1852, 68.   [40] Prestwich 2004.   [41] Maddicott 2010, 420.

[42] Ormrod 1995, 91.

[43] Willard 1934, 162. Exemptions were granted to churches holding lands, to towns, or to individuals, for instance to reward military service; Harding 2002, 211–21.

assessments were replaced by quotas in 1334, however;[44] by the 1370s, assessments were frozen at the levels of 1334, and taxation became regressive, though the crown strove to counteract this trend, as Ormrod has noted in a nuanced assessment.[45] It is no accident that English constitutional history became more turbulent as the tax burden shifted. Nonetheless, Parliament as an institution was sufficiently entrenched so as to serve as the locus for most subsequent conflict and change.

The next section examines the striking contrast with France in the period of institutional emergence.

6.2   France: Noble Military Service, Taxation, and Estates-General

In 1407, Christine de Pizan (1364–c.1430), a French-Italian author writing for the Duke of Burgundy on the constitution of princely power, lambasted the inequity of noble tax exemption. She radically claimed, "the rich . . . ought to support the poor, and not exempt the rich, as is done nowadays, leaving the poor the more heavily burdened." She continued by objecting that, as of "right,"

the rich and high officials of the king or princes who have their rank and power as a gift of the king and princes and are able to carry the burden, are exempt from taxes, and the poor who have nothing from the king have to pay. Is it not reasonable if I have given a great gift to my servant, and give him a rich livelihood and his estate, and it happened that I had some need, that he comes to my aid more than one who has nothing from me? It is a strange custom that is used nowadays in this kingdom in the setting of taxes . . . I say these things for the poor. Compassion moves me because their tears and moans come bitterly forth.[46]

This "strange custom" was more than simply unjust, I argue; it undermined institutional consolidation. In the early period, the nobility was expected to pay "tax in blood."[47] Though documentation is "scattered," it shows "that nobles sometimes paid taxes to avoid serving and sometimes escaped paying because they served." However, nobles became effectively exempt in 1445, six years after the Estates-General approved raising taxation annually – the step identified by Tocqueville as the turning point for French absolutism.[48]

Why did the French distributional and representative patterns evolve this way? Assemblies flourished whilst war with England escalated after the 1360s and until 1440, as bellicist theories would predict. However, as

---

[44] Ormrod 1995, 91.   [45] Ormrod 2008, 643–47.   [46] Christine de Pizan 1994, 20.
[47] Contamine 1972, 176, my translation.
[48] Henneman 1983, 5, 16–17. Customary variation existed between north and south.

Table 6.2 *Frequency of Estates-General per decade contrasted with military troops raised per year, per thousand of population*

	Years	Meetings of Estates General per decade	Average size of military force in any year (thousands)	Average military troops raised per thousand
Pre-noble tax exemption	1300–1440	2.14	13	1
Post-noble tax exemption	1441–1619	0.44	42	2
	1441–1789	0.31	120	6

Sources: For meetings, see Soule 1968; Desjardins 1871; Major 1960b. For military troops, see online Appendix D.

Ertman points out, "French rulers had little use for the Estates General" after 1440.[49] That is paradoxical, because military campaigns continued not only unabated, mainly against the Burgundians, but at a higher level of troop mobilization against Italy under Louis XII (1498–1515; Table 6.2). Until 1440, meetings averaged over two per decade and average forces raised about 13,000. While meetings declined after 1440 however, average troop size exploded to 42,000 until 1617, and 120,000 until 1789. The monarchy did not reinstate a central assembly even during the Thirty Years War, at the height of the Military Revolution,[50] except once in 1614; it relied on regional negotiations instead.[51]

A strict bellicist logic would predict instead that the more pressures rose, the more rulers would call on assemblies. Especially since, as Ertman astutely notes, the French crown had achieved its greatest victories during the period of intense "constitutionalism" before 1440 – which could not have been lost on the king and his agents. So why did general assemblies cease to be called, relying on the more cumbersome local meetings? Existing explanations emphasize weak constitutional forces and absolutism. Downing follows the historian J. Russell Major in claiming that the crown did not "seek to weaken or destroy the estates"; nonetheless, whether intentionally or not, they were only called again twice in the next 120 years.[52] Ertman explains the suspension of assemblies as part of a "progressive decline" of Estates in Latin Europe, because assemblies were "plagued by basic structural weaknesses." This weakness prevented them from blocking the absolutist tendencies in the royal revival of Roman law. The attitude of "working together with their

[49] Ertman 1997, 87.   [50] Roberts 1956; 1967; G. Parker 1976; 1996.
[51] Potter and Rosenthal 1997; Beik 2005, 200–206.   [52] Downing 1992, 118–21.

Estates" was "foreign to the princely mind" except in moments of crisis, a view that echoes Major's argument. French kings "chose instead to draw on neo-Roman political and legal traditions to centralize power in their own hands."[53]

But why would they do that when assemblies had helped them win the Hundred Years War? As argued already in Chapter 5, it was not Roman law that encouraged absolutism but weak French capacity to enforce crucial elements of it, especially plenipotentiary representative powers. Only the *central* assembly, the Estates-General, was structurally weak. French rulers were so weakened by war, they could not compel the nobility to either attend central institutions or contribute fiscally. Local organization was not less effective in blocking royal power than English resistance was; it was just decentralized. The crown abandoned the Estates-General after a protracted effort to compel the nobility that resulted in the nobility appropriating even greater powers over the revenue concerned.

In fact, representative activity mirrored noble compellence. In the fourteenth century, the nobility was repeatedly asked to approve collection of taxes for the Hundred Years War from their subjects. Both noble compellence and meetings of the Estates-General are observed between 1300 and 1440: about two meetings per decade occurred on average. Both plummeted after that.

Meetings declined in large part at least because the nobility's burden did. The tax burden changed for everyone, as in the 1350s "the French began to pay annual taxes without regard for the state of war or peace."[54] This was a period of emergency as King John II (1350–1364) was captured by the English. The bargaining that occurred under severe war pressure thus indeed led to a "permanent system of taxation."[55] However, this did not lead to enduring representative institutions; it led to noble privileges instead. Nobles succeeded in blocking the Estates-General from imposing higher rates on them, even though noble tax rates were low (about 2 percent in the 1340s).[56] The great appanage princes who ruled over the provinces, like Burgundy, instead requested to retain a third of the taxes collected. When some of them did not secure this, "they defied the collectors and even instigated armed attacks against them."[57] The pressure on seigneurial revenues between 1300 and 1450 may have exacerbated these conflicts.[58]

---

[53] Ertman 1997, 87, 89; Major 1980, 15.   [54] Henneman 1978, 948; 1976, 2.
[55] Major 1980, 15.   [56] Henneman 1971, 152.   [57] Fryde 1979, 848.
[58] The evidence on seigneurial decline is now somewhat challenged; Small 2009, 76–84.

Eventually, the princes succeeded in keeping a part of the taxes collected from their lands after the 1360s. In 1389, Louis d'Orléans was allowed to receive half the *gabelle* and the *aides*, as was the Duke of Anjou in 1392 and the dukes of Burgundy, Berri, and Bourbon in the following years. In 1394, Louis d'Orléans got all of the taxes, as did the rest of the royal princes between 1397 and 1402.[59] By the end of the fifteenth century the great principalities often converted the king's taxes for their own use.[60] Incentives for the local nobility to bargain in a central assembly weakened as individual exemptions proliferated.[61] Only five meetings were called for six decades after 1360, while war with England raged.

Representative activity spiked again as the English occupied Paris in the 1420s.[62] This echoes the bellicist logic again; representation did increase under military pressure and the tax regime changed. After endless bargaining with local assemblies, in 1439 the royal direct tax (*taille*) replaced the seigniorial one, ending the feudal regime.[63] However, assemblies lapsed after that, until 1560. Even Tocqueville thought they had granted the king the right to levy annual taxes without assent. Historians have corrected that "completely erroneous theory."[64] Instead, they point to inadequate demand for subsequent meetings, with strong variation between the (more compliant) north and the south.[65] But this did not vary in the previous period; only noble taxation did. Nobles were no longer taxed after 1445, like their English counterparts, and they were no longer incentivized to demand consent. When the king could not compel the most powerful, polity-wide institutions lapsed.

The full causes of representative decline are more complex than this dynamic, and crucial evidence is lacking (for instance, on loans and debt), but outcomes accord with the expectations set by the hypotheses of this study. The more the nobility was engaged, the more likely Estates-General were to be called. The effective exemption of the nobility (as well as the clergy, royal officials, and bourgeois oligarchies of large towns) by the 1440s removed the major motor of polity-wide representation and reflected the crown's weak infrastructural powers.[66] Despite regional variation, enough provinces were so uncooperative as to make the Estates-General not a productive mechanism for tax collection.[67] French fiscal troubles suggest that one intuitive hypothesis about representative weakness there – that France was richer and therefore the crown

---

[59] Fryde 1991, 273; Henneman 1999, 117.   [60] Perroy 1943–45, 183–84.
[61] Major 1980, 29.   [62] Thompson 1991.
[63] Major 1960b, 25–47; Clamageran 1867, 488–89.
[64] Major 1960b, 32–33; Wolfe 1972, 34, 30–35.   [65] Major 1960b, 32–39.
[66] Rigaudière 1994, 177; Major 1980, 37–39.   [67] Major 1960b, 35–36.

needed to make fewer concessions[68] – does not mean that the crown could easily access that wealth.

6.3   Comparative Extractive Capacity of England and France

Throughout the book, I have argued that the English crown's precocious capacity to compel its subjects, especially the most powerful ones, increased its per capita extraction, even before Parliament made its beginnings in the 1220s. In this section, I present data to support this claim.

As noted in earlier chapters, the extractive strength of the English state has been highlighted by historians, but it has typically been placed after the fifteenth century.[69] Only Michael Mann's pivotal study on the early English state went back to the period of origins examined here, strikingly demonstrating both the early fiscal capacity of the English crown, especially since the 1300s, and its increase during times of war.[70]

In this section, I expand on Mann's findings by setting English extractive capacity in a broader framework. Medieval historians have long emphasized English superiority in both fiscal and military extraction. On revenue, Joseph Strayer noted that the English could match the French "man for man" and "pound for pound" already in the 1290s, despite having less than a fifth of their population and "much less" than a fourth of its wealth.[71] On military extraction, the historian Michael Prestwich remarked that in the fourteenth century, during the Hundred Years War, English armies were "the most formidable in Europe, and achieved astonishing success at Crécy in 1346 and at Poitiers ten years later."[72] The data below show that these points were part of a systematic pattern.

First, on the military front, through an original dataset compiling evidence from a broad array of historical sources[73] between 1200 and 1800, I show the remarkable advantage that England had compared to the French. To assess state capacity, per capita number of troops is the appropriate measure;[74] the absolute sizes of armies are relevant for questions of international relations. Except for a period in the seventeenth century (which frequently forms the basis of comparison about military strength), England consistently outnumbered French armies on a per capita basis

---

[68] Maddicott 2010, 402–403.
[69] Brewer 1989; O'Brien and Hunt 1993; 1999; Hoffman and Norberg 1994.
[70] Mann 1988.
[71] Strayer 1970b, 52. Scholars today estimate English population at a third of France's.
[72] Prestwich 2006, 75; see also Verbruggen 1997, 167; Corvisier 1992, 305.
[73] See online Appendix D.
[74] See Boucoyannis 2017. Scholars often use data on casualties from Clodfelter 2008, but their inferential value is assumed, not proven; Karaman and Pamuk 2013; Dincecco and Wang 2018.

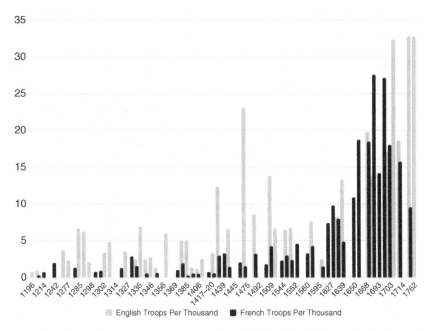

Figure 6.1 Number of troops raised, England and France, per thousand
of population, 1200s–1700s
Sources: Armies: Online Appendix D. Population: McEvedy and Jones
1978 for France and Broadberry et al. 2015, 20 for England.

(Figure 6.1). It raised three times more per capita between 1200 and 1400
and 60 percent more over the whole period. Such mobilizational power
explains the disproportionate role England was to play during the premodern period on the Continental military arena and beyond.

Fiscal extraction displays the same pattern. Comparing revenues for
the period before 1500 is a very hazardous task, given data quality. No
continuous series exist for France, though some do for England; separating central collection from local expenditures is mostly impossible; and
actual yield mostly cannot be deduced from amounts expected. Figures
can occasionally be supplemented by detailed historical studies of
expenditures in individual wars, but these figures too are far from unprob-
lematic, since spending may reflect the importance of the specific battle,
which need not be identical for both sides.[75] Readers interested in

[75] Barratt 1999b.

a detailed discussion of the sources used and adjustments made should consult online Appendix A. All premodern figures are provisional.

First, I examine English extraction. Figure 6.2 shows that in the later twelfth century, when the judicial infrastructure was being systematized, extraction was not much less than at the turn of the seventeenth century! Moreover, extraction doubled in the 1280s before Parliament acquired its "model" form with full representation, reflecting strong royal powers. Taxation increased drastically after 1300, but this reflects the inclusion of indirect taxation, which in Chapter 9 will be shown to originally have tenuous connections to Parliament. Nonetheless, this period of parliamentary consolidation saw extraction reach peaks that were not matched until after the Civil War. Parliament certainly did not limit extraction. Instead, extraction declined when the regime underwent its most "despotic" phase, during the late sixteenth and seventeenth centuries under the Tudors and Stuarts – as this argument predicts. Ironically, this irregular period has served as the baseline for assessments of English capacity.

Further, novel estimates by economic historians Broadberry, Campbell, Klein, Overton, and van Leeuwen allow us to challenge an intuitive assumption about this increase, that it reflects rising wealth due to trade. These new estimates show that real per capita taxation grew quite independently of real GDP growth per capita (Figure 6.3).[76] They also confirm that per capita taxation as a percentage of per capita GDP was higher in the 1300s than at any point until the 1660s (about 2.3 percent), as Mark Ormrod argued,[77] to an average of 1.9 percent from 1130 to 1640 (Figure 6.4).

English capacity emerges more clearly in the next graphs, which compare with per capita extraction in France. They show that the English extractive advantage preceded the formation of Parliament. Figure 6.5 shows an estimate of the "disposable war revenue" of John and Philip Augustus in 1202/3 and 1210–14. English revenue was more than double, even triple French resources at a per capita level. The advantage was amplified as the daily cost of troops was lower for the English. As until 1205 John controlled much French territory and extracted revenue from Normandy, per capita extraction is also reported without Norman revenues (which amounted to only 19 percent of disposable war revenue); the English advantage remains. Technically, however, that revenue belonged to the French king as

[76] The pattern is similar if the consumer price indexes developed by Allen n.d. and Clark 2014 are used.
[77] Ormrod 2011, 218.

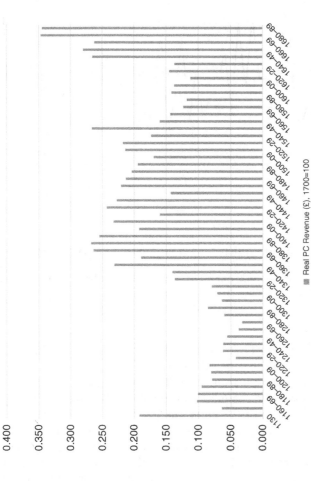

Figure 6.2 Real English taxation per capita (1154–1689), in 1700 £.

Sources: See discussion in Figure 4.1 and online Appendix A. Here supplemented by Steel 1954 for 1377–1455, Ormrod 1994 for 1462–85, and O'Brien 1993 between 1485 and 1688. For population: Broadberry et al. 2015, 20 until 1541, and Wrigley et al. 1997 after 1541.

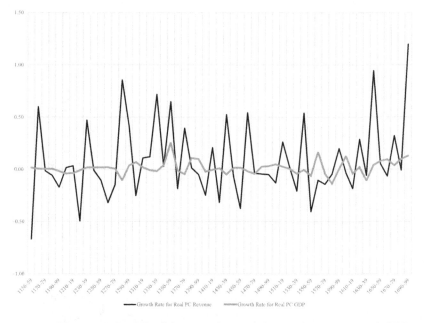

Figure 6.3 Real English per capita growth rates for taxation and GDP, 1154–1689
Sources: See Figure 6.2. For GDP after 1270, Broadberry et al. 2015 and for 1130–1270 Walker 2010.

John's feudal overlord. That John could appropriate it against him reflects the weakness of the French crown.[78]

The same ratio emerges from overall taxation estimates. Between 1200 and 1250, when Parliament was emerging, the average ratio of English to French per capita revenue was 2:1. Between 1300 and 1500, the average ratio was 3:1. When we exclude four very high, though well-sourced, ratios, the ratio is still 2:1 (see Figure 6.6 and Figure 6.7).[79] That the exchange rates used may be, if anything, under-reporting the English advantage is suggested by the ratio based on revenue figures expressed in silver for the period between 1322 and 1345: it reaches up

[78] Estimates are from Barratt 1999b, 93, 97. Aquitaine was also under John's jurisdiction but is not counted in his revenue. That Philip did not control this revenue is what these ratios are meant to capture: he should have done.
[79] In online Appendix A, I explain how I adjust figures when French sources only report ordinary revenue. These are therefore provisional figures, taking as generous an estimate of the French side as evidence permits.

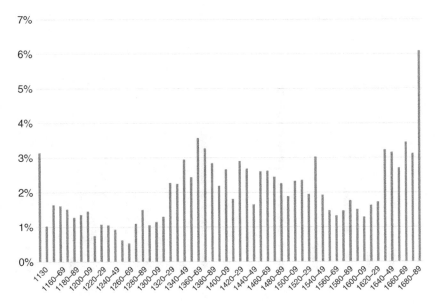

Figure 6.4 Ratio of English per capita taxation to per capita GDP, 1130–1689
Sources: See Figure 6.3.

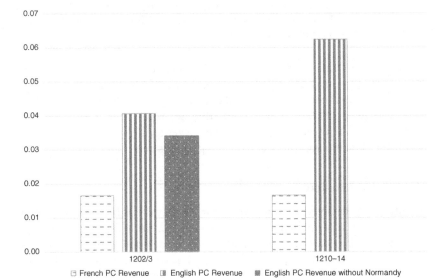

Figure 6.5 English and French per capita war revenue, 1202/3, 1210–1214
Source: Barratt 1999b, 93, 97.

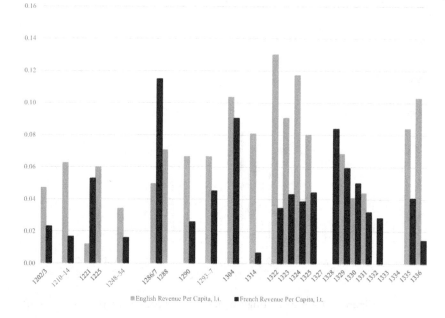

Figure 6.6 English and French per capita taxation, in *livres tournois*, 1202–1336
Sources: Online Appendix A. Exchange rates between the English pound and the French *livre tournois* are derived mainly from Spufford 1996 in ways described in online Appendix A.

to six to seven times French levels and has an average of 3.6:1 (a discrepancy that suggests caution with all these figures).[80] It is only in the 1500s that France was able to catch up and exceed English extraction, as the data in Karaman and Pamuk suggest – and that was reversed by 1700.[81] Figure 6.2 has shown how the sixteenth and early seventeenth centuries were a low point for England compared to the two previous centuries.

6.4   Conclusion

Contrary to widely held stereotypes, the medieval English state thus had an extractive capacity that exceeded that of its most prominent adversary, France. This is not surprising, however, since "the country with the largest number of taxpayers in Western Europe, France, also had, until

[80] Ormrod 1992. Exchange rates are problematic, but they account for fluctuations in prices and debasements, whilst giving more conservative estimates.
[81] Karaman and Pamuk 2013.

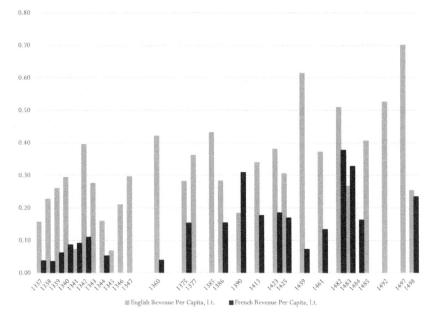

Figure 6.7 English and French per capita taxation, in *livres tournois*, 1337–1498
Sources: See Figure 6.2 and Figure 6.6.

1790, the largest number and highest proportion of fiscal exemptions," according to historian Richard Bonney.[82] One key to this divergence, I have argued, lay in the ruler's power to tax the nobility, which had "trickle-down" effects on the population.

Taxation of the nobility, the most powerful social group in any pre-modern polity, helped enable a representative institution to become an inclusive organ of governance. It is not taxation alone that generates this outcome, but the royal capacity to compel powerful actors. Where the nobility was not compelled or taxed, as in most Continental states and most prominently France and Castile, few incentives existed for that group to seek a regular presence in such institutions or to counteract the power of the crown. Opposition to royal power happened mostly locally and in a decentralized way. By contrast, once the nobility was collectively organized within Parliament, it could overcome its collective action problem. This did not limit extraction, however.

The bargaining logic, which has long dominated accounts of institutional emergence, thus arises at a secondary level. It follows an antecedent

---

[82] Bonney 2012, 93.

stage, predicated on state capacity, in which noble judicial service meant a regular presence in Parliament – the dynamics explored in Part I. In Durkheimian fashion, the "contractual" exchange on taxes had institutional results where norms already imposed obligations on the actors most capable of eventually exercising resistance to the crown and demanding accountability. "No compellence of elites, no representative institutions" could well be the motto of the European historical precedent. When taxation declined from the 1550s, the most "despotic" period of English history ensued.

Part III

Trade, Towns, and the Political Economy
of Representation

7 Courts, Institutions, and Cities: Low Countries and Italy

So far, the account has explained fiscal dynamics in terms of ruler power and concerns about justice. A major alternative derives parliaments from very different dynamics: political scientist Carles Boix, for instance, argues they are "a consequence of urban strength – and causally irrelevant to growth."[1] A rich, empowered bourgeoisie defeated arbitrary government and absolutism, in such accounts, and its origins lay in the commercial and technological revolution that transformed the European economy after the year 1000.[2] The Low Countries, especially, typify the "urban belt" of Europe, which ran from Italy and Spain to England. Similarly, for some economic historians, the participatory government in European cities resulted from urban "independence" from the state – this even allowed European urban (and thus economic) development to outpace the Islamic world and the East more generally.[3]

Trade was of course important for urban growth, as Henri Pirenne argued a century ago.[4] Many parameters of his thesis have been challenged, but the commercial growth after the millennium is undeniable.[5] Cities, moreover, dominate accounts of the agricultural and industrial revolutions,[6] as well as the efflorescence of political participation. They were indeed innovative laboratories of electoral politics, bottom-up social organization, and market mechanisms.[7] They systematized key features of modern democracy, not least the regulation of the economy, public works, the provision of welfare[8] as well as state credit.[9] Were they also an alternative path to representation?

If parliaments resulted from urban growth, the necessary condition for representative emergence posited here, namely ruler strength, would be either endogenous or not necessary. The following three chapters address different parts of this line of argument and of the challenge of equifinality

---

[1] Boix 2015, 204.   [2] See also, van Zanden et al. 2012.
[3] van Zanden et al. 2012, 13; Bosker et al. 2013.   [4] Pirenne 1925.
[5] See the discussion in Buylaert 2015.   [6] DeLong and Shleifer 1993; de Vries 1984.
[7] Najemy 1982; Padgett and Powell 2012; Wickham 2015.
[8] Jones 1997, 401–402; Waley and Dean 2010, 57–62.   [9] Stasavage 2003; 2007a.

it presents. First, however, we need to ask if the institutions that emerged in these city-states are the same as the dependent variable in this book, the emergence of polity-wide representative regimes; unit homogeneity is typically assumed, not analytically derived. After all, if urban institutions were so fundamental, why did the most robust and long-lasting parliament emerge in the region, England, with the lowest rates of urbanization in Europe in the formative early period, 4.4 percent in 1300, compared to 20.8 percent in Italy and 22.4 percent in Belgium?[10]

We also need to explain why the most highly urbanized regions, like Italy, Belgium, and Spain, devolved into principalities or absolutism by the early modern period (with the Netherlands as a partial outlier).[11] These small islands of advanced organization did not naturally scale up to integrated polities. Like Athenian democracy, they failed to solve the fundamental problem of inclusion of broader populations outside the city walls on an equal or at least sustainable basis. Was this a random historical outcome or an inherent feature of urban incapacity to stem the concentration of power and to include disparate groups, suggesting that urban republicanism was not as effective as a self-sustaining equilibrium? In fact, social scientists are echoing Weber's insight about the oligarchic tendencies of mercantile polities.[12] Charles Tilly suggested a U-shaped relation between cities and state formation.[13] More radically, economic historian Bas van Bavel has even posited a "fundamental incompatibility of market economies with long-run prosperity, equity, and broad participation in decision making."[14]

To establish urban primacy, finally, it is not enough to note that economic and urban growth preceded the emergence of parliaments. After all, as noted already, economic growth in China led neither to urban proliferation nor to representative institutions.[15] Unless one is able to show that urban groups initiated representative institutions which became polity-wide and governed surrounding territories, the correlation does not explain those institutions. "If large-N studies make incorrect assumptions about causal paths, they will lack explanatory power."[16]

To address these concerns, this chapter focuses first on the classic examples of urban governance, Italy and the Low Countries. I claim city-states aren't strictly speaking representative regimes, so they differ from

---

[10] Bairoch et al. 1988, 259 use the name Belgium for the eastern Low Countries.
[11] Italy had some notable exceptions in the aristocratic republics of Genoa, Venice, and, to a lesser extent, Lucca.
[12] Weber 1958; Jones 1997; Stasavage 2014; Puga and Trefler 2014.
[13] Tilly 1990; Blockmans 1989.
[14] van Bavel 2016, 251. See also Stasavage 2014 for a conditional statement.
[15] Hoffman 2015; Dincecco and Wang 2018.   [16] Sambanis 2004, 273.

the dependent variable in this study. Even if these differences are not deemed to be dispositive, however, we will see how the republican institutions that did emerge were not the spontaneous outcome of commercial efflorescence. Most studies focus on the period when urban participatory institutions were fully formed, yet communal forms emerged earlier, from the eleventh century, which is typically overlooked. Correcting this oversight reveals how judicial dynamics and power over the most powerful social actors – the key mechanisms in this account – were also critical in enabling urban participatory institutions. This chapter examines Italy and the Low Countries, whilst Chapter 8 tests these claims on the case of Catalonia. Lastly, Chapter 9 examines whether mercantile groups actually shaped representative institutions through the two classic cases in neo-institutional analysis, England and Spain, only for their role to emerge as endogenous to ruler power. Echoing Acemoglu and Robinson, I show how "the differences in the organization of trade ... reflected the different political institutions of these countries."[17]

7.1 The Differences between City-States and Representative Regimes: Selectorate and Incentives

City-states are not systematically distinguished from representative polities in the literature. In studies focused on state emergence, city-states reflect a different path to the one of territorial states or empires.[18] However, studies with regime variation as the dependent variable posit unit homogeneity with territorial states.[19] They assume that since all types of regimes had similar functions to differing degrees (voting and administration of taxes) they are comparable.

As van Zanden, Buringh, and Bosker note, however, northern Italy "'missed' the development of [the] institutional innovation" of a parliament.[20] City-states removed a central element of representative regimes: an executive power with some interests and resources separate from those of its subjects.[21] Cities became republican only when they became de facto independent of any overlord. The Holy Roman Emperor was juridically sovereign over north-central Italian cities, but this did not affect daily governance during periods of republican rule, a compromise sealed with the Peace of Constance in 1183.[22]

---

[17] Acemoglu et al. 2005a, 454.
[18] Blockmans 1989; Tilly 1990; Spruyt 1994; Downing 1992.
[19] Stasavage 2011; Abramson and Boix 2012; Dincecco and Wang 2018.
[20] van Zanden et al. 2012, 14.   [21] Venice is an exception discussed below.
[22] Still, the emperor retained a role and intervened in the region after that; Raccagni 2013; Lee 2018.

Self-governing communes were associations to preserve peace and good customs that emerged between 1080 and 1150.[23] Most communes developed republican institutions by the thirteenth century. For "the first time since republican Rome,"[24] the general body of citizens (not subjects), the *universitas civium*, "practiced their own foreign policy, were fiscally independent, could raise an army and enforce the death penalty, and could mint coins," as well as "forge independent commercial policy."[25] This was not a system "of representation, the subordinate, class-divided parliaments of a hierarchic *Ständestaat*, but of common participation, government by all."[26]

Republican government entailed many radical practices. Citizens could be elected to office by nomination and/or lot. Officials were often rotated at two, three, six, or twelve months to counter corruption.[27] The Venetian doge was himself elected. When, for practical purposes, the *universitas civium* was replaced by general councils as elective bodies, these could often include 10 percent of the population, for instance, out of an adult male population of 11,000, as in Padua.[28] The English Parliament might have about 240 representatives in the House of Commons and a maximum of 110 nobles in the House of Lords, out of an adult male population of around 1 million in 1300.[29]

The more radical and democratic the political features, however, the more backsliding occurred. Communes suffered from elite factionalism from the 1200s.[30] As assemblies grew in size, the more specialized councils and committees formed "for speed and efficiency."[31] In Florence, for instance, in the 1300s, these powers belonged to the *Signoria*, a body composed of nine members; eligibility was restricted primarily to Guelph guild members, though selection was through a combination of lot and election.[32] This radical republican system was mostly confined to Tuscany and did not shape the whole regime for too long. Despite the popular revolutions after 1343 that placed guilds in power, by the 1430s the regime had veered in a signorial direction.[33] By 1532, it officially had a Medici Duke.

Republican institutions, in any case, made fiscal extraction very different: citizens, not a ruler, decided on policy *and* level of taxation, so incentives to attend an assembly were both different and higher. In

---

[23] Waley and Dean 2010, 31.   [24] Jones 1997, 334.

[25] Epstein 2000b, 277. See also Wickham 2015, 15–16; Jones 1997, 406.

[26] Jones 1997, 334.   [27] Jones 1997, 411; Brucker 1962, 59, 61.

[28] Jones 1997, 407. This still meant that 90 percent or more of townsmen were disenfranchised; Jones 1997, 573–76; Brucker 1962, 70.

[29] See Chapter 3.   [30] Coleman 2004, 48–56.   [31] Jones 1997, 407; Becker 1960, 431.

[32] Brucker 1962, 59ff., 66.

[33] Jones 2010, 7–10. Jones describes it as "despotic," but the term is no longer widely used.

territorial states, as we have seen, representatives initially had limited capacity to constrain the crown. In city-states, as the historian Anthony Molho has shown, those who voted on taxes were often dominated by those who had lent to the state and were expecting to be reimbursed through tax proceeds, even as oligarchies came to prevail.[34] Extraction was even more coercive in these polities; it actually mirrored the inversion dynamic identified throughout the book. Those that originally had strong republican traditions, for instance Venice and Florence, were able to impose forced loans in the fourteenth century that later consolidated into long-term debts.[35] By contrast, "many of those ruled by signori (for example, Milan) relied instead on a floating debt of voluntary short-term loans,"[36] suggesting relative ruler weakness. That forced loans were more common in republican regimes echoes the strong connection between obligation and institutional outcomes observed in England: high levels of participation were possible where the capacity to impose obligation was overall high.[37] After all, civic office itself was an obligation and fines penalized non-compliance.[38] But it is also a paradox from the perspective of this account: how was this power achieved without an executive? The next section addresses this point.

A further fundamental distinction is that representative institutions, where territorially anchored, integrated a composite society that included groups separated by occupation, geographical distance, social status, and other characteristics. By contrast, as historians have concluded, that city-states failed to effectively accommodate rural populations within the republican framework was a key reason why republican governments collapsed.[39] Their republican structure reflected a *failure* to install representation. The economic historian Stephen Epstein has further argued that conflict between landed and commercial interests could not be resolved, not least because "extreme [institutional] openness created conditions of 'permanent revolution' that threatened the city-state's survival as a distinctive mode of organised power."[40]

It is on these dimensions that most city-states also differ from cities with municipal governance, such as those in the Low Countries, also examined below. Although the latter were self-governing, they lacked the attributes of sovereignty that city-states had gained: Flanders and Holland were subject to counts, dukes, or kings. The "counts of Flanders always remained in place as the ruling power,"[41] as did the Hollander count, as

---

[34] Molho 1971. Stasavage has confirmed this more broadly; Stasavage 2007a; 2011.
[35] Mueller and Lane 1997, 454–58; Epstein 1996a, 112.
[36] Munro 2003, 515–16; Lane and Mueller 1997, 359–543.   [37] Jones 1997, 410.
[38] Jones 1997, 410.   [39] Jones 1997, 564–73; Epstein 2000b, 287–90.
[40] Epstein 2000b, 277.   [41] Blockmans and Prevenier 1999, 7.

will be seen. This, however, also explains why their representative institutions were more long-lasting than those of city-states. Accordingly, municipalities are better placed on a continuum between the city-states of Italy and territorial states, such as England.

7.2   Similarities: Common Origins in Central Power and Justice

Representative and republican regimes differed in how power was distributed and governing structures were ordered but they shared a prehistory of effective centralization. This similar prehistory solved collective action problems and enabled communal institutions. These commonalities indirectly support the main hypotheses in this account about power centralization and judicial integration.

7.2.1   City-States in Northern Italy

The Italian cities reflect the logic presented in this book in three ways. First, a feudal prehistory was critical for the emergence of communal institutions (though regional variation, especially between the Po Valley and Tuscany, was strong). Judicial institutions were also crucial. Finally, equally important was communal power over the most powerful. However, as noted, to the degree that many of these polities established a more bottom-up, commercial foundation without a strong executive, they were unable to effectively resolve tensions and control their countryside and eventually lapsed into more signorial forms of government.

The importance of feudal precedents becomes apparent when we examine explanations of institutional origins. The economist Avner Greif explained two key communal institutions in Genoa from the 1100s, the consuls and the *podestà*, as an effort to address economic inefficiencies produced by family rivalries and power competitions.[42] The consuls were elected officials and the *podestà* was an outsider placed as "an executive administrator, above all the head of the judiciary"[43] to transcend local rivalries – which they did for some time. These were common practices throughout Tuscany and Lombardy. Genoa's wealth rose exponentially in this period; its nominal trade grew fifty times between the 1160s and the 1300s and was "roughly ten times the receipts of the French royal treasury."[44] Greif connects these political institutions to commercial needs in a persuasive way, whilst critiquing the

---

[42] Greif 1994.   [43] Waley and Dean 2010, 40, 42; Greif 1998.
[44] Greif 1994, 284; Jones 1997, 196.

functionalism of old economic history that saw political systems as "a response to the gains to be attained from establishing them."[45]

However, neither consuls nor, certainly, the *podesteria* are in themselves definitive of the *participatory* nature of republican governance. Without an account of how *assemblies* formed and elections prevailed, the core of the regime remains unexplained, though records on this are much scantier than on consuls.[46] Assemblies, however, cannot be reduced to the exigencies of commercial growth. Their major precedent had judicial functions and origins. In Italy, "unlike in most of the rest of Latin Europe, highly formal court proceedings were a regular feature of political life." Until the eleventh century, the *placita generalia* were assemblies that adjudicated cases, mainly on land. They were "extremely regularized" and "large-scale public occasions," convened by the emperor or their local representatives (marquises, counts, bishops) or their envoys, where attendance was obligatory.[47] Assemblies additionally elected bishops, who also had major administrative functions.[48]

The new communal assembly, called *concio, arengum*, occasionally even *parlamentum*, also "undoubtedly" operated as a court of law especially for landholding cases in the first half of the twelfth century, as the historian Edward Coleman pointed out, though specialized courts also later emerged.[49] Continuity with judicial practice similarly existed at the level of elected consuls, many of whom were increasingly *iudices*, judges who "controlled public acts," especially from the 1130s.[50] Assemblies acquired broader roles, both in political decision-making and legislation; only criminal cases continued to be judged there. Taxation, here too, is not included in the list of main functions until later.[51] Ultimately, communal assemblies differed from the old judicial assemblies on a dimension that will recur in this analysis as causing regime weakness: no single executive convoked them, as the bishop of old, unlike in parliamentary cases.[52] As discussed below and also seen in Poland, Hungary, and elsewhere, the lack of executive only facilitated capture by elites, leading to oligarchy and instability.

Assembly practices thus drew both from historical traditions dating back to the seventh century[53] and from feudalism, which endowed lords with judicial powers and was very strong in Northern Italy.[54] Lombardy

[45] Greif 1994, 272.   [46] Coleman 2003, 194–95.   [47] Wickham 1997, 179–80.
[48] Coleman 2003, 194.   [49] Coleman 2003, 206–207.
[50] Wickham 2015, 10, 38–39, 90–91, 179–80.
[51] Coleman 2003, 206–207, 203–206; Wickham 2003, 19–20.
[52] Wickham 2014, 47–48.
[53] Coleman 2003, 209. The historical traditions are masterfully traced in Witt 2012.
[54] Black 1994; Magni 1937.

produced one of the most important European law-books treating the feudal transmission of land, the *Libri Feudorum*.[55] It recorded legal practice in northern Italy: eleventh-century lands were granted by the major landholders, whether secular or ecclesiastical, typically conditionally.[56] Even a strong critic of the concept of feudalism, medievalist Susan Reynolds, claimed that the "whole idea of feudalism originated from [it]";[57] it was the concept's application to northern Europe, not Italy, she deemed contentious.

The medieval/Renaissance communal and republican stages were thus interjected in a feudal landscape.[58] Rulers, both secular and ecclesiastical, were important in the early stage. Bishops frequently filled the vacuum of secular authority, particularly in the administration of justice. Bishops and lay lords originally oversaw the urban consuls administering justice, as in Milan: the status of consuls originally "derived from a place in the court or entourage of kings, counts, and bishops,"[59]though they eventually "overshadowed" the lords. Practices varied widely, but the "presence of the Count" was necessary for the final resolution of conflict in the early period, as urban consuls could not adjudicate. Counts "continued to hear some suits" into the 1150s at Pavia.[60]

In most social science accounts, however, the early period receives little attention. Even when origins are examined, the narrative is typically one of cities overthrowing the authority of the Holy Roman Emperor or of local princes, counts, and bishops.[61] Lords appear almost incidentally, typically as the grantors of emancipation or as the owners of the land in which towns had free tenure.[62] Further, arguments about the feudal origins of government were associated with a conservative, reactionary view of politics in the early twentieth century, as it placed government origins in private associations rather than public authority.[63]

The topic remains controversial, with some historians emphasizing the communal aspect and others identifying feudo-vassalic elements. As the historian Chris Wickham has argued, however, recent scholarship has provided a more nuanced understanding of how feudal structures shaped the gradual emancipation from imperial authority. Most major landowners, for instance, lived in cities and "that was the basic reason why Italian cities were so much larger, more powerful, and more socio-

---

[55] *Liber Legis Langobardorum* 1896.   [56] Reynolds 1994, 215–30.
[57] Reynolds 1994, 181. Also, see Giordanengo 1990, 61–62; Wickham 2015, 58–62.
[58] Jones 1997, 560; Epstein 1996a, 109.   [59] Wickham 2003, 19.
[60] Waley and Dean 2010, 32, 31.   [61] Spruyt 1994, 130–39.
[62] van Werveke 1965, 26.
[63] Marongiu 1968, 119–20, and 121 for Marongiu's objections to this view. Also, see Tabacco 1989, 185; Wickham 2014, 43.

politically complex than those of Latin Europe."[64] Moreover, the emancipation of the communes also involved the submission of the countryside, the *contado*.[65] But the cities adopted feudal relations with the countryside themselves.[66]

Further, cities may have lacked kings or princes, but they had a judge, the *podestà*, demonstrating again the centrality of justice in integrating polities. He was typically an outsider brought in by communes when internal strife had become unmanageable. However, the emperor Frederick Barbarossa was important in establishing the institution, as he appointed many officials in Lombardy and Emilia after 1160.[67] Further, many "of these early officials were feudatories," either counts, as in Verona, or lords of surrounding lands. Landholding was thus a critical component of the arrangement. The powers of the office, however, declined during the thirteenth century until it devolved into a "chief justice with police powers."[68] The weakening of some central coordinating figure contributed to the centrifugal tendencies that eventually undermined the republics.

Most critically perhaps, communes also achieved what this account has identified as another key condition for representative emergence: power over the most powerful, at least initially. In fact, many *popolo* revolts in the mid-to-late thirteenth century ensured that "magnates were required to post a large security against the possibility that they might commit a crime, and were subject to severe penalties if they did harm a *popolano*."[69] The Florentine Ordinances of Justice, a set of laws passed in 1293–95, restricted both laborers *and* magnates from government, and Florence later appointed an outsider short-term to pursue denunciations of magnate abuse, the Executor to the Ordinances.[70] Nobles lost their legal prerogatives and tax immunity – a pattern resembling England.[71]

This power over the most powerful was indeed achieved without a ruler; however, it did not produce enduring institutions. Despite these (and other) precautions, the communal phase was not self-sustaining over the long term, as city-states did not remain autonomous.[72] From the 1250s, feudal lords slowly reemerged in response to civil strife:

at the height of commercialization, city after city in anti-feudal Italy began surrendering liberty again for lordship, for government by "domini" or "tyrants" preponderantly feudal, not merchant but landed magnates, barons, nobles, prelates. The land of merchant republics was a land also of despots.[73]

[64] Wickham 2015, 8, 9–20.   [65] Waley and Dean 2010, 33–34.
[66] Jones 1997, 558–64.   [67] Waley and Dean 2010, 40–44.
[68] Waley and Dean 2010, 41, 42.   [69] Lansing 2010, 35.   [70] Lansing 2010, 39–45.
[71] Jones 1997, 419–20, 516.   [72] Venice excepted.
[73] Jones 1997, 231; 1965; Becker 1960; Dean 2004.

The concept of a despot is more fluid than what stereotypical understandings imply, as historians have cautioned.[74] Nonetheless, lordship and conditional forms of landholding remained prevalent in Northern Italy into the modern period. In Lombardy, "a large number of fief-holders enjoyed, as late as the eighteenth century, civil and criminal jurisdiction and the right to make laws and even to coin money. They were usually entitled to … taxation as well as to the profits of justice, in the form of levies for the administration of the courts and penal fines and confiscations." By 1714, two-thirds of the duchy of Milan still consisted of fiefs and the powers of central government were limited in those domains. Lands were still held "of the duke," as in England.[75] Contemporary accounts seek the higher social capital of the North in its civic component, but the feudal one may be as important.[76]

7.2.1.1 An Exception? Venice[77]   Devolution to oligarchy is also observable in a case that did retain a semi-executive, Venice; together with Genoa, it was also the most long-lasting city-state, as this account predicts, though only until the Napoleonic invasion in 1797.[78] In some ways, however, early Venice seems to reflect the narrative contested here. Its republican, elective character was affirmed when rising mercantile groups ended the de facto dynastic succession of doges in 1032, further installing two elected judges to restrain dogal power. These restraints were strengthened when the doge lost militarily to Byzantium in 1172 and was assassinated; the dogeship was then transformed into a republican magistracy. Other institutions, such as the Great and Minor Councils or the judicial tribunal of the Forty and the State Attorneys, further controlled the doge.[79] This period also ushered a wave of fiscal innovation, from limited-liability to double-entry accounting.[80]

Venice thus seems to confirm the model of mercantile power creating open economic and political orders. In fact, however, mercantile control eventually restricted participation to a section of the elite, especially after 1297. The nobility became a closed order, limiting access to maritime trade, and thus generating "political closure, extreme inequality, and social stratification."[81] Mercantile origins did not endogenously produce greater participation. Venice's longevity is, however, probably also tied to

---

[74] Law and Paton 2010; Dean 2012.   [75] Black 1994, 1150, 1151, citing Magni 1937.
[76] Putnam et al. 1993; Guiso et al. 2016.
[77] The same arguments apply to Genoa's regime, which also had an elected doge; Epstein 1996b.
[78] Lane 1966; 1973; Martin and Romano 2000; McNeill 1986; Queller 1986.
[79] Lane 1973, 90, 92, 95–101.   [80] Puga and Trefler 2014, 767–68; de Roover 1965.
[81] Puga and Trefler 2014, 753. But cf. Ruggiero 1979.

its more successful reorientation after the fourteenth century towards the surrounding countryside (the *terraferma*) than other city-states. It also crucially renegotiated the tax burden after the fifteenth century, reducing inequalities.[82] The implication of this argument is that an executive power, even of limited powers, contributed to these differences.

Some city-states, as in Lombardy, were unable to dismantle rural federations operating under quasi-feudal conditions. The more ruthless domination of the countryside, the *contado*, by Florence, produced "a peculiarly inactive countryside," ridden with "anomie."[83] In all cases, the rural population was not integrated into the civic machinery of governance. "Inequality between town and country was intrinsic to city-states." About 5 percent of taxed population held up to half or more of property or wealth and 50 percent held as little as one-twentieth or less in the 1280s.[84] The tax burden was overall much higher in the country.[85] For many historians, inequality explains the gradual decline of communal and republican regimes: "Without a widened franchise the culmination of divided oligarchy seemed fated to be dictatorship, party or personal dominion."[86]

In short, to the degree that Italian city-states were able to mobilize similar mechanisms to England, especially power over the most powerful and some judicial centralization, they developed striking participatory institutions; to the degree that executive power was weak or dispersed, their regimes did not survive – a pattern that will be echoed in cases like Hungary and Poland as well.

7.2.2   Cities in the Low Countries

Cities in the Low Countries also achieved robust civic government from the early Middle Ages. Many accounts focus on Holland, but until the fifteenth century Flanders was the most developed region. In 1400, its urbanization, at almost 40 percent, was double that of Holland; it was only in 1500 that the latter edged ahead.[87] In both cases, though, comital power was fundamental in creating the conditions for participatory politics at the polity level.

Their constitutionalism is typically attributed to economic factors, for instance, "rich soils" and "agriculturally suitable areas" that created

---

[82] Epstein 1996a, 109–10.   [83] Epstein 1996a, 110.   [84] Jones 1997, 234–35.

[85] Jones 1997, 566–69, 571; Epstein 1996a, 103–106; Alfani and Ammannati 2017.

[86] Jones 1997, 581–650; Epstein 2000b, 287–90. Of course, other factors also contributed; Jones 1997, 524–83.

[87] Bairoch et al. 1988, 259. De Vries 1984, 32, using a different metric, also places the Netherlands below Belgium in 1500.

population densities and urban growth, making institutions endogenous to technological and economic change.[88] However, these agricultural conditions in the Low Countries were the result of a precocious feat over nature, as discussed below, that depended on political power structures. Further, agricultural, urban, and commercial growth also occurred in fertile parts of premodern China and India, such as the Yangzi Delta and Gujarat,[89] so how the European urban belt avoided both absolutism and underdevelopment must yet be explained. Military technology often serves this purpose. Towns with sufficient wealth could defeat the reactionary, land-based forces, ensuring the survival of parliamentarism, in such accounts.[90] But these developments date at best from the early 1300s and the potentially equalizing effects of the gunpowder revolution only operated from the 1450s. Institutions were formed by both those points.

Other economic approaches see political institutions as endogenous to market exchange earlier than the fifteenth century. The stable conditions necessary for trade were created by city competition from the 1250s, Oscar Gelderblom has argued.[91] This is a non-state alternative to the neo-institutionalism of Douglass North that saw an effectively constrained state as a key actor.[92] Similarly, for van Zanden, Buringh, and Bosker, institutional constraints emerged by incorporating new economic classes after 1200.[93] These are compelling narratives, but both trade and institutions were present before 1200.[94] Economic growth was underway by 1050 and trade already flourished in the 1100s, but so did comital authority.

The question is whether this prior growth had commercial, bottom-up propulsion or whether political authority, either of counts or bishops, was instrumental. Although some commercial growth can be explained without much reference to central authority, its extension over a whole region cannot. The alternative proposed here is threefold. Public authorities provided the necessary infrastructure, as economic historian Sheilagh Ogilvie has argued in her major work.[95] The weaker comital power was and the more autonomous the cities, the more conditions for long-term economic and institutional growth weakened. Second, rulers' capacity to compel subjects under fairly uniform legal frameworks owed much to conditional patterns of relations, which shaped representation as well. Finally, since Flemish counts were weaker than English kings, representative practice was more uneven in the Low Countries. The pattern in early Holland was similar.

---

[88] Boix 2015, 209, 204.   [89] Pomeranz 2000, 7–8; Wong 1997.   [90] Boix 2015.
[91] Gelderblom 2013.   [92] North 1990.   [93] van Zanden et al. 2012.
[94] Nicholas 1992, 70–123.   [95] Ogilvie 2019.

Counts provided infrastructure in two main ways. First, in both Flanders and Holland, rich soils were not a natural given but the product of an astonishing program of intervention, the reclamation of land from the marshes below sea level, the building of dikes, canals, and dams – "taming the Waterwolf," as the Dutch termed it.[96] This land provided a tabula rasa that was not burdened by local strongmen possessing ancient rights. Available land was originally unable to feed its population.[97] Historians differ on the role of counts before the 1110s,[98] but the question is not simply how initiatives begin (for which counts may have been less important) but how they extend polity-wide to lift an entire region. Even if counts lacked the power to carry out these large hydraulic projects alone early on, their role was crucial.[99] They had regalian rights over land and "gave the coasts to the abbeys on condition of diking and turning them into agricultural or pasture land."[100] Counts also offered personal freedom and the right to own land or to self-government.[101]

Further, for trade to grow the coasts had to be connected to the interior: "Philip of Alsace [1168–91] accordingly evolved a master plan to provide the Flemish coast with ports that could be linked with interior towns such as Bruges." Moreover, "counts had sponsored most canal construction before 1200," though cities undertook the task subsequently.[102] Comital intervention also varied by region, occurring late only in the northeast, after 1230.[103]

Similarly, in Holland, a "centralized, bureaucratized state" may not have existed,[104] but this did not mean the absence of central authority. Even when initiative for such communal works lay with the communities, resolution of conflict depended on higher authority.[105] Faced with need, collective action is not hard to mobilize; instead, action stalls when conflicting interests cannot be resolved. But in Holland, the board formed by communities to regulate such conflicts, the Rijnland Water Board, was led by the bailiff, the highest-ranking officer of the count. This was particularly necessary already since 1150, because simple drainage techniques could not address soil subsidence – complex hydraulic works were required.[106] Dutch fertile soils were as endogenous to political authority as Flanders'.

---

[96] TeBrake 2002. Reclamation occurred in Italy with different consequences; Curtis and Campopiano 2014.
[97] Nicholas 1991, 27–28.   [98] Dhondt 1948 is challenged by Nicholas 1991.
[99] van Bochove et al. 2015, 13; van Bavel et al. 2012, 352; Dijkman 2011, 12. Bishops often provided the only public authority.
[100] Nicholas 1992, 98, 99; 1991, 24–25, 27.
[101] Curtis and Campopiano 2014, 6; van Bavel and Schofield 2008, 21.
[102] Nicholas 1992, 129, 110.   [103] Nicholas 1991, 27.   [104] TeBrake 2002, 489.
[105] TeBrake 2002, 492–93.   [106] TeBrake 2002, 494.

Second, city growth was also dependent on comital authority – commercial activity did not suffice to turn settlements into the major trading urban centers that many Flemish towns became, concentrating between 20^{107} and 36 percent[108] of the population by 1500. Cities became more independent from the 1100s, but this followed the imposition of peace, first through the Church (Truce and Peace of God), then through the Peace of the Count (*pax comitis*) before the 1120s.[109] It was also predicated on counts granting charters that provided crucial rights to all major cities, including relating to trade.[110] In Holland, towns lacked coercive powers over the countryside, a crucial precondition for market growth.[111] Though historians take such lack as given, it was not a natural outcome; the strong jurisdictional powers of the count described below were instrumental. These patterns shaped the legal and judicial structure of Flemish and Dutch cities, in ways discussed separately next.

7.2.2.1 Flanders and the Power of the Count: Conditional Landholding, Justice, and Assemblies   Early Flanders shows connections between conditional landholding, ruler penetration of localities through judicial structures, and representative activity that resemble England's, already from the 1100s. Counts controlled the land, although the nobility eventually weakened as most wealth was controlled by the towns. Evidence on noble service and fiscal dependence is not as readily available, though nobles were taxed. But relations with towns were forged through the count's increasing judicial centralization. This involved both collective responsibility and the petitioning identified as key. To the degree that judicial integration was limited by the strength of urban courts and assemblies, the functional layering and institutional fusion observed in England did not materialize. As this section shows, the increased autonomy of towns therefore simply inhibited polity-wide integration and representation, eventually weakening the regime.

In Flanders, like Italy, the urban efflorescence of the 1200s was preceded by institutional learning under central authority. The count was "the most eminent warlord in Flanders, the wealthiest landowner, and the feudal lord of the most prominent men of the land."[112] By 1200, his territorial holdings were considered "immense" by local standards:[113] they were about the size of Catalonia or Burgundy (about 12,000 square km). They included some of the most important commercial

[107] de Vries 1984, 39.
[108] Buylaert's 2015, 34 figure is for the county of Flanders alone.
[109] Koziol 1987; Dhondt 1948.   [110] Ganshof 1949, 77–78; 1951.
[111] van Bavel et al. 2012, 360.   [112] Demyttenaere 2003, 153.
[113] Dhondt 1950, 7; Lot et al. 1957, 365; Ganshof 1949, 108–10.

centers, such as Ghent, Saint-Omer, Bruges, and Ypres. Counts were originally weak, but they increased their power over the cities after 1128.[114] This secured the de jure monopoly on violence and establishing peace, just as English kings had done.[115] In the twelfth century, Flemish counts only trailed after Henry II of England and Frederick Barbarossa.[116]

Counts granted fiefs to local lords, whilst retaining an advantage over them and curtailing their autonomy, as in England.[117] But as the legal historian Dirk Heirbaut has argued, Flemish counts exploited feudalism "as an instrument of princely power" mainly in terms of service, whilst retaining control of castle land for instance.[118] Below the nobility, subjects gradually "received the right to construct their houses on land which the Count or the landlord owned, as long as they paid a ground rent (*landcijns*) for the use of the land occupied" – paralleling the English legal structure and also observed in Holland.[119] Term leaseholds were widely spread by the fourteenth century.[120]

The land regime also shaped how the count controlled the judicial system. Twelfth-century counts replaced the hereditary feudal viscounts, who administered justice in both cities and countryside in the old system of castellanies, with comital bailiffs.[121] Vassals performed judicial service within this framework, as in England.[122] Seigneurial courts did not have the independence observed in France – comital institutions prevailed.[123] Flemish fiscal organization accordingly has been compared to that of the English in the early twelfth century, "ahead of that in Normandy and the French royal domain."[124]

Nonetheless, unlike in England and France, the towns were so wealthy that the landed nobility was weak in comparison.[125] Unlike Italy, however, the towns were not as dominant over the countryside because the count's power penetrated polity-wide, especially through legislation. Urban law was standardized from the 1160s, especially by Philip of Alsace, "a legal innovator" in many respects.[126] These comital law codes were crucial for commercial growth, not least by changing

[114] Verhulst 1999, 127–31; Dhondt 1950, 12–21; Nicholas 1992, 62–88.
[115] Koziol 1987.   [116] Nicholas 1992, 150.
[117] Nicholas 1992, 67; Ganshof 1949, 40–46.   [118] Heirbaut 2001, 34 and passim.
[119] van Bochove et al. 2015, 21; Nicholas 1992, 107.   [120] Nicholas 1992, 127–28.
[121] Nicholas 1992, 87–89; Ganshof 1939, 45ff., 52; 1932, 10; Blommaert 1915.
[122] Ganshof 1939, 52–53; Heirbaut 2001, 29.
[123] Ganshof 1939, 45. Counts, as vassals of the French king, lacked jurisdictional sovereignty; appeals were submitted to the Paris *Parlement*; van Caenegem 1966. Appellants from urban courts were pressured not to take their cases there, but jurisdictional subordination existed.
[124] Lyon and Verhulst 1967, 86.   [125] Nicholas 1992, 159–60.
[126] Nicholas 1992, 120–21.

marital laws, as the historian David Nicholas has argued.[127] Law was gradually homogenized under the banner of the *utilitas publica*, which based the count's superior right to impose the peace on Roman law. Major crimes became offenses against the count and his *pax comitis*, so he alone had jurisdiction over them. This state-building enterprise in the twelfth century produced a communal identity that transcended local urban contexts – though not as effectively as in England, as we will see.[128] As historian Jan Dumolyn noted, the basis of this identity was "the eleventh- or twelfth-century urban sworn association partially empowered to regulate and govern its own affairs by a contractual relationship with the prince."[129]

Counts restricted urban autonomy by intervening in urban tribunals, unlike in France or Germany.[130] They originally chose the aldermen (*schepenen, scabini Flandrie*),[131] who were judicial officials, with jurisdiction initially over crimes and wrongs but eventually also over administrative and economic matters. Aldermen particularly regulated the critical wool trade with England, probably since the 1160s, certainly since the 1240s.[132] Though originally appointed for life, by the 1240s annual selection prevailed[133] – but this allowed the count more power to contain the patriciate, not greater municipal independence.[134]

Urban independence gradually grew: new aldermen were selected by sitting members, not the count, though some remained at his discretion.[135] After the 1240s, the count's control over aldermen had weakened, and later fluctuated.[136] In other words, periods of institutional gestation under the leadership of the count occurred before the institutions begun to develop relative self-rule.[137] Urban autonomy looms large in accounts of commercial growth, such as Gelderblom's, but these ignore how embedded mercantile institutions were in comital structures.[138] They also ignore how important the counts were for international trade: counts forged agreements for safe conduct with the English that were vital for trade after 1200 – a crisis in Anglo-Flemish ruler relations in 1270–74 was, for instance, "catastrophic" for the Flemish economy.[139]

Even if urban courts had been sufficient for *commercial* growth, their autonomy was certainly in tension with a polity-wide *representative*

---

[127] Nicholas 1992, 136–38.
[128] Dumolyn 2000, 488; 2007, 113; Dhondt 1950, 6; Boutemy 1943, 53–55.
[129] Dumolyn and Haemers 2015, 179.   [130] Ganshof 1939, 50–51; Gilissen 1954, 541.
[131] Ganshof 1939, 51; Dumolyn 2000, 489.   [132] Boone 2010, 463.
[133] Duesberg 1932, 29, 31.   [134] Dumolyn 2015, 398.   [135] Gilissen 1954, 555–57.
[136] Ganshof 1939, 54–55; Dumolyn and Lambert 2014, 100.
[137] Verhulst 1999, 127–31, 144.   [138] Dumolyn and Lambert 2014.
[139] Nicholas 1992, 176–78, 164–66.

regime. To the degree that supra-local institutions emerged it was instead because their early stages display the themes identified throughout the book, judicial integration, ruler imposition of collective responsibility, and petitions. This is obscured because, as for Italy, scholars tackle assemblies only in their mature form, after 1300, when indeed commercial growth had strengthened cities.[140] Yet, an itinerant comital council is observed at least since the 1050s, just as in England and France (the *curia comitis* or "het hof"), originally composed of the count's vassals. It particularly dealt with infractions of the count's peace.[141] Trade required at least pockets of peace beyond the city walls, at the supra-local level, and this too depended on the count. He created jurisdictional homogeneity by judging any affair related to fiefs and vassalic obligations, as with the English Parliament. Vassals also had judicial duties and accompanied comital officers in itinerant inquests.[142] A structure of obligation bound the towns as well. When the count recognized the "commune" or sworn association of Saint-Omer in 1127, for instance, he "imposed a duty of collective vengeance if a citizen's injuries at the hands of an outsider were not redressed."[143] The capacity to impose a collective frame of responsibility was thus key for Flemish institutional development too.

As noted previously, collective responsibility engenders collective demands. Collective action from the 1270s was tied to the same wave of petitions we have seen in England and France in the same period. Social unrest escalated in response to the economic crisis of the period. It triggered strong conflict, not just violent riots (enemies would be expelled and their houses demolished), but also in the judicial and legislative arena via petitions.[144] These grievances were presented to the count, often in assembly or in the alderman's court; they brought together the social groups that economic approaches see as independent agents of institutional change. These petitions, as well as the rebellions they precipitated, presented familiar grievances, as Dumolyn has extensively shown: taxes that were regressive and misapplied, corruption of comital officials, and participation in the council through nomination of aldermen, among others.[145]

Accordingly, a trade-based approach must be qualified. First, the communal spirit was forged in relation to the count. Once again, collective action that appears to be born though commercial interest alone emerges through a preceding structure of obligation, imposed from above. And it is typically artisans, i.e. dependent workers, not merchants

---

[140] Blockmans 1976, 216; van Zanden et al. 2012.
[141] Ganshof 1939, 49–50; 1949, 103; Demyttenaere 2003, 161 and passim.
[142] Ganshof 1932, 53.   [143] Nicholas 1992, 120.
[144] Dumolyn and Haemers 2015, 169.   [145] Dumolyn 2015, 395, 399, 400.

that spearhead these demands. After all, the government of the thirteenth-century Flemish cities was not exclusively mercantile, but was instead "patrician," composed also of urban landowners, as in Ghent.[146] Finally, in as much as cities became too powerful to remain in a system under the count's direction, integration was impeded and a polity-wide regime less effective. In fact, much of the period can be examined through the conflict between the "Three Cities" (Ghent, Bruges, and Ypres) and the "Commun Pays" of Flanders brought together by the count.

As towns became increasingly assertive in the thirteenth century, comital power fluctuated greatly:[147] by the 1300s, the cities were referred to collectively as the "bonnes villes" rather than by reference to the "*scabini Flandrie*," which had expressed urban corporate identity under comital authority since the 1200s.[148] Commercial growth indeed empowered the artisanal class and the guilds, ushering the "corporative" stage in Flemish politics, which spread across cities.[149] But this left the count unable to deal with the Three Cities when they attempted to divide the county in the early 1300s.[150]

In some arguments, this juncture illustrates how war helped Flanders transition from an aristocratic to a popular regime.[151] At the famous battle at Courtrai in 1302, Flemish urban groups indeed routed the French cavalry and Flemish aristocracy. However, although guild corporations acquired a position in city government, what was almost "democratic" within a city was not the same as polity-wide representation. Instead, city divisions produced conflict and defeat.[152] They allowed the French to prevail in 1304. While the Brugeois were winning, the other cities "left the field, a pattern that would recur and plague concerted Flemish military actions for the rest of the medieval period," leading to a punitive peace with the French.[153] The background to this crisis had been the Flemish count's inability to manage the Anglo-French rivalry or control his nobles who defected to the French.[154]

Ironically, the first polity-wide system of revenue for the count was ushered by the heavy taxation raised to meet the French fines for the urban feat in 1302.[155] Representative activity picked up in response to these pressures. But it included the "*commun pays de Flandre*," which integrated all three orders, clergy and nobility included.[156] Assemblies

---

[146] Nicholas 1992, 133.   [147] Verhulst 1999, 144; Derville 2002.
[148] Dhondt 1950, 28; Boone 2010, 463; Blockmans 1998, 56.
[149] Dumolyn 2015, 384; Dumolyn and Haemers 2015.   [150] Dhondt 1950, 29ff.
[151] Boix 2015, 157–59.   [152] Gilissen 1954, 563–64.   [153] Nicholas 1992, 195.
[154] Nicholas 1992, 181ff; Boone 2010, 466; Dumolyn and Haemers 2015, 180.
[155] Nicholas 1992, 186.   [156] Dhondt 1950, 36–37, 32.

also included smaller towns and the castellanies, which together shouldered 70 percent of the tax burden. Only a third of taxation was paid by the Three Cities and the artisanal groups increasingly leading them, though more countryside was included through the Franc of Bruges and that contribution rose to half in the fifteenth century.[157] Crucially, by "the fourteenth century, the counts of Flanders taxed all inhabitants directly, forbidding lesser lords to ask for aides."[158]

It cannot therefore be asserted that representative institutions "emerged and remained in place in those areas that had a sufficiently wealthy and cohesive class of 'burghers' that could block the landed and monarchical elites and sustain the process of endogenous growth that eventually led to the industrial revolution."[159] Burghers may have created precocious pockets of radical politics, as Flemish cities had a continuous history of informal meetings averaging at about thirty per year in the fourteenth and fifteenth centuries,[160] dealing mostly with commercial policy.[161] But that is not the same as polity-wide representation for *governance*. For the latter, input was necessary from groups across society, the rural population, clergy, and nobility, which occurred in less than 6 percent of total meetings[162] – foremost, legislation and justice was necessary.

The count's role was increasingly key here. Steep conflict with the big cities in the 1300s was handled judicially, with charters confiscated after 1328, making sessions of the comital council, the *Audientie*, the final point of appeal even for citizens of smaller towns against their own governments.[163] But existing institutional proliferation meant that no single forum was available where both judicial and political/fiscal functions were fused, as in England, weakening central institutions.[164]

Later Flemish history was complicated as the county was subsumed under the Burgundian Netherlands and ruled first by the Valois (from 1384) and then the Habsburgs (from 1477). Explaining this trajectory exceeds the scope of this account, but some observations can illustrate the implications that flow from it. Representative activity continued at the provincial level; after 1464 it also occurred in the Estates-General that brought all Burgundian provinces together. Yet, Blockmans, for instance, posits a "decline of the representative system in the Low Countries"

---

[157] Dhondt 1950, 37; Blockmans 1976, 227.   [158] Dumolyn 2007, 115.
[159] Abramson and Boix 2019, 832.   [160] Blockmans 1976, 216.
[161] Blockmans 1998, 56.   [162] Blockmans 1976, 224.
[163] Ganshof 1939, 58; Nicholas 1992, 236–37; Dumolyn 2000; Boone 2010, 467–68.
[164] Dhondt 1950, 32. Judicial functions were separated from the count's court in the thirteenth century. A supreme court was composed of councilors and great feudatories, while the "council" became an advisory body; Nicholas 1992, 234.

already from the 1430s, which presumably laid the ground for the collapse of the constitutional framework after the northern provinces split (and the Dutch Republic was born) in the 1570s, with Flanders remaining under imperial control. The familiar narrative of powerful rulers exploiting outside resources to suppress representation is particularly apt here.[165]

Yet Burgundian representative activity in the early 1500s was still higher in frequency than anywhere in Europe, even England.[166] This argument suggests that to the degree that we see such activity at all, ruler power must be enabling it and that such power should be encouraging greater collective action among groups. However, to the degree that such activity fails to shape the regime at the polity level, that power must have been ultimately insufficient; a key indicator of such failure was the lack of plenipotentiary powers among representatives. The Burgundian period displays all these traits.

The dukes of Burgundy returned to the institution of the "Pays Commun," not the "Bonnes Villes," i.e. they upheld an inclusive institution in Flanders, not one confined to the urban sector. Flanders was exceptional in including small cities and the rural sector, echoing English patterns.[167] This is when we see *estate* representation, including the nobility and clergy, from 1384.[168] Critically, the expanding Flemish elites were now committed to supporting "the common good" of the Burgundian state, "abandoning [their] traditional autonomism."[169] Feudal relations remained crucial, since failure to perform obligations led to confiscation of property, as attested by many confiscation registers.[170] But various local entities had their own Estates (Brabant, Hainault, Liège for instance).[171] Polity-wide representation faltered as cities adopted the imperative mandate, not full powers, for their representatives – the center of authority remained local.[172]

This feature undercut the capacity of the Estates to operate effectively at the supra-local level of the Estates-General after 1464. Participation was indeed propelled by the deep social conflicts that trade generated. However, as Blockmans argued, economic and social differences kept groups separated, and it was the Habsburg princes that brought them together to the extent they did.[173] Crucially, whilst they voted on taxes, they never legislated. So, technically, this institution does not even

---

[165] Blockmans 1976, 237.
[166] Blockmans 1976, 223–24, 219. The caveats about frequency apply less in cases where convocation was also bottom-up; Blockmans 1976, 229–30; Boone 2010, 471.
[167] Blockmans 1976, 225–26.   [168] Blockmans 1976, 224.   [169] Dumolyn 2006, 431.
[170] Dumolyn 2000, 520.   [171] Buch 1965, 35–37.   [172] Buch 1965, 37.
[173] Blockmans 1976, 236–37.

conform to the definition of this study. Even though it governed as an executive for a brief period in the sixteenth century, particularism undercut its power; it was more of an "assembly of Parlements" than a parliament, leading to its eventual eclipse in 1632.[174]

In short, precocious commercial activity and assembly practices to deal with the needs of trade did not generate an enduring polity-wide regime that translated local preferences into applied law. Accordingly, city independence was not the crucial factor nor what distinguished East from West; in fact, the greater the city independence, the less constitutional the polity-wide outcome.[175] Moreover, to the degree that the Flemish assemblies focused on by social scientists after 1300 were effective, they had a prehistory of institutional interaction which became polity-wide only when counts had an advantage in power and recognized the benefits of accommodating the demands of merchants. This led to less conflictual relations with the communal movements than in Italy, Germany, or France.[176]

7.2.2.2 Holland: Landholding, Comital Power, and Collective Responsibility Similar patterns are observed in Holland. International trade shifted from Bruges in the 1200s to Antwerp in the late 1400s and Amsterdam by 1585.[177] After 1579, Holland became the leader among the seven provinces of the Dutch Republic, which often outshone England in economic performance. It exemplified a rather exceptional combination of bottom-up rule with commercial interests. This combination depended on a "social discipline" that was predicated on family networks and Calvinism, as argued by sociologists Julia Adams and Philip Gorski respectively.[178] Nonetheless, the decentralized nature of the Dutch Republic has also made economic growth, fragmentation, and representation appear associated.[179] The economic historian de Vries has emphasized however that, although the Republic was decentralized, it functioned "as a single economy."[180] Holland dominated the union, as it provided almost 60 percent of its budget.[181] The foundations for this condition went back to the medieval period, as van Zanden noted.[182] These insights echo the main claims advanced in this book.

[174] Buch 1965, 38–41, quote from p. 39.
[175] Defenders of city independence also note the problems of an "excess of communal power"; van Zanden et al. 2012, 13–14.
[176] Dumolyn and Haemers 2015, 167–68; Verhulst 1999, 144. Nicholas 1991, 20–21 sees comital weakness in urban mobilization and violence, but that would be compared to England, not northern Italy where rulers were virtually absent.
[177] Gelderblom 2013, 16.   [178] Adams 1994; Gorski 2003.   [179] Gelderblom 2013.
[180] de Vries and van der Woude 1997, 189, 172–94.   [181] Rowen 1988, 84.
[182] van Zanden 2002, 635–37.

Holland early on displayed key features highlighted in this account: relatively strong comital power, a weakened nobility (and clergy) often conscripted to judicial service, land held from the count, effective structures of collective responsibility, and exceptional taxing powers. Comital power was not strong enough to prevent institutional proliferation, especially at the supra-local level. This precluded the formation of a single polity-wide representative that governed, so no institutional fusion occurred at the center.

Nonetheless, relative comital power is evidenced in the neglected "prehistory" of the county of Holland. As discussed, this authority was already displayed during the marshland reclamations between the tenth and the fifteenth centuries – land cleared was held in tenure from the count.[183] Conditionality was also important. When Holland is noted as lacking a "truly feudal past," this meant the absence of manorialism (i.e. the subjection of peasants to a lord) and local lordships, not the conditionality invoked in this account.[184] This absence is contested for many regions.[185] In any case, manorialism was absent and peasants free when the power of manorial lords was undercut, typically by a higher authority.

Holland in the Middle Ages was no "society of orders"[186] – perhaps more than England – because counts limited the jurisdictional powers of the nobility and the Church.[187] Cities also remained small in size, as "the thirteenth- and fourteenth-century counts were strong enough to prevent the towns from extending their jurisdiction over the country-side."[188] By the mid-seventeenth century, "only 8 per cent of the villages in Holland had become subject to urban jurisdiction."[189] When rural areas were integrated, the regimes achieved greater territorial anchoring.

Did urban competition cause these conditions, via growth?[190] Would it thus also lie behind the representative activity that flourished? Though competition was certainly operating, it cannot explain the emergence of the "incipient national economy" noted by de Vries.[191] Integration required rather, first, that neither nobles nor cities dominated property rights.[192] In fact, from "the tenth to thirteenth centuries, the counts and bishops established a political structure consisting of local jurisdictions administered by government agents (sheriffs) and villagers." As in England, "nobles and clergymen did not preside over jurisdictions of

---

[183] van Bochove et al. 2015, 13; van Bavel et al. 2012, 352, 366–67; Dijkman 2011, 12; van Zanden 2002, 636.
[184] de Vries and van der Woude 1997, 159–65.   [185] van Zanden 2002, 636.
[186] de Vries and van der Woude 1997, 160; van Bavel et al. 2012, 366.
[187] Zuijderduijn 2014, 22.   [188] van Bavel et al. 2012, 367, 355, 359–61.
[189] Zuijderduijn 2014, 23.   [190] Gelderblom 2013.   [191] de Vries 2001, 81.
[192] van Bavel 2016, 147.

their own," with some limited exceptions.[193] In 1351, count William V forbade both groups from settling disputes. They did, however, serve as judges in regional courts.[194] As in England, a sheriff ensured compliance throughout the county; he and other officials were checked by the inquests we've seen elsewhere.[195] The system was thus polity-wide, but more fragmented than in England, "consisting of regional courts of appeal and a supreme court in The Hague, and later in Malines."[196]

Second, integration of a "national" economy also required the integration of land markets.[197] These depended on secure property rights, such as registration of transactions, mortgages, and fewer transaction costs. All these were handled by public courts.[198] In most of Holland, private registration by "lords and notaries … was almost non-existent," unlike France and Flanders, even England. Public registration was in some parts compulsory,[199] making mortgages more secure.[200] By the sixteenth century, village courts seem "interchangeable" with public ones.[201] This integration homogenized interest rates and wages across town and countryside – thus generating a "national" economy.[202] City courts may have been vital for the precocious growth of urban trade, but polity-wide integration was necessary for overall growth.

Ultimately, the "real question," as Gelderblom noted, "is under which circumstances local magistrates, whether traders, artisans, lawyers, or otherwise, were willing to put aside their private concerns and serve the merchant community at large."[203] The explanation he provides – that "they expected to gain" – shares the functionalism questioned already. This book's argument suggests that such collective action was a response to collective obligation. Some critical collective action between cities, in fact, responded to sovereign demands for loans on the basis of collective responsibility.

As the economic historian Jaco Zuijderduijn has argued, counts of Holland used cities as intermediary corporate bodies bound by collective responsibility to raise loans in capital markets already by 1300. Foreign creditors thus knew that public debt was secured by all towns contracting – the law of reprisals was harsh. If Haarlem reneged, Delft merchants were also responsible. The towns of Holland and Zeeland were forced "to formulate common goals to bargain for during negotiations with the sovereign." In the 1500s, Charles V and the States of Holland (the

[193] Zuijderduijn 2014, 22.   [194] van Bochove et al. 2015, 14.
[195] van Bavel et al. 2012, 357, 367.   [196] Zuijderduijn 2014, 21–23.
[197] Dumolyn and Lambert 2014.   [198] van Bavel 2010, 62–63.
[199] van Bavel 2008, 23; Zuijderduijn 2014, 25.   [200] van Bochove et al. 2015, 13–14.
[201] Zuijderduijn 2014, 41.   [202] van Bavel et al. 2012, 363–66.
[203] Gelderblom 2013, 11.

Estate representatives to the court of the Count of Holland) developed a more centralized system of province-wide debt by extending this system, which bound the cities to a common frame.[204] The superior capacity of the Dutch Republic to mobilize domestic and foreign resources rightly identified by Downing as key to preserving its constitutionalism was endogenous to a previous advantage of ruling authorities.[205]

How did this advantage affect representative practice? Representative origins lie in the medieval period, though accessible sources are still limited.[206] The Count of Holland held a Common Council (*commune concilium*), which subjects could petition from at least the thirteenth century. The count acted as judge, as surviving registers attest. But the institution became increasingly professionalized. It was also distinct from the broader feudal council that was composed of vassals.[207] Moreover, when the Estates-General emerged under the Burgundians, continuing under the Habsburgs after 1477, as we saw, they assembled the States (representatives) of all individual counties, which remained fragmented. They were exemplary of what the historian Koenigsberger called "composite assemblies," agglomerations of widely varying political institutions.[208] Dutch representatives also had imperative mandates[209] – to the consternation of authorities.[210] Institutional proliferation, not fusion, occurred. This is partly why, as noted already, the "Estates of the central provinces never obtained the competence to legislate" in the Burgundian-Habsburg period either – meaning that the composite Estates-General also does not qualify as a polity-wide organ of governance, as defined in this analysis.[211]

Even taxation was initially handled by the provincial Estates.[212] The voting system at the local level procured impressive results; it provided about 80 percent of the Republic's revenue, with Holland producing 60 percent of that.[213] Data suggest that this was the most impressive premodern per capita revenue extraction, exceeding England's.[214] Such collective action was possible because of the structures of provincial collective responsibility outlined above, but it was also enhanced after the Burgundians erected "a whole hierarchy" of judicial institutions. They dispatched an itinerant Aulic Council in the fifteenth century, and

---

[204] Zuijderduijn 2010, 346 and passim.   [205] Downing 1992, 212–38.
[206] Scholarship is mostly in Dutch; Burgers 2009; Kokken 1991; Ward 2001.
[207] Burgers 2011, 107–10; Nijenhuis et al. 2009, 9.
[208] Koenigsberger 1988, 101–103; Tracy 1990; Gorski 2003, 46–48.
[209] Koenigsberger 1978, 214–15; 1988, 102–103.   [210] Koenigsberger 1988, 113–14.
[211] de Schepper and Cauchies 1997, 267.   [212] Koenigsberger 1988, 106–107.
[213] Gorski 2003, 47. Towns had eighteen votes and the nobility only one in Holland, with variation elsewhere.
[214] Dincecco 2011, 46–59; Karaman and Pamuk 2013, 606.

"put an end to the sovereignty of customary justice in civil and feudal matters," by harnessing the appeal process, as in France. All this flowed from the monarch's status as "supreme judge,"[215] with, however, more limited powers of execution than in England. The Netherlands thus also shows how radical practices at the local level do not naturally scale up to the polity level – judicial integration was key. Whether the decentralized nature of the regime also accounts for Dutch decline after the seventeenth century, as Julia Adams has argued and this account implies, can be corroborated when the political underpinnings of economic sustainability are further probed.

7.2.2.3 Swiss Cantons

The Swiss cantons also appear as exceptions to this account and suggest even more strongly a bottom-up organization, as well as a capacity to survive without a unified executive. Some important qualifications must be made, however, albeit briefly. The cantons had small populations, ranging between 400,000 and 600,000 inhabitants by 1500.[216] As argued already, coordinating small groups of people is easier compared to large populations across extended territories.

Second, they did not have a truly representative regime as defined in this account beyond the local level. The Swiss Diet, the *Tagsatzung*, assembled since the 1400s canton delegates to deliberate mainly on foreign policy and administration; it had only rudimentary (i.e. exceptional) legislative and judicial duties.[217] The confederation instead functioned as an alliance of semi-sovereign communes, with independent jurisdiction. Crucially, however, to the degree that it did operate as a unit, it was predicated on a key condition identified in this account and seen in both the Italian and Low Country cases: power over the most powerful. The Swiss cantons achieved "the elimination of the nobility" to a degree "found in no other region in Europe."[218] The corollary to this is that, as in England, both urban and rural communes had independent representation: the nobility was not able to control the countryside as in France and Castile.[219] Military pressures seem not have been a major impetus early on, as defense expenditures only amounted to about 5 percent of total expenditures.[220]

Finally, communes attained greater independence whilst remaining under the jurisdiction of the emperor, though sources focus on their

---

[215] de Schepper and Cauchies 1997, 250–51, 264–67.   [216] Bairoch et al. 1988, 259.
[217] Würgler 2014; 2008, 34–35; Sablonier 1998, 658, 660–61. For a nuanced overview, see Scott 2012, 164–92.
[218] Sablonier 1998, 651; Church and Head 2013, 30, 33.
[219] Sablonier 1998, 656–63; Church and Head 2013, 19–20.   [220] Körner 1999, 335.

conflict not the interdependence that caused it.[221] As in other cases, the emperor's powers must have structured judicial relations early on. Even for the survival of the confederation into the modern period, some historians argue that an external executive was necessary to suppress the canton quarrels of the 1700s, provided by French intervention.[222] Another case that merits a full comparison, that of the early American states, also suggests the necessity of central executive power: after 1787, the attempt to build a bottom-up, decentralized union gave way to the need to install a more powerful executive, echoing the argument of this book.[223] Even if early forms of representation emerged in a decentralized way, some level of central executive intervention was necessary at the polity level.

7.3   Conclusion

The chapter focused on city-states, showing how their origins parallel those of territorial representative institutions, such as England's, on some dimensions. Land rights were controlled by counts or lords and public administration involved jurisdiction, a pattern that in northern Italy was still operative into the eighteenth century under princely governments. The stronger the executive government, the more representative the regime: Flanders sustained more effective institutions, unlike Italian cities, because "the counts of Flanders always remained in place as the ruling power."[224] This applied throughout the Low Countries, "where the towns did not succeed in winning complete autonomy. They did not cease to form part of the territorial principalities within which they had sprung up. Their institutions had a mixed character, half princely, half urban."[225] This also ensured the participation of the countryside.[226] In Holland, as de Vries noted, government was institutionalized at the provincial level, so as to check domination by cities.[227]

Failure to integrate social groups is accepted as a major cause of institutional and regime divergence in the Italian cases. To the question, "why could *urban* republics not become effective *territorial* republics,"[228] the answer seems to be that "the conflict between landed and commercial interests was seldom resolved successfully." Republican governments were not able to co-opt rural populations in

[221] Sablonier 1998, 650–53.   [222] Würgler 2008, 36.
[223] Wood 1969, 463–68. The United States also started with similarly low population until 1730.
[224] Blockmans and Prevenier 1999, 7.
[225] van Werveke 1965, 28; see also Gilissen 1954, 541–43; Lyon 1978.
[226] Blockmans 1978, 194.   [227] de Vries 2001, 81.   [228] Epstein 2000b, 298.

a structure that permitted the jurisdictional integration needed for a polity-wide regime.[229]

England, by contrast, was distinguished by a broad network of small urban centers. Urbanization in 1300, as we have noted, is estimated at about 4.4 percent, that is about a fifth of that in the Low Countries, when only cities above 5,000 inhabitants are included.[230] But about half of the urban population of England was then living in small towns, numbering between 300 and 2,000 inhabitants, and not captured by such datasets.[231] If these are included, urbanization could potentially be around 13 percent.[232] These were "local outlets and collection points" providing "vital points of contact between the different levels of the commercial economy."[233] They were integrated into a network of commercial activity because of the English crown's high capacity to regulate internal affairs and create "free-trade" areas.[234] Cities are often considered engines for growth, yet about 80 percent of wealth in the early period was concentrated in the countryside.[235] It was the English crown's capacity to harness urban and rural entities across this territory, mediated through its parliamentary structures, that enabled its later growth. Sequencing matters.

In other words, if Europe's urban development "outpaced that in the Islamic world," it is not because "the development of forms of local participative government in Europe ... made cities less dependent on the state."[236] The more independent cities were from any supra-local "state," as in Italy, the more their long-term political (and economic) trajectory suffered. Accordingly, we also cannot seek representative origins in the urban advantage of Europe over other regions.

Trade increased the resources available to communities, but it could not itself dictate the shape of institutional solutions to the problem of governance: law and the classical tradition provided the initial foundations to these, as Perry Anderson noted long ago, with the Church as intermediary.[237] It is not an accident that the regions that generated these political forms had also witnessed the revival of classical forms in Carolingian and Romanesque architecture and art from the ninth century and of textual traditions, including political ones, especially since the twelfth century.[238] As Wickham notes, communal forms emerged not just in commercial but non-commercial towns as well.[239]

[229] Epstein 2000b, 298; Jones 1997, 233.   [230] Bairoch et al. 1988, 259, 297.
[231] Dyer 2002b, 2, 5; Beresford 1967.   [232] Campbell 2008, 911.
[233] Dyer 2002b, 16, 12.   [234] Britnell 1981; 1978.
[235] Mayhew 1995, 58; Dyer 2002b, 16.   [236] Bosker et al. 2013, 1418.
[237] Anderson 1974a, 131; Tabacco 1989, 321–44.
[238] Conant 1973; Benson et al. 1985; Witt 2012.   [239] Wickham 2015, 8–9.

8   Courts, Institutions, and Territory: Catalonia

Another major case combining commercial expansion and a strong representative tradition was medieval Catalonia. For some historians, it was second only to England in its constitutional arrangements.[1] The Catalan regime even preceded England's when it affirmed in 1283 that laws should be issued with the counsel and assent not only of nobles and church leaders but of townsmen as well[2] – in England these points were only officially affirmed in 1311/1322.[3] Catalonia developed a precocious commercial and maritime empire in the thirteenth to fifteenth centuries. It epitomized regional resistance to Bourbon Castile until 1714, when the Crown of Aragon[4] was absorbed by the latter. It has held a prominent place in accounts of early modern revolution, as an example of societal opposition to encroaching absolutism and an outgrowth of strong municipal structures that sustained self-government.[5]

Catalonia therefore reflects both the common assumption of representative rule under commercial expansion and the narrative of all-powerful Continental monarchies suppressing local institutions and commercial growth. It thus exemplifies the theories questioned in this book. In fact, however, the Catalan *Corts* had a prehistory in the medieval period that parallels England's. The *Corts* were a body with judicial functions that became the main representative institution. As historical scholarship has shown, Barcelona's strong municipal phase of the fourteenth century was preceded by a period of strong comital power and land consolidation starting in the 1100s.[6] The centralized, unifying powers of the count-prince were stronger than in Italy, more similar to Flanders, and weaker

---

[1] Merriman 1911; McIlwain 1932, 695–96.   [2] *Cortes de Cataluña* 1896, 145.
[3] McIlwain 1932, 698–99.
[4] The Crown of Aragon formed when the county of Barcelona united with the Kingdom of Aragon after 1137. Valencia was added in 1238.
[5] North and Thomas 1973, 85; Koenigsberger 1978, 195; Goldstone 1983, 145; van Zanden et al. 2012, 18.
[6] Font Rius 1985, 463–65; Bensch 1995, 45–84.

than in England. These conditions weakened the regime over time and undercut its capacity to survive into the modern period.

Given its commercial development, Catalonia is a more appropriate unit of comparison in examining the trade thesis than either the Kingdom of Aragon, the poorer, insular, noble-dominated region to its west or the composite Crown of Aragon.[7] Catalonia "was the true centre of the Aragonese Empire." The Aragonese nobility was more independent than the Catalan one, it had more limited land obligations to the crown, including to serve, was not taxed, did not contribute as much to the Reconquista, and in general resisted the growth of central government.[8] As historians have noted, this makes Aragon closer to Hungary and Poland, examined in Chapter 10, pushing the whole Crown towards the model of an "aristocratic republic,"[9] which, as we shall see, generally proved unable to survive overtime. The Catalans had a strong count-prince in the count of Barcelona;[10] eventually also facing Italian competition, they understood the need for central governance and cooperated more.[11]

The first section describes the frequency of the Catalan *Corts*. The following ones show how the Catalan trajectory reflects the logic suggested in this book: how patterns of land concentration and conditionality help predict institutional outcomes, how judicial concerns were dominant, and how representative activity interacted with fiscal pressures only later. The robust municipal institutions of the mercantile fourteenth century are thus shown to have historical foundations in strong comital power.

8.1   Frequency of Meetings

As Bisson has argued, the origins of the Catalan *Corts* should be placed after the 1160s. They averaged almost four per decade in the 1200s.[12] These are lower frequencies than in England, where twenty parliamentary meetings were held on average per decade until 1300. As discussed,

---

[7] See, however, the treatment in Møller 2017.   [8] Merriman [1918] 1962, 451–53.
[9] Shneidman 1970, 109–10; Merriman [1918] 1962, 430.
[10] The count of Barcelona claimed a position of primacy among other Catalan counts, hence the title of prince, but he was also count-king.
[11] Shneidman 1970, 109, 205.
[12] Bisson 1996. These figures come primarily from the contemporary parliamentary records, which summarized the business of the assembly, sometimes listed some participants (in greater detail for the later periods) and promulgated ordinances and laws for the realm. This is one of the richest archives in continental Europe; Bisson 1986, 190. These records are collected in 26 volumes in the *Cortes de los antiguos reinos de Aragón y de Valencia y principado de Cataluña* (1896). I have supplemented them with the detailed analysis in Kagay 1981, which reaches to 1327.

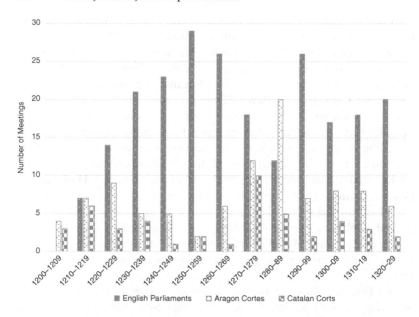

Figure 8.1 Comparative frequency of parliamentary meetings, England, Aragon, and Catalonia per decade, 1200–1329.
Source: Cortes de Cataluña 1896; Kagay 1981. Catalan and Aragonese figures include all meetings, even when towns were absent. As Bisson 1996, 45 has argued, it "is useless to speak of 'pre-parliaments'" in Catalonia, as early meetings performed the same functions, so I draw no distinction.

frequency does not necessarily measure the strength of social interests: it was the *Corts* that requested that they be reduced to once every three years in 1301, as opposed to yearly as set in 1283.[13] Moreover, Catalan representatives were formally as obligated to come with specified powers as English ones.[14] Yet Catalan frequency was lower than Aragonese, even though the Catalan nobility was taxed but the Aragonese was not (Figure 8.1).[15] Frequency only informs about regularity; inferences about power or consent must be derived in conjunction with other factors.

Frequency is not necessarily determined by the count-prince's strength either. For instance, a meeting was held almost every year after James the Conqueror (1213–76) ascended to the throne at the age of five. However,

[13] Kagay 1981, 264; MacKay 1977, 116.   [14] McIlwain 1932, 700.
[15] Merriman [1918] 1962, 453.

previous strong rulers had set the stage for this pattern, as analyzed further down. Nonetheless, his powerful rule did lead to more frequent meetings for the whole of Aragon, when he conquered new territories during the campaigns of the 1220s and 1240s, including the kingdom of Valencia by 1244.[16] Meetings sharply declined in the 1250s, when serious rivalries with France were dealt with diplomatic concessions instead of war, suggesting weakness. Meetings were held about every three years into the 1300s[17] just as territorial gains again accumulated,[18] suggesting greater military activity was related to assembly frequency.[19] As we will see next, however, these fluctuations reflect variation in the infrastructural strength and homogeneity that eventually allowed municipal institutions to flourish in the fourteenth century.

8.2   Concentration of Land, Conditionality, and the Power of the Count-Prince

As assemblies regularized after the 1160s,[20] the first question is how land and power were distributed before and around that date. Surrounding counties were absorbed in the eleventh century, after the counts of Barcelona gained de facto independence from the French crown around the turn of the millennium. More land came under the control of Ramon Berenguer IV (1131–62) compared to his domestic competitors,[21] especially after the union with Aragon in 1137 and the capture of major towns from the Muslims in the 1140s.[22] Expansion continued into the late twelfth century under Alfons I (1164–96), who reasserted control over a "string of castles."[23] After 1192, "the territory controlled by the House of Barcelona was greater than the combined holdings of the other counts."[24] Once the count-prince's strength had grown, representative activity increased. As military expeditions incurred "staggering" costs,[25] parliament indeed started becoming more regular, whilst concessions were tied to the danger of enemy invasion.

However, expansion occurred in the context of conditional landholding patterns. The type of landholding was crucially important in determining the continuing control of the ruler over his subjects and his capacity to penetrate into local judicial structures. A conditional system

---

[16] Bisson 1986, 63–68.
[17] By the late 1300s, some sessions extended over two years or more; I have counted each year as a separate observation.
[18] Shneidman 1970, 166; Bisson 1986, 97.
[19] Similarly, Blank et al. 2017. The Aragonese patterns are analyzed in Møller 2017.
[20] Earlier meetings are also attested; Kagay 1981, 20–47.   [21] Bisson 1986, 31–33.
[22] Tortosa in 1148 and Lérida in 1149.   [23] Bisson 1984, 95.
[24] Shneidman 1970, 165.   [25] Bisson 1984, 123.

of land tenures was applied to lands of the Spanish March that were integrated into Catalonia, where the count-prince retained the right to revoke a grant. The process was codified when Ramon Berenguer IV published the *Usatges*, around 1150; this described fief law and other customs and remained in effect until 1716.[26]

The count-princes accordingly asserted control over much territory also through judicial means, by claiming sovereignty over castellans.[27] They won a series of suits held after the 1170s using archival documents demonstrating original comital grants. Diplomatic victories, not just war, secured the allegiance of important competitors.[28] This process culminated in the compilation of the earliest surviving register of feudal oaths and conventions in the Crown of Aragon, the *Liber Feudorum maior*.[29]

In both concentration and conditionality, Catalan count-princes were more limited than their English counterparts, but more effective than in Aragon or than later Castilian kings. Some vassals, like the count of Foix, could occasionally muster greater forces than the count-prince. Vast estates, "sometimes as much as one fifth of the conquered territory" had to be granted to the Church. This meant that bishops too were summoned as feudal vassals, as they were in England, and not in their ecclesiastical capacity.[30] Other land was sometimes granted allodially, i.e. unconditionally. But both feudal and allodial lands "owed some form of political allegiance – the evidence is conclusive that owners of allods had to swear allegiance to the Crown."[31]

The system, moreover, had some important differences from the traditional system of feudalism, as Thomas Bisson argued.[32] Conditionality in landholding was somewhat weaker in Catalonia than in England, which undercut the ties between ruler and ruled. Especially after 1202, the count-princes could not restrict landlord power over peasants or secure peasant access to royal courts, as in England.[33] Further, they did not control the countryside as English kings controlled the counties through their courts;[34] towns, the nobility, and the Church remained the direct overlords. Catalan noble rights were thus stronger than those demanded in Magna Carta.[35] This affected parliamentary representation and territorial anchoring, as we shall see.

[26] Sánchez Martínez 1995, 29; Bisson 1986, 34; Kagay 1999, 60–62. Cf. Kosto 2001b.
[27] Kagay 1999, 78–81.
[28] Viscounts were subdued this way; Bisson 1984, 86, 87; Sabaté i Curull 1997, 39.
[29] Bisson 1984, 97; Sánchez Martínez 1995, 33; Kosto 2001a.
[30] Shneidman 1970, 193, 202, 248.   [31] Shneidman 1970, 156, 193, 393.
[32] Bisson 1989; Albert 2002.   [33] Benito i Monclus 2003, 484–503.
[34] McIlwain 1932, 700–701.
[35] McIlwain 1932, 702–703; Procter 1936, 544–46. A more systematic comparison would be valuable.

Nonetheless, land reverted to rulers when heirs were lacking, both for peasants and for county vassals, though evidence is not systematic. Catalan lords owed military service, but count-princes often had to pay for offensive wars, which they usually did by granting lands. Aragonese lords, by contrast, were less burdened by such duties, given their allodial status. Consequently, the count-princes relied on them less, drawing support mostly from the Catalans.[36] This greater control over the Catalan aristocracy also meant that aristocratic clans were less fractious in Barcelona than they were in Italian city-states, originally stemming oligarchic pressures relatively better.[37]

8.3   Pacification, Judicial Integration, and Ruler Power

The main incentive for English nobles to attend Parliament, as we have seen, was that all land was held of the crown. This explains why questions of adjudication and legislation were the overriding concern throughout all periods. Similarly, in Catalonia, much conflict was over jurisdiction, especially between castellan and ecclesiastical seigneurs (Figure 8.2).[38] However, Catalan subjects had a more elementary concern, until at least the middle of the thirteenth century: pacification. They expected count-princes to impose the Peace and Truce of God (*pax et treuga*), which was a form of adjudication. This reflected more anarchic local conditions (and hence weaker ruler powers) than in England, where the Peace "barely put in an appearance."[39] Both forms originated in church efforts to suppress private conflict: the Peace provided a right of asylum and protection of the unarmed in the ambit of a church; the Truce prohibited private wars during periods of religious significance.[40] These allowed the count-prince some control over baronial areas.[41] Other concerns, for instance, war, succession, taxation, officials, the authority of the Church, coinage, and more, had far lower frequencies in the early period.[42]

Pacification relied on two main institutions, the vicar (*veguer*) and the practice of the "guard and bailiwick" (*guarda i batllia*). The vicar was especially important in integrating Catalonia's urban centers, not least Barcelona. Vicars were not selected from the powerful castellan lineages, so the count-prince could control them better.[43] As in all other European cases, we cannot understand the urban efflorescence in Catalonia without acknowledging the integrating effects of the count-prince's justice. The

---

[36] Shneidman 1970, 194, 195–96.   [37] Bensch 1995, 5.
[38] Benito i Monclus 2003, 483.   [39] Kaeuper 1988, 153.
[40] Lalinde Abadia 1966, 69–70; Head and Landes 1992, 7.
[41] Sabaté i Curull 1997, 278.   [42] *Cortes de Cataluña* 1896, 8–153.   [43] Bisson 1986, 50.

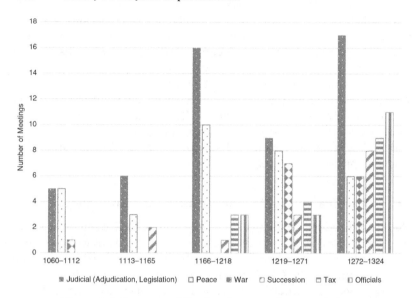

Figure 8.2 Purposes of Catalan *Corts* meetings, 1060–1327
Source: See Figure 8.1.

revival of the old vicariate system at the assembly of Fondarella in
1173–74 helped unify the judicial system in Catalonia, demonstrating
the count-prince's renewed power, just as *Corts* meetings increased.[44]

Vicars extended comital power into municipalities. They were originally appointed by the count-prince to enforce the peace and hold his
hearings locally with the bishops. They had authority over the officials
heading municipal government, including the counselors that flanked the
four keepers of the peace and truce (paciarii) that swore to them and thus,
ultimately, to the count-prince.[45] Vicars also integrated the functions of
local judicial magistrates, who had been administering justice in some
towns with relative autonomy probably since the late 1140s and by the
1200s operated in many major towns.[46] However, as early as the 1190s
the count's vicar held "a regularly functioning court" in Barcelona, which
now "served as the site where townspeople could come to receive justice
from an officer of the sovereign."[47] By 1301, vicariates operated throughout the kingdom, although seigniorial jurisdiction had also made major

[44] Salrach 1987, 384–85; Bensch 1995, 79–80.   [45] Font Rius 1985, 494.
[46] Lalinde Abadia 1966, 70–83.   [47] Bensch 1995, 73, 79.

gains.[48] Vicars were also important in supervising the urban assemblies found in many towns and composed of "good men" from all orders, the probi homines, representing about 3 percent of the population.[49] A level of legal uniformity was hence achieved over the five different legal systems in the region, though Aragon's legal system remained distinct.[50]

Through the *guarda i batllia*, the count-prince offered protection to peasants for an annual fee. Between 1151 and 1198, small proprietors entered under this protection on an extensive scale in Catalonia *Vella* (old Catalonia, of the east), as seen by the proliferation of contracts. Protection was also offered to travelers, to town inhabitants and especially merchants, and to monastic tenants. But the count-princes still had to compete with other lords, local seigneurs, and military orders, who also offered protection to peasants to assert jurisdiction.[51]

Catalan towns and their municipal institutions, however, formed the "primary base or cell in the organization of the whole of the political society."[52] This network of interconnected units was not a spontaneous growth; it was institutionalized by charters granted by the early count-princes. Such charters placed royal towns on a higher level than seigniorial ones. James I in particular chartered a series of towns after the 1240s, including Barcelona.[53] The municipal structures that were so important in the fourteenth century, as we will see, were predicated on strong ruler capacity to integrate justice across this network in the previous century.

8.4   Institutional Fusion at the Corts with Limited Territorial Anchoring

The judicial integration of the various counties subordinated the county courts to the central court, the *Corts*. This made the *Corts* the most important judicial institution, one that the nobility had many incentives to attend. It could thus operate as a regular and central institution of governance, since it displayed functional layering and institutional fusion, as in England and Castile, but unlike France. Like France and Castile, however, the Catalan *Corts* incorporated only towns as representatives of the third estate, not counties independently organized as in England. This

---

[48] Sabaté i Curull 1997, 278.   [49] Font Rius 1985, 464, 480, 494; MacKay 1977, 108.

[50] Sabaté i Curull 1997, 228, 231, 278; Shneidman 1970, 199–200, 209; Kagay 1988, 65–67.

[51] Benito i Monclus 2003, 550–54, 567–70; Ortí Gost 2000, 622–26.

[52] Font Rius 1985, 471; Guilleré 1997.

[53] The period of intense activity of municipal constitutions ended in 1284; Font Rius 1985, 477–79, 490–94, 496–97.

reflected weaker powers over the nobility and its subordinate population, which restricted the territorial anchoring of the regime.

Judicial activities were central to the role of the count-king across the Crown of Aragon, not just Catalonia. Rather than a roving bandit, James I was a roving judge, as were his predecessors and his European counterparts, traveling throughout his kingdom accompanied by jurists specializing in the multiple local laws and customs (*fueros*):

It "was true that I had civil and canon lawyers in my household, but that I was bound to have such lawyers by me: every king's court ought to be accompanied by canon, civil, and fuero lawyers, for there were many law-suits in all those branches. I myself, by the grace of God, had three or four kingdoms to my share, and law-suits came before me of many different kinds. If I had not with me those who could judge and sentence such suits-at-law, it would be a shame to me and to my court, as neither I nor any layman could know all the law-writings there are in the world."[54]

Cases were usually heard in the small council, the *curia*. By contrast, a fuller meeting was held when it involved a great noble or bishop, as with the claim of a countess to the county of Urgell in 1228 or the "king's accusation against the Viscount of Cardona for breach of a truce imposed on him in 1252" or again in 1274, against him on account of his "refusal to obey the king's writ of summons to the host."[55] Cases could also involve local crimes, such as murder, where James ordered financial compensation as well as support for the widows and orphans from the incident.[56] Failure to attend the *Corts* was, as in England, an act of insubordination. The Aragonese barons were particularly prone to reject the obligation. James condemned them for not being "willing to accept judgment from me: this is the most novel pretension that ever men raised against their lord."[57] Detailed evidence is lacking to demonstrate participation rates of different social classes. However, unlike in France or later Castile, participation appears more regular and mandated.[58]

The *Corts* also functioned as a forum where the count-prince and the Catalan nobility resolved broader rights of jurisdiction. At the great court of 1214, for instance, the count-prince was forced to accept only Catalans as vicars to administer justice.[59] This demand aimed at regulating, not rejecting, the count-prince's authority – similar to the dynamic in Magna Carta. But nobles retained greater rights to exclude the count-prince's agents from their jurisdictions, rendering exempted territories abodes for those persecuted by comital justice. These rights were affirmed in the

---

[54] *Chronicle of James* 1883, 519.   [55] Procter 1936, 533.
[56] *Chronicle of James* 1883, 515, 623.   [57] *Chronicle of James* 1883, 520–21.
[58] McIlwain 1932, 697, 700.   [59] Bisson 1986, 59.

Corts of 1228 and 1283, further consolidating noble power. Jurisdictional conflicts were thus recurrent.[60]

The *Corts* further legislated on the rights of the nobility vis-à-vis the peasants. On this issue as well, Catalan nobles were more autonomous than English ones, as already noted (though not more than the Aragonese). As the historian Paul Freedman has argued, peasant conditions "may legitimately be termed serfdom." The *Corts* of 1202 secured their right to "maltreat" and imprison their men (*rusticos*) and to deny them the right to appeal to county courts.[61] This was the *ius maletractandi*, which regulated peasant servitude.[62] These were rights English lords lost as royal courts prevailed (Part I). The count-prince therefore did not have direct control over the countryside and the rural population lacked representation independent of the towns. This urban predominance ultimately weakened territorial anchoring and hence the polity-wide reach of the regime. These weaker powers are also reflected in the late imposition of full powers on representatives – these were requested in 1281, but they do not appear systematically after that.[63]

Two more factors that were significant in the English system do not find systematic counterparts in the Catalan case: England's relatively direct system of courts and the necessary authorization by the center for court action (the writ system of the common law). The Catalan system was less structured, with overlapping authorities between offices such as the bailiffs, the vicars, and the majordomo.[64] In all, these differences reflect the variation in the capacity of the respective rulers to install an integrated judicial system.

Although Catalan petitions have not received systematic attention as in England, they were part of standard *Corts* procedure.[65] They were also instrumental in fusing local demand with central legislation, as in England: already from 1283 it was recognized that the participation of the third estate was central and one of the most important constitutional documents, the *Privilegio General*, was granted in response to petitions from nobles and town representatives.[66] By the 1350s, common petitions (*greuges generals*) were submitted by the *universitas Cathaloniæ*, as were individual ones from all social orders.[67]

The Catalan *Corts* thus fused judicial activities with political ones, achieving the institutional fusion that generated both greater

---

[60] Sabaté i Curull 1997, 228.   [61] Freedman 1991, 90, 116, 89–118.
[62] Benito i Monclus 2003, 114–19, 483–504.
[63] Kagay 1981, 160, 162, 279–81, 312, 340, 370–74. They also probably appear in 1214; Bisson 1996, 40–41.
[64] Shneidman 1970, 207–208.   [65] See throughout Kagay 1981.
[66] Procter 1936, 544–46.   [67] Hébert 2014, 468, 506ff.; McIlwain 1932, 703.

centralization and greater robustness over time. Compellence of the nobility was key here as well, but as this was weaker than in England, urban institutions developed more independently, undercutting the long-term cohesion of the regime.

8.5   Parliament, Noble Fiscal Obligations, and Taxation

The argument in this book suggests that where institutional fusion is observed, ruler powers to compel the nobility must be higher. A key indicator was taxation of the nobility and, indeed, a main trait of the Catalan regime was that, unlike in Aragon, Valencia, and later Castile, the Catalan nobility was taxed, both the rural aristocracy and the urban patriciate,[68] though not as systematically as in England. Accessible sources do not allow the detailed picture that was presented for the English case about taxation (or participation in judicial procedures); however, evidence about loans and debt suggests a similar pattern to England especially in the critical early institutional development of the county, despite weaker ruler powers.

Catalan count-princes relied on domestic lending from powerful vassals and allies. In the early period of institutional beginnings, Ramon Berenguer IV (1131–62) obtained loans by pawning county property.[69] As Bisson showed, a "striking revival of county borrowing" occurred under Peter II (1196–1213), due to military expeditions between 1210 and 1213 – with borrowing rising sixteen times over a few years. "In some years – 1204–1206, 1209, 1212 – loans must have constituted the main source of county income. The creditors were chiefly lay magnates and allies – the king of Navarre, the viscount of Béarn, the count of Urgell, plus other Catalonian barons."[70] Unpaid loans were a recurring source of conflict.[71] Most of the lenders were thus regular and important participants in the meetings of the *Corts* and their fiscal outlays provided them with powerful incentives to support the extension of the crown's capacity to extract from the whole territory – echoing the Eumenes effect observed in England. Bisson finds similar incentives in Catalan bailiffs as well, who were often creditors of the king, thus explaining why they were more centralized compared to their counterparts in France.[72] Later loans were raised against ordinary and extraordinary income from the realm.[73] Personal ties were thus a crucial factor in securing liquidity for the crown but also in incentivizing social actors to support parliament.

---

[68] Sánchez Martínez 1995, 37; Kagay 1981, 174.   [69] Sánchez Martínez 1995, 32.
[70] Bisson 1984, 129, 130.   [71] Kagay 1988, 63.
[72] Bisson 1984, 154; Bensch 1995, 71.   [73] Bisson 1984, 141–42, 156.

Taxation, however, did not spearhead Catalan parliamentary meetings nor were the urban, mercantile groups the key actor – again as in England. Taxes did not become central in assembly meetings until well into the thirteenth century – whereas assemblies had achieved some regularity since the 1160s. Moreover, towns did not approve taxes until even later, in the fourteenth century. Of about sixty-four meetings until 1327, sixteen (25 percent) dealt with taxation per se (Figure 8.3).[74] Taxation was raised more regularly after 1214 and became a major preoccupation after 1283, i.e. after a full century of meetings.[75] Coinage was a more frequent preoccupation in Aragon (in 14 percent of meetings), but in five Catalan meetings count-princes also promised not to devalue in exchange for grants by subjects. Count-princes also raised funds by alienating towns and villages, but this was mostly a later phenomenon.[76] Although these practices were more clearly a bargaining exchange between the ruler and subjects, they reflected weaker ruler powers overall; alienations, especially, decreased the landed wealth of the count-prince.

Finally, explanations predicated on commercial urban groups and their bargaining power are challenged since towns had a limited role in the *Corts* in the century before the 1270s – less than half of the meetings had representatives (considerably less than in the whole of Aragon, where half the meetings had townsmen). Even when present, as in the *Corts* of 1228, only the named nobility and clergy granted the subsidy for war (though towns pledged their fleet).[77] Catalan towns were represented by the king, who was their feudal *senyor*.[78] They participated fully after 1283, but royal enforcement of concessions to them lagged, as Bisson noted,[79] as they did with Magna Carta. Moreover, it was not until the 1360s that the municipal contributions were decided by all the estates together with the count-prince, as examined in the next section.[80] The prior period of comital strength was critical to this outcome.

8.6   Municipal Organization Endogenous to Comital Strength

Despite this prehistory, the early modern history of Catalonia consolidated the romantic image of a "free" Crown of Aragon versus an "enslaved" Castile, a strong republican regime with its own *fueros* that valiantly opposed the despotism of the Castilian crown.[81] Yet, as the historian Stephen Bensch emphasized, none "of the urban communities … is known to have clamored for the independent regimes they received from

---

[74] See similarly Møller 2017, 186 for Aragon and Chapter 2 for England.
[75] *Cortes de Cataluña* 1896, 143ff.   [76] O'Callaghan 2003, 30–31.
[77] Kagay 1981, 97–100.   [78] Ortí Gost 2000, 641.   [79] Bisson 1982, 193.
[80] Ortí Gost 2000, 641.   [81] Elliott 1963, 16.

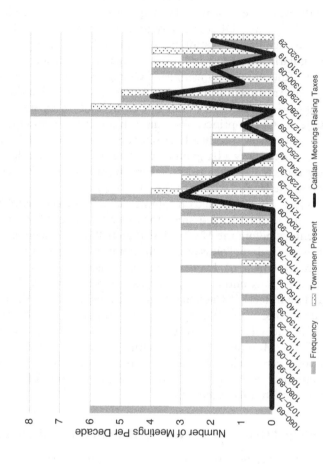

Figure 8.3 Presence of nobles and townsmen and taxes raised in the *Corts* of Catalonia *Sources:* See Figure 8.1. I include taxes incurred to prevent currency debasement and supplement Kagay with Bisson 1986.

the king in the 1240s, for with autonomy came responsibilities, as King Jaume I and his successor would frequently remind the city."[82]

Barcelona's strong municipal institutions indeed appear to confirm the narrative of strong commercial interests resisting despotic authority, exchanging rights for taxation in the midst of war, and prevailing only when the ruler was weak. By the 1370s, the Catalan *Corts* were precocious. They were raising taxes for the public good (*rei publice*) of Catalonia, which was clearly distinguished from the king's wars.[83] Critically, and as expected from the logic of this book, taxes applied across groups, including the Church and nobility, unlike France and Castile, and to the royal domain.[84] As in England, this state-wide system of taxation emerged after a "profound national sentiment" prevailed in the 1300s.[85] Moreover, taxes were collected and administered by the General Council (*Diputació del General*), a committee of the *Corts* that was also responsible for the laws and liberties of Catalonia since 1365 and which represented the *Generalitat*, the entire Catalan community.[86] This was indeed a republican constitution closer to Italian city-states and with far greater powers than the English Parliament. Moreover, war was a constant background to these concessions by a king unable to collect sufficient taxes, and mounting municipal debt was crucial.

But once again, the same qualifications raised about city-states apply here. Previous studies typically retrojected the republican character of the fourteenth and fifteenth centuries to the early, formative period.[87] However, between 1150 and 1270 Barcelona was governed as a royal seigniory, offering a long period of institutional learning before independence was possible.[88] It gained some self-rule by 1300 but not full collegial autonomy until 1370. Justice was key to this institutional learning: magnates selected by the count-prince already judged cases in the county court of Barcelona since the 1130s. Land held in tenure was a major concern (a third of some surviving cases around 1150 concerned inheritance, possession, and alienation).[89] The count fostered the urban growth of this period, similarly to Flanders and differentiating the region from Italian patterns; the Catalan count-prince did not relinquish the administration of justice in the towns.[90]

---

[82] Bensch 1995, 316.

[83] For instance the *fogatge* (hearth tax); Sánchez Martínez and Ortí Gost 1997, xvii.

[84] Sánchez Martínez 1995, 11.

[85] Sánchez Martínez 1995, 11 citing Genet and Le Mené 1987, 241.

[86] Sabaté i Curull 1997, 279; Bisson 1986, 118; Elliott 1963, 46; Herb 2003, 14.

[87] Ortí Gost 2000, 617–18; Font Rius 1985, 463–65.

[88] See Daileader 1999 for why the Catalan consulates lasted so briefly.

[89] Kosto 2001b, 81–82.

[90] Guilleré 1997, 270; Abulafia 1995, 657; Lalinde Abadia 1966; Ortí Gost 2000, 619–20.

Some historians have adopted Tilly's emphasis on war,[91] especially as it initiated the fiscal independence of Barcelona from the count after the municipality obtained the franchise of the *questià* in 1299.[92] Others, however, such as the historian Font Rius, have noted that the Council of Barcelona originated in the "regularization of ... judicial functions" associated with the administration of local life described earlier, including the extensive public works required.[93] Regardless, the count's jurisdiction was enhanced by both the polity-wide vicariates widely operating by 1300, as we have seen, and the uniform toll system that resembled England's.[94] Municipal privileges were after all granted to towns that passed from seigniorial to royal control.[95]

However, increasing municipal independence decreased the count's powers, benefiting landlords as well. By 1359, the nobility and Church controlled over 60 percent of hearths, as the count alienated large parts of royal property to pursue an imperial policy: by the seventeenth century, only 25 percent of towns and cities were held directly by the count.[96] Given the jurisdictional immunities in place, this continued the exclusion of the lower rural social orders from the *Corts*. Consequently, Bisson argued, "the exclusion of the lesser knights [from the *Corts*] consolidated a formidable alliance of landed magnates and urban oligarchs through which a 'pactist' program hostile to fiscal and agrarian reform was confirmed."[97]

The oligarchical tendencies observed by Weber and confirmed by Stasavage and others shaped later Catalan history too. The strong Catalan municipal institutions may have allowed precocious commercial expansion (a Mediterranean empire in fact) and resistance to Castilian authority, but they did not prevent civil war and losing the war against John II in 1472, being overshadowed by Castile, or the eventual loss of independence in 1714.[98] A stronger ruling capacity might have even enabled Catalan dominance of the other units; minority populations do rule over larger regions with lower institutional integration. But centrifugal dynamics were even more intense in Aragon, so although Catalonia overshadowed Aragon institutionally, it was not centralized enough to shape its recalcitrant neighbors.

---

[91] Sánchez Martínez 1995 emphasized war, but for the Crown of Aragon.
[92] Ortí Gost 2000, 571.   [93] Font Rius 1985, 463–65, 463–503; Rubinat 2002, 49–50.
[94] Sabaté i Curull 1997, 279, 278.   [95] Font Rius 1985, 470.
[96] Merriman [1918] 1962, 477; Sobroqués 1957, 75; Ortí Gost 2000, 632–34.
[97] Bisson 2003, 265; McIlwain 1932, 697; Guilleré 1997, 270–71; Ortí Gost 2000, 619.
[98] Elliott 1963, 5.

The Endogeneity of Trade: The English Wool
Trade and the Castilian *Mesta*

The widely posited links between the urban belt of Europe, trade, and representative institutions are not supported by either the Italian city-states, the cities of the Low Countries, or Catalonia, previous chapters have argued. Historical legacies were crucial in those cases, as the institutions formed either did not include broad sections of the population or failed to integrate localities in the legislative process (which also affected their survival). Nonetheless, the hypothesis is an intuitive one, especially given the commercial character of the main case that fulfilled all those conditions, England, so it merits further scrutiny. Trade was central to the English economy and to Parliament since the 1300s: even today, the Lord Chancellor sits on a "Woolsack" dating from the time of Edward III (1327–77), symbolizing the fount of English wealth.[1] Exports to Europe generated remarkable revenue.[2] The wool trade was also crucial for Douglass North's neo-institutionalist account of the contrasting impact of trade, exemplified positively through England and negatively through Castile.[3]

Parsing out the logic that connects trade and representation requires scrutinizing the mechanisms that might transform commercial activity into political outcomes. The main current hypotheses revolve around the dynamics of mobile capital and bargaining, which draw on a thriving literature in modern political economy. As discussed in the opening chapters, mobile capital is more commonly identified with trade-generated wealth, which is not tied to land and is therefore amenable to "exit."[4] As mobile wealth is harder to monitor, it is assumed to endow

---

[1] Pollard 1920, 22–23.   [2] Lloyd 1977; Power 1942; Unwin 1918a; 1918b.
[3] North and Thomas 1973, 4, 128–30; North 1981, 150–52; 1990, 113–14. North's views on Spain eventually changed, as he discarded assumptions about the efficiency of existing institutions, as Hough and Grier (2015, 1–64) incisively show. Hough and Grier offer a bold revision of English and Spanish developments, although they postulate London as a city-state, which cannot be applied to the early period examined here.
[4] Hirschman 1970.

actors with greater bargaining power to demand representation and more constitutional governance.

This dynamic further entails some specific hypotheses that require more thorough examination. One of these has already been rejected by historians. It used to be thought that as trade-generated wealth elicits indirect taxation, which was assumed to require a small bureaucracy, it obviated the rise of a coercive state that could suppress rights. Conversely, agricultural systems necessitated direct taxation; this required greater use of coercion, which was more congruent with absolutism – a hypothesis that seemed to be corroborated by French use of direct taxation.[5] John Brewer's classic study of eighteenth-century England refuted the link between indirect taxation and a small bureaucracy.[6] This, however, does not settle the question of how both mobile capital and indirect taxation impact the origins of representation.

I address this question in the first section that examines two additional assumptions about the English case: that actors with bargaining powers will request constitutional gains in return, which implies that mercantile interests align with those of the public, and that such actors will be able to act collectively to secure their goals. The second section considers the case of Castile, which has often been invoked to exemplify a "strong" crown that suppresses political rights and economic growth. Following the conclusions of Chapter 5, I show how existing conditions were contrary to those assumed and how the suboptimal effects of trade flowed from state weakness. Echoing Acemoglu and Robinson, I show how "the differences in the organization of trade . . . reflected the different political institutions of these countries."[7] The analysis further undercuts hypotheses that reduce representative emergence to commercial dynamics.

9.1   Capital Mobility, the English Wool Trade, and the Links to Representation

9.1.1   Taxes on Mobile Capital not the Key for Representation

Mobile capital is variously conceived in the literature. It typically means either the capital connected to the wool trade that produced indirect taxation or movable goods that constituted the wealth of taxpayers and were taxed directly.[8] Neither, however, can be tied to representation through a bargaining logic.

---

[5] Levi 1988, 111–12; Bates and Lien 1985, 53–55; Zolberg 1980, 695; Hopcroft 1999; Moore 2004, 300.
[6] Brewer 1989.   [7] Acemoglu et al. 2005a, 454.
[8] Medieval England had no sales taxes; Ormrod 1999, 32.

Two types of indirect taxation were charged on wool, customs and subsidies. None of these taxes, however, can explain a regular demand for Parliament. Customs were duties on imports and exports of wool and other commodities and the "largest item of regular income" around 1300 and still in 1433.[9] They were called customs because of their customary nature, *"consuetudines,"*[10] meaning that after they were granted they were not negotiated again.[11] They were thus ordinary, i.e. not bargained for, royal income until the seventeenth century.[12] The custom of 1275 was indeed granted by Parliament; however, though merchant towns had possibly the highest representation in that session before 1500, they were not called again for almost a decade. The next custom of 1303 was raised from foreign merchants and "became permanent without ever being confirmed by Parliament" after 1322.[13]

Medieval "subsidies" on the other hand were financial aid provided by subjects to the ruler, originally for emergencies, though some later became regular.[14] However, extraordinary wool subsidies, such as the *maltolt* (bad tax), were also not granted by Parliament initially but by the merchants. Parliament took de facto control of wool subsidies after prolonged conflict in the 1330s and 1340s and de jure after the 1360s.[15] Yet Parliament was fully formed since 1295, as we have seen.[16] Further, the wool trade was already declining by this point,[17] so some historians argue that revenue decline, rather than royal weakness, allowed the king to cede control over it.[18] Negotiations over wool taxes therefore did not contribute to the *emergence* of representative institutions or rights in England, though they were intertwined with their growth.

The association of representation and indirect taxes on commercial wealth is additionally challenged by aggregate data. These show that, in the early period of institutional origins in England, direct taxes were the main source of income, often dwarfing revenue from trade. It was not until the 1330s that indirect taxation began to rival direct forms and as I argue elsewhere,[19] the later period also saw backsliding in some key dimensions of interest in this account, especially the growth of local powers that could more effectively resist taxation, undermining the regime (Figure 9.1).

[9] Brown 1989, 65.   [10] Morgan 1911, 113.   [11] Lloyd 1977, 60, 124.
[12] Sacks 1994, 42; Prestwich 1990, 125.
[13] McKisack 1962, 5; Power 1942, 46, 41–43; Ramsay 1925b, 281.
[14] Brown 1989, 67–70; Harriss 1975, 426.
[15] Power 1942, 41, 46–48; Ormrod 1999, 32; Harriss 1975, 429.
[16] Maddicott 2010, 277–375; Fryde 1996, 533–49.
[17] Ormrod 1987, 39; Carus-Wilson and Coleman 1963.   [18] Harriss 1975, 446, 448.
[19] See Chapter 3 and the Conclusion.

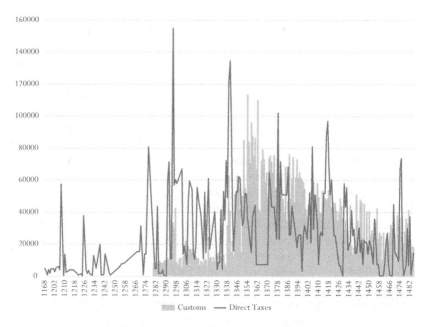

Figure 9.1 Direct taxation and customs in England, in £, 1168–1482
Source: Mark Ormrod, European State Finance Database, available at
www.esfdb.org/table.aspx?resourceid=11689

Direct taxes, by contrast, were raised on "movable property," namely
a core English tax base of "cows, oxen, grain, household goods," as Bates
and Lien note. This was wealth which they claim "could be hidden,"[20] thus
endowing its holders with bargaining powers tied to representative outcomes. Taxes on movables indeed helped establish "national" taxation
based on consent and were decided in Parliament. However, it was effective state compellence in such tax extraction that mobilized social demands
against the king in the early period more so than any bargaining advantage
of the taxpayers. In fact, tax assessments were carried out by the sworn
inquest of neighbors up to the 1350s.[21] Enforcement was initially strong:
for instance, officials simply seized cattle to force even earls to pay.[22] This
explains the phenomenal yield of direct taxes in some years: it was systematically around or well over 90 percent between 1290 and 1346.[23] When

[20] Bates and Lien 1985, 55.
[21] Stubbs 1896, 223–26; Bartlett 2000, 166–67; Brown 1989, 71–72; Willard 1934,
183–229; Willard and Strayer 1947, 168–280; Mitchell 1951, 111–55. Sworn inquest
of neighbors was also employed in Castile; I thank M. Drelichman for the point.
[22] Miller 1975, 18–19.   [23] Ormrod 1991, 152–53.

the capacity to hide wealth through undervaluation spread after the 1330s,[24] parliament was already established. Such "bargaining power" did not help the institution emerge; if anything, it weakened it (a point taken up in the Conclusion and supported by the Continental cases).

9.1.2   Bargains over Taxes on Mobile Capital: Sectoral Privileges, not Constitutional Rights

Even if bargaining powers of social groups had been strong, why should we assume they would be used to claim common rights rather than sectoral privileges? The empirical record from the developing world suggests the latter, as Bates and Lien noted,[25] especially in the literature on clientelism and neopatrimonialism.[26] In Haber, Maurer, and Razo's study of Mexico, for instance, economic actors do not demand public goods; "first and foremost [they] care about the sanctity of *their* property rights."[27] This is not simply a modern non-Western pathology. Historian Sheilagh Ogilvie has argued similarly in her analysis of medieval guilds;[28] I show it is also the dynamic in the English wool trade.

When trade groups granted taxes in England in the period of parliamentary emergence, no constitutional bargain was involved, just a sectoral one. Merchants would exchange taxes for *commercial* quid pro quos: the 1275 "Ancient Custom" was granted for the resumption of open trade with Flanders that the crown had stopped.[29] The 1303 "New Custom" was granted by foreign merchants in exchange for the *Carta Mercatoria* that secured them free trade.[30] It was "accepted as the price of royal protection," primarily for travel by sea.[31] In 1336–37, with the Hundred Years War starting, merchants granted taxes in exchange for a monopoly on the export of wool through compulsory staples – ports designated to control exports – in the Low Countries, established with royal support. In 1363, a small group of traders obtained such a monopoly, the Staple at Calais (then under English control).[32] When the king offered nothing, English merchants rejected tax demands.[33]

Parliament itself did extract political concessions when it acquired the right to approve wool taxes by the 1370s,[34] but this often did not generate

---

[24] By 1309, the lay subsidies were taxing less than 50 percent of the total movable wealth of the kingdom and that proportion diminished thereafter; Nightingale 2004, 28.
[25] Bates and Lien 1985, 62–63.   [26] Kitschelt and Wilkinson 2007.
[27] Haber et al. 2003, 10. However, their dependent variable is economic growth, not the long-term development of institutions examined in this book.
[28] Ogilvie 2019, 78.   [29] Power 1942, 43–44; Brown 1989, 66.   [30] Lloyd 1977, 124.
[31] Harriss 1975, 425–26; Gras 1918, 59ff., 257ff.
[32] Lloyd 1977, 145–47, 211–12; Ormrod 1987, 38.   [33] Power 1942, 45; Baker 1961, 5.
[34] Harriss 1975, 408–409, 505–506.

a constitutional gain, only a positional one. Members had "clearly recognised that unless Parliament was prepared to continue the subsidy it would be obliged to vote the king larger and more frequent amounts of direct taxation. On the whole the former course of action was preferred . . . History was to prove that a higher rate of wool subsidy was a lesser evil than the poll tax."[35] Parliament was thus not exchanging taxes with rights but avoiding a direct tax on all with an indirect one on wool. This does imply greater bargaining power on the part of certain groups in Parliament. However, this power moved the tax regime into an increasingly regressive direction by the 1400s.[36] It also reflected the weakening power of the crown and the increased power of nobles in the localities, which, as discussed in the Conclusion, contributed to the greater political instability of the period of "bastard" feudalism.[37]

Moreover, we cannot assume that merchant interests aligned with the public welfare. Merchants selling wool on the Continent granted taxes to the king easily because, as a result of their monopoly powers, "they were able to pass on a good deal of the tax . . . [either] in the form of higher prices to the continental purchaser . . . [or] in the form of lower payments to the English grower."[38] Mercantile interests, themselves divided, had constitutional effects through a logic diametrically opposed to the capital mobility model. Wool merchant concessions often generated a "solidarity of interests" in groups *opposed to them* in Parliament: "the lay and ecclesiastical magnates and the knights of the shire. They were wool growers – the former the large producers . . . and the latter the small ones."[39]

Some historians have argued that no inherent antagonism between domestic social groups existed, but Harriss, for instance, still concedes that it was the threat of royal favor towards merchant monopolies that galvanized Parliament to demand a role in these negotiations after 1330.[40] Critics have also shown that merchant groups did not have convergent interests either under Edward III;[41] but if they lacked common interests, we cannot assume they acted effectively to achieve constitutional effects either. Urban preferences are revealed in petitions to be diverse.[42] Just as in Robert Brenner's seventeenth-century account, it was the lesser merchants threatened by elite monopolies who sided with Parliament.[43] Outsider status rather than mercantile interest per se was

---

[35] Lloyd 1977, 236.   [36] Ormrod 2008.   [37] Coss 1989.
[38] Power 1942, 41; Wilkinson 1937, 72–76; Ormrod 1995, 93. McFarlane 1962 and Harriss 1975, 421–22 saw the burden shifted onto Flemish buyers, but merchants were still the least affected by the tax they freely granted.
[39] Power 1942, 41–42.   [40] Harriss 1975, 447–48, 420–49.   [41] Lloyd 1977, 144–92.
[42] Dodd 2007, 266–78.
[43] Harriss 1975, 437–41, 447–48; Brenner 1993. Moore 1967, 7 also notes the lack of connection between trade and democracy; for him, however, it was the united opposition

the critical mechanism. Moreover, and crucially, Parliament was the already-present arena in which these conflicts unfolded.

This divergence of interest should be unsurprising. Adam Smith emphasized that the interests of "those who live by profit," of the merchants and manufacturers, are not naturally aligned with those of the community and that parliaments should never accept their demands, except after prolonged consideration and critique.[44] The conventional view, of a natural, rather than context-specific, affinity between mercantile interests and constitutionalism stems from nineteenth-century bourgeois historiography and cannot be projected to the period of origins.[45]

9.1.3   Mercantile Interests and Collective Action Endogenous to State Capacity

Finally, the claim that parliaments are "a consequence of urban strength"[46] must show that urban, commercial groups acquired the capacity to act collectively in pursuit of their goals before parliaments were constituted. How whole groups of people are placed in "similar positions vis-à-vis the flow of resources" is a fundamental question.[47] Merchants were summoned by the crown on the same basis as Parliament since 1275 (up to 1327 through the sheriff) in the separate assembly of the merchants, though informal meetings also occurred.[48] The king's capacity to do so constituted merchants into a politically organized group in the first place. "The key to the king's control over [the merchants] was his right to stop overseas trade at will"[49] – and especially his capacity to do so. He controlled the staples and enforced trade-enhancing ordinances. These were remarkable feats for a medieval monarch, ones critical for the trajectory of the English trade (though it did not stem its decline).[50]

This capacity had multiple implications. It was both constitutive and limiting of mercantile power. By forcing merchants to bargain with him collectively through the Estate of Merchants, the king endowed them with an institutional presence. At the same time, the monopoly privileges to trade through a single Staple, such as Calais, consolidated their economic power in the international market. In short, the state gave a corporate identity to the very class of people – here, wool merchants – who are

---

of town and countryside against the crown that was consequential. My account explains why such convergence, to the degree it occurred, was possible.
[44] Smith [1776] 1981b, I.xi.p.10.
[45] Guizot 1851. Stasavage 2011 posits such an affinity under certain conditions, but assemblies are an independent variable in his account, unlike mine.
[46] Boix 2015, 204.   [47] Mahoney 2010, 20; Peter A. Hall 1986, 19.
[48] Power 1942, 39–40.   [49] Lloyd 1977, 174.   [50] Lloyd 1977, 101–102.

claimed to have induced the state to concede representation and limits to its power.[51] Merchant capacity to act in a coordinated manner cannot be assumed to be exogenous to the state – it depended on one that could penalize defectors.

9.2   The Castilian *Mesta* and the Inefficiencies of Political Weakness

Spain had an urban sector that was double if not quadruple that of England, as we have seen. It also had a thriving wool trade in the medieval period, similarly tightly interdependent with the European market. Yet by the early modern period, it was considered neither wealthy nor constitutional. The most common explanations, at least in non-specialist literature, have focused on problems of political authority. Neo-institutionalists in particular had focused on the mercantilist policies of the absolutist Spanish crown, claiming it used the wool trade to establish a monopoly that undermined economic growth.[52]

Spain therefore might support the hypothesis that where rulers were too strong, they could intervene in the economy and distort the outcomes anticipated by commercial activity. If urban groups did not succeed in shaping parliaments, as they did in the Low Countries or Italy, it was because powerful kings thwarted them. Acemoglu and Robinson, for instance, discussed Spain's mercantilism as a function of a "much stronger" crown and Ekelund and Tollison castigated Spain's oppressive taxation.[53]

Much scholarship has indeed treated the *Mesta* as the baneful institution exemplifying the mercantilist, monopolist tendencies of the Spanish crown.[54] This view has been jettisoned by Castilian historians, however.[55] They have noted that the Castilian *Mesta* was not a monopoly or a cartel,[56] but an export industry competing on the international market. It was a collective body in which "all owners of transhumant flocks were automatically members."[57] It became "national" under Alfonso X. Large wool producers did not receive monopoly rights; instead, royal policy aimed to reduce the high transaction

[51] See Edwards and Ogilvie 2012 on guilds.
[52] North and Thomas 1973, 4, 128–30; North 1981, 151; Ekelund and Tollison 1997.
[53] Acemoglu et al. 2005a, 454; Ekelund and Tollison 1997, 129.
[54] Klein 1920; Vicens Vives 1969; North and Thomas 1973; Ekelund and Tollison 1997, 124–53; Moore 1967, 7.
[55] Nugent and Sanchez 1989; Phillips and Phillips 1997; Ruiz Martín and García Sanz 1998; Drelichman 2009.
[56] As in North and Thomas 1973, 4–5; Ekelund and Tollison 1997.
[57] Phillips and Phillips 1997, 37.

costs of securing pasture lands, due to local conflict and grazing rights fees (*montazgos*).[58] In short, royal "intervention" aimed to secure conditions which were already operating in the English economy due to the unchallenged authority of the English kings. English towns were not subject to tolls because they were under royal jurisdiction, as were counties, thus effectively creating "free-trade" areas that accelerated commercial activity.[59]

In the Spanish context, pasture has been viewed as an inefficient choice compared to agriculture, serving monarchical rentierism. Yet in England pasture was fundamental to economic growth.[60] Communally owned lands were gradually partitioned to allow for grazing through the Enclosures, starting in the fifteenth century.[61] That "sheep ate men" was the necessary step in modernizing the English economy, for some scholars at least, despite its profound social dislocations.[62] In a pattern observed elsewhere in this book, similar developments across the two countries (here in the economic realm) are interpreted in contrasting light, when the difference lay in state capacity to respond to them. In fact, pasture is now seen as an efficient Spanish response to the international market.[63] As seen in Chapter 5, however, Spanish kings had much weaker infrastructural control over territories and populations than their English counterparts.[64] Commercial activity did not translate into political institutions as in England because of the political framework already in place and the power deficit of ruling authorities. This also limited the role of trade in the economy, though data seem lacking for the earlier period. In the first half of the sixteenth century, most ordinary crown revenues came from the 10 percent sales tax, the *alcabala*. Even when this amounted to about 30 percent of total revenue, wool revenue did not exceed 3 percent.[65]

*

In this chapter, I questioned assumptions of the literature claiming to link economic growth, especially trade, with political institutions. Such arguments can only be demonstrated through the mechanisms translating changes in the economy to changes in the institutional structure. Case studies are therefore appropriate means of testing them, especially since they allow the careful tracing of temporal precedence. The English case

---

[58] Phillips and Phillips 1997, 28–59.   [59] Bartlett 2000, 336; Bolton 1980, 130–31.
[60] North and Thomas 1973, 4, 130; Ekelund and Tollison 1997, 124–53.
[61] Allen 1992; Neeson 1993.   [62] Polanyi 1944.
[63] Phillips and Phillips 1997; see also Nugent and Sanchez 1989; Drelichman 2009, 235.
[64] See also Drelichman 2009; Drelichman and Voth 2014; Summerhill 2008; Grafe 2012.
[65] Drelichman and Voth 2010.

showed how the greater state capacity established in previous chapters was also critical for the effects of the wool trade. Process-tracing establishes the precedence of Parliament and the crown's role in constituting mercantile groups as a political bargaining force – an early instance of the structuring role of institutions in political economy. Merchants acquired a political profile because the crown interacted with an assembly for that purpose. Their early interests were not only not constitutional in nature, they were often contrary to public welfare and, consequently, bargains with political authority aimed at sectoral privilege, not the common good. Where state capacity was weak, as in Spain, similar economic activities were not harnessed by central institutions and did not enhance institutional outcomes. These conclusions suggest that instead of assuming that the European model of political centralization, partly based on trade, fails to explain other regions, such as Africa,[66] we should reconsider the model's origins.

[66] Osafo-Kwaako and Robinson 2013.

Part IV

Land, Conditionality, and Property Rights

10 Power, Land, and Second-Best Constitutionalism: Central and Northern Europe

England may have developed a robust parliament, but it did not display radical democratic practices – rulers, for instance, were never elected. Instead, it was in central-northern Europe, in Hungary, Poland, the Holy Roman Empire, Denmark, Sweden, even Russia that elections of rulers were held. Hungary was one of the few constitutional regimes of Europe since the early medieval period. It "has often been pointed out, especially by Hungarians, that there is a certain analogy between English and Hungarian constitutional history."[1] Poland also had a remarkable "republican" tradition, with a Parliament since the fifteenth century. Yet in all these cases, absolutism ultimately prevailed in the early modern period. In Poland, noble veto powers became so effective that collective action was impossible when serious military threat was looming, leading to the dissolution of the Polish–Lithuanian Commonwealth by 1795. The Hungarian nobility also failed to marshal a coordinated front and Hungary dissolved under the Ottoman onslaught in the 1520s, being partially absorbed into the Habsburg Empire. Sweden oscillated between absolutism and constitutionalism, whilst Denmark that had similar beginnings lapsed entirely, as did Russia and the Holy Roman Empire.

Why, despite such precocious beginnings, did these cases not sustain representative institutions? The main alternative explanation of this divergence focuses on military pressures. Ertman for instance discerned a lack of "sustained geopolitical stimulus" in the Continental cases before 1450, which prevented the build-up of the state. He also crucially pointed to weak central structures and a strong, entrenched nobility as distinguishing these cases.[2] Downing similarly pointed to the Polish internal failure to mobilize in response to geopolitical pressures.[3]

However, English pressures have not been demonstrated to be proportionately heavier than Hungarian or Polish ones before 1450. The English fought against the French, Scots, Welsh, and in the Crusades between the

---

[1] Coolidge 1910, 360; Smith 1850.   [2] Ertman 1997, 272, 268–78.
[3] Downing 1992, 140–56.

1150s and 1300 (the critical period of institutional formation), but Hungarian engagements during the formative thirteenth and fourteenth centuries were likewise multipronged. Hungarians participated in the Crusades, but also faced Russia, the Cumans, Byzantines, Mongols, Lithuanians and Poles, and battles in the Balkans.[4] Moreover, what counts as military "pressure" is endogenous to the capacity to withstand it: the Mongol invasion in 1241 could have counted as such if Hungarian forces had not been simply overpowered. When rulers were weak, they preferred to sign a treaty with rivals, like the Hungarian Charles I in the 1320s.[5] The Polish Piast kings also had to fight the Teutonic order, Brandenburg, Lithuania, Bohemia and others from a meager base to reconsolidate the fragmented Polish kingdom after the 1320s, doubling its size.[6] These pressures don't register as strong because royal powers were too limited to present a sizeable resistance; opponents simply prevailed and territory was lost or a truce was signed. Although pressures increased after 1450, they cannot be confirmed as negligible earlier.

So how can we explain the "entrenched nobility" that Ertman and Downing aptly identified as a key obstacle to constitutional practice in the Central European cases,[7] if military pressures differed little? The argument in this book suggests that its roots lie in the power relations between king and nobility in the period of origins and especially the nature of landed property rights distributed by the king. The common denominator across these cases is that kings had weaker capacity and could not compel the most powerful as effectively, so most constitutional dynamics transpired with lower social groups – what I have called second-best constitutionalism. Instead of strong groups contracting to limit the ruler's power, as conventional narratives claim, the king coordinated with the lower nobility to contain the great lords. This reverses the English pattern, where either fear of an insurgent crown forced barons to include broader groups, as we have seen, or when the crown itself expanded access to new groups, it could still compel the most powerful.

I begin with the two cases of Hungary and Poland, discussing first their similar land regime, and then tracing the links between their various "constitutional moments" and the key variables in this account, namely ruler power, conditional land grants, judicial structures, petitions, and taxation, to assess levels of functional layering, institutional fusion, and collective action at the aggregate level.[8] As at many points throughout the book, absent data on military troops, tax revenues, and other forms of

---

[4] Makkai 1990a, 18–19, 24, 26–28, 39–42.   [5] Engel 1990, 38.

[6] Gieysztor 1979, 99–101, 111–12; Knoll 1972, 28–32, 42–82.

[7] Ertman 1997, 265–66; Downing 1992, 140.

[8] Collective responsibility is not covered in available sources.

coercion over both ranks of the nobility, royal strength is mostly deduced from observed outcomes. But the proposed claims seem to accord with historians' assessments. I conclude with a consideration of key ways in which Sweden, Denmark, and the Holy Roman Empire can also be explained through this book's logic.

10.1   Hungary and Poland

The land regime in both Hungary and Poland was similar to the rest of the premodern world, from England to the Ottoman Empire. In Hungary, initially, "all land was held of the ruler, originating in an act of donation and ennoblement."[9] Similarly, when the Piast kings rebuilt the Polish kingdom, they were considered lords of the lands of the kingdom of Poland, with patrimonial rights to grant land at their discretion.[10] Their capacity to enforce these rights varied, as did the mode in which lands were distributed, whether conditionally or not. Unlike in England, but similar to France, local lords in both cases retained jurisdictional rights and greater autonomy. This, accordingly, weakened the territorial anchoring of the crown in the localities, thus making the assemblies an affair of the nobility – Poland for instance was a "Republic of Nobles."

Nonetheless, the parliamentary activity that *was* observed can be traced to mechanisms identified in this account, all predicated on some level of dependence on the ruler. Land ownership was still conditional on relations with the crown, especially military service; 2,400 Polish estates were confiscated through court verdict for failure to serve in 1497, for instance.[11] In Hungary, "upon the expiry of the nobleman's line or his conviction for perfidy, his property reverted to the ruler."[12]

Another commonality with England was crucial. As the historian Martyn Rady notes, "One of the outstanding features of medieval Central European society as a whole is that its nobility stood for the most part in a direct relationship to the king, not holding their property at one or several removes from the ruler by process of subinfeudation and thus not dividing their fealty."[13] Since "military service was due to none

---

[9] Rady 2015, 85. Hungary was a composite entity with much local variation, but due to space constraints, I will focus on the general traits of the main territories.

[10] Frost 2015, 12. The *corona regni*, the royal domain, became property of the state after the Piasts.

[11] Skwarczyński 1956, 301; Rady 2000, 144.

[12] Rady 2015, 85. In the Hungarian context, *nobility* was not defined in terms of land tenure but on the basis of fidelity to the crown. Those who held land only through tenure (rather than through royal gift) were "conditional nobles" or not really nobles at all; Rady 2000, 44, 79–95.

[13] Rady 2015, 74.

but the king," Polish relations were also "similar in this respect to English feudalism."[14] They entailed typical feudal obligations, like knighting the king's son.[15] I next examine the two cases separately.

10.1.1 Hungary

Assembly activity in Hungary appears in the eleventh century, followed by the grants of two charters that have elicited comparisons with Magna Carta in the thirteenth. It continued into the early 1300s, then lapsed until the 1380s, only to gain strength over the following century, before collective action weakened, leading to defeat by the Ottomans in 1526. The following sections explain how this development can be illuminated by the factors identified in this book.

10.1.1.1 The Eleventh Century: Royal Control of Land and the Emergence of Parliament   Like English kings, Hungarian ones began the process of state-building already holding most of the territory of the realm. King Stephen (1000–38) controlled approximately two thirds of the country's revenues.[16] "[B]eyond doubt in Stephen's time, the king and his family became by far the greatest landowners of the kingdom. They retained for their own use huge and contiguous domains."[17] The kingdom was divided into about forty counties (*megyék*), later increased to seventy-two.[18] A royal governor headed each county, the count (*ispán*), with military and jurisdictional authority as well as the right to appropriate one third of the local income, like the "third penny" of English earls – the rest went to the king.[19] This county system remained a core institutional feature of the Hungarian kingdom for the next five centuries, structuring provincial power relations and providing a relatively homogeneous administrative system that allowed strong organization of representative practices, though less so than in England.

As elsewhere in Europe, the king held judicial sessions, the "days of the law" at Székesfehérvár once a year – though he held itinerant sessions more often.[20] Their purpose was "redressing the grievances and settling

---

[14] Skwarczyński 1956, 301. So, when some scholars reject feudalism as inapplicable to Poland, they are referring to the decentralized and overlapping sovereignties that proliferated in western Continental Europe.

[15] Gieysztor 1966, 322.   [16] Molnár 2001, 25.

[17] Engel 2001, 80. Much of the royal demesne consisted of forest, but still had high value as hunting grounds and royal residences, as elsewhere in Europe (see the English Charter of the Forest (1217); Stubbs 1913, 344ff.; Hudson 2012, 455–94; Bartlett 2000, 170, 139).

[18] Engel 2001, 41; Rady 2000, 19.   [19] Engel 2001, 40, 73; Bartlett 2000, 209.

[20] Eszláry 1959, 108–109; Rady 2015, 50.

the differences of the military ruling class,"[21] similar to the English Parliament. Barons and prelates participated in judgments, though attendance was problematic. In a dualism that lasted into later centuries, legislation was formulated by the Royal Council. It was composed by the highest nobility, the *ispáns*, and the bishops, who witnessed the major decisions issued by Hungarian kings throughout the twelfth century.[22] But this met originally at Esztergom, 50 miles away.[23] Nonetheless, the sparsely surviving legislation since the eleventh century gradually transformed Hungarian society from one composed of semi-nomadic steppe people to settled agriculturalists "with rights and duties like those of the rural population of contemporary England or Northern Italy."[24] Yet the institutional fusion observed in England did not appear here – early assemblies have thus not left a solid institutional imprint.[25]

10.1.1.2 Thirteenth Century: Conditional Landholding, the Servitor Class, and Second-Best Constitutionalism   Evidence picks up again in the early 1200s, when the king still controlled most land, estimated at more than half or even 70 percent.[26] The key "constitutional" moments generating charters of rights occurred in 1222 and 1267.[27] Unlike England, however, neither of these moments involved the higher strata of the nobility, which the Hungarian crown was less able to control. Rather, a new group of nobles was created by the crown by rewarding military service and loyalty to counterbalance the higher nobility, producing second-best constitutionalism.

The higher nobility had been empowered by the extensive land grants by Andrew II (1205–35), the *New Institutions*. A group of about twenty barons received land from the crown "forever" (*perpetuo iure*) and unconditionally, as an allod (*haereditas*).[28] Without conditional relations, barons became a centripetal force challenging the king's control, despite owing their offices to him, diverging from the English pattern.[29] The new lower nobility, the *servientes regis*, had ties with the king that were more conditional and hierarchical, especially in the early period, holding land as a royal donation. They owed military service not in return for this land, however, but because they now belonged to the "royal household," a fictional entity assembling those tied to the king through ties of fidelity

---

[21] Bónis 1965, 289.
[22] When lay and ecclesiastical lords witnessed a donation by King Béla II in 1137, he claimed it occurred with the will and consent of the whole kingdom (*totius regni voluntate et consilio*); Eckhart 1939, 213.
[23] Eszláry 1959, 109–13; Engel 2001, 40.   [24] Bak 1999, xxxv.   [25] Eckhart 1939, 215.
[26] Molnár 2001, 32; Makkai 1990a, 20.   [27] Rady 2014; Molnár 2001, 32–34.
[28] Engel 2001, 91–93; Függedi 1986, 43.   [29] Rady 2000, 31–35, 38.

(*fidelitas*) and protection.[30] In this period, they were also still subject to taxation, only gaining full exemption after the fourteenth century.[31]

It was this group that petitioned the king for a charter of rights, the Golden Bull, in 1222 (and in 1231).[32] They demanded to be placed under the king's direct jurisdiction to counter the higher nobility.[33] As in Magna Carta, relations of dependence generated judicial demands; the *servientes* wanted *more* royal government, not less.[34] Petitioners demanded that justice be delivered regularly, so court meetings were to be held annually in Székesfehérvár "to hear cases" and that the king protect the *servientes* against the magnates and remove them from the jurisdiction of the lords. But they also asserted stronger claims than their English counterparts, for instance, to have the right to name heirs by will. They asked that their lands revert to the crown only when no relatives existed; that royal lands not be granted in perpetuity, as this allowed their holders to develop independent power in the localities, threatening them; that they were not obliged to follow the king on military expeditions abroad; and that they be exempt from some taxes.[35]

The same dynamic underlies the second constitutional moment, when a new lower nobility forced the king to reconfirm the Golden Bull in the assembly of 1267 and to give them a role in government and the administration of justice. As in 1222, they demanded that they be judged by the king and palatine, not local lords. They too were recruited into the royal army and granted land in the provinces and noble status to counterbalance the baronial class.[36] Barons had grown in power again, especially after the Mongol invasion in 1241, which killed more than 20 percent of the population.[37] Under such pressures, assemblies had been sparse until the last quarter of the thirteenth century.

Nonetheless, as in England, this second constitutional moment occurred whilst county judicial structures were being strengthened. Historians typically describe this as the transition from the "royal" to the "nobiliary county," as a step to greater autonomy for the new service nobility. However, the transition resembles the "territorial anchoring" we observed in England: the court system was guided by the crown; it was an "organ of the state apparatus."[38] Developments were not linear and backsliding occurred as royal power receded in some areas while baronial power grew. Nonetheless, the crown ordained that the service nobility

[30] Rady 2015, 70, 79; 2000, 3, 35–44, 144–46; but see footnote 12.
[31] Rady 2000, 145–46.   [32] Makkai 1990b, 25; Rady 2000, 39.
[33] Holub 1958, 94–95; Rady 2015, 70–71; 2000, 35–38.
[34] The Bull is translated in Bak 1999, 32–35.   [35] Engel 2001, 93–95; Rady 2014.
[36] Makkai 1990b, 30; Barta 1975, 65–66; Engel 2001, 120.
[37] Engel 2001, 98–100, 102; Makkai 1990a, 26–28.   [38] Makkai 1990b, 30, 28–30.

elect four judges/sheriffs (the *iudices servientium*, later *nobilium*, or *szolgabírák*) from its ranks, delivering county justice typically on property rights claims.[39] Original court powers were limited, however. Béla IV (1235–70) remedied this by recognizing the lands of the service nobility as free and by "unifying the judiciary powers of the *ispáns* and sheriffs and creating county courts with enforcing powers."[40] Judicial business was carried out in county assemblies (*congregationes*) held multiple times per year, which were also convened by a royal official.[41] This judicial activity made county courts central to local life. The "noble county" thus acquired quasi-corporative form by 1280.[42]

This judicial infrastructure coordinated by the state was also crucial for the growth of representation. In a decree of 1267, Béla ordered that "each county was obliged to send two to three representatives to the royal legislative assembly."[43] As in England, county courts handled this obligation. However, unlike England, the crown introduced the lower nobility to these practices to counterbalance the high nobility, the barons – an instance of second-best constitutionalism.[44] Demands were more radical than in England accordingly: in 1298, a law stipulated that the Royal Council be staffed by members elected by the Diet, but this was not observed.[45]

Petitions were as central here as they were in all other cases. They were submitted to the royal court and chancellery, especially by the landed nobility pursuing matters of inheritance or possession.[46] The "clamour of petitioners" was so high that kings had to devise mechanisms to either limit them by requesting them in writing or divert them to regular institutions, for instance, the itinerant palatine or the high judge. Yet the institutional fusion observed in England was not reproduced effectively, given weaker ruler powers, and assemblies did not yet consolidate. Moreover, the practice of collective responsibility cannot be traced through accessible sources. However, clans and family structures (*aviticitas*) were central in shaping landholding and inheritance until 1848, so their role should be further studied.[47]

10.1.1.3 Fourteenth to Sixteenth Centuries: Royal Strength, Judicial Infrastructural Growth, and Parliamentary Fluctuations The constitutional moments observed in the fourteenth century were also instances

[39] Engel 2001, 120; Eszláry 1959, 267–69.   [40] Makkai 1990a, 30.
[41] Eszláry 1959, 269–71.   [42] Eszláry 1959, 262–71; Engel 2001, 120–21.
[43] Makkai 1990b, 29–30.
[44] The terms used were *parlamentum publicum, parlamentum generale, congregatio totus*; see Eszláry 1959, 227.
[45] Eckhart 1939, 214.   [46] Rady 1999, 303; 2001, 639–40; Bónis 1965, 300.
[47] Rady 2015, 51, 85–101.

of second-best constitutionalism, mostly predicated on the service nobility, not the barons. These occurred under the Angevin kings, whose reigns (1301–82) have been called the "apogee" of Hungarian power.[48] Despite royal strength, assemblies were only held until 1323, a constitutional moment happened around 1351/52, and then assemblies are not recorded until the 1380s (Figure 10.1). This does not challenge my argument, which is confined to necessary conditions. The claim is not that all rulers were budding constitutionalists determined to hold parliaments when their power was strong – only that if we do observe enduring polity-wide parliamentary activity, we should expect stronger ruler powers.

But the decline merits an explanation. Its answer lies again in royal incapacity to subdue the baronial class and thus achieve effective territorial anchoring throughout the kingdom. This condition also explains why, even when assemblies became increasingly frequent after 1387, through dynamics that resemble those of city-states more than England, elites were unable to sustain collective action over the long term, leading to defeat by the Ottomans. To the degree that assembly activity did occur, however, it was preceded by judicial centralization and at least temporary ruler strength. The following two subsections show in greater detail how Hungarian developments reflect this logic.

The Angevins, Representative Fluctuation, and Judicial Infrastructure, 1300–1382. The early reign of Charles (1301–42) echoes the model of parliaments forming in response to weakness. Charles embarked to restore royal power by reclaiming lands granted away by previous rulers and to curb baronial powers through civil war but also legal reform.[49] Assembly activity until 1323 happened under an embattled crown countering the barons by co-opting the lower nobility. This alliance helped Charles to win the civil war. However, the point is that, as such, assemblies did not last. Instead, the king governed with a much-reduced Royal Council, composed of select barons and prelates, where he continued to judge.[50]

Alternative hypotheses can't explain the decline of representative activity after 1323 either. Bellicist logic suggests that rulers had few incentives to strengthen administrative structures when military pressures were weak.[51] However, the argument cannot be extended to this case, as no decline in military pressures can be ascertained in this period; if anything, between 1316 and 1340 there were "only two years when no 'royal

---

[48] Engel et al. 2008, 57.
[49] Eszláry 1963, 217–19; Engel 2001, 124–25; Molnár 2001, 42–45.
[50] Engel 2001, 141–42; Eckhart 1939, 216.   [51] Ertman 1997, 277.

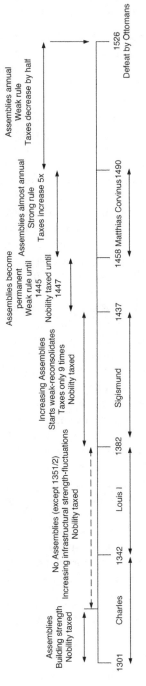

Figure 10.1 Hungarian trajectory, 1301–1526

campaign' was proclaimed."[52] Another hypothesis would be that assemblies lapsed because Hungary experienced a "resource curse": the largest European gold mines were discovered, accounting for three quarters of European production after 1320. This was added to an already large production of silver.[53] However, a sudden windfall is not sufficient to undermine constitutional practices: if infrastructural control had been strong, a new resource could have supplemented revenue, it need not have displaced it.[54] Rather, for assemblies to survive over time royal power over the most powerful had at least to be sustained and it was not.

Nonetheless, that central assemblies lapsed did not mean local judicial and representative practices did so too. Instead, the crown tried to undercut the high nobility by granting the lower nobility similar rights and by reorganizing both county and local judicial institutions.[55] Under Charles, royal officials, the vice-*ispáns*, supervised criminal, land, and peasant-related justice in the county courts, the *sedes iudiciaria* (i.e. seat of judgment, *sedria* in short). They ensured that the local nobility served as elected magistrates (the *iudices nobilium* or *szolgabírák*, with antecedents since the thirteenth century, as seen). Court burdens were considerable, as the court met twice a month.[56] This resembles the English pattern of "self-government at the king's command." More occasional was the triennial assembly called *congregatio generalis*, the supreme judicial forum of the county summoned by the king. This also elected office-holders and representatives. The local nobility selected twelve jurors to represent them.[57] As the assembly included and judged residents of all ranks, it created the concept of a community that embodied the entire realm in the central Diets.[58] This assembly included not just the barons and prelates but the lower nobility (gentry) as well and non-noble free-holders (until the fifteenth century) – an equalizing trend that evokes English conditions. Other assemblies, ordered by the king as inquisitions, examined a broad array of judicial cases. As Rady notes, the authority of the crown was enhanced by these measures.[59]

The next constitutional moment under Louis I (1342–82) occurred during another jurisdictional expansion aiming to undercut baronial privilege, in 1351–52. The one major Diet meeting had judicial purposes – legislation was issued by the Royal Council.[60] Louis further homogenized

---

[52] Engel 2001, 142, 130–32, 140.   [53] Engel 2001, 155; Molnár 2001, 46.
[54] Herb 2005; Haber and Menaldo 2011. This point is made about Sweden by Nilsson 2017, 148–49.
[55] See Eszláry 1963, 195–247 for an overview of the whole period.
[56] Rady 2000, 164–66; Eszláry 1963, 227–28, 233–34.   [57] Holub 1958, 97.
[58] Rady 2000, 166–67; Engel et al. 2008, ch. 2, §§76–78.
[59] Rady 2000, 166–69; Eckhart 1939, 218; Eszláry 1963, 231–33, 237–47.
[60] Eszláry 1963, 77–78.

the legal status of lower knights and the upper nobility, aiming to weaken the latter: he extended to all most liberties and rights of inheritance granted in 1222.[61] This echoes the English pattern of imposing legal equality across orders. Crucially, however, English kings first granted common law rights to *lower* tenants and only conceded these to the higher nobility after they collectively organized through Parliament, indicating higher original royal powers.

Louis' reforms aimed to re-centralize administration as counts grew more independent. For instance, from 1350, property rights cases moved from county to central, i.e. royal, law courts. Royal itineration was also key, as a top royal official administered the general eyre of the palatine, which became "the only local forum where the county gentry could meet a person who represented supreme authority" after 1342.[62] Louis restricted the inheritance rights of extended kin in favor of the crown, thus reducing clan power.[63] By the 1360s, he re-centralized county powers by concentrating two or more counties under one royal official, so that the government of the entire kingdom was administered by ten or twelve knights commanding troops (*seigneurs de bannerets*).[64] After 1370, he asserted the "king's right" (*jus regium*) on all lands for which title could not be proven.[65] But the family unit was strengthened, as land was entailed, "meaning that the noble estate was the common property 'in perpetuity' of the ancestor, i.e. of the original owner,"[66] similarly to England but perhaps even more restrictively.

These policies look remarkably like those of Henry II and Henry III, examined in Part I. Yet they are viewed as evidence of county "decline" by some Hungarian historians.[67] What really indicates a "decline," however, is that at the same time, barons were "trampling" on the local nobility, thus inhibiting royal jurisdiction at higher rates than in England in the formative early period. So when counts lost the monopoly over the right to convict and punish criminals, the *ius gladii*, it was not royal institutions that took over, but local lords instead.[68] The crown also had to exempt the lower nobility from a tax, which great lords evaded, enabling them to recruit more peasants. This is similar to a pattern in Russia (see Chapter

---

[61] Engel 2001, 175.   [62] Engel 2001, 179.

[63] Louis generously allowed that daughters could be "promoted to a son" so that they could inherit, through the legal device of the *prefectio in filium*; Engel 2001, 177–78; Rady 2015, 88, 92–93.

[64] Eszláry 1963, 294, 200–201.

[65] This affected landholder interests and was not resolved until 1410, when the mechanism of transferring to the occupant "latent royal rights" was introduced; Engel 2001, 149.

[66] Engel 1990, 44.   [67] Engel 2001, 179–80.   [68] Rady 2015, 6; Engel 2001, 180.

12), showing how tax exemptions of lower groups often occur when the crown cannot control the most powerful lords.[69]

By Louis' death in 1382, only a third of the kingdom was under his control, with the Church as the only other major single landholder.[70] Following the pattern noted already, where control over the high nobility weakened, inclusion of the lower classes, the non-nobles, suffered. They were sidelined in the county courts after the 1380s and were finally excluded in 1433–35. Assemblies thus "became almost exclusively an institution of the nobility,"[71] reflecting the weaker territorial anchoring of the Hungarian regime. This veered the regime into the aristocratic trajectory that proved fatal a century later. When barons grew in power in England, by contrast, as after the 1380s or during the War of the Roses (1455–85), Parliament was already institutionally consolidated.

So, it's not that Hungarian rulers lacked incentives to create an administrative apparatus before 1450; they took similar measures to those observed in England from the 1200s. However, they faced stronger baronial resistance early on and failed at points.

Assembly Resurgence, Power Distribution, and Decline, 1380s–1520s. The subsequent period poses two questions: first, how parliaments started meeting more regularly after royal power suffered the downturn just described and how they were even further consolidated after the 1440s when, at the same time, royal power was fluctuating sharply and the baronial class often displayed semi-sovereign status. Assemblies were called occasionally after the 1380s; they became permanent after 1437, almost annual under the strong king Matthias Corvinus (1458–90), more frequent under the weak kings that followed, but then collapsed when they could not raise enough taxes to fund resistance against the Turks in 1526, leading to the break-up of the country. An account of origins cannot cover the whole of parliamentary development in each case, but some brief points will show how it is consistent with the logic proposed here.

Military pressures cannot explain the increase in assembly frequency after 1387, as they were also high before 1382,[72] though they indeed increased further in the 1400s, at a time of royal weakness and under the Ottoman threat, as Ertman notes.[73] The main point here is that these assemblies depended on the local court structures revamped by the Angevins, as described above, and further strengthened in the following period. County courts became the court of appeal for nobles of all status

---

[69] The nobility was, however, still obliged to allow the periodic debasements of the coinage by the king; Rady 2000, 146.
[70] Engel 2001, 148.   [71] Rady 2000, 169; Eszláry 1963, 231–32.
[72] Engel 2001, 157–69; 1990, 40–42; Bak 1990, 55–56.   [73] Ertman 1997, 286–87.

by 1405,[74] endowing counties with a corporative character.[75] Service was as binding here as it was in England: once elected, judges had to serve for a year unless they presented a valid reason or paid a fine, as in England.[76] Local judicial operations procedurally interlocked with central assemblies: all local court business was suspended during parliament sessions.[77] Crucially, just as in England, royal jurisdiction expansion had occurred by establishing rules of procedure, not substantive law, throughout the realm, as Rady has noted.[78]

Moreover, the representative outburst after 1437 may have met the same death as many others had it not been followed by two strong leaders, regent John Hunyadi (1446–53) and then his son and king, Matthias Corvinus (1458–90). From 1446, the Royal Council had to meet regularly to hear petitions, displaying some institutional fusion.[79] Matthias further consolidated his kingdom into "the leading power of central Europe."[80] He reasserted control over major barons and extensively reformed the central judicial system,[81] also raising taxes more than fivefold – and representation again spiked.[82]

However, the weakness of subsequent leaders led to an institution that ultimately collapsed. By 1500, the Diet had even acquired the right to elect officials assessing and collecting taxes as well.[83] It veered in a democratic direction, as the local nobility gained the right to be summoned individually, not by county representatives, amounting to thousands present.[84] Accordingly, the plenipotentiary powers of early representatives were supplemented with instructions (and eventually with imperative mandates).[85] As a result, tax revenue collapsed in the early 1500s from 800,000 florins under Matthias to under 200,000,[86] leaving the kingdom unable to face the Ottoman attack in 1526.

Economic approaches, as we have seen, tend to ascribe such weakness to commercial, especially urban, weakness and dependence on the state. Indeed, Hungary's urban population is estimated at only 3.4 percent of the total with Austrian and Czech lands, whereas the highly urbanized regions in Europe were over 20 percent. But England's rate was 4.4 percent in 1300 and was even slightly less until 1500.[87] The problem rather was that, as in Castile and France, the Hungarian third estate was represented in parliament only by royal towns.[88] Royal weakness accounted for

---

[74] Engel 2001, 222.   [75] Rady 2000, 166–67; Engel 2001, 219–20; Bónis 1965, 290.
[76] Eszláry 1963, 227–28.   [77] Eszláry 1963, 97; Bónis 1965, 301–305.
[78] Rady 2015, 15.   [79] Eszláry 1963, 199.   [80] Engel 2001, 299–300.
[81] Rady 2015, 52, 50–55; Engel 2001, 302.
[82] Rady 2005, 6. Weaker kings allowed nobles to attend individually, not through representation; Eckhart 1939, 218–19.
[83] Rady 2005, 8–10, 18.   [84] Eszláry 1963, 88.   [85] Holub 1958, 100, 104–107.
[86] Rady 2005, 3, 7.   [87] Bairoch et al. 1988, 259.   [88] Eszláry 1963, 338–43.

that: many towns and the surrounding countryside were under noble or ecclesiastical jurisdiction, so they were represented through their lords. Hungarian towns appear weak because they were outnumbered by nobles.[89] Wherever the crown could not control the nobility, as will be seen for parts of the Holy Roman Empire, towns suffered. Towns were also only entitled to "hear and report" in parliament and did not obtain legislative powers, which we have also seen to be an indicator of weak central powers.[90] Yet, royal cities provided "the principal source of royal revenues."[91] Nor was urban freedom lacking in Central Europe.[92] Another factor may have been critical: in Hungary, towns were mostly populated by foreign groups, especially Germans, who were not well integrated into the public sphere; this may have inhibited further urban growth.[93] Urban size and importance cannot be treated as exogenous to the political power balances in place.

In any case, representative practice in Hungary had had regularity due to the judicial integration of the realm and the Diet's judicial functions. These caused it to be called until 1848 in the Habsburg-ruled provinces of Hungary, even when it was not a governing body.[94] What made such integration possible was spikes in royal authority. When such authority lapsed, the territorial anchoring of the regime suffered, as did the crown's power over the most powerful, undermining not just representation but the regime itself.

10.1.2 Poland

Hungarian patterns were not exceptional; Polish ones were very similar, even though accessible sources do not permit as detailed a process-tracing. In the 1570s Poles proudly declared they were electing their kings and co-legislating with them, later asserting the right of resistance; their "Republic of Nobles" survived into the eighteenth century.[95] Seventeenth-century Poland was much closer to the modern democratic model than its English counterpart ever was before the nineteenth century. The assembly was in fact so strong that nobles possessed full and equal veto powers (*liberum veto*). This attested to both noble class power

---

[89] Eszláry 1963, 339; Bak 1990, 65.
[90] Holub 1958, 99; Eckhart 1939, 219; Bónis 1965, 294.
[91] Eszláry 1963, 338, 341, 250; Engel et al. 2008, ch. 2, §§79–87.
[92] Eszláry 1959, 371, 338–43.   [93] Eszláry 1963, 248–50; Engel 2001, 260–62.
[94] The Diet continued to be called until 1848 in the parts of Hungary under Habsburg rule; it was not a governing body, but its judicial functions preserved its regularity.
[95] Fedorowicz et al. 1982; Uruszczak 1997, 196; Miller 1983, 65–67.

and crown weakness. It also paralyzed action leading to the dismemberment of the state in 1795.

Yet, like Hungary and the city-states that appeared to challenge my thesis, at critical points Poland depended on the dynamics foregrounded in this account. A polity-wide representative institution, the *Sejm*, was consolidated in 1495. But representative activity was extended first at the local level after the 1440s and 1450s, ultimately drawing on institutional innovations of the 1380s. These in turn would not have been possible without the reassertion of royal authority after the 1320s, following the fragmentation of the kingdom in the previous century. Two kings renowned for their strength spearheaded this transformation, Casimir the Great (1333–70) and Louis I (1370–82; he was also king of Hungary and unified the crowns). They consolidated what historians have called the "*Corona Regni Poloniae* at the height of its power."[96]

Ultimately, this account concurs with Ertman's ascription of Poland's eventual collapse to "structurally weak monarchs" who could not prevent state institutions being appropriated by a patrimonial elite.[97] However, these conditions were not caused by variation in war pressures; rather, they were often endogenous to existing power balances, as elsewhere. Kings still sought to erect administrative structures, but their resources were weaker.

The process of state consolidation pitted Polish kings against powerful local magnates, dukes and palatines with formidable local governing and jurisdictional powers. So kings replaced dukes with royal agents (*starostas*), who took over the local judicial institutions (*wiece*).[98] *Starostas* were called "royal arms" (*brachia regale*) and performed a function similar to that of sheriffs – like them, they were removable at will.[99] Yet they too eventually gained too much power, turning into rival forces. But Casimir unified state chanceries and codified customary law to create a Polish "common law," whilst ruling by Royal Council.[100] Interest in creating an effective administration was not lacking, therefore. Just like the University of Cracow was founded in 1364 but neglected until 1400,[101] administration-building was hampered by limited resources. After 1374 the new king, Louis I, had to even decrease tax collection, from 12 gros per manor to 2, due to noble resistance – he had tenuous control over the country.[102]

Louis too faced powerful magnates, who claimed the right to advise kings at the center and who dominated the main local assemblies, the

---

[96] Gieysztor 1979, 107; Bardach 1977, 251.   [97] Ertman 1997, 285–86, 315.

[98] Russocki 1976, 105–106. Regional variation existed that cannot be done justice here.

[99] Gieysztor 1979, 108.   [100] Gieysztor 1979, 108–11; Uruszczak 1997.

[101] Gieysztor 1979, 133; Knoll 1968, 248–49.   [102] Lukowski and Zawadzki 2006, 34.

judicial *wiece*.[103] It was, accordingly, from a position of weakness that the next constitutional moment emerged, when Louis extended privileges to the whole of the nobility with the statute of Koszyce in 1374. He extended privileges to broader sections of the population in exchange for military service, whilst reducing the tax burden (and securing the succession of a royal daughter).[104] The very thinly sourced historical works present the moment as a concession to a nobility led by the magnates, so it is not clear if this was a case of second-best constitutionalism – where a king faced with powerful magnates co-opts the lower nobility by granting rights. But the promise to the lower nobility to suppress the justiciars, who delivered justice, undermined magnate interests, which is why it was not achieved until much later.[105]

Nonetheless, after the crown imposed this juridical framework of rights, it helped unify the Polish nobility into a large class, the *szlachta*, which provided them with a collective identity and turned them into the "*communitas nobilium*."[106] The first Polish Diet (*Sejm*) was called shortly thereafter, in 1384–86, though the lower nobility did not yet have electoral rights.[107] Functional layering did not fully occur – law was made by the Royal Council, which accorded to the nobility its *habeas corpus* rights, for instance (the *captivabimus*).[108] Crucially, the central assembly did not involve taxation negotiations.[109] Although nobles (as well as clergy and some towns) were personally exempt from taxation, they still had to approve taxation over their underlying populations.[110] Accordingly, as in France, taxes were decided at the local and provincial level, the *sejmiki* and provincial *sejms*, which were predicated on the aforementioned judicial structures.[111] Though the crown encouraged this, it is best seen as reflecting royal weakness, also observed in the assembly's power to select the queen's husband, as Ertman noted.[112] In fact, "early Jagellonian Poland was dominated by the great nobles."[113]

This second stage better exemplifies second-best constitutionalism. As part of his struggle against the magnates, the king supported the gentry and "the young barons of the kingdom" as well as the towns. At the next constitutional moment, when the Nieszawa liberties of 1454 were

---

[103] Górski 1976, 255; 1968, 40.
[104] Bardach 1977, 261; Lukowski and Zawadzki 2006, 34–36.
[105] Górski 1976, 255–56; Bardach 1965, 262.
[106] Górski 1976, 254–55; Bardach 1965, 262.
[107] Ertman 1997, 293; Górski 1976, 258.   [108] Górski 1966, 123.
[109] Bardach 1965, 266.
[110] Bardach 1965, 262, 266–67. See the discussion in Myśliwski 2008, 274–75.
[111] Górski 1966, 124; Bardach 1965, 266–67. The judicial *wiec* remained separate, however.
[112] Ertman 1997, 293, 285.   [113] Miller 1983, 71.

granted, the king again favored the gentry and "opened the way to the parliamentary system by widening [their] liberties while restricting those of the oligarchy."[114] So after the 1450s the monarchy gave "the gentry a consultative role distinct from – and as a counterweight to – that of the magnates."[115] As the historian Frost points out, however, this still did not amount to a "watershed" in Polish politics nor the right to consent to new laws, only the *sejmiks'* right to consultation.[116]

One thing that the *Sejm* did demand, strikingly, was functional layering. Kings served as supreme judges in the *Sejm* as in England, but laws had to be passed asking them to "hold regular judicial sessions twice a week … during the *Seym* debates so that the two might overlap" and so that adjudication did not lag. But kings were unable to "manage the mass of cases submitted" to them after the 1520s, as noble petitions and judicial disputes were streaming into the *Sejm*.[117] Still, some petitions even began to shape legislation, as elsewhere (though, as for Hungary, they seem not yet systematically treated by historians). Royal courts were also in demand, especially for appeals, as litigants wanted to avoid local courts controlled by power-holders; local courts consequently declined by the late 1400s, similarly to England, but nobles were subject to their own courts.[118] Similar building blocks, however, had different aggregate outcomes due to ruler weakness.

Ruler strength also affected the institutional development of the *Sejm*, which was first divided in two chambers under Jan Olbracht (1492–1501). Such division was explained in Chapter 2 as a consequence of ruler strength, albeit here this strength was very temporary. Indeed, Olbracht had a strong following in the lower nobility: he accorded them a series of privileges, by removing them from the jurisdiction of the *starostas* and tenants-in-chief, i.e. the magnates, and by restricting the rights of peasants and townspeople.[119] The chamber division was, moreover, enabled by the local judicial institutions that were strengthened in the previous decades, allowing the local nobility to elect representatives.[120]

Thereafter, however, the Chamber of Deputies became so independent that collective action was undermined. But it was the king who first ensured that it became a co-equal branch of government after 1505,

[114] Gieysztor 1979, 120, 121.
[115] Miller 1983, 71–72; Wyczański 1982, 92; Bardach 1977, 273; Lukowski and Zawadzki 2006, 49.
[116] Frost 2015, 240, 237–41. Frost also disputes the counterweight thesis, but does not explain why.
[117] Uruszczak 1997, 195.
[118] Uruszczak 1997, 191–92. Non-state based adjudication was, however, well-entrenched; Uruszczak 1997, 190, 192–96.
[119] Górski 1966, 135; Miller 1983, 73.   [120] Górski 1966, 137.

with the statute of *Nihil Novi* which stipulated that "nothing new" could be decided without its input.[121] This was granted so "that the monarchy would never again be at the magnates' mercy."[122] The more radical rights ascribed to the Polish representative body indeed stemmed from royal weakness. Eventually, however, the imperative mandate prevailed, displaying the Polish nobility's greater independence that led to the *liberum veto* – any member could reject a decision, taking the principle of *quod omnes tangit* to its logical conclusion.[123] Bellicist logic correctly notes that these developments occurred under military pressure and central weakness. But these precocious constitutional steps under a weak crown, while increasing concessions to the lower nobility and producing the "democracy of the *szlachta*" by the 1570s, ultimately undermined the *Sejm*'s capacity to operate as an effective organ of governance.[124]

The problem, however, was not the lower nobility's increased strength; it was royal incapacity to control the magnates. Magnate armed forces "were often equal in size to the peacetime army of the Crown."[125] The local nobility sought support from a crown too weak to offer a counterweight, unlike originally in England. Critically, the crown had to accept that *starostas* became "immovable landed officials for life," i.e. conditionality was undermined.[126] The Senate accordingly gained in strength, whereas taxation decisions remained in the local diets. But this meant great imbalances between regions, greater resistance, and fewer revenues. It also meant that the territorial anchoring observed in England, which bound agrarian and urban populations to the center, did not occur. When external pressures became overwhelming in the early 1700s, as earlier in Hungary, the entrenched rights of the institution obviated a solution to the collective action problem and Poland was eventually dismembered.

10.2   Sweden and Denmark

Similar patterns are observable in Sweden and Denmark. The main feature to be foregrounded from the perspective of this book is that the crown was elected during the formative early period.[127] This suggests it was relatively weaker and depended on the most powerful actors of the realm. Population was low before 1300 – around 600,000 in Sweden,

---

[121] Burkhardt 2015, 160–61; Uruszczak 1997, 183.
[122] Miller 1983, 73; Górski 1966, 136.
[123] Bardach 1965, 272, 281–83; Miller 1983, 78–79. See Chapter 4.
[124] Górski 1966, 136–37; Gieysztor 1979, 149–56.
[125] Gieysztor 1979, 192 for quote, 193–96.   [126] Górski 1966, 136.
[127] Helle 2003, 347.

slightly more in Denmark.[128] These traits affected representative practice, since Scandinavian royal assemblies "never became permanent political institutions," unlike Western European ones.[129] Rather, they too developed a more institutionalized form of the Royal Council, especially after 1280.[130] Both cases developed constitutional practices, but both also succumbed to absolutist rule, though Denmark remained that way into the modern period. Only a brief overview can be offered here, showing how weaker executive power in Denmark underlay this divergence. Sweden was closer to England, but its kings lacked the capacity to integrate society as effectively.

Reliable comparative data on extraction and assemblies are lacking, so the analysis must remain suggestive. As in all cases, land was held of the crown. Sweden in particular resembles England in having conditional tenures and no subinfeudation, both signs of relative royal strength. Fiefs were apparently not heritable.[131] Royal control was strongly tied to Church initiative in both cases.[132] As again in England, provinces had a homogeneous administrative structure,[133] generated by the crown in alliance with bishops. The king was the supreme judge in both kingdoms by the late thirteenth century[134] and judicial activity was originally central to the provincial assemblies (the "things").[135]

The Swedish crown was relatively stronger than its Danish counterpart. Private jurisdiction was almost totally absent there after the 1200s.[136]Another indicator was the free peasantry. The peasants are typically discussed as an independent, idiosyncratic element of both societies.[137] Yet, in Sweden they were subject to direct royal taxation that stemmed from the commutation of either purveyance (the supply of goods to the itinerant king) or military service.[138] The term "peasants" seems to denote a lower social class than was included in the English and other parliaments; however, their legal status seems closer to English tenants or even freeholders[139] and it is unclear if they were poorer.[140]

---

[128] Vahtola 2003, 566, 564.   [129] Helle 2003, 351.
[130] Skovgaard-Petersen 2003, 361–63; Ertman 1997, 308–309.
[131] Emilsson 2005, 22–23.   [132] Schück 1987, 9; Hørby 1997, 197–99.
[133] Ertman 1997, 307, 312.   [134] Helle 2003, 349.
[135] This is only indirectly acknowledged, as judicial functions lapsed in the 1400s; Schück 2003a, 689.
[136] Lindkvist 1997, 223.   [137] Skovgaard-Petersen 2003, 355; Nilsson 2017, 126.
[138] Lindkvist 2003, 231.
[139] Orrman 2003, 300–303; Lönnroth 1955, 126; Emilsson 2005, 24, 30. The true distinctiveness of the Swedish system is the lack of serfdom.
[140] The new data from the Maddison project suggest that after 1300 Sweden had higher per capita revenue than France (English comparative data n/a); www.ggdc.net/maddison. Other estimates place France higher than England and Sweden lower than both; Álvarez-Nogal and Prados de La Escosura 2012, 23.

The relations of dependence, as in England, aggregated to collective rights – only here these included the right to elect the king. Danish peasants, by contrast, were also believed to be free but were in fact tenants of lay or ecclesiastical lords, reflecting even weaker royal powers.[141] This weakness also enabled the influx of German nobility that developed feudal relations with the local population, as Ertman noted, creating a strong centrifugal force that put Denmark on a different trajectory.[142]

Other key indicators, however, suggest that both Scandinavian kings were relatively weaker than English ones. Noble tax immunity was crucial; in exchange for the land they received nobles only provided military service and they retained a privileged position throughout the period, especially through the Royal Council.[143] Noble tax immunity in fact pushed the two lower estates in Denmark, the burghers and clergy, to support a hereditary absolutist monarchy that could break noble power after 1660.[144]

Royal relative weakness was also reflected in the judicial system. Local Danish assemblies were very active, voting on taxes and even on royal elections. As they retained separate provincial laws, however, the crown could not achieve the territorial anchoring observed in England that flowed from judicial control. A national law was instituted only in 1683.[145] Swedish kings imposed a uniform law code from the mid-1300s, which enabled relatively stronger territorial anchoring of the crown in the provinces.[146] However, Sweden's semi-federal character kept judicial functions localized originally.[147] So the population was less integrated in the central judicial or legislative activity of the realm in both cases – as argued, lack of institutional fusion typically reflects royal weakness. This helps explain why Swedish representative *practice* did not involve legislation by broader social orders: the "legal right of 'commonalty' to participate in decisions affecting the entire kingdom was limited to royal elections and taxation," not legislation.[148]

Nonetheless, as this book suggests, representation emerged under a strong king, Magnus Eriksson (1319–64). He was strong enough to pass the aforementioned common rural land law, the Landlaw that lasted until 1719.[149] Strong royal powers also underlay the next step in representative practice, under the rising but challenged king, Gustav Vasa (1523–60). Faced with a powerful nobility, he incorporated the free peasants into a national central system of representation after 1527

---

[141] Skovgaard-Petersen 2003, 355.   [142] Ertman 1997, 306–308.
[143] Skovgaard-Petersen 2003, 360–61; Schück 2003b, 399.   [144] Ertman 1997, 310.
[145] Skovgaard-Petersen 2003, 358, 356–59.   [146] Helle 2003, 348.
[147] Lindkvist 1997, 219–23.   [148] Schück 1987, 27.   [149] Schück 2003b, 404–409.

(later called *Riksdag*), generating another case of the second-best constitutionalism observed in Poland and Hungary.

Gustav expanded royal strength the most, after liberating Sweden from the Kalmar Union with Denmark and Norway and getting elected from a strong base. In addition to the silver/gold reserves he amassed, he increased tax collection, contrary to old views – though taxation was not important in early meetings.[150] He also expropriated extensive Church lands before England's Henry VIII did and made the monarchy hereditary.[151] Royal power was also asserted by enforcing the conditionality of relations with the critical group: the same peasants that were being included in parliament now faced strict rules that failure to pay taxes three years in a row reverted their land to the crown.[152]

Scholars with access to primary and further secondary sources can uncover how petition-making and collective responsibility interacted with political centralization. But available evidence suggests that the weaker powers of the Swedish monarchy compared to England, ironically leading to its more "democratic" character, undermined the constitutional structure for an extended period. This led to the mix of constitutionalism and autocracy that has divided scholarly views and made Swedish history less linear than the English one. In Denmark, where local lords were strong, absolutism prevailed, as it did in neighboring France.

10.3   The Holy Roman Empire

The Holy Roman Empire was a major player in medieval and early modern Europe. It was an inordinately complex agglomeration of hundreds of kingdoms, principalities, counties, duchies, Free Imperial Cities, prince-bishoprics and other units.[153] It never developed an effective polity-wide governing institution, however. The local assemblies (the *Landtage*), though widespread, eventually declined; as they did not define the regime as a whole, it is commonly judged "absolutist." Given the findings of this book, it is not surprising that it displayed many of the constitutional building-blocks found in England, some to an even higher degree. It exhibited intense levels of local resistance, for instance, as the historian Blickle has provocatively argued.[154] Yet for the Imperial Diet, the emperor's role was key: he issued the summons and could ennoble princes and thus admit them to its chamber.[155] He also served as judge.[156] Similarities even in petition-making are striking.[157] The main

---

[150] Nilsson 2017, 152–54, 127.   [151] Schück 1987, 45.   [152] Emilsson 2005, 54.
[153] Gunlicks 2003, 13.   [154] Blickle 1997a, 58–61.   [155] Neu 2015, 191.
[156] Berman 1983, 486–87.   [157] Kümin and Würgler 1997.

difference, I argue here, lay in ruler power. Systematic evidence on early values of key variables for this account, for instance distribution of land, collective responsibility, or the imposition of service, is not readily accessible. The task instead is to suggest that they are congruent with the book's logic; future studies can test the claims in more detail.

Ruler weakness is observed at both the imperial and local levels. The emperor's original task was to sustain the Peace of God, as in other weaker states like France.[158] He was originally elected, like Polish and Hungarian kings,[159] so his power was shared with the lay and ecclesiastical princes. As with France and Castile, the Diets included towns and nobles but the rural population mostly lacked independent representation, reducing the territorial anchoring of the regime.[160] Judicial integration was accordingly weak. The Diet was separate from the two judicial institutions, the Imperial Chamber Court and the Aulic Council, which after the 1490s decided cases that affected the whole empire, not the individual territories – similarly to the personal imperial court that preceded them.[161] No institutional fusion was achieved, therefore, and the Diet never acquired the governing functions its equivalent in England did; contemporaries complained it was ineffective.[162] The radical adoption of unanimity in voting on religious issues after 1555 (which implies weaker capacity to compel subjects into agreement) further "made imperial politics much more difficult."[163] Size mattered of course, but the deeper reason, as Ertman noted, was that emperors lacked a "geographically compact base."[164]

Moreover, imperial courts could not penetrate the localities.[165] Imperial weakness is now re-written by historians as a symptom of jurisdictional autonomy retained by local princes, a process underwritten by imperial legislation in the thirteenth century.[166] Local diets (*Landtage*) accordingly proliferated at that level after the 1400s. These units were also quite small; Hesse had a population of 250,000, Württemberg probably 450,000, whilst Prussia was more sparsely populated.[167] Yet, in some provinces nobles and major towns sought independence as Imperial Knights and Cities, so they "disappeared from the diets, which henceforth were attended only by the clergy and the towns."[168] Deprived of the most powerful actors, the diets were accordingly weakened; elsewhere, the nobility dominated them.[169] So the estates "never succeeded

---

[158] Berman 1983, 493–95.   [159] Gunlicks 2003, 12; Berman 1983, 485.
[160] Blickle 1997a, 40.   [161] Fuchs 2003.   [162] Burkhardt 2015, 168.
[163] Schulze 1986, S50.   [164] Ertman 1997, 234.
[165] Du Boulay 1978, 345; Gunlicks 2003, 13.
[166] Arnold 1991, 6, 186–210; Berman 1983, 509–10; Reuter 2006, 406–12.
[167] Kümin and Würgler 1997, 41; Carsten 1959, 4–5.   [168] Carsten 1959, 3, 423.
[169] Carsten 1959, 425.

in translating their considerable financial leverage into effective participation in areas of government other than direct taxation" at the polity level, despite handling petitions. They did not become "co-rulers" as in England, Poland, Hungary, and Sweden.[170] Despite having greater powers than the English Parliament in fiscal and foreign policy, even war, they had no judicial functions nor could they initiate legislation; they only presented grievances through petitions, as in Hesse.[171] So they ultimately weakened after 1648.

Princes and emperors, this account implies, thus faced powerful landlords originally and were less able to compel them systematically either through taxation[172] or service. This resulted in weaker territorial anchoring of ruler power in the principalities and weaker judicial integration. Urban weakness, often deemed to enable absolutism,[173] is better seen as endogenous to weak ruling powers. The decline of towns in parts of Germany after the sixteenth century noted by Barrington Moore[174] was preceded by the commercial tax privileges of the nobility, whilst towns shouldered most of the tax burden.[175] The nobility's "strong anti-urban" bias[176] could only be consequential where state protection of towns was weak – a weak bourgeoisie would thus be the result of urban decline not the cause. Where German princes "were much weaker" than English kings and the nobility and free cities gained tax exemptions whilst others carried the fiscal burden, the foundations for robust and inclusive representative institutions were lacking.[177] Conversely, where the prince was stronger than the nobility, the diet was stronger too, as in Württemberg – there the diet also received petitions, displaying institutional fusion, and the countryside was also represented, albeit not independently.[178] Why Prussia built a strong state out of similar conditions without developing a constitutional regime after the seventeenth century cannot be fully answered without recognizing both the parallels and differences with England on many levels.

*

This chapter has aimed to show an alternative path to parliamentary practice that emerges when the crown cannot compel the higher nobility as comprehensively as English kings could. The latter did not allow military service to displace other obligations, including taxation. Weaker kings elsewhere had to allow this and to include lower social

---

[170] Ertman 1997, 241, 224.   [171] Carsten 1959, 442; Kümin and Würgler 1997, 42–44.
[172] Isenmann 1999.   [173] Anderson 1974b, 252.   [174] Moore 1967, 418.
[175] Carsten 1954, 170–73; 1959, 439.   [176] Carsten 1954, 172.
[177] Carsten 1959, 1–148, 442, 423, 439.
[178] Kümin and Würgler 1997, 44; Carsten 1959, 3–6.

strata to counteract the higher nobility, generating in some cases at least second-best constitutionalism. This dynamic is closer to the bargaining model challenged in this book, as rights were conceded to these lower groups as a result of weakness. But this was not a model that produced effective and durable polity-wide governing institutions. Nonetheless, the Hungarian, Polish, and Swedish cases showed that to the degree that assemblies continued, this was predicated on the infrastructural, especially judicial, build-up under strong kings, as well as the conditional relations between the ruler and the subjects involved in the constitutional practices. To the degree that rulers were even weaker, as in the Holy Roman Empire and Denmark, the representative activity that did occur did not succeed in shaping the regime and eventually atrophied.

11 Conditional Land Law, Property Rights, and "Sultanism": Premodern English and Ottoman Land Regimes

Conditionality of landholding has emerged as central to representative emergence across the cases examined in this book so far, from England to Hungary and Poland. It generated the bottom-up demand that made parliament regular, since it endowed rulers with jurisdiction over disputes, as well as the obligation that sustained institutional interaction. Conditional property rights predicated on strong state capacity also underlie the economic growth many have attributed to exogenous change such as trade. The Flemish, Dutch, Italian, and Catalan sections have shown how a political order based on conditionality preceded the "security of property rights" emphasized in neo-institutional accounts. Might conditionality be sufficient to generate representation?

The question does not require a counterfactual to be answered; cases abound, as conditionality was widespread throughout the premodern world. Holding land conditionally from a ruler was typical of most premodern regimes – including the Ottoman Empire and Russia, examined in this and the following chapters. This has been obscured because scholars have focused instead on the specific concept of feudalism and have sharply distinguished its Western from its non-Western forms.[1] As we have seen, Western feudalism is taken to denote weak central powers, an association observed in the Continental European cases – though not England. So no connection has ever been established between land regimes in East and West. Instead, in the Eastern cases, ruler ownership of land is conceived as symptomatic of absolutism and inimical to the secure property rights believed to underlie the West.

The revision proposed in this book, however, suggests that existing polarities drawn in the literature fail to register some crucial commonalities. Focusing on conditionality uncovers some striking parallels between cases traditionally viewed as opposed, namely constitutional England and the "sultanic" Ottoman Empire. Once the powers of the English crown over the land regime are acknowledged, Ottoman property rights appear

---

[1] For instance, in Japan; Bodde 1981; Duus 1976.

in a new light: below I argue they resembled English conditional tenure. If such a similarity in property rights can be shown for two regimes as diametrically opposed as these, then another key mechanism tying the economy to political outcomes is challenged. As argued already, any arguments prioritizing trade or economic growth must show how wealth translated into demands for constitutionalism. In Part III, we saw that mercantile wealth does not meet this challenge.

The main alternative would be land: some link must connect landed wealth to parliament, turning economic gains into legally protected rights, if the hypothesis holds. This is the approach for instance in North, Wallis, and Weingast's exploration of the emergence of open political orders, where special attention is devoted to the English land law.[2] Their argument, however, also does not explain how these economic dynamics translated into specific institutions; courts are treated as given and Parliament makes only incidental appearances in their book. An implicit functionalism must serve to explain institutional outcomes.[3] If, however, similar property rights are observed in cases without representative institutions, they cannot suffice to explain those outcomes.

To show this, this chapter tackles Ottoman "sultanism" as a classic foil to Western constitutionalism to show fundamental similarities in property rights with the most constitutional regime in the West. The Ottoman Empire is a "hard case," as it varies in religion, legal heritage, and cultural contact with the West more than any other case examined. Why, despite similar property rights regimes in England and the Ottoman Empire, institutional outcomes diverged is a question I address in Chapter 13, where the similarities with Russia are also explored.

Ever since Montesquieu, the Ottoman Empire's apparent "lack" of property rights has made it an exemplary "sultanic" regime in the social scientific literature, the opposite of constitutional polities.[4] Sultanism, as Weber defined it, was an extreme form of patrimonialism, claiming not just "full personal powers" for the ruler but an "arbitrary free will free of traditional limitations," thus leading to "fiscal arbitrariness."[5] For sociologist Perry Anderson, its "economic bedrock ... was the virtually complete absence of private property in land."[6] The Ottomanist Halil İnalcık invoked Persian Mirror-for-Princes literature that stipulated that the "land and the peasant belong to the sultan," exemplifying Marx's

---

[2] North et al. 2009, 77–109.

[3] This problem applies broadly; van Zanden et al. 2012; Boix 2015.

[4] Montesquieu [1748] 1989, books 2 and 3; Anderson 1974a, 365, 565; Acemoglu and Robinson 2012, 120.

[5] Weber 1947, 347, 357; 1978, 231–32.   [6] Anderson 1974a, 365.

"Asiatic mode of production."[7] The economist Timur Kuran qualified such readings by positing that property rights were not absent, only weak, in the Ottoman case.[8] Nonetheless, he still ascribed this weakness to the fact that the sultan could invoke the Islamic principle that "all property belongs to God" to engage in arbitrary confiscation.[9] Even in Karen Barkey's revisionist study, the lack of land ownership by the military elite prevented any ties between landholders and peasants, thus suppressing civil society.[10]

The "sultanic" nature of the Ottoman regime was already challenged in the eighteenth century and is now widely jettisoned as a stereotype by Ottomanists.[11] The Ottoman Empire is increasingly placed by a rich historiographical tradition in the context of early modern European polities. Its government emerges as pluralist and responsive to social concerns, both by showing how theory and practice diverged and by reconsidering the theoretical foundations of the sultanate.[12] Similarities with England have also been highlighted, but in its seventeenth-century "despotic" phase.[13] Despite these more nuanced views, however, the fact remains that the Ottoman Empire did not develop representative institutions indigenously (or a liberal, "open" economy). The empire is thus most typically compared with European absolutist regimes, principally France.[14] This chapter rejects property rights as a possible explanation of this divergence.

In what follows, I first show how Ottoman and English laws involved similar conditional property rights to land by distinguishing between Hanafi and Ottoman law. I then examine a key example of assumed weak Ottoman property rights, the military-administrative land units called *timars*, and compare them with Western fiefs, to show that they are fundamentally different entities. When comparing more equivalent property rights at the peasant level, we observe striking similarities to English ones. Moreover, both land regimes had common fiscal effects, land endowments that allowed tax evasion, the *vakıfs* and *uses*; I argue that their impact on the economy depended on state strength. I then show that property rights were also not more protected in England: in fact, expropriation was more extensive and arbitrary than in the Ottoman Empire.[15]

---

[7] İnalcık 1994, 105–107. But see İnalcık 1992.

[8] Kuran's aim is to revise the narratives about Ottoman economic backwardness; Kuran 2011, 127; 2001, 854–55, 860–61.

[9] Kuran 2001, 854; Shatzmiller 2001, 49.   [10] Barkey 1994, 36, 40–41, 89–93.

[11] See the remarkably enlightened assessments of the empire by the British Ambassador to the Porte, Sir James Porter (1710–76), for instance; 1771, 49ff.

[12] The literature is substantial and only a few works can be referenced here: Fleischer 1986; Imber 1997; Barkey 1994; 2008; Kafadar 1995; 2008; Darling 1996; 2013; Goffman 2002.

[13] For instance, see Tezcan 2010.   [14] Barkey 1994; Balla and Johnson 2009.

[15] Another striking similarity exists between the common law and *kadı* justice, as noted by Weber; Weber 1978, 892, 976–78.

The key to all these divergences, I argue, lay in the English crown's superior capacity to impose its will, not in its weakness or limits. Comparing an empire with a relatively small kingdom might appear incongruous, but the Ottoman Empire before 1370 was not much larger than England.[16] As noted, arguments based on size don't explain why a political unit could not develop a robust core and expand imperially over greater territory. England eventually did just that.

11.1   Ottoman and English Property Rights: Conditionality and Power

11.1.1   Private Property and Conditional State Control: Hanafi vs. Ottoman Land Law

Assumptions about Ottoman property rights being absent or weak stem from the belief that either Islamic law provided few or no protections to property rights or that the customary Ottoman tradition ascribed land ownership to the state. These assumptions, however, are misleading.

Ottomans mainly followed the Hanafi school, one of the four orthodox schools of law in Muslim jurisprudence.[17] Far from rejecting property rights, sale contracts under Hanafi law made property private and outside the reach of the state – hence strong sultanic opposition to it.[18] Hanafi law also imposed partible inheritance, thus securing the rights of *all* heirs of a property owner following rules of priority[19] – a far more equitable arrangement than the primogeniture that was obligatory in England until 1925.[20] If little land was held privately, it was partly because property holders wished to avoid such religious, not state, restrictions, opting for *vakıfs* instead, examined below.[21] Though private holdings (most of them urban) required a grant from the sultan, as did *vakıfs*, *tımars*, and peasant land,[22] this differed little from English conditions, as we will see.

Property rights, however, are assumed to be absent in the Ottoman Empire mainly because most land (about 87 percent in 1528) was held under a customary regime known as *miri* land.[23] This is normally

---

[16] Kafadar 1995.

[17] The best exposition of its main parameters is Colin Imber's study; Imber 1997.

[18] İnalcık 1994, 111.   [19] Schacht 1964, 169–73; Abu Zahra 1955, 161.

[20] And then it only ceased being the default in the absence of a will but can still be deployed in wills; Baker 2002, 269.

[21] Imber 2019, 160.   [22] Imber 1997, 128–29, 156–62; 2006, 236.

[23] İnalcık 1973, 110.

interpreted as "the sultan's" land,[24] suggesting personal ownership. However, when this regime acquired official legal justification by the highest judicial official of the empire, Ebu's-su'ud (c.1490–1574),[25] as the Ottomanist Colin Imber has shown in his major study, the terms were far more radical than in England. *Miri* land was specified as land held by the *Treasury*, which was "nominally the joint property of the Muslim community."[26] The sultan was thus not the actual owner, but the acting agent of the community, with the land at his "disposal . . . to administer on behalf of the community."[27] Similar ideas were expounded privately by the Scot George Buchanan at the same time, but his book was condemned by acts of the English Parliament in 1584 and 1664 and burned by the University of Oxford in 1683.[28] The claim that "the people, not kings, have property rights over the commonwealth" was first articulated in absolutist France, as the normative/empirical inversion pattern would predict.[29] Claims that were only made as revolutionary legal fiction in Europe were the official Ottoman doctrine at the same time. Moreover, both regimes derived the ruler's title to all land through conquest.[30] This land regime, finally, did not express "sultanist" preferences: a major aim, as Imber emphasized, was to "prevent [the realm's] excessive fragmentation through inheritance,"[31] which English law prevented through the most unequal practice of primogeniture.

A similarly qualified picture about the Ottoman property regime emerges from considering a basic military office, the *tımar*. I argue that since it was a bureaucratic office, it cannot inform us about property rights.

11.1.2 Western Patrimonial Fiefs and Ottoman Bureaucratic Offices, the Tımars

Classic and revisionist accounts of the Ottoman Empire focus on the *tımar* to exemplify the contrast with Western conditions.[32] *Tımars* were the smallest category of land grants awarded to members of the Ottoman military class, known as *sipahis*.[33] They were conditional upon the

---

[24] Imber 2011, 53. See Mahmasani 1955, 181 for full legal distinctions.

[25] Imber 1997, 8–20, 12.

[26] Imber 2006, 238. Also see Vikør 2005, 337; İnalcık 1994, 104.

[27] Imber 1997, 120–21.

[28] Macmillan 1906, 233; Skinner 1978, 342–43. Possibly because, as the tutor of the future James I, Buchanan subjected the "child-king to regular beatings" (Croft 2003, 12), James was not as taken with his ideas as Süleyman I was with those of his jurist.

[29] Lee 2008, 370.

[30] Gray and Gray 2009, 56; Simpson 1986, 2–4; İnalcık 1994, 103; Imber 2006, 218.

[31] Imber 2006, 238; 1997, 129.   [32] Anderson 1974a; Barkey 1994.

[33] For larger grants, see Kunt 1983, 9, 12–29. On *tımars* more general, see Imber 2010, 354–58; İnalcık 1973, 105–109.

performance of obligations to the ruler, as European military fiefs were, and this has supported the view the two offices were comparable. Yet they have seemed deficient in a number of features that characterized their Western counterparts. For instance, they did not involve ownership rights over land, they were not heritable, nor were they alienable. All these elements, however, demonstrate that *tımars* were offices closer to the Weberian ideal of bureaucracy, not forms of property rights.[34]

Western fiefs, indeed, granted property rights over land and over peasants living on the land, under a hierarchical relationship known as lordship.[35] The English crown's tenants-in-chief, for instance, originally acquired these rights of lordship over land and people in exchange for military service and exercised them through seigniorial courts.[36] Local political and judicial power was originally fused (though in England royal courts eventually supplanted local courts). However, rewarding service with jurisdiction over people and land was how Max Weber defined estate-type patrimonialism, one of the organizational types he claimed Western states had to progressively *eliminate* for rational, modern forms of bureaucracy to emerge.[37] Yet these traits are emblematic of the early English system's strong patrimonial character, as we have seen, and as Weber passingly noted.[38] *Tımar*-holders, by contrast, did not have lordship rights over land or over peasants living on the land.[39] Instead, service was rewarded with land revenues.[40] *Tımars* were thus not fiefs nor were they deficient as property rights; they were a different thing, an office, as İnalcık stressed.[41]

English fiefs were also heritable; they could succeed from father to son from the eleventh century and inheritance was established by the thirteenth.[42] Although secure succession is typically seen as a victory of property rights, here it was another victory for patrimonialism: it perpetuated rights over people. Moreover, "succession was no danger to the lord: it was an advantage ... The real gauge of the strength of the feudal relationship [was] the lord's disciplinary power: his ability to disinherit the tenant for disloyalty."[43] This ability, as argued in Chapter 2, was initially stronger in English kings than elsewhere, despite the strength of royal tenants-in-chief. Ottoman sultans were by contrast only engaging with officials at their employ. *Tımars* were not initially formally heritable,

---

[34] Ottomanists apply the term fief extensively, however; Gerber 1994; Imber 2011.

[35] Hudson 2012, 334–36, 630–32; Bloch 1965, 163–75; Reynolds 1994, 59–60.

[36] Pollock and Maitland 1898, 531–32; Dawson 1960, 184–87, 192–228.

[37] Weber 1978, 232–33, 235–37; Ertman 1997, 8.   [38] Rudolph and Rudolph 1979.

[39] Özel 1999, 230–31.   [40] İnalcık 1973, 111.   [41] İnalcık 1994, 115.

[42] Hudson 2012, 347–57, 645–53; Baker 2002, 265–68.

[43] Palmer 1985, 6; Hudson 2012, 347.

as bureaucratic principle would dictate.[44] However, heritability was permitted by decrees passed in the 1530s, though these granted only the right of sons to *a timar* fief, not to any particular one – i.e. to the office and status, after competence had been demonstrated.[45] Inheritance of specific *timars* was prohibited to prevent a "local landed class" from forming, though a decree in 1585 permitted it as well.[46] Such "property rights," however, only weakened Ottoman political cohesion.[47]

The same concern about land concentration also precluded the alienation of *timars*. In England, fiefs were alienated since the thirteenth century. Once again, however, any rights of alienation over a bureaucratic office would imply greater patrimonialism and venality – a trait that seriously undermined some Western cases.[48] When we consider Ottoman *peasant* rights to alienate below, we will note rights similar to England at that more appropriate level.

The Ottoman system, therefore, like the English one, was not arbitrary but rule-governed: lack of representative institutions did not mean ruler restraints were absent. Even when the sultan had the right to revoke a particular *timar*, he was bound by custom and imperial law to provide its holder with a replacement.[49] The sultan could also revoke a *timar* when a holder died without heirs (*musadara*) or fell from grace.[50] But this resembles the English royal prerogative of escheats, which applied under the same conditions,[51] and of forfeitures, which occurred when a tenant "commit[ted] a theft, betray[ed] his lord, ... desert[ed] him in a hostile encounter or military engagement, ... [was] defeated in trial by battle or ... commit[ted] a breach of the feudal bond."[52] Weber's contrast between feudal contractualism and sultanic arbitrariness is therefore unfounded.[53]

Yet, rather than emphasizing Ottoman "modernity" on this dimension, some simply conclude that the Ottoman and Western versions of feudalism were different.[54] But the difference is usually located in the stereotypical polarity between a societally strong West and societally weak East, a contrast between the decentralized character of European feudal

---

[44] *Timar*-holders were also rotated throughout the empire and faced fierce but regulated competition for vacant *timars*; Barkey 1994, 36, 65–66, 92; İnalcık 1994, 115–16.
[45] Imber 2019, 167–69.
[46] Imber 2006, 229–30; Itzkowitz 1980, 39–49; İnalcık 1994, 114–15.   [47] See note 56.
[48] Doyle 1996; Salmon 1967; Marsh 1962.   [49] Çirakman 2001, 55.
[50] Gerber 1987, 10.
[51] Pollock and Maitland 1898, 351–56; Stevenson 1940; Baker 2002, 239.
[52] *Leges Henrici Primi* 1972, 43, 7; Pollock and Maitland 1898, 351–56; Stevenson 1940.
[53] Weber 1978, 1075. Arbitrariness was only possible in principle against the Janissaries; İnalcık 1992, 58.
[54] Kunt and Woodhead 1995, 34.

monarchies and the "strong" Ottoman state.[55] This, however, assumes the French and Continental model of feudalism, where central authority was indeed weak. It omits the more relevant comparison with English feudalism, which, as argued throughout this book, was highly centralized and very effectively imposed, especially after the late twelfth century. As Marc Bloch noted, "in certain respects, no state was more completely feudal,"[56] at least until the fifteenth century. The Weberian perception of Ottoman patrimonialism fits better the seventeenth-century changes to this regime when the *timar* system largely lapsed and regional power-holders, like the *a'yans*, concentrated land, military, and fiscal powers.[57]

These observations suggest that patrimonial and bureaucratic practices have complex interactions with state capacity, as noted in Chapter 3. The Ottoman case before the seventeenth century indicates that bureaucratic institutions may be employed when ruler capacity is relatively weak but consolidating: the more a ruler faces intractable social forces, e.g. heterogeneous communities, the more rational structures are applied to exert power. Sultans actively fostered bureaucracy by co-opting impressively large groups of scholars, as Ottomanists Atçıl and Şahin have shown.[58] Russian and French early modern administrations present a similar bureaucratic orientation. Russian governors even displayed more bureaucratic features when compared to French intendants.[59] Patrimonial practices, on the other hand, when they involve the privatization of power, may be a symptom of declining authority, as the later Ottoman or French developments (after the seventeenth century) suggest; but under stronger state capacity, as in England during the period of parliamentary emergence, they may enhance institutional formation.

In any case, the comparison of fiefs and *timars* supports the view of the Ottomanist Haim Gerber that Ottoman society as a whole was "closer to th[e] bureaucratic ideal-type."[60] So an "advanced" bureaucratic trait – office rewarded with revenue not lordship – has been assumed to be a deficiency in the Ottoman case, a "failure" to develop property rights.[61] And a patrimonial practice – rights over people in return for state service – is taken to show European respect for property rights.

Fiefs and *timars*, however, were assigned to upper social groups. Property rights lower down the social scale must also be considered.

---

[55] Itzkowitz 1980, 48–49. These assumptions are common in Western scholarship too; Teschke 2003, 171; Anderson 1974a, 25.
[56] Bloch 1961, 146; Hollister 1976, 105, 99–106.
[57] McGowan 1981; 1994; Adanir 2006.   [58] Şahin 2013; Atçıl 2017.
[59] Armstrong 1972. These traits are noted by Russianists; see Kollmann 2012, 25–26; Poe 2006, 453–58. For the limits of this tendency, Davies 2006, 472.
[60] Gerber 1994, 18–20, 127–73. Note the qualifications in Barkey 1994, 32.
[61] Anderson 1974a, 365.

Here, similarities with the English system are striking, with the Ottoman system even showing marginally stronger rights on some dimensions. If weakness was observed, it was in the *enforcement* of rights (i.e. due to a weak state capacity) not in their definition or legal status.

11.1.3 Peasant Rights to Land: The Common Frame of Tenure

A long tradition of Marxist scholarship popularized the position that community ownership of land underlay the Asiatic mode of production, where peasants were deprived of any ownership.[62] Modern social science, as we've noted, has inherited the view that secure individual property rights are distinctive to the West. However, peasant rights in the early period of the Ottoman Empire (from at least the fourteenth century) had key similarities to English ones. In neither system could a person own land absolutely; they only had full rights to sell, buy, or rent objects above land, such as trees, animals, or plate.[63] Ottoman law also permitted house sales, but English common law did not, considering them to be part of land except if they stood on pattens.[64] On this dimension, the Ottoman rules seem more inclusive. Also, just as in England, much village land could be under common pasturage.[65]

Rights were instead tenurial, not based on ownership, throughout the social scale. Although English theorists by the thirteenth century employed Roman terms such as *dominium* (which meant either lordship or ownership) and *proprietas* (ownership),[66] the main concern of the law was with possession (*seisin*) and rights.[67] Moreover, a tenant had rights only "because he and his land owe[d] services to the king or to some other lord."[68] Similarly, the Ottoman state preserved ultimate authority over land from at least the 1300s, the *dominium eminens* of Roman law (called *raqaba* or *rikab*). The right was established by conquest and it separated ownership from use. The "ownership of the substance (*raqaba*)" was distinguished from "ownership of the usufruct (*tasarruf*) ... The ruler in effect owns the substance of the land, while the occupants own the benefits. This was a fiction," but it defined the law of tenure.[69] As mentioned above, the real owner was not the sultan, but the Treasury

---

[62] Marx 1973, 484.   [63] Imber 2019, 169–70; 2006, 236; Anderson 1974a, 565.
[64] Baker 2002, 380.   [65] Gerber 1987, 14; Orwin 1967.
[66] Pollock and Maitland 1899, 5; Pollock 1898, 230.
[67] For a careful distinction of common law from Roman concepts (and for all English concepts discussed here), see the definitive overview of medieval English laws by John Hudson 2012, especially 670–76.
[68] Pollock and Maitland 1899, 5.   [69] Imber 1997, 120.

on behalf of the people. In practice, land use was granted to individuals in ways that did not fundamentally differ from English conditions.

The English common law also gave use rights, though this varied by class. About half the population before the fourteenth century were unfree peasants, known as villeins.[70] Though not slaves, they were serfs bonded to a lord on a hereditary basis, attached to the land, and restricted in movement. They were allotted land for cultivation in exchange for service to the lord, which was uncertain and had only local protections.[71] They could only appeal to manorial courts and thus lacked protection in state courts, as the villein held land "at will" of the lord who ran the court.[72]

Ottoman peasants were also distinct from slaves (*kul*).[73] They held land under two types of contract. One could be "freely concluded" and involved only a lump sum rent but no taxes (*mukataalu* lands). The other denoted subjugated status (due to being non-Muslim) but simply entailed service to the state and the *sipahi* and the obligation to pay taxes (*tapulu* land). The key here is that property rights accorded even to subjugated peasants were in some respects stronger than those of villeins and equivalent to those granted to the *higher* ranks of free peasants in the English system. Whilst English villeins depended on the local lord, the *reaya* acquired *tapulu* land through a sales contract with a state agent, which was registered in court and certified by a *kadı* judge. The *reaya* could thus enforce their contract in a state court, in full accordance with the *Shari'a*.[74] Assuming regular tax payments and three years of cultivation, the *reaya* had "security of tenure,"[75] as we have seen in Sweden too.[76] "Sultanic law recognized that if a peasant held the actual possession of land long enough, and no one disputed it, this constituted legal possession."[77] Tenants could not dictate the conditions of tenure, but this held in both systems.

Conditions for English peasants improved after the demographic and socio-economic changes of the Black Death: servile villeinage gradually disappeared.[78] Tenurial rights were increasingly recorded on a court roll,

[70] Bailey 2014, 330.
[71] Pollock and Maitland 1898, 356–83; Simpson 1986, 158–60. Hyams 1980 has shown the customary regulation of these relations, however – they were not lawless.
[72] Hudson 2012, especially 666–67; Baker 2002, 468–70. For a nuanced assessment of villein conditions, see Hatcher 1981.
[73] Slaves were usually prisoners-of-war or purchased slaves employed as agricultural laborers. Even *kul* cannot be identified with Western slaves: some could attain high status in imperial service, so had little in common with English villeins.
[74] İnalcık 1994, 108–10; Imber 2011, 43.   [75] Imber 2006, 236.   [76] Chapter 10.
[77] İnalcık 1994, 110, 111.
[78] Bailey 2014, 3–86; see also Chapter 12 in the present volume.

a copy of which was given to the tenant (hence, copyhold tenure). Though copyholders had more secure rights than villeins, they still did not enjoy the full rights of freeholders. They could not sue in a royal court, so common law remedies remained unavailable to them, as they had been to villeins. However, if the lord violated manorial custom, copyholders could appeal to Chancery. Only gradually did their legal status change: a copyholder could recover title to land in case of trespass by using a real common law action (of ejectment), i.e. a remedy that could be tried in a royal court – but only after the 1570s.[79] English peasants only acquired the coveted state protection enjoyed by freeholders and Ottoman peasants late. If actual conditions were better for English peasants originally, this cannot be ascribed to the legal framework.

What about the assumed hallmark of secure property rights, inheritance? Even the highest ranks of English tenants, the fee simple holders, could not bequeath their property at will; inheritance was determined by common law strictures,[80] which seem more restrictive than Ottoman ones. By the thirteenth century, most free tenures in England could only be inherited by the first-born, though such succession seems to have been already customary from the eleventh century, not least due to royal involvement.[81] Primogeniture preserved estates intact over generations, so it is assumed to serve landlord interests. But, with only small exceptions, "the nobility and gentry were ... in effect forbidden to make in their lifetimes arrangements for the benefit of younger sons or daughters" or relatives, to arrange for marriages, or to pay debts after death, except by gift when alive (inter vivos), which had drawbacks.[82] Wills were also invalid in common law until the Statute of Wills was passed in 1540 in response to overwhelming social pressure.[83] The individual thus did not originally have full freedom of disposition; it had highly restricted, well-regulated rights, with often highly inequitable outcomes. And although eventually such rights were transformed in a way that protected individual will very strongly – for instance, the testator's right even to disinherit became uncontested[84] – these developments long postdated the emergence of Parliament, so cannot explain institutional variation at this level between the two cases.

---

[79] Simpson 1986, 155–65; Baker 2002, 308.

[80] Baker 2002, 265–68; Hudson 2012, 645–53; Bean 1991, 547.

[81] Hudson 1994, 148, 65–153. Local custom varied, however, especially for socage and gavelkind; Holdsworth 1923b, 171–97; Simpson 1986, 51, 62. Some parts of England applied ultimogeniture, where the last son inherited all; Baker 2002, 266, 165–68.

[82] Bean 1991, 548; Hudson 2012, 655–61.   [83] Baker 2002, 256–57.

[84] Only in 1938, after the Family Provisions Act, could a court undercut the testator's will in favor of reasonable provisions for family dependents.

Ottoman law provided somewhat greater individual discretion, as the *çift*, the main land unit, passed by default to the son or was divided among many sons under a different status.[85] Even daughters' inheritance rights were codified in 1568, provided they paid tax.[86] Islamic law allowed the testator to allocate one third of his possessions at will, with the rest going to the family group with strict orders of priority.[87] As noted, Hanafi law imposed partible inheritance. In a recurrent irony, the fairest solution – ensuring all descendants were provided for – appears in the non-constitutional setting; it also often had suboptimal economic results, however, as it fragmented landholdings often making them economically non-viable.[88]

English and Ottoman law imposed similar restrictions on alienation as well. Alienation of Ottoman lands was formally barred: "In principle ... *miri* land could not be bought and sold."[89] Only loans and leases were allowed. In practice, however, peasants did buy and sell land "as though they were its owners," as affirmed by contemporary jurists in *fatwas*.[90] Early sixteenth-century legal texts referred to such transactions as sales of the right of residence (*hakk-i karar*). This required the permission of the *timar*-holder (the *sipahi*) and a tax payment to him.[91]

At the bottom of the scale, English villeins could also only alienate their tenement with their lord's consent.[92] But even their more secure successors, copyholders, were formally at least limited, as they could not alienate their tenancy independently; they could only surrender it to their lord, who alone had the right to transfer – a formality that held until 1925.[93] Nonetheless, in practice, copyholders also alienated and kept the proceeds of sales like their Ottoman counterparts. Freeholders had the power to alienate since the twelfth century.[94] Whether these practices make England truly different can only be assessed by examining whether Ottoman transactions were more constrained *in practice* than in England and for what reasons.

It is important also to note what social purposes were being served by restrictions on alienation; doing so shows how demands for rights were similar across cases but also how increasingly English freedoms were

---

[85] Imber 2006, 236. The *çift* was the basis of the *çift-hane*, or family farm, system.
[86] Imber 2011, 51–52. See Hudson 2012, 648 for similar English practice for tenants-in-chiefs' daughters.
[87] Coulson 1971, 213–14 and passim.
[88] The claim that fragmented holdings discouraged economic productivity underlies the Brenner thesis (Brenner 1976), but is not without critics; cf. Aston and Philpin 1985.
[89] Imber 2006, 236.   [90] Imber 1997, 121.   [91] Imber 2006, 236; Vikør 2005, 337.
[92] Pollock and Maitland 1898, 382; Hudson 2012, 666–67.
[93] Baker 2002, 309; Megarry and Wade 2012, 27.
[94] Hudson 1994, 157–281, 208–29; 2012, 657; Baker 2002, 261.

predicated on state power. Alienations were barred in both cases originally to prevent the concentration of land and to protect heirs.

In England the crown could (originally at least) exercise power over the more powerful and limit the concentration of power among tenants-in-chief through strong restrictions, especially after 1256: tenants-in-chief could not alienate without persuading the crown that it would not lose income through the sale and without obtaining a royal license.[95] Land transferred without license was seized or a fine was imposed. Tenants-in-chief only acquired effective freedom of alienation after 1327, i.e. after parliament was fully formed, though licenses and fines remained.[96] That was the condition for allowing lower tenants to freely alienate their holdings from the twelfth century. By contrast, in the Ottoman Empire the danger of unrestricted alienations "allowing land to accumulate in the wrong hands" remained pressing, as Imber noted[97] – absent state capacity to manage such a trend, alienations were formally barred. Nor did Ottoman restrictions flow from weaker property rights; on the contrary, once *miri* land was sold under Islamic law, it was so protected that it could not revert back to *miri* status.[98]

Further, alienation of *miri* lands was restricted in Ottoman law in 1601 due again to equity concerns: land sold to settle debts of the deceased deprived heirs of their inheritance.[99] Alienation was similarly originally restricted in England to "maintain equality among the sons":[100] it prevented the father from selling, which typically dispossessed other sons. Early English freeholders were also originally restricted by their descendants' right to inherit, especially regarding land they had themselves inherited (as opposed to purchased).[101] When primogeniture prevailed, however, other offspring lost protection and substitutes had to be found. Alienation allowed a parent to endow their other children before death. It was thus liberalized because it "mitigate[d] the harshness of primogeniture."[102] Alienation accordingly cannot be reduced to pressures from rising land prices;[103] rather it balanced pressures created by the inequity royal law could impose.[104] But the enabling condition was royal capacity to keep the most powerful under relative control, at least originally. Ottoman incapacity to both protect all heirs and prevent land concentration explains why alienation remained restricted.

---

[95] Plucknett 1956, 542; Bean 1968, 66–79.   [96] Bean 1968, 74, 100–3; 1991, 549.
[97] Imber 2011, 48.   [98] İnalcık 1994, 111.   [99] İnalcık 1994, 111.
[100] Plucknett 1956, 528–29.   [101] Hudson 2012, 653–62.   [102] Simpson 1986, 52.
[103] North and Thomas 1971, 801.
[104] Primogeniture was customary (and Norman) in origin but its polity-wide application was state-dependent.

In short, a comparison of the two systems of real property suggests that the common foundation of state control of land generated very similar patterns of legal rights. Of course, far more detailed studies are needed to probe regime differences than is possible here. These points aim simply to suggest that the assessment of Ottoman property rights requires a fuller comparison with England and that, before culturalist arguments are invoked to explain political and economic outcomes, a better assessment of state capacity is required. Variation, we will see next, was more at the level of enforcement than legal principle, and this was a problem of infrastructural control. As Gerber emphasized, "much of the predation that took place in the Ottoman Empire [in the seventeenth century] was not an outgrowth of central policy but rather a violation and subversion of it, mainly by disobedient central governors."[105] If property rights *security* differed, this reflected poor infrastructural capacity, not a more "despotic" or arbitrary regime. This is further seen in two further aspects of land relations, examined next: land endowments and expropriations.

11.2   Common Responses to Ruler Control of Land: *Uses* and *Vakıfs*

The similar land regime in England and the Ottoman Empire also led to remarkably similar devices to avoid ruler control of land rights: *uses* in England, *vakıfs* in the Ottoman Empire.[106] In both cases, land was turned into an endowment founded in perpetuity that vested beneficiaries with its use. The Ottoman *vakıfs* (*waqfs* in Arabic) were mainly of two types, the religious or public service *waqf* (*waqf khair*) and the family endowment (*waqf ahli* or *dhurri*).[107] The former especially shaped the social fabric of Islamic communities, as *vakıfs* disbursed public goods: hospitals, mosques, colleges, even water fountains were founded and maintained through them into the twentieth century.[108] English *uses* allowed the nominal property-holders to differ from the beneficiaries who received its income, enabling the perpetual untaxed succession of the latter. Lands were often vested in a monastery for the use of descendants of the donor. This device originated mostly in the need, of crusaders for instance, to

---

[105] Gerber 1994, 21; Faroqhi 1992, 13.

[106] The similarities between the two have suggested an Islamic origin for English *uses* or trusts, but this remains conjectural; Gaudiosi 1988; Cattan 1955, 212–18. Nonetheless, the English version is closer to the Islamic one than to the Roman antecedent, the legal form of *fidei commissum*; Hennigan 2004, 96–102, 56.

[107] Shatzmiller 2001; Kuran 2001, 855–56. The cash *waqf*, by contrast, involved capital, not land, although the prohibition of usury created legal problems; Imber 1997, 143–46; Mandaville 1979.

[108] Abbasi 2012; Cattan 1955, 203–205; Powers 1999.

leave estates under the care of others,[109] but developed as a legal mechanism of tax avoidance in response to the same structural condition, state control of land.[110]

Initially, both these legal instruments appear as instances of what North, Wallis, and Weingast in their latest major account called "perpetually lived organizations." These are organizations "whose existence is independent of the lives of their members," for instance corporations. Their impersonality provides the foundation of "open political orders" and thereby also economic growth.[111] The "perpetuity" of *vakıfs*, however, has been tied to economic underperformance in the Ottoman context. For instance, for Kuran, the *vakıf* typifies the "immobilization" (or "static perpetuity") that prevented the Ottoman economy from growing like the West. Their prevalence is also tied to the fact that Islamic law never developed corporations,[112] entities with legal personhood which are central to many accounts of why the West diverged economically.[113] The corporation will be discussed in the next chapter (only to suggest that its role for the emergence of representation was probably adverse).

An explanation is required, however, as to why similar institutions, *uses* and *vakıfs*, had such divergent effects in the two cases. Such an explanation might also shed light on the necessary conditions for representative emergence: maybe the factors that enabled the spread of *vakıfs* whilst inhibiting the rise of corporations and of an open political order in the Ottoman case also account for why representation never developed. In what follows, I argue that variation in state strength accounts for these outcomes: *uses* failed to "immobilize" the English economy because of the higher capacity of the English crown to regulate property rights. I conclude with empirical data that confirm the weaker capacity of the Ottoman state.

Vakıfs and *uses* responded to the restrictions on inheritance that were described in the previous section. Both legal systems constrained the freedom of a landowner to "employ the revenues of his land after his death"[114] and imposed further burdens. The rules were substantively opposite (partible inheritance vs. primogeniture) but elicited the same response. Endowments served as "legal loopholes" exempting land from taxation, especially death duties, and circumvented the prohibition of

---

[109] Baker 2002, 248–53; Bean 1968, 104–79.
[110] Kuran 2014, 18–19 briefly also considers trusts and entails as alternatives, highlighting their more democratic decision-making mode and other flexible traits. These are discussed below.
[111] North et al. 2009, 23, 240–42.   [112] Kuran 2011, 110–15, 128; 2001, 843.
[113] North et al. 2009; Kuran 2005; Williamson 1985.   [114] Bean 1968, 104.

wills.[115] It was not therefore the "weakness of private property rights [that] made the sacred institution of the waqf a convenient vehicle for defending wealth," but the all-too-potent effect of Islamic protections of inheritance rights; nor was "official predation" the problem but tax duties and state regulations,[116] as in England.

These incentives were so strong that by "1502 it could be asserted that the greater part of the land of England was held in use."[117] Much of this was through the monasteries, which held between a fifth and a quarter of the land of England.[118] Similarly, about three quarters of Ottoman land and buildings may have been under *vakıfs* – but unlike England, this lasted until the collapse of the Ottoman Empire.[119] Why did *vakıfs* prevail while *uses* did not "immobilize" the English economy?

One explanation of the continued prevalence of the *vakıf* in the Middle East sees it as a symptom of the "wealth transmission norms of Islamic society," in contrast to "the Anglo-American norm . . . of distributional self-determination." The latter is assumed to be "entirely consistent with general cultural preferences and economic theory that accentuate individuality and relatively unregulated private property ownership."[120] Similarly, Kuran has argued that *vakıfs* reflect a greater collectivism and "communal vision" in Islam, which was sustained due to a fear of factionalism and tribalism. In the West, by contrast, the division of political power in the West among kings, emperors, and cities prevented such communalism.[121]

There is little that is "self-determining," however, in the forms of landownership that dominated English society into the twentieth century, family settlements.[122] Entails in particular bound all descendants to accept that only one heir could retain control of an estate, whilst depriving him of the right to alienate or devise by will; it aimed to preserve family wealth intact by excluding other descendants. Even when a temporal limit was attempted with the "Rule against Perpetuities" in 1682, property-holders still sought ways to circumvent that until the crippling tax duties of the twentieth century.[123] English property rights as a whole involved overlapping rights, creating multiple ties of dependence and entanglement, not the absolute private ownership postulated by some modern liberal theory: tenure consisted of "pyramidal relationships of reciprocal

---

[115] Darling 1996, 88; Abou-El-Haj 1991, 46; Baker 2002, 249–50.
[116] Kuran 2001, 854–55; 2011, 127. Kuran acknowledges the role of inheritance and taxation, but not how the former indicates property rights were not weak; Kuran 2001, 856–58.
[117] Baker 2002, 251.   [118] Baker 2003, 709.   [119] Kuran 2001, 849; Fratcher 1973.
[120] Schoenblum 1999, 1203.   [121] Kuran 2005, 796–99.   [122] Baker 2002, 280–97.
[123] Baker 2002, 280–84, 293–96.

obligation," whilst estates could vest a property to different individuals for different "slices of time."[124]

Kuran instead contrasts *vakıfs*, which were founded by individuals who determined the nature of the organization into the future, to Western corporations, which were determined by the collective will of their members. This is because the *vakıf* had fixed rules, whereas corporations could remake them.[125] If so, however, far from reflecting a "communal vision" in Islam,[126] they reflect greater powers of the *individual* in that system to define their property rights, even across time, in absolute ways. The claimed "inflexibility"[127] of this instrument results from the greater capacity of the founder to restrict encroachments on his or her will after death.[128] But this is no different than with entails. The difference between the *vakıfs* and corporations, therefore, is not between a communal and an individualist vision; it has to be located elsewhere, between different conceptions of which individuals have priority.

In endowments, should the founder or later members have final say? The intuitive individualist approach is that those who generated the wealth should have it, as *vakıfs* stipulated. The corporation's rules take the founder's powers away and vest them on ever changing individuals. They therefore force the founder(s) to accept restrictions on their will in the future. It is not greater individualism that distinguishes the corporation, but greater subjection to collectively defined goals. Accepting a legal, impersonal frame requires precisely the subordination of multiple individual wills – which is what allows corporations to grow in size, a feature which is crucial for economic growth and economies of scale and which was lacking in the region, as Kuran importantly emphasized (and as it still is). The empirical record suggests that such restrictions were possible when the general political framework could compel power-holders effectively: it is not an accident from the perspective of this account that, as Kuran notes, it was not Italy, but England and Holland that developed the business corporation to its full form.[129]

This conclusion is strengthened when we consider why *uses* did not "immobilize" the English economy, like *vakıfs* did in the Middle East. The answer is complex, but state intervention was key: it pushed landholders in different directions, by generating strong social resistance. The crown passed the *Statute of Uses* in 1536, which curtailed their tax advantages. This was so strongly opposed that the aforementioned *Statute of*

---

[124] Simpson 1986, 47–48; Megarry and Wade 2012, 64, 58.   [125] Kuran 2005, 800.
[126] Kuran 2005, 800.   [127] Schoenblum 1999, 1201.
[128] Women could also found *vakıfs*; Filan 2007.
[129] Kuran 2001, 880–81; 2005, 806–807.

Wills was conceded in 1540, enabling the disposition of freeholds by will.[130] *Uses* were therefore sidelined not though a natural, endogenous development of more "efficient" property rights but after state-led action.

The crown was also crucial in regulating an outgrowth of *uses*, trusts, which spread after 1536. Trusts managed land when its legal ownership was separated from its beneficial ownership, especially to secure inheritance over generations, particularly for charity and the vulnerable. But they could not so easily avoid tax duties: the Chancellor worked to identify and neutralize those trusts that posed "a financial threat."[131] State capacity was therefore key in the containment of these practices, though as I have suggested and will argue further in the Conclusion, the capacity was gradually weakened from the later medieval and into the early modern periods – hence the need for radical action, such as the drastic expropriation of monastic lands examined next. Nonetheless, the "immobilization" of the Ottoman *vakıf* regime, by contrast, may be better seen in the light of *less* intrusive state action; there was no Ottoman "dissolution of the monasteries" and a class of "grandees" formed that undermined the sultan.[132] The reality is therefore the opposite of common assumptions, which have suggested that Ottoman rulers had the power to block self-governing units, unlike in Western Europe.[133]

The underlying theme in the above analysis has been the disparity in infrastructural capacity and a relative Ottoman weakness compared to England. Ottomanists, such as Rifa'at Ali Abou-El-Haj, have long warned that contemporary descriptions of despotism were "idealized fantasies" that should not be confused with reality.[134] This is supported by comparative data on tax extraction, compiled by Karaman and Pamuk. Though all premodern data are problematic, these suggest Ottomans collected far less than Western monarchies. In 1550, they extracted about 5.6 grams of silver per thousand of population to England's 8.9 grams and France's 10.9 grams. By 1600, England and France were extracting at least three times per capita more than the Ottomans, and by 1700 England was extracting more than ten times more. When expressed in terms of wages of unskilled workers to compare real values, the Ottomans were raising between 63 (at best) and 22 (at worst) percent of what England and France were raising between 1550 and 1650 respectively, though English tax revenues in the 1500s and 1600s were

---

[130] Baker 2002, 255–57.   [131] Jones 1998, 183, 173–99.   [132] Abou-El-Haj 1991, 46.
[133] Kuran 2011, 112.
[134] Abou-El-Haj 1991, 33, 29–44. Strength assessments vary, especially by period; Darling 1996, 298.

suppressed, as observed in Chapter 6.[135] On this metric at least, Ottoman capacity was weaker than that of its European counterparts, though as Karen Barkey and others have argued, the empire developed sophisticated methods to manage its domestic and external challenges.[136] Countering Eurocentric narratives that depict non-Western polities as "weak" is a laudable goal, but it is also important to identify features of state capacity that eventually allowed European dominance.

11.3   Expropriation

Claims about Ottoman weakness conflict with common narratives about the arbitrary confiscations of various sultans, however. Expropriations are considered to inhibit both economic change and the political openness that is necessary to generate it, in most economic studies,[137] but also in conventional Ottoman historiography. Yet Ottoman capacity was weaker than England's on this dimension too.

A claimed example of the arbitrary exercise of sultanic power was when the sultan Mehmed II (1444–46 and 1451–81), the conqueror of Constantinople, "decided to abolish private and *vakf* properties."[138] However, more recent studies show that Mehmed did not alter existing land arrangements, only those concerning land revenues. Further, the state appropriated revenues only where owners were missing – and it redistributed some as *timars* to new holders.[139] The "reform" was even later reversed. Nonetheless, its basis was a state claim that differed little from England's.[140] As is typical, late developers are classified as arbitrary or interventionist for taking similar action to England, only with less power.[141]

In another instance, Selîm II (1566–74) abrogated the trusts of Orthodox monasteries in 1568. But he too drew on legal principle, a *fatwa* of jurist Ebu's-su`ud. Two legal grounds were invoked: first, the trusts were formed on rural land, which remained royal demesne absent a sultanic grant, and second, Hanafi law forbade individuals to "create trusts directly for the benefit of churches and monasteries"; they could only be for the benefit of the poor. If the grant was not specified correctly,

---

[135] Caution is required with all premodern data. *Timar*-holders collected taxes locally, so Ottoman extractive capacity is probably under-reported, though local expenditures also occurred in Europe; Hoffman 1994, 226–40. Moreover, per capita conscription was also less than in the West; Murphey 1999, 44–49. Ultimately, the Ottoman system did not have the infrastructural capacity to meet the challenges of the eighteenth century. By the 1780s, it was raising 4–10 percent of what England and France were in real terms; Karaman and Pamuk 2010; 2013.

[136] Barkey 1994.   [137] Kuran 2011; Acemoglu et al. 2004.   [138] İnalcık 1994, 106.

[139] Özel 1999, 242, 238–39.   [140] İnalcık 1973, 109–10.

[141] Gerschenkron 1962; Chang 2002.

it was void. The aim was not to dispossess the monks, however. It made the trusts legal and raised cash for the sultan. The monks retained the right of occupation by paying an entry fine, raised from a tax on the Orthodox; only the land was returned to the Treasury.[142] Expropriations by "absolutist" rulers, thus, though easily seen as symptoms of unchecked power, were regulated.

Expropriations in England, by contrast, showed in fact greater state capacity to confiscate extensive property and to reallocate it at will – occasionally with thinner basis in law. Henry VIII from the 1530s sold two thirds of monastic lands to private buyers within ten years. This involved about 20–25 percent of English land:[143] it was the most extensive reallocation of land since the Norman Conquest. The initial pretext, moreover, was not legal title but religious conformity, pursued through Cromwell's "visitations" from 1535. To prevent the lands from reverting to the founders' heirs, Parliament was even enlisted to pass the "Suppression of Religious Houses Act" of 1535, which expropriated lesser religious houses.[144] The English state did not respect property rights more; it was comparatively far more effective in surgically suppressing them, according to need – not least by employing Parliament to do so.

11.4   Conclusion

To conclude, comparing English and Ottoman property rights regimes undercuts the still common association, at least within social science though not among Ottomanists, between a "sultanic," non-constitutional regime and the lack of property rights. Neither property rights in general nor conditionality in particular suffice to explain representation. The comparison establishes how similar the conditional character of property rights was in the two cases, stemming from the common foundation of state control of land. Manifold differences exist, only some of which can be covered in an overview such as this. But on some key dimensions, for instance, alienation, heritability, and court enforcement of rights, Ottoman rights emerged as highly similar, even stronger de jure at points. And *tımars* demonstrate the stronger bureaucratic character of the early regime, not its arbitrariness.

Further, the comparison of *vakıfs* to English *uses* and trusts similarly suggests that their effects were a function of royal power. A book on representative origins in the West cannot cover the full range of factors enabling or inhibiting such legal instruments. But it can suggest that if *vakıfs* did hamper economic development and thereby possibly

---

[142] Imber 1997, 160.   [143] Baker 2003, 709.   [144] Youings 1971.

constitutional practices, such effects were endogenous to weak state capacity. Some of the key inefficiencies typically ascribed to "over-stretched and authoritarian states"[145] resulted from the underlying weakness in enforcing property rights. *Vakıfs* prevailed in the Ottoman Empire because the state lacked the relative power to delimit them. Given their profoundly important social role, of course, it is not clear it would necessarily have wished to. By contrast, the English economic trajectory, though far from smooth, veered in a more "efficient" direction because state action, and especially regulation, prevented extensive loss of jurisdiction over productive assets in the economy. The state was often able to drastically intervene and curtail economic rights where expedient and therefore preserved better its fiscal capacity, as both the Dissolution of the Monasteries and the Enclosures[146] suggest. Even during periods of fiscal weakness, it still performed better than the Ottoman state. In any case, during periods of "backsliding" in these dimensions, as especially under the Stuarts, constitutionalism faltered too. As I argue in the Conclusion, if the aristocracy had failed to preserve its power base in the ensuing centuries, voting reform may have even happened earlier. Next, we turn to another non-Western case that displayed similar patterns of conditionality but different political outcomes, Russia.

[145] Kuran 2001, 844.   [146] See Chapter 9.

12   Land, Tenure, and Assemblies: Russia in the Sixteenth and Seventeenth Centuries

Russia expanded greatly from the late fifteenth to the seventeenth centuries, especially under Ivan IV "the Terrible" (1547–84). His rule encapsulates Russia's image as a "despotic," tyrannical regime, displaying notorious brutality. He reportedly fried men "in special man-sized frying pans."[1] During his reign of terror, known as the *Oprichnina*, Ivan slaughtered over 3,000 people, exiled 190 princes, and devastated regions with confiscatory taxation. Moreover, he consolidated a feature of the Russian regime widely accepted as definitive of its patrimonial and despotic character: obligations flowing from service upon all social classes, even the elites. The "phenomenon of service landholding is one of the fundamental bases of the theory that Muscovy was a patrimonial state."[2] Secular landholders owed not only military service; they even had the "obligation to 'build' palaces for the grand prince and [houses] for the district officials and governors," including lords holding immunities.[3] This meant that "estates … were defined by their obligations, not their rights."[4] This dependence caused the subservience that, for many scholars, distinguished Russia from the West. It not only foreclosed a constitutional trajectory,[5] it even prefigured its communist future.[6] This "statist," despotic view confirms the perceptions of early modern visitors, who relayed both the tsar's tyrannical behavior and subjects' servile response.

It causes "astonishment," therefore, especially in such scholarship, that this period also saw unprecedented (though not enduring) representative activity in Russia.[7] From the 1540s, Ivan IV himself began convoking Assemblies of the Land with large attendance. No less than eight of them even elected a tsar when dynastic lineage failed[8] – an inconceivable function for contemporary English or French parliaments. Even in studies that have strongly questioned the despotic interpretation of the Russian regime, this paradox is typically left unexplained.

---

[1] Kivelson 1997, 656.   [2] Weickhardt 1993, 677.   [3] Floria 2000, 14.
[4] Halperin 2002, 502.   [5] Hellie 2000, 12; Alef 1983, 34.
[6] As discussed in Poe 2002, 474–75; Hellie 2006a, 384.
[7] Keep 1957, 100; Hosking 2000, 305.   [8] Ostrowski 2004, 129–30.

Revisionist studies have, however, explored other remarkable parallels with Western practice. On many dimensions, center–periphery relations, land rights, demands for justice, petitions, the judicial system itself, traits we have observed in England and elsewhere in the West, also appear in Russia. For instance, the development of property rights in Russia has been conventionally seen as "exactly contrary to its course in Western Europe"; independent rights in the early period were replaced by the servitude consolidated by Ivan IV, ensconcing "despotism."[9] However, as the legal historian George Weickhardt has strikingly shown, some land rights in Russia in the seventeenth century closely "approached that of the English 'fee simple,' ... the most unqualified type of ownership in Anglo-American common law"[10] – in ways very similar to those explored in the previous chapter for the Ottoman Empire.

Other scholars further uncovered a social and political life in historical sources that parallels many Western early modern patterns. According to Nancy Kollmann, far from an absolutist autocracy, Muscovy was controlled by clans of aristocrats that limited the crown's powers, echoing historical findings on France and Spain.[11] Tsars had to govern with them, requiring consensus to secure implementation.[12] Further, the judicial system also displayed a balancing between local communities and central structures, with equality lying in the application of the law, if not its content.[13] It even abolished capital punishment before the West.[14] For Valerie Kivelson, similar autonomy can be discerned in the seventeenth-century provincial gentry, which succeeded in pursuing family-focused interests even against central encroachments, in ways that parallel findings on family networks in the West.[15]

Critics of this revisionism, however, such as Donald Ostrowski and Marshal Poe, point out that it does not explain the contrast between its own findings and the "despotic" image conveyed by Western contemporaries, except to present this discourse as a "façade."[16] Indeed, Kollmann describes the "persistent emphasis in Muscovite sources on the sovereign's exclusive autocratic power" as "striking, given that the boyars [the highest serving elite] also held real, albeit not institutionalized, power."[17] Revisionism also leaves unaddressed the broad imposition of service and dependence, which critics view as evidence of patrimonialism and, effectively, backwardness.[18]

---

[9] Pipes 1994, 525–26.   [10] Weickhardt 1993, 665; 1994.   [11] Kollmann 1987.
[12] Ostrowski 2006, 217–18, 224–25. See also Rowland 1990.   [13] Weickhardt 1992.
[14] Kollmann 2012, 421–23.   [15] Kivelson 1996.
[16] Ostrowski 2002, 538–40; Poe 2002, 480.   [17] Kollmann 1987, 8–9.
[18] Pipes 1994; Poe 2002.

Here, by contrast, I show how Russia was like England precisely on this element that causes most difficulty for the non-despotic reading, service to the state. In Parts I and II, service emerged as a necessary condition for constitutional emergence in England and its variation helped explain different outcomes in the West. From this book's perspective, therefore, representative activity under a ruler asserting his power through service and conditional relations is not paradoxical but what the preceding argument has led us to expect. One does not need to accept the book's argument about the necessary connection between the two to admit that service is at least not sufficient to explain despotism.

Moreover, the disjuncture between ideology and practice is also predicted by the normative/empirical inversion identified throughout the book. Though power was being asserted under the late Ruriks in unprecedented ways, it was comparatively much weaker than in medieval England. Society was much more loosely controlled by the tsar; in fact, freedom was initially greater at points than in the West, as I will suggest. Even Russian serfs could change lords once a year,[19] a freedom unthinkable for their English counterparts, who inherited their condition for life down the male line (like Russian slaves) and could be sold with the land.[20] It is thus not surprising that "the adjective 'free' or 'at will' (vol'nyi) signified disorder and disturbance, disruptive willfulness."[21] The rhetoric was extreme precisely to counteract that. The incentives on the tsar to terrorize those within his reach, this argument suggests, increased the more he could not subdue those out of reach, especially the boyars and princes, helping explain the subservient behavior of those present.

Ultimately, the analysis presented in this book helps synthesize the varied explanations Russian scholars have offered for the divergence with the West. Differences between the regions are fewer than expected at the micro level of daily practice; they become salient at the aggregate level of polity-wide institutions, as some have argued. Either political culture remained at the personal level, eschewing the impersonal, bureaucratic traits of Western monarchies, or Russia lacked the "established social groups and solidarities" that allowed the West to move towards a more modern political culture, or enserfment prevailed.[22] But these differences have yet to be explained.

This book has argued that England in particular differed in the more effective supra-local organization of subject participation, which was predicated on state strength – not on greater limits on central authority,

---

[19] Graham 1987, 31.   [20] Pollock and Maitland 1898, 412–32.   [21] Kivelson 2002, 484.
[22] Kivelson 1996, 9–15, 151–56, 276–78; Kollmann 2012, 425–26; 1987, 181–83; Weickhardt 1993, 678.

as conventional narratives have it. If that is so, then the differing Russian trajectory would be due to ruler weakness. Yet so much evidence militates against this view. What this chapter will argue instead is that what appears as evidence of overpowering rulership in Russia, even serfdom, is the result of weaker control over the most powerful social groups.

To support these claims, I first explain the land regime and relations between the tsar and elite groups, to show how the representative activity that did occur depended mainly on conditional relations with a newer, less powerful elite based on service – producing second-best constitutionalism, similar to Hungary and Poland. Then I present evidence for three indicators of ruler weakness – weaker control over the *boyar* nobility and society more broadly, poor taxing capability, and mass enserfment – in order to explain the outcomes observed, congruently with the predictions of this account. Absent effective control over the most powerful elite, neither institutional fusion could occur between judicial and fiscal functions nor could collective action be coordinated at the supra-local level. Since no alternative mechanisms were deployed to provide regularity and inclusiveness, especially of the most powerful, the representative activity that did emerge could not consolidate or define the regime.

It should be emphasized that no teleology is assumed in this account, nor that, by not developing representative institutions, the Russian regime somehow "failed." Even if state capacity had been sufficient, Russians might not have wanted to develop along similar lines to the West, setting other values or traditions as paramount.[23] Instead, comparison is used for analytical purposes, to test whether some conditions deemed necessary can be identified in this case. Moreover, although historians perform very careful comparisons and will reject them if isomorphism is not evident,[24] this study applies a looser strategy, by looking at similarities, rather than identity, in form and function. Democracies today operate across regions with great variation, yet they still form part of a recognizable category, as long as certain relations hold. An equivalent criterion is applied here to the historical past.

12.1   Conditional Land Rights and Second-Best Constitutionalism

Just like rulers from medieval Europe to the early American state,[25] Russian princes from the fourteenth century granted conquered land to

---

[23] Note this objection in Ostrowski 2004, 135. He emphasizes the alternative tradition of steppe *quriltai*, an advisory council.
[24] Brown 1983, 81–83; Kollmann 1987, 185.   [25] Frymer 2017.

military men, creating a service class that evolved over time, the *boyars*. When these fragmented principalities were gradually absorbed by Muscovy, the princes and their servitors transferred allegiance to Muscovy's prince (who eventually was named tsar).[26] *Boyars* acquired land allodially, as *votchina*, which guaranteed inheritance (even to daughters since the twelfth century), thus establishing a power base.[27] The highest ranks of *boyars*, as well as princes and administrators, were part of the *Boyar Duma*, the Royal Council that governed the realm. Membership in the *Duma* was fluid, ranging from a couple of dozen families in the early fifteenth century, to less than 40 *boyars* in the early 1600s, to close to 150 by 1690.[28] The tsar had "to rule the country in consultation" with them.[29] "Almost every Muscovite decree begins with the redolent phrase 'the tsar decreed and the boyars confirmed.'"[30] Although older scholarship assumed this was empty rhetoric and the tsar's power was absolute, recent works have made a compelling case for their role. The following sections support this view.

The increasing independence of the *boyars* and acquisition of new land since the fifteenth century led Russian tsars to build a new class of servitors, frequently described as gentry and more dependent on the ruler than the *boyars*. They were cavalry owing military service to the tsar and are estimated to have reached about 17,500 in the mid-1500s.[31] Their lands were termed *pomest'e* and were distinguished from the hereditary *votchina* of the *boyars*.[32] *Pomest'e* land could not technically be sold. Eventually, it could be inherited, as long as the heir assumed military service,[33] but if a servitor died without heirs, the land returned to the Treasury, as did the Ottoman *timars* and the lands held by tenants-in-chief in England.

The new military servitors were "less clannish" than the *boyars*,[34] a crucial trait that only enhanced the tsar's capacity to control them, as discussed in the next chapter. They received about half of the land that Ivan III (1462–1505) confiscated after he conquered Novgorod, which amounted to about 82 percent of total cultivated land, retaining the rest for the royal household.[35] From the 1490s, these Muscovite cavalrymen replaced the Novgorodian landowners; they were granted lands with peasants whose taxes paid for their military service.[36] This move aimed

---

[26] The highest rank was Grand Prince; the title "tsar" was established in 1547 by Ivan IV.
[27] Pipes 1974, 46.   [28] Crummey 1983, 22–23; 1987, 12–15; Hosking 2001, 92–96.
[29] Poe 2006, 437, 460.   [30] Kivelson 2002, 492.
[31] Ostrowski 2006, 225–26; Kivelson 1996, 26–29.
[32] Pipes 1974, 92–93; Ostrowski 2006, 230–31; Graham 1987.
[33] Weickhardt 1993, 664, 677–78.   [34] Pipes 1974, 92.   [35] Pipes 1974, 93.
[36] Hellie 2006a, 382.

to halt the "grave abuses" of the entrenched elites.[37] It was, according to historian Anne Kleimola, a protection device against a populace that blamed the elite, not the state, for local corruption and abuse.[38] But the incapacity to control elite behavior typically indicates state weakness.

Although the gentry *pomest'e* resembled Western fiefs, some scholars draw a sharp distinction. The two types differ of course, and this study cannot present their full historical complexity. It can, however, challenge the logic that specialists have invoked to dismiss comparability: according to historian Richard Pipes, Russian fiefs were established under apparently strong tsarist rule, at the height of monarchical centralization, whereas Western fiefs exemplify "'feudal' decentralization."[39] Yet, as in the Ottoman case, this assumed contrast conceives of feudalism as fragmentation – i.e. it assumes that the French or German versions of feudalism were definitive. It ignores the English version, where fief-granting was administered by a highly centralized crown, as noted in the previous analysis.[40] High levels of concentration in the hands of and dependence on the crown were *the* features that shaped regime type in England. Feudal decentralization did not produce constitutional outcomes; that is where absolutism prevailed.

As the English case predicts, dependence on the tsar shaped how local governance evolved in this period. The gentry secured through petitions – the same mechanism observed in the West – the right to governance by local councils of elders, the *guba*, in the 1530s. This servitor class thus effectively managed local government at the behest of the tsar: it administered law and order in the provinces, controlled mobility and the distribution of service lands, it collected taxes, mustered military forces, and certified servile contracts.[41] By the 1550s, land surveys and uniform coinage and weight measures were being promoted throughout the land.[42] Justice was also centralized by the early 1500s: the state became "the exclusive agent of sanctioned violence (corporal and capital punishment, judicial torture) and eliminated private blood violence."[43]

By "the mid-sixteenth century almost the entire population owed substantial obligations to the state."[44] Russian agents were locally selected and unpaid, with personal liabilities if they failed in their obligations, just like medieval English sheriffs and other royal agents. Russian historians debate whether this experiment was genuinely democratic or a "sham"

---

[37] Martin 2007, 409.   [38] Kleimola 1977, 28.   [39] Pipes 1974, 100.
[40] Reynolds 1994, 480, and more extensively 323–95; Kaeuper 1988, 152–53; Hollister 1976, 105, 99–106.
[41] Martin 2007, 385; Kivelson 1996, 143–46.
[42] Bogatyrev 2006, 253; Martin 2007, 404–405.   [43] Kollmann 2012, 25.
[44] Zlotnik 1979, 244, 250.

masking state extension;[45] but it strongly resembles the medieval English context that generated the most robust parliament, as described in Parts I and II. Even the "scattered landholding" of the Moscow elites, which is seen to have "exacerbated the service-induced rootlessness of the gentry,"[46] resembles English patterns, where estate fragmentation was initially a key mechanism of undercutting noble power.[47] Landholding fragmentation thus cannot help explain divergent Russian outcomes.

Service emerges as key also for Russian representative activity. The assemblies that emerged in the mid-sixteenth century mainly involved the gentry who were most dependent on the tsar. Far from a paradox, this is the main prediction of the argument advanced here, illustrating second-best constitutionalism. These Assemblies of the Land (later named *zemskii sobor*) were first called in 1549 due to war and ended in 1653.[48] Depending on the criteria of social composition, about fifteen to sixty assemblies are identified. They had no formal procedure, elections, or quotas; "sometimes the instructions requested that as many representatives as desired should come."[49] Despite this, they took radical political action: they elected tsars, occasionally with broad representation that included black peasants; Mikhail Fedorovich was thus elected in 1613, ending the Time of Troubles.

The paradox of representative practice in the violent rule of Ivan IV has been muted because Western historians mostly questioned the portrayal of the period in Soviet scholarship as that of an "estate-representative monarchy." Instead, the assemblies were presented simply as an instrument of the tsar, mainly because no estates existed in Russia, no legally recognized corporative entities with established rights.[50] As Pipes argued, "Participants in [assemblies] were considered to be performing state service and received pay from the treasury; attendance was a duty, not a right."[51] Yet again, however, as we have seen, these traits defined English practice. In England, the state even forced communities to cover the expense of representatives, causing bitter disputes – again indicating higher royal powers in England.[52] These points, therefore, cannot account for the differential outcomes in the Russian case either.

Some scholars have dismissed many Russian assemblies due to the absence of non-nobles,[53] but this is also not dispositive. As we have seen in England, the Commons were only present in 17 percent of

---

[45] Kivelson 1996, 144–45.   [46] Kivelson 1994, 199; 1996, 87, 99.
[47] Prestwich 1990, 60; Bartlett 2000, 219.
[48] Brown 1983, 78; Pipes 1974, 107. The term *zemskii sobor* was invented in the nineteenth century; Brown 1983, 90; Hellie 1987.
[49] Pipes 1974, 107; Brown 1983, 79, 82, 84.   [50] Brown 1983, 78–90.
[51] Pipes 1974, 107.   [52] See Chapter 4.   [53] Brown 1983, 81.

meetings before 1307 (the critical period of emergence), and important decisions were taken in their absence – nobles were the main actors. Without the systematic compellence of the nobility, the English Parliament would have gone in the direction of France and Castile, where the third estate and ultimately absolutism predominated. Likewise, the early absence of "corporate chambers" in Russian assemblies (an upper and a lower house only emerged in 1649) does not disqualify them. As seen in Chapter 2, the English houses of Lords and Commons also solidified late, as a result of common burdens.[54] Even the (s)election of representatives had procedural parallels.[55]

Russian assemblies were rather typically attended by the "members of the middle service class," which depended on the tsar for its land, with "church officials, merchants, advisers to the tsar, civil administrators, and in the seventeenth century, townsmen" also attending.[56] The most consequential difference with England was, I argue, instead the variation in ruler power. Russian tsars were weaker compared to medieval English kings in compelling especially their strongest domestic competitors (the *boyars* and princes); tsars were after all elected.

Weaker infrastructural powers meant that attendance overall could not be compelled – the key advantage observed in the English case. There, as seen, kings relied on a robust, polity-wide system of counties organized around a court under royal command with strong enforcement powers. By contrast, Russian assembly members were "either drawn from whichever members of the service ranks happened to be in Moscow at the time or chosen by local government officials."[57] Candidate selection "had to take into consideration not only who was of the appropriate service rank as well as who did not have other service obligations at the moment but also who had sufficient wherewithal to afford the expenses involved with travel to and from Moscow, not to mention living there for the duration of the Assembly sessions. It is little wonder these governors had difficulty finding delegates and often encountered resistance from the pool of potential candidates."[58] Such resistance was, as we have seen, not weaker in England, yet the process still provided a steady stream of representatives, because royal enforcement was more effective.

---

[54] Keep 1957, 115; Ostrowski 2004, 115, 116.   [55] Keep 1957, 102.

[56] Brown 1983, 81; Hellie 1987, 229–31; Kivelson 1996, 198.

[57] Ostrowski 2004, 117; Hellie 1987, 229.

[58] Ostrowski 2004, 117. Ostrowski ascribes the choice to governors, whereas Kivelson 1996, 198 notes that for the gentry the selection was of "the best" representatives from that class, a principle that differs little from English practice. Though we tend to think of elections as more democratic, they were in fact more efficient in collecting information than relying on an outside administrator.

Since attendance is widely seen as a right demanded from below, failure to secure it seems to support the assumption that Russian rulers simply suppressed it. Instead, the previous account has illuminated the obligatory component of representation in Western cases, especially England. This makes it easier to attribute the low and haphazard attendance in Russia to the infrastructural weakness of the regime.

12.2   Indicators of Ruler Weakness

The claim of tsarist weakness, however, goes against widespread stereotypes. What evidence supports it? Revisionist scholarship has concurred on this front,[59] but three indicators can only be examined here: the tsars' weak control over the *boyars*; their poor taxing capability, especially over the most powerful social actors; and, paradoxically, the mass enserfment of peasants by the gentry. These in turn precluded the institutional fusion between the different instruments of governance observed in England and the supra-local collective organization of the gentry. It also meant that collective responsibility was not as organized above the local level in Russia, a part of a broader pattern of difference with the West that will be examined more fully in the next chapter.

12.2.1   Weak Control Over Society, Especially the Boyars

The question of the power balance between the tsar and society, especially the *boyars*, goes to the heart of the long-standing debate on whether Russia was a despotism. The brief treatment below cannot exhaust the question. Rather, key issues raised in the historiography will be addressed through the insights of this account, supporting the revisionist interpretation.

This revisionism notes that despite the autocratic façade, underlying power dynamics were very fragmented.[60] In this view, drawing on the groundbreaking work of Edward Keenan, "the real ruling force in the Kremlin" was "a network of interconnected patriarchal boyar clans."[61] The main implication of such a condition, according to the conventional metric applied in this study, is that the tsar would not be able to tax the *boyars* and other powerful groups. This is shown in the next section.

In Russian historiography, however, tsar despotism is derived from a posited lack of full property rights for the servitor classes, even the

---

[59] See for instance Kollmann 2012, 425.   [60] Kollmann 1987, 146–80.

[61] Kivelson 1994, 198; Keenan 1986; Crummey 1983. Bogatyrev 2000, 221 disagrees, but evidence on taxation suggests that on the dimensions relevant to this account, the balance was against the tsar.

boyars. Pipes focused on two observations: property rights depended on service and rulers curtailed them through arbitrary restrictions and confiscations. Service exemplified the regime's character as unfree and absolutist. In "no other European land was the sovereign able to make all nonclerical landholding conditional upon the performance of service to him."[62] "It meant nothing less than the elimination of private property in land." Absolutism is identified with total control of economic resources: "It was the combination of absolute political power with nearly complete control of the country's productive resources that made the Muscovite monarchy so formidable an institution."[63]

Service may have made Russia "backward" or "medieval" compared to contemporaneous Western conditions, but it cannot explain or define "despotism," since it mirrored the period of parliamentary emergence in England. Treating service as a regressive trait assumes a teleological understanding of Western development, progressing away from conditional service to "freedom" and "absolute property rights." Pipes' argument was in fact powerfully countered by Weickhardt, who, as mentioned, showed how key forms of Russian property were similar to English common law forms.[64] Moreover, the restriction of more "absolute" rights (observed up to the 1400s) in favor of more conditional ones based on service cannot inform us about the power balance with the leading social group, the *boyars*, pace Pipes.

Instead, tsars imposed conditional service in the late 1400s when the *boyars* had levels of freedom unparalleled in the West, especially England. Just as English nobles, *boyars* were major landowners,[65] but unlike them in the early period of parliamentary emergence, their land was allodial and thus could be freely sold. A *boyar* clan member could repurchase a relative's sold *votchina* land within forty years.[66] Although almost all *boyars* performed military service, this was not a tenurial obligation as in England. They served to gain income, albeit bound by concerns of honor.[67] They were not as dependent as the English tenant nobility, having an obligation to make some contribution to the state but free to serve any prince; they could even serve a foreign ruler, such as the Great Prince of Lithuania, a right affirmed in treaties. Service had been "optional."[68] They could leave a prince "at a moment's notice" through

---

[62] Blum 1961, 169.

[63] Pipes 1974, 93, 94. I focus on Pipes because, although his views are not as prevalent among specialists, they exemplify stereotypes that are still current.

[64] Weickhardt 1994.   [65] Kollmann 1987, 37–46.

[66] Hellie 2006a, 384. This practice was not exclusively Eastern and "patrimonial"; in the West it was called *retrait lignager*; Pipes 1974, 93; Baker 2002, 262.

[67] Kollmann 1999.   [68] Hellie 2006a, 382–83.

the right of renunciation (*otkaz*).[69] This displays a transactional, contractual structure that was inconceivable in the English or French monarchies, originally at least.

Unsurprisingly, the rhetoric applied was absolutist and extreme: faced with such centrifugal forces, ideology becomes a tool to bend a recalcitrant social reality in a more centralized mold. The term *gosudar*, master of slaves, spread as Muscovy was subduing formidable independent princes.[70] The tsar also faced the appanage princes, who, though family members, had large retinues and autonomy.[71] Even Pipes concedes this: "Behind the façade of monopolistic and autocratic monarchy survived powerful vestiges of the appanage era ... Annexation was often a mere formality."[72]

The implications of such weakness are important. They explain why the tsar would not acknowledge law-making authority in another body, another major argument of the despotist thesis:[73] the de facto existence of such rights was what tsars were combating. Just as in France, absolutist rhetoric aimed to counter the fragmentation and initial strength of social groups, as the normative/empirical inversion suggests. Measures that appear autocratic were mild by comparison. Ivan III, in the 1470s, treated departure as treason, worthy of land confiscation.[74] But confiscation was the penalty for a simple felony in England; treason was brutally punished. Edward I had disloyal opponents hung, disemboweled, and quartered, with summary judicial procedures, as did his successors.[75]

Tsars employed other tools, moreover, that look familiar given the preceding account. They started extracting oaths for service, as well as security deposits in case of breach of oath – again, requirements hardly different from those in early Western monarchies and inevitable in a process of asserting sovereignty over new territories.[76] Critically, however, in a trait that later I show to also reflect comparative weakness, tsars had to rely on the collective responsibility of kinship groups to ensure compliance with such oaths, given the strong clan structure of the *boyars*.[77] Enforcement of obligation remained difficult: as *boyars* often avoided service, a "stream of decrees threatening dire punishment" was issued.[78] This was possibly why tsars drastically increased the size of the *Duma*.[79]

---

[69] Pipes 1974, 47.   [70] Bogatyrev 2000, 18.
[71] Crummey 1987, 110–14; Martin 2007, 333–35.   [72] Pipes 1974, 89.
[73] Poe 2002, 482.   [74] Farrow 2004, 34; Kleimola 1977, 26–27; Pipes 1974, 88.
[75] Bellamy 1970, 33–39, 119, 132, 152, 201.   [76] Kosto 2012.   [77] Dewey 1987.
[78] Pipes 1974, 89.
[79] Poe 2006, 451 also ascribed a sharper increase in the late 1600s to weakness. See also, Martin 2007, 372–74; Ostrowski 2004, 133 and note 28 above.

As noted in the previous chapter, the major indicators of state arbitrariness in this literature,[80] as in much property rights scholarship,[81] are limitations on land transfers and confiscations. Tsars indeed restricted transfers to monastic institutions.[82] But so did English kings, especially Edward I through the Statute of Mortmain, at the height of parliamentary consolidation in the late 1200s. Land bequeathed to a monastery paid no inheritance taxes to the state in both cases; the Church is a perpetual organization, so these restrictions concerned tax enforcement.[83]

As Weickhardt has noted, confiscations were also hardly absent in England.[84] The Dissolution of the Monasteries by Henry VIII in the 1530s, as we have seen, was one of the largest confiscations of property in Europe.[85] The initial pretext was religious conformity – an extra-legal motive, for which Parliament was enlisted.[86] The unparalleled English capacity to appropriate land is also seen in the Enclosures, where land rights of large sections of the population were privately expropriated over centuries, eventually with parliamentary approval.[87] But expropriation was also widely prevalent in the period of parliamentary emergence, as seen in Chapter 6: kings confiscated lands of at least 44 percent and 32 percent of recorded nobles in the decades before and after 1250 respectively.[88] It was precisely the greater capacity of the English crown to threaten its most powerful subjects that mobilized them to collaborate and solve their collective action problem – enabling representative institutions.

By contrast, existing data, though incomplete, suggest that expropriations of land were quite limited in Russia. Landowners had at most a 4 percent chance of confiscation in the eighteenth century, according to some studies at least.[89] Despite the rhetoric and violence, the overall capacity of tsars to regularly compel their most powerful subjects was weaker. This is strikingly displayed in an episode widely invoked to prove exactly the opposite, the *Oprichnina*. In 1564, Ivan the Terrible split the country in two to confront the *boyars*, placing half under his direct control.[90] He confiscated land from *boyars* and lower servitors alike. Moreover, Ivan's henchmen "collected as much rent from their peasants in one year as usually was collected in ten years," resulting in up to 85 percent of the area being abandoned.[91] This was the classic exemplar of tsarist tyranny.

However, Ivan's retreat from Moscow was generated by fear – of court intrigue, of foreign relations failures, of danger to his family.[92] It was the

---

[80] Pipes 1994; Poe 2002.   [81] North and Weingast 1989.   [82] Martin 2007, 404–405.
[83] Prestwich 2005, 129–31.   [84] Weickhardt 1994, 532.   [85] Baker 2003, 709.
[86] Youings 1971.   [87] Polanyi 1944.   [88] See Table 6.1.   [89] Weickhardt 1994, 533.
[90] Bogatyrev 2006, 259–61.   [91] Hellie 2006b, 293–94.   [92] Bogatyrev 2006, 257.

incapacity to control most *boyars* that elicited the move. The public part of the kingdom, the *zemschina*, was ruled by the *boyar* council and was out of his control. More service than *boyar* land seems to have been confiscated, although the evidence is not clear-cut.[93] Many of the exiled princes were able to return. The critical point is that the tsar was unable to control a substantial part of the polity, so Muscovy "found itself with two administrations, two armies and two separate groups of territories" – one controlled by the tsar, another by the *boyars*.[94] Tax collection plummeted after the 1560s to less than a tenth in Novgorod, "once the wealthiest region in all the Russian lands."[95] This reign of terror, as typical, stemmed from weakness (although "paranoia" is also detected[96]), not strength. The greater the weakness and threat, the more the resort to violence and cruelty.

A key reason why, despite such facts, the image remains reversed – with Russia considered far more arbitrary than premodern England – is that ruler action, deeply expropriatory as it was, took place in a central institutionalized setting in England, whereas in Russia it involved extra-institutional action of the tsar against individuals, thus appearing more arbitrary. As Kleimola notes, repressive measures did not target classes as a whole, but were mostly atomized.[97] The observed "power" of tsars had more to do with the lack of institutionalized barriers, which allowed them to use violence against individuals, than to their effectiveness in controlling society. This encapsulates the definition of despotism in the seminal treatment by Michael Mann: it is the "range of actions which the elite is empowered to undertake without routine, institutionalized negotiation with civil society groups."[98] But institutions were absent due to royal weakness. In England, their presence flowed from royal strength, at least initially.

12.2.2 Poor Taxing Capability of Tsars

The episode I have described as one of weakness, the *Oprichnina*, actually culminated a decades-long effort to strengthen the state. The striking rise in taxes in the intervening period, at least in nominal terms, is an indicator of this. The rate per taxable unit rose seven times in the first half of the sixteenth century and similar increases in revenue are estimated for one region, Novgorod, according to some studies.[99] These increases hit peasants particularly hard, hence amplifying the tyrannical image of the

---

[93] Farrow 2004, 35.   [94] Crummey 1987, 162.   [95] Martin 2007, 414–15.
[96] Hellie 2006b, 293.   [97] Kleimola 1977, 28.   [98] Mann 1984, 188.
[99] See the studies cited by Martin 2007, 405–406.

regime. They also involved a restriction on the widespread exemptions that shaped the Russian tax regime, especially for secular landlords: "the turn of the sixteenth century brought a fundamental restructuring of the norms governing" immunities.[100] The spike in taxation is congruent with the rise of state power I have suggested was a necessary condition for institutional emergence. However, it is not adequate to prove strong state capacity overall, which enables institutions to survive; this can only be established on a relative and comparative basis. Extractive capability is relative to the wealth of the country and to the extractive rates of other countries.

Historical evidence at least suggests limited extraction. The Russian tax system after the fifteenth century is mostly known through immunity charters, which indicate weak infrastructure, as we've seen in France.[101] The most privileged status was enjoyed by the nobility and Church in particular since the feudal wars of the fifteenth century.[102] Unlike in England, military service land was tax exempt.[103] Further, by the seventeenth century taxation declined, despite claims that that was the "height of monarchical centralization."[104] Lands that were the major source of tax revenue included court lands that were directly under the tsar's control and "black" lands populated by peasants that the tsar could freely grant to private proprietors.[105] However, by "the early seventeenth century black lands had almost disappeared from the heartland of the Moscow state, and with them vanished most of the independent [tax-paying] peasants living in self-governing communities."[106]

The claims about monarchical centralization thus belie the massive privatization of state land observed on the ground. By the late 1650s, 67 percent of the households subject to fiscal and other obligations (*tiaglo*) were in *boyar* and *dvoriane* land and 13 percent in the hands of the Church; the crown controlled only about 9 percent. Four out of five Russians "ceased to be subjects of the state," a condition formalized in the Code of 1649.[107] Tax collection was inevitably undermined: despite local increases, it remained far below the levels that could be supported by the wealth of the country. In England, not only were the peasants taxed, as we have seen, but the nobles themselves were liable as well, undercutting their wealth more deeply than in Russia. The incapacity to impose broadly-based state taxation underlies again an absolutist rhetoric which conceals infrastructural weakness.

---

[100] Floria 2000, 21–22; Dewey 1964.
[101] Dewey 1964; Froianov 1986, 42–48; Kashtanov 1971.   [102] Floria 2000, 18.
[103] Kivelson 1996, 46.   [104] Pipes 1974, 100.   [105] Blum 1961, 93.
[106] Pipes 1974, 104.   [107] Pipes 1974, 104.

Comparative data are highly speculative and only available for a later period, yet they establish a baseline that can be revised by further historical research. According to extrapolations by economist Angus Maddison,[108] Russia had about half the GDP per capita of Britain in 1700 (610 to 1,250 1990 Geary-Khamis dollars). Data on taxation starting in 1700, by Karaman and Pamuk, suggest that Russia's tax revenue per capita was only 7 percent of what England raised, 3 percent of what the Netherlands raised and 14 percent of what France did (but 78 percent of what the Ottoman Empire did).[109] It would thus need to raise about seven times as much to reach English levels of real per capita taxation. Though taxation doubled in the next fifty years, it still fell behind Western states. Extraction seems therefore considerably less than what was possible, although, as suggested above, revenue in 1700 was possibly less than earlier.[110] Russian state capacity, though rising before representation emerged, was weak relative to European and especially English standards.

12.2.3 Mass Enserfment of Peasants by the Servitor Class

Within social science, especially economic history, no feature has exemplified Russian despotism (and explained its economic stagnation) more than the expansion of serfdom[111] in the seventeenth century,[112] while Western serfdom declined after the Black Death. Russian scholars have drawn a bleak picture of oppression: in the Code of 1649, among "the hundreds of articles defining the power of landlords over their peasants there is not one which sets on it any limits." The Code even recognized peasants as chattels, making them "personally liable for debts of bankrupt landlords."[113]

This sounds despotic indeed, but what explains it? A conventional economic logic attributed Eastern serfdom to the poor labor-to-land ratio: the need for a military force and the scarcity of labor over extensive lands forced the state to use coercion.[114] Labor scarcity, however,

---

[108] I use the older quite speculative data, as the recent estimates by the Maddison Project do not include Russia; Maddison 2003.

[109] Karaman and Pamuk 2013.

[110] For an earlier period, pre-1400, historian Janet Martin strikingly estimated that the fur trade (the most important economic resource) probably equaled the tribute paid to the Golden Horde; Martin 1986, 163. A full GDP estimate of course would need to include all economic activity, of which trade was one part.

[111] Brenner 1976; Aston and Philpin 1985; Blum 1961; Hellie 1971; Robinson and Torvik 2013.

[112] Weickhardt 1993, 678; Hellie 2006b, 296.   [113] Pipes 1974, 104–105.

[114] Domar 1970.

normally entails greater bargaining power for laborers, as it did in the West after the Black Death, not enserfment, as Robert Brenner noted.[115] So, did "a central coercive authority" keep "lords from competing for labor" instead, as North and Thomas claimed?[116]

In fact, the Code was implementing servitor landlord interests, not any "statist" agenda of the tsar.[117] It was "gentry landlords and urban communes [who] agitated for increasingly active state intervention in enforcing these norms, recovering runaways, penalizing those who harbored fugitives, and closing loopholes for escape into border regiments and frontier towns."[118] The state ceded such rights to the gentry as it could not prevent the *boyars* and the Church from encroaching on gentry lands and their peasants. Without rent-payers the gentry could not render military service. Competition was thus not suppressed by the state in Russia; rather, contracts (between gentry and peasants) were being violated by the powerful – a market failure the state tried to correct. Again, power over the most powerful emerges as a vital conditional for optimal outcomes.

That such power was deficient in the Russian case is suggested by a typically overlooked difference with England. Outright slavery in Russia usually removed persons from tax-paying rolls, so was unwanted by the state, whilst many serfs had been "converted into slaves" by the 1670s.[119] Serfs in any case were taxed through their lords.[120] English villeins and serfs, some of whom could be among the wealthiest members of their communities,[121] were instead taxed directly and increasingly so after the Black Death.[122] Despite stiff resistance to innovations like the Poll Taxes of 1377–81,[123] English kings could circumvent the lords and access all subjects directly. As seen in Chapter 6, they raised more per capita in taxation in this period.

The English infrastructural advantage also undergirds what scholars have described as the failure of the "seigneurial reaction" in England, a major theme in the "Brenner debate": English lords, deprived of extra-economic powers, tried to coerce serfs and villeins after 1348, by allying with the state to pass laws regulating wages.[124] Regulation failed, however, and serfdom ended because of peasant resistance,

---

[115] Brenner 1976.   [116] North and Thomas 1971, 779.   [117] Kivelson 1994, 200.
[118] Kivelson 1997, 649.   [119] Hellie 2006b, 295, 294n33; 1971; Blum 1961, 273–74.
[120] Pipes 1974, 104.
[121] Raftis 1997; Bailey 2021, ch. 1. In simplified terms, serfdom related to status, villeinage to unfree land tenure.
[122] Ormrod 2008.   [123] Fenwick 1983.
[124] Putnam 1908; Given-Wilson 2000; Palmer 1993. The debate on serfdom has been repositioned by the most extensive recent treatments by Mark Bailey 2014; 2021.

culminating with the Revolt of 1381.[125] Russian lords by contrast succeeded, in this logic.

First, it must be pointed out that the "seigneurial reaction" was highly effective initially, but typically when the crown was strong. Nominal wages did rise but this happened *before* the second Labor Statute (1351). Its "failure" is moreover judged against its unrealistic stipulation that wages be fixed at levels lower than those of the 1330s. In fact, under most of Edward III and Henry V, both assessed as strong rulers,[126] real wages and income appear, remarkably, stationary, even at some points declining,[127] or at least growing at a slower rate than GDP per capita,[128] while the population halved. Enforcement lapsed especially under and after the weaker Richard II (though other factors of course contributed). The "exceptional"[129] level of enforcement in the 1350s and 1360s transpired not least because those charged with enforcing the Statutes were often magnates and gentry who stood to gain by it, serving as justices of the peace (JPs). JPs are widely viewed as exemplifying the surrender of royal justice to local elites, leading to corruption.[130] Dissenting views have emphasized the importance of strong royal rule in sustaining the new judicial institutions at times.[131] Either way, the peace commissions they administered applied royal law[132] and were aided by 664 royal officials appointed to enforce the Statutes.[133]

Moreover, even when English royal power waned, serfdom was being transformed through royal institutions. By 1381, the main concern was "civic, not tenurial, freedom," as landlords could mobilize a "new public jurisdiction": since the royal ordinance of 1349, "everyone 'physically capable'" under 60 had to "serve or be imprisoned."[134] Some historians even speak of a "second serfdom."[135] Serfdom thus receded not because workers had "sufficient power,"[136] but because the royal judicial infrastructure in England permitted the relative control of labor through laws and regulations. In Russia, such infrastructure was weaker in the sixteenth century and personal forms of domination prevailed. It's not just that the courts managed social relations more consistently in England; it

---

[125] Hilton 1969; Brenner 1976.

[126] Bubenicek and Partington 2015, 155; Ormrod 2013.

[127] Indices vary, but the pattern is common; Phelps Brown and Hopkins 1962; Munro 2012; Humphries and Weisdorf 2019.

[128] See Clark 2014 on real building laborer wages and Broadberry et al. 2015 for GDP.

[129] Poos 1983, 50.   [130] Maddicott 1978b.

[131] Bubenicek and Partington 2015. See also Palmer 1993 and the critique in Musson 2000.

[132] Bubenicek and Partington 2015, 156.   [133] Putnam 1906, 527.

[134] Harding 1984, 187; Bennett 2010.

[135] Harding 1984, 187; Beier 2008; Given-Wilson 2000, 98. But cf. Bailey 2014.

[136] Acemoglu and Robinson 2012, 100.

is also that English lords had weaker levels of extra-economic means of coercion due to the expanding state.[137] So, restrictive measures with the same intent in the two cases appear as regulations in one case and serfdom in the other.

These successive laws, moreover, were passed in Parliament at a time when the Commons, as we have seen, were gaining in power, meaning that higher levels of cooperation could be expected than in Russia, despite resistance.[138] That in England serfdom did not prevail is surely related to its capacity to regularize restrictions on labor movement through polity-wide laws that were so effective they still required a frontal attack in Adam Smith's *Wealth of Nations* four centuries later.[139] They were only removed from the statute books "after heated debate" in 1814, yet workers could still be criminally prosecuted for breach of contract through master-servant laws until 1875.[140] England did not forgo coercion; it regularized it through law.

Finally, overt coercion was avoided in England due to another conse-quence of state strength: demographic pressures were occurring in perhaps the most articulated and well-enforced systems of land tenures. The "decline of serfdom" meant the upgrading of villein (unfree) tenures into contractual ones, either life tenancies or leases for years. This ultimately led to copyhold tenures that were gradually incorporated into the common law system, as we've seen.[141] As historian Mark Bailey has argued in his reassessment of serfdom's decline, villeins were already quite enmeshed in royal courts, despite being formally excluded,[142] and manorial courts, which handled their cases, were increasingly reflecting common law practices.[143] Whether manorial courts enforced the interests of the lords[144] or were dominated by the far more numerous peasant elites,[145] the tenurial transition in England resulted in the expansion of a far more efficient organization of production, enabling the creation of larger farming units.[146] Economic growth, coupled with the more "subtle forms of social control"[147] existing institutions provided, made the re-establishment of serfdom in England both less necessary and less possible.

After all, Russian policy did not aim to create serfdom: the word serf was not even mentioned in the Code of 1649, which only specified what happened to peasants who fled.[148] Russian tsars were simply less able to depersonalize coercion through law, because the state had inadequate

---

[137] Wood 2002.   [138] Given-Wilson 2000, 85–90, 94–97.

[139] Smith [1776] 1981a, I.x.c., 41–59.   [140] Bennett 2010, 7; Steinberg 2016.

[141] Bailey 2014, 316–36 dates this to the sharp decline in land prices after 1350.

[142] Musson and Ormrod 1999, 131–33.   [143] Bailey 2021, ch. 4.

[144] Dyer 2002a, 283.   [145] Bailey 2021.   [146] Dyer 2002a, 357–62.

[147] Musson and Ormrod 1999, 95–96.   [148] Hosking 2000, 308.

power over the most powerful and therefore also a weaker judicial infrastructure. Whereas in Russia the *boyars* were the major threat who could
poach servitor peasants, in England, as the sociologist Richard Lachmann
pointed out, the landlords were relatively more constrained by the crown
and Church, at least after the Black Death.[149]

12.3   Consequences of Ruler Weakness: Institutional Fragmentation

The Russian regime therefore shared many features with England especially; it differed on dimensions reflecting weaker ruler powers. Weakness
produced the observable "despotism" as a coping mechanism, but it also
precluded the key necessary condition for an enduring constitutional
regime. In England, strong state capacity enabled an institutional fusion
of judicial and fiscal functions which consolidated Parliament. It also
forced the powerful sectors of society into concerted action in response
to high service and taxation demands, thus solving elite collective action
problems. The following section traces the divergent Russian outcomes,
arguing that weak state power suffices to explain them, similarly to
France. Regardless of whether local actors had constitutional preferences
or not, the capacity was absent to implement them.

The "absolutist" character of the Russian regime in some Russian
historiography (the "statist" approach) is exemplified in the tsar's council, the *Duma*. Yet this judgment selects institutional traits that have
striking similarities with English practice. For instance, Richard Pipes
noted that *Duma* attendees did not have corporative status; they received
instead "personal invitations," dismissed as a sign of the illiberal, controlling character of the regime.[150] However, an individual summons for the
nobility was also a European practice, as seen.[151] England was distinguished by the higher control of the crown over this selection, as it was
only late in time that some families gained a customary, but still not legal,
right of parliamentary attendance.[152]

Further, although the *Duma* was only attended by *boyars*, this again had
parallels with the West, where royal councils did much of the governing.
As we saw, early assemblies that survived were dominated by the nobility,
like England, and where towns were dominant, as in France and Spain,
the estates either withered or did not become fully representative. The

[149] Lachmann 1985, 360.   [150] Pipes 1974, 107; Brown 1983, 86–88.
[151] Russian practice may even draw on Norman antecedents; Pipes 1974, 106. That the
Duma's competence and role were undefined (Poe 2006, 460) also does not distinguish
it from early Western institutions.
[152] Powell and Wallis 1968, 222–25.

boyars had similar roles to Western nobilities: they participated in decree-
ing some of the most significant acts of the government, law codes, foreign
treaties, and other precedent-setting measures.[153] The *Duma*, like all
premodern royal councils, also had official judicial functions.[154] The
tsar was actively involved in cases from the late fifteenth century. The
ruler's justice was "one of the highest privileges that could be bestowed
upon a subject."[155] As in Western cases, land disputes were the main
source of at least surviving lawsuits from that time.[156] As business
increased, tsars delegated cases, either to their sons or to *boyars* who
held separate courts, the latter since 1497.[157]

This institutional proliferation undercut the dynamics of functional
layering and fusion we have seen to be critical. *Boyars* also served as
judges into the 1600s and appeared in the petitions Chancellery, as in
England.[158] Generally, however, chancelleries (*prikazys*) were staffed
with servicemen "because nobles scorned such routine activity."[159] The
power dynamics involved in *boyar* judicial service are not clear. Was this
service imposed or a privilege sought by the Russian upper nobility? We
do know that the gentry petitions of 1648 requested their removal, so they
must have been using the posts for personal enrichment. Tsars called
boyars to service on an ad hoc basis,[160] though; as numbers of *boyars*
serving seem unavailable, it is not possible to directly compare levels of
service and relative powers to compel. Nonetheless, the common pattern
of similar practices at the micro level occurring in cases with different
institutional outcomes is observed here too.

The representative institution, however, was the Assemblies of the
Land, introduced above, that drew broader social groups. These were
not tied to the *Duma* nor to regular judicial business, as representative
meetings were in the English Parliament. They were thus irregular and
also ad hoc, like the French Estates-General. They were convoked "on
issues like war, dynastic succession, and peace."[161] Bellicist theories
would attribute the meetings to these pressures, but the bargaining logic
does not explain observed patterns. In fact, it was the "non-taxpaying
social groups" that originally supported the meetings.[162] When taxation

---

[153] "Other, less important decrees, such as *kormlenie* ('feeding'), *votchina*, and *pomest'e*
grants, judicial immunities, local agreements, etc., were clearly the prerogative of the
ruler alone"; Ostrowski 2006, 225, 217.
[154] The *Duma* became an appellate court in 1649; Davies 2006, 469.
[155] Kleimola 1975, 10–11. This judicial role was still central in the law code of 1550;
Kivelson 1996, 234.
[156] Kleimola 1975, 8.   [157] Kleimola 1975, 13, 15.   [158] Kivelson 1996, 231–32.
[159] Graham 1987, 30.   [160] Kleimola 1975, 13.
[161] Kollmann 1987, 185; Poe 2006, 461; Bogatyrev 2006, 259.
[162] Kollmann 1987, 185.

was discussed, in 1615 and 1618, it was at the end of the Polish–Muscovite war (1605–18). Nor did the renewal of war in 1654 lead to their recurrence; about three were held after 1681 and they ceased thereafter.[163] Military pressures do not suffice to produce enduring representation – unless a regular pre-existing institutional structure integrated representative activity.

The eclipse of such activity has received various explanations by Russian historians. One has been already addressed, that delegates "were called as a matter of service obligation (and sometimes viewed said service as onerous), not as a matter of 'right.'"[164] But this in fact explains why there was any representative activity at all from the perspective of this account. Another is that land being held through service explains why no common law "ancient custom" or law of resistance existed, as it presumably inhibited the freedom and power of landholders.[165] However, we've seen that it was precisely the common frame of obligations derived from landholding that coordinated English elites in articulating such rights – which they did to a more restrained degree than on the Continent. English common law was the product of dependent landholding.

The most common explanation for the lapse of representative institutions among Russian historians, however, is that there was no collective consciousness in Russia, that social actors lacked corporate identity as estates, in contrast to the West.[166] I examine this in the next chapter, bringing the Ottoman Empire into the comparison.

*

This chapter has shown that conditional rights to land underlie what many see as a paradox in Russian history, a spate of representative activity under highly centralizing rulers. This was generated in response to demands for justice that differed little from Western cases. However, Russian state capacity was shown to be comparatively weaker, enabling it to compel systematically only the lower nobility, thus generating the pattern of second-best constitutionalism observed in Hungary, Poland, Castile, and elsewhere. Many traits of the regime traditionally interpreted as indicators of strength, even arbitrariness, emerge rather as symptoms of infrastructural weakness. Most crucially this is seen in the incapacity to aggregate judicial activity systematically at the supra-local level. This meant weaker territorial anchoring in the localities, as the next chapter discusses. The building blocks of social interaction were similar; it was their organization by the state that differed.

[163] Ostrowski 2004, 129–30.   [164] Poe 2006, 461; 2002.   [165] Hellie 2000, 16.
[166] Brown 1983, 78–90; Kollmann 1987, 3; Kleimola 1977, 25.

Part V

Why Representation in the West: Petitions, Collective Responsibility, and Supra-Local Organization

13 Petitions, Collective Responsibility, and Representative Practice: England, Russia, and the Ottoman Empire

Representative outcomes in East and West differed and previous chapters considered possible explanations. Fully comparing cases is hardly possible in such a broad study, so I have examined the factors that leading social scientists, especially historians, have identified as crucial. The main conditions militating against constitutional outcomes in such accounts have been "state control of land," the imposition of conditional service, and the "weak" conditional property rights these entail. Yet these hypotheses counter the genetic account of English institutions offered in this book, which shows these factors to be fundamental. The account thus has expanded the dimensions on which non-Western regimes display crucial similarities with Western ones, especially England. It thereby has supported arguments in Russian and Ottoman history that have revised stereotypical assumptions about these regions.

Yet, profound differences do exist between these regimes and Western ones, so accounting for them remains challenging. Intriguingly, scholars working in very different fields have converged on a similar assessment of the underlying difference: in the West, depersonalized forms of exchange developed enabling collective action, whereas the two non-Western cases, Russia and the Ottoman Empire, remained confined to personalized exchange. Personalization precluded a language of rights, which by definition apply to whole groups, not individuals. From Russian history to Ottoman economics to general social science theory, the above verdict seems recurrent.

Russian historians have rejected simplistic views of the regime as "despotic," as seen in Chapter 12,[1] by stressing the emerging pluralism and language of claims against the state, especially in the seventeenth century, whilst identifying their limitations and divergence from the West.[2] Valerie Kivelson argued that Russian "subjects" differed from Western European "citizens" by being confined to pre-democratic forms of political

---

[1] Poe 1998; Hellie 1998.
[2] Keep 1970; Kollmann 1987; 1999; Kivelson 1996; 1997; 2002.

expression, namely petitions, but also supplications, riots, and consultation. The absence of representative institutions flowed from "the
absence among subjects of a self-conscious claim to freedom as
a citizen's right."[3] For Nancy Kollmann, Russian autocracy was different
from the West's "in that it allowed a multiplicity of interests to be
represented without tolerating social pluralism in politics." Power was
the sovereign's private prerogative, but it carried no obligation.[4] This
same atomism meant that in Russia actors in court politics "did not
constitute a privileged corporative class, and their political struggles
were not expressions of class-based antagonisms. Struggles at court
were not over policies and rights, but over personal power as defined in
terms of kinship and personal alliances."[5]

From such a view, it was unsurprising that assemblies failed; deputies
"could not proceed from a consciousness of their *interests* to
a consciousness of their *rights*,"[6] part of the general lack of social cohe-
siveness in Russia.[7] The provincial gentrymen remained linked to the
center in a "limited, individualized, and fragmentary" manner. Their
autonomy allowed them to engage in "highly particularistic, local
competitions."[8] This created the impression of "the Muscovite gentry's
seeming lack of interest in political participation."[9]

So, as Kleimola also emphasized, it was not the lack of dissent but of
collective dissent that distinguished Russia.[10] This cannot therefore be
attributed to differences in *demand* for rights across cases: a very strong
sense of "what [the gentry] expected as their due, an understanding of
their 'rights'" existed. The difference was, instead, that this demand was
"couched in the language of right and wrong rather than that of *corporative*
charters of laws," as in the West.[11] Individual abuses were actively
opposed; there was only insufficient *institutionalized* effort to stop them.

This language of corporative demands and extensive institutionalization echoes classics of sociological theory and seminal historical accounts
where corporate estates are central to the development of the modern
state and constitutional order.[12] It was the self-conscious organization of
similarly placed individuals under a corporate entity, an estate, that
allowed them to claim rights against the state, in such accounts. But
these themes also echo the conclusions of major social science studies of
economic development and social order proceeding from very different
premises. These focus on the absence/presence of corporations or other

---

[3] Kivelson 2002, 489.   [4] Kollmann 1987, 1.
[5] Kollmann 1987, 3; Kleimola 1977, 25.   [6] Keep 1957, 119.   [7] Hellie 2000, 13.
[8] Kivelson 1996, 152; Kleimola 1977, 25.   [9] Kivelson 1994, 211–12.
[10] Kleimola 1977, 29.   [11] Kivelson 1996, 152, italics added.
[12] Poggi 1978; 1990; de Lagarde 1937; Lousse 1935.

"perpetually lived organizations."[13] Chapter 11 briefly discussed corporations, bodies legally authorized to act as individuals, created by royal charter or legislative act and endowed with perpetual rights. They were adopted in the West in different domains, such as municipalities, universities, or in commerce.[14] Their absence helps explain why the Ottoman economy diverged from the West for economist Timur Kuran. Such formal and informal bodies underlay the transition from the "natural state" to modern "open access orders," for Douglass North and his co-authors Wallis and Weingast: they allowed the depersonalization of social relations, which, in turn, generated organizations able to pursue complex goals beyond the capacities of individuals.[15]

Although specialists may disagree about the adequacy of these explanations, they do capture an important aspect of reality – corporations were after all absent in both Russia and the Ottoman Empire and collective rights had low articulation.[16] Do these points help explain variation in representative practice? Historians seem to gravitate in the same direction. The absence of a cultural template – corporate bodies, citizens' rights – often suffices to explain differential outcomes. But what the preceding genetic account of Western, especially English, institutions has shown is that these cultural templates were not a fortuitous presence in Western intellectual flora. Nor was the capacity for collective action – which is necessary for any concept of general rights to be articulated – a natural given that grew spontaneously in Western social structures. It cannot be reduced to economic factors, I have argued, as these were endogenous to the political conditions in place.[17] Military pressures don't explain variation systematically either, except in ways that also reflect prior levels of political organization. Weakly organized polities cannot wage extensive war and the "lack of military pressures," as seen in the early history of Russia or Poland for instance, often simply reflected the lack of wherewithal to meet them.

Rather, where they shaped constitutional outcomes, the cultural templates emerged in direct relation to the powers of rulers to impose uniform obligations. The Western cases diverged foremost whenever the state could summon to the center groups across society and systematically impose collective obligations that were state-defined rather than tradition-derived; other variations were endogenous to this primary condition. The language of rights developed to the degree that state power forced social actors to transcend their differences and think of their interests in more collective terms. It was their common subjection

---

[13] Cahen 1970; Kuran 2005; North et al. 2009, 23.   [14] Davis 1905.
[15] North et al. 2009.   [16] Owen 1991, 3; Kuran 2005.   [17] See below and Chapter 7.

to royal power that elicited inclusive representative outcomes at the polity level, not their independent corporate structure. In fact – and this is a widely ignored paradox – the more robust the corporate structure of estates in the West, as in France, Italy, or the Holy Roman Empire, the weaker the representative outcomes; that is where absolutism thrived. The common emphasis on the "corporate" structure of Western social groups in fact misleads our understanding of the conditions for a broadly-based representative polity, as distinct from narrow representative practice, as argued below.

Two components of the narrative advanced here on Western representative practice – the legal principle of representation and the demand for justice mediated through petitions – were, however, independent of royal power, as we have seen. Their absence could also account for divergent outcomes in non-Western cases.[18] The first task of this chapter is therefore to show that both components were present outside the West. It is not thus cultural templates or any demand for rights that initially differed. Though present, these components were, however, just not cultivated at the supra-local level, and the question is why, especially since the land regimes across cases shared the dependence of land rights on the ruler. The chapter's second task is then to show that what differed was the initial capacity to organize demands for justice, to impose obligations across social orders, and to enforce interaction at the center, initially on the ruler's terms. This involves an analysis of how collective responsibility was organized across societies and the role of corporate structures.

This analysis does not imply that, if state capacity had been consistently present in the two non-Western cases, the outcome would have been necessarily identical with the West. My argument is not one of sufficiency but of necessity. It only suggests that even if preferences had been identical, the capacity was absent, and that factor has to be registered before assumptions about "collectivist" identities or authoritarian preferences are projected on the non-Western cases.

13.1   The Kernel of Representative Practice: Legal Representatives in the Ottoman Empire and Russia

Before it developed philosophical dimensions and matured into a language of rights shaping politics, representation had simpler, practical origins in everyday legal practice, enhanced by the Roman principle of plenipotentiary powers, as we have seen. Parts I and II showed that

---

[18] The abstract concept of representation is key for the emergence of capitalism in de Soto 2000.

English representatives had full powers that ensured that decisions made at the center with the king were binding in represented localities. Further, decisions were enforced because of state capacity. The legal practice of representation thus helped shape political representation. Yet it was known and practiced in both the Ottoman and especially the Russian empires, as I show below.

In fact, as Weber has pointed out, the idea of representation, of one agent standing in for many, is already embodied in the theory of rule – hardly a Western exclusivity.[19] The idea of "representation from above," of the ruler being represented by his agents, existed before the people came to be represented.[20] The question is what triggers the extension of the principle to the broader population. Despite common stereotypes, no ideational impediment existed for the extension to broader groups in the non-Western cases. I show this by examining first the Ottoman, then the Russian case.

The legal kernel of representation as a judicial form was theorized and practiced in Islamic law.[21] Legal representatives, the *vekils*, were bound by an articulated set of rules, which distinguished between the principal (*muwakkil*) and the agent himself (*vekil*).[22] For instance, *vekils* were in some cases not permitted to testify on behalf of their clients, when judges believed that the litigant "would be more likely to reveal the truth."[23] The Muslim law of partnerships recognized each partner as the *vekil* of the other.[24]

Group representation was also known in the Ottoman Empire, primarily through religious groups. Jewish communities have left extensive documentation of group representation and bargaining collectively with the sultan over taxation.[25] Courts treated them occasionally as having legal personhood when it suited state interests.[26] A key form of social organization in major centers like Istanbul were guilds, though they were fragmented: no unified organization of Jewish communities (and hence representation) was able to emerge.[27] They did not have "traditional centers or established hierarchy on which the Ottomans could rely as a basis for an administrative system or on which the subjects could rely as a basis for countering and resisting the Ottoman regime."[28] Neither did the Ottoman state create one.

---

[19] Weber 1978, 292–98; 1947, 143–45, 416–23.   [20] Hoyt 1961, 16.

[21] Ibn Rušd 1996, Book 43; Tyan 1955, 257–59; Jennings 1975; Rubin 2012.

[22] The Arabic version is *wakil*; the Ottoman transliteration is *vekil*. On English attorneys, see Hudson 2012, 586–88.

[23] Tyan 1955, 258.   [24] Gerber 1981, 113.   [25] Rozen 2010, 33–34.

[26] Kuran 2011, 186.   [27] Rozen 2010, 69–70.   [28] Epstein 1982, 113.

In Christian communities in the Balkans and the Aegean, community leaders also assumed responsibility for common obligations and actions and acted as representatives in court and central government. Christian monasteries bargained aggressively with the sultan. The monks of Mount Athos stridently opposed the repossession of their monasteries by Selîm II in 1568: "if you do not order an imperial document of confirmation, we will sell our possessions and pay back the gold we borrowed and we will scatter all around the world; it is certain that our monasteries will be deserted and our taxes, which we customarily pay in a lump sum (*maktu*) each year, will be lost."[29] The monks bargained hard; no institution followed, however. The sultan just complied.

Center–periphery relations with Muslim communities were similarly not collectively harnessed at the center by the Ottoman administration. Nothing peculiar to Islamic *doctrine* has been claimed to proscribe collective organization on an equal basis. Egalitarianism permeated Islam no less than it did Christianity,[30] feeding the incipient notions of popular sovereignty described in Chapter 11. The Hadith states, after all, that "All people are equal, as equal as the teeth of a comb."[31] A doctrinal origin of the political divergence thus cannot be sustained.[32] Instead, organizational, institutional factors appear more salient. As seen, representation is attested first in the Catholic Church, the most hierarchical Christian denomination (as the obligatory nature of representation would predict).[33] In Islam, ecclesiastical organization was looser and did not foster such practices nor did any alternative political actor.

Political representation is directly observed in Russia, as discussed in Chapter 12. Representatives were also used in court, as Russian medieval law codes attest albeit fleetingly, with special provisions posited.[34] Plenipotentiary powers were defined in the Novgorod Judicial Charter.[35] Legal representatives appear in court records even among the peasantry. For instance, a judgment charter in 1501 mentions three peasants representing "all the peasants of the Likurzhskaia canton" against two of "the metropolitan's petty noblemen," and such instances were common.[36] Representatives were also used in the Russian criminal system, though it is unclear how formalized and binding their terms of action were.[37] In other words, the legal foundation for representation was present in Russia just as much as in England, although "neither notaries

---

[29] Kermeli 2008, 194.   [30] Marlow 1997.
[31] Heyneman 2004, 51; Davis and Robinson 2006.   [32] As in Møller 2018.
[33] Chapter 4.
[34] Before the Code of 1649, Russian law codes were very slim; Kivelson 2002, 481.
[35] Four articles reference representation in the Charter, nos. 5, 18, 19, and 32; Kaiser 1992.
[36] Kleimola 1975, 24.   [37] Kollmann 2012, 38, 359, 42, 72, 78, 218, 169.

nor lawyers existed as a formal profession until the Great Reforms of the 1860s"[38] – a point that would be central to any full explanation of this divergence. Little evidence exists, however, on whether Russian representatives had full powers to bind local communities, though in law that was observed.[39]

The principle of representation was presumably also available to the Christian monasteries and churches, as in the Ottoman Empire. These did secure, especially after the sixteenth century, tax and other immunities,[40] and negotiations likely involved a representative. But these exchanges have not been tied to the political representation that did emerge.[41] The synodal organization and conciliar ecclesiology of the Orthodox Church, which held meetings called *sobors*, possibly influenced assemblies in the political realm.[42] Ultimately, although representation was practiced for about a century, it did not shape the regime in an enduring way. Christianity per se does not sufficiently explain polity-wide representation. It's certainly not, however, that the concept or cultural template of representation were unavailable in these cases. Might differential demands for justice explain why?

13.2   Bottom-Up Incentives and Collective Action: Petitions for Justice

In Part II of the book, the sustained demand for justice was shown to explain the regularity and institutional fusion that was necessary for institutions to become consolidated and inclusive, but which war-generated fiscal pressures could not generate. Petitions further aggregated these demands at a supra-local level, transmitting local concerns to central authority. They were thus key in imprinting parliament with its principal function, legislation.

Petitions, however, were far from exclusive to Western polities, as we have seen. Rather, they were and are part of a near universal vocabulary of grievance, encountered across regions and periods. Innumerable petitions survive, mostly still unexplored, in the archives of regimes as disparate as not only Russia and the Ottoman Empire, but Iran, China, Japan, India and elsewhere, from the ancient into the colonial, communist, and

---

[38] Kollmann 2012, 49.
[39] In the Pravosudie Mitropolich'e: "20. And a judge himself is to represent [in court] his own bishop, and he is not to send a copy from the trial [to the bishop for confirmation]," which suggests full powers for the representative; Kaiser 1992.
[40] Dewey 1971.
[41] No study of monastic negotiations with the tsars seems to exist, unlike for the Ottoman Empire.
[42] Bogatyrev 2000, 137.

modern eras.[43] This is why we cannot assume that there was variation between East and West in the demand for rights. Social conflict and the demand for rights are endogenous to intra-societal exchange and are thus endemic to all societies, regardless of geopolitical or economic conditions. They may be amplified or transformed under military or economic pressure, but the fundamental demand is always present.

At least, no systematic studies yet exist to demonstrate differential patterns in petition-making across cases; instead, the general themes appear to be remarkably similar to the English petitions that generated parliamentary legislation. The same prosaic concerns, corruption of officials, miscarriage of justice, excessive taxation and local petty crime were raised in radically different social and economic contexts.

However, the difference that did emerge over time was precisely the collective organization of petitions in the West, especially in England. There, local demands began to slowly aggregate into general claims that could affect central decision-making: "common petitions" became the primary basis of legislation in England, as seen in Chapter 2. But such *collective* submission would not have occurred if the state had not forced disparate groups to be present on common terms at the center nor if they were not all bound by common heavy obligations, including taxation but especially judicial service, nor if the state's reach did not extend uniformly throughout the territory and across social orders, as it did in England.

Non-Western petitions, conversely, exhibited a recurrent pattern: they were narrowly local and ad hoc. Without collective organization, petitions failed to have the *systemic and sustained* effects they did in England, even though they were fairly consistently responded to and did sometimes lead to legislation. When such collective petition-making occurred in Russia over a few decades, representative activity flourished. But in neither case did supra-local petition-making consolidate to shape regime type over the long term; the question is whether differences in the demands for justice accounted for this.

Next I describe available historical evidence on petitions in these cases to suggest that petitions differed not in demand but in their collective organization.

13.2.1   Ottoman Empire

Karen Barkey begins her revisionist discussion of the Ottoman peasantry with the story of a peasant who walks alone for two days to submit a tax complaint to the regional judge, the *kadı*.[44] To striking effect, she shows

---

[43] See note 109 in Chapter 1.   [44] Barkey 1994, 85–86.

how the atomistic access to justice helps explain a paradox of Ottoman history: peasants did not rebel as in the West. Together with the organization of production and the lack of patron–client relations between local power-holders and the peasants via land, localized justice provided an outlet for discontent that prevented collective action among the peasantry.[45] The comparative context in this book suggests that these patterns would be endogenous to sultanic weakness: we would expect different outcomes only when the ruler could compel his subjects to service and presence at the center on an obligatory and collective basis.

It is certainly not the case that subjects did not *seek* justice at the center. Following the seminal work by historian Suraiya Faroqhi, Ottoman petitions have been attracting the systematic attention they deserve and the evidence is overwhelming.[46] Their importance in the administration of justice by the sultan had long roots in Seljuk and Ottoman practice throughout the Middle East, as shown in the panoramic view of justice in the region since antiquity by the historian Linda Darling.[47] Petitions were read in the "great *divan*" four days a week. The *divan* was the supreme organ of government, but in origin it was a high court of justice. It was housed at Topkapı Palace, designed with open walls to symbolize "free access of the empire's subjects to imperial justice."[48] The forum of petitions also served as court of appeals against *kadı* judgments.[49]

Sultans performed these duties regularly, as recorded in chronicles already from the 1390s. Mehmed the Conqueror ceased to preside in person over imperial councils after about 1475, but he heard the sessions behind a grated window in the "Mansion of Justice," where all business was discussed. Procedure was stipulated in his Law Book. Other high officials, especially the Grand Vizier, eventually took over. The Chamber of Petitions was lavishly rebuilt under Süleyman the Magnificent in the 1520s.[50]

Petitions were submitted, as in the West, on varied issues either by ordinary individuals (*arz-ı hal*) or by officials, such as governors or *kadıs* on behalf of communities (*arz-ı mahzar'lar*). The latter appears as a symptom of a "top-down administration," typical of absolutism. However, as seen, the English crown also appointed agents to mobilize the county structure throughout the kingdom, the sheriffs. Moreover, as discussed,[51] common petitions were initially produced by the nobility –

---

[45] Barkey 1994, 104, 85–140.
[46] Faroqhi 1986a; 1992; Barkey 1991; 1994; Gerber 1994, 154–73; Darling 1996, 246–80; 2013, 132, 143–44; Karaman 2009; Baldwin 2012.
[47] Darling 2013, 88–90, 132–33, 139–41, 146–49, 164–71.   [48] Darling 1996, 287, 248.
[49] Imber 2006, 224–25.
[50] İnalcık 1973, 89–90; Imber 2006, 224; Darling 2013, 143–44.
[51] See section 3.1.1.2.

collective petitions were not a spontaneous process. The difference rather was that the nobility was compelled to attend Parliament while English sheriffs were able to summon representatives across *all* administrative units at the same time and for the same purpose. This endowed the process with a systematic character that the bottom-up demand for justice, of which there was no shortage in the non-Western regions, did not suffice to produce.

A major theme was corruption of officials, as in England, especially tax collectors or judges.[52] The sultans would dispatch inspectors. This was not just a Near Eastern practice, as İnalcık claims, but widespread in the West too, as we have seen, especially England. Some would even perform inspections personally in disguise, as did Süleyman I, Ahmed II, and Murad IV.[53] Petitions usually triggered an imperial response, known through a rescript, which typically ordered the *kadı* to investigate. This could be escalated if a local official had transgressed, as patronage networks had to be activated to secure restitution.[54]

Responsiveness was high; some evidence suggests few requests were rejected.[55] Guild petitions from seventeenth-century Istanbul also had their requests "almost always granted."[56] This echoes French evidence, which similarly suggests that individual tax petitions may have been more successful than those by provincial estates.[57] Further, petitions, although localized, often shaped the legal system as a whole, as also in England. For instance, the *kanunname*, consisting of decrees issued in the sultan's name and distributed to all the judges in the empire, often derived from individual petitions.[58] Identifying a regime as "unlimited" or "arbitrary" simply because it lacked a central representative institution, emerges, yet again, as unwarranted.

This is especially salient with taxation disputes, which were widespread.[59] Darling has shown how sophisticated – albeit beset by inefficiencies – was the process of disputing the tax burden (surviving records start during the sixteenth century).[60] It was thus not that "bargaining over taxation" did not happen in the Ottoman Empire; petitions show it was relentless. It was just more localized, atomized, and judicialized. Even when collectivities were petitioning, they were not coordinated across the realm and had no forum for collective action. Such a forum, where judicial and fiscal demands *could* be adjudicated, was

---

[52] Gerber 1994, 154–73.   [53] İnalcık 1973, 91–92.   [54] Faroqhi 1992, 2–3.
[55] Darling 1996, 281.   [56] Yi 2004, 198.   [57] Major 1960b, 42.
[58] Darling 1996, 281; Imber 2011.
[59] İnalcık 1973, 91; Darling 1996. Countless petitions survive introducing tax farmer candidates; Faroqhi 1992, 4, 5.
[60] Darling 1996, 246–80.

not lacking; the Palace already served this purpose. Rather, subjects were not summoned there on a systematic, obligatory, and collective basis, as with Parliament, where they had to deliberate in common to present petitions that conveyed more general concerns instead of just local grievances.

Scale is important of course, because it made such central coordination inordinately harder. But it certainly did not preclude the English outcome, where core territories achieved this integration, whilst outlying territories, like Scotland and Ireland and eventually the British Empire itself, were ruled in more "imperial" fashion. Coordinating a highly varied judicial and tax system over 20 to 30 million people in 280 provinces with a permanent staff of maybe 72 and local part-timers, as in the 1620s, may have been impossible;[61] that the empire yet became a major power under such terms is even more impressive. But it was not impossible over a smaller core area in an earlier period. The point here is that it was not too much strength that precluded supra-local collective organization, but too little.

In Russia, however, a central focal point was instituted, and this helps explain the representative practice that was observed. One needs to explain rather why it did not endure.

13.2.2   Russia

Petitions were also the major instrument of submitting demands to the tsar and redressing grievance in Russia. Their usual content does not differ from that of English or Ottoman petitions, at least as far as surviving patterns suggest.[62] Taxation was a major topic and immunities were extensively granted in response to petitions,[63] as were exemptions from judicial and administrative service. Land disputes[64] and corruption and abuse of power, by both officials and powerful elites,[65] were recurrent concerns. Subject pleas were submitted to the Grand Prince, the tsar, who was strongly encouraged by the clergy to dispense justice.[66] At first, the tsar judged together with *boyars*, until they acquired their independent venue after 1497, as seen.[67]

Some Russian petitions had broad social impact, as noted by historians, echoing English dynamics. For instance, the Russian judicial system was reformed in the 1520s after law and order collapsed throughout Muscovy;

---

[61] Darling 1996, 279; Gerber 1994, 14.   [62] The issue awaits systematic quantification.
[63] About 500 immunity charters remain from the fifteenth and early sixteenth centuries and 1,039 between 1504 and 1584; Dewey 1964, 643–44.
[64] Kleimola 1975, 15, 13.   [65] Kivelson 1996, 199–200, 225–27, 231–34.
[66] Kleimola 1975, 11; Crummey 1987, 151.   [67] Kleimola 1975, 13.

following a wave of petitions, Moscow sent agents to the provinces to stop crime in response. This established the state's intermediary role in criminal justice, producing a "triadic" legal process.[68] A petition by a group of landholders in 1539 in response to local anarchy and state weakness generated the *guba* system, mentioned in the previous chapter. The *guba* elders were established as provincial brigandage-control officers and extended throughout the realm after their local success. They were (s)elected in a manner similar to the selection of Members of Parliament in seventeenth-century England. All estates voted, but not all could hold office; "worthy and prosperous gentrymen" were needed for positions of authority.[69]

The "deluge" of petitions in the mid-sixteenth century led to greater institutionalization: a special Chancellery formed to handle submissions to the Grand Prince (the *Chelobitnyi Prikaz*).[70] Petitions continued to be central into the seventeenth century. They were also crucial in the major reforms announced in the decree of 1619, which emerged "not only as a response to petitions from many people (primarily gentry) but also as the result of extensive consultation." Petition campaigns also occurred in the 1630s and 1640s. Themes were "corruption, bureaucratism, patronage and favoritism, banditry and violence, paternalism and protectionism" – concerns that differed little from recurrent English grievances. Judicial concerns were also central: in 1637, petitioners asked that trials be held in provincial towns and that judges be chosen locally, requests that continued to be presented in later petitions.[71] By the 1640s, a special institution had emerged where "People Petition[ed] Against Strong People."[72] The gentry's main complaint was the one discussed in Chapter 12, that peasants were removed by the "strong people of Moscow," namely the *boyars* and high administrators, but also by church authorities and monasteries.[73]

The seventeenth century, in fact, saw a wave of *collective* petitions. These had a moral and religious language absent from local ones, showing clear Church influence. Echoing the pattern observed in Magna Carta, which requested greater regularization of the king's justice, petitions shifted from being against to being in favor of regulation, as Kivelson noted. Early petitions were from the service class, but eventually, by the 1660s, local petitions would even include the higher Moscow nobility. Accordingly, petitioner demands eventually generated broad-based legislation, paralleling English developments. The great uprising of 1648 was

[68] Hellie 2006a, 360–86; Kaiser 1980.   [69] Kivelson 1996, 143–51, 145.
[70] Kleimola 1975, 11.   [71] All quotes are from Kivelson 1996, 211, 215, 216, 225.
[72] Hosking 2000, 157; Kivelson 1996, 220.   [73] Kivelson 1996, 219–20.

fueled by the "national petition campaigns" of the service nobility of the previous decades. These were not individual but collective petitions and they shaped the law code of 1649.[74]

Tsars attempted to limit petitioner demands, which may seem to confirm an absolutist interpretation. They would not serve as final arbiter in disputes and the people were punished for even trying to gain access to them.[75] But as we've seen, English kings also used force to prevent petitioners from thrusting petitions into their hand, which imposed an obligation to address them.[76] Restrictions everywhere attempted to meet overwhelming demand: when Ivan IV refused to answer petitions he was a "terrified teen"; ten days of "bloodshed and destruction" followed.[77]

Further, the state avoided persistent petitions requesting localized justice, which was extensively, though not always effectively, provided in England. Litigants could go to Moscow three times a year to have their cases heard in the early 1600s, but this conflicted with service obligations. Their demands were further frustrated later in the century, as local petitions were mediated through the governor who would not send petitions to the center. This too suggests an "impersonal bureaucratic administration of the centralized state."[78] However, as Part I showed, local justice was more available in England in the period of institutional formation because the crown had successfully penetrated the localities to counter the jurisdiction of local lords. Despite the tsar's impressive displays of power, his capacity did not subordinate local institutions to the center as effectively. Judicial supply was more contested and fragmented in Russia. What appears as an autocratic motion in the Russian case reflects a position of relative institutional weakness.

In terms of social impact, however, petitions in the Russian sixteenth and seventeenth centuries produced outcomes that were closer to those observed in England than Ottoman ones. Common to all these petition drives was the crucial class behind them, the service gentry which owed its land and service to the tsar. As we have seen, the petitioning gentry was also crucial for the assemblies that flourished in this period. But these practices did not shape the regime as a whole and thus in an enduring way.

Why? Two major hypotheses on why East and West diverged institutionally could help answer this question and remain to be examined. As noted in the Introduction, they propose different forms of collective organization – collective responsibility and corporate estates – as crucial in shaping political trajectories.

---

[74] Kivelson 1996, 258–59, 199, 211, 225–26, 216–27.   [75] Kivelson 1996, 238–39, 243.
[76] See Chapter 2.   [77] Kivelson 1996, 242–43.   [78] Kivelson 1996, 224–27, 140, 227.

13.3   Collective Responsibility and Corporate Bodies

As we have seen, historians and neo-institutionalists like Douglass North have claimed that formalized, impersonal collective organization, for instance through corporations, is what spearheaded the West in generating open political orders. At the same time, however, historians and anthropologists have long identified a cognate concept, collective responsibility, as the form of social organization that obstructed Eastern political development. An apparent tension exists between these positions: after all, corporations are just more formalized versions of collective responsibility. Probing this tension can help specify the critical dimension on which Western polities, especially England, diverged from Eastern ones: state-coordinated supra-local organization.

13.3.1   Collective Responsibility, Eastern and Western

A widespread trait of premodern societies, collective responsibility is recorded as an effective means of conflict resolution and social order maintenance even in the smallest communities within and far beyond Europe.[79] The system held a broader group (whether kin, village, or administrative unit) responsible for the actions or obligations of an individual member. Communities showed remarkable capacity to mobilize populations at the local level to get communal work done through this mechanism. As Mancur Olson noted, collective action is easier in small villages.[80] Murder and other crimes were policed this way, but so were tax obligations. "Sureties," whereby either individuals or communities were pledged to fulfill the responsibilities of one person or the whole community, were pervasive not only in Western Europe, Russia, and the Ottoman Empire, but throughout the premodern world since antiquity, from Egypt and Africa to Japan and China.[81]

Part I, however, has shown the striking level of collective responsibility achieved by the English crown in the period of parliamentary emergence. Mobilization especially of the most powerful was fundamental for representative institutions that were more inclusive and thus more robust. The crown bound subjects to a wide array of obligations, especially judicial ones, that created the appearance of self-government, but which was "at the king's command."[82] Counties had to engage in public works, repairs to the king's property, serve in courts, provide supplies, enforce the peace,

---

[79] Weber 1978, 1022–25.   [80] Olson 1965, 53–57 citing Homans 1950.
[81] Les Sûretés Personnelles: Civilisations Archaïques, Antiques et Orientales 1974; Les Sûretés Personnelles: Moyen Âge et Temps Modernes 1971.
[82] White 1933.

inform inquests, and so on. Russian scholarship has presented a picture of striking similarity at the micro level, where subject obligations were pervasive, as locals were burdened with a long list of functions, especially in justice enforcement, taxation, and administration.[83] Ottoman administration, we will see, also depended on similar mechanisms of enforcement.

However, in Russian scholarship collective responsibility is treated as a symptom of an autocratic, oppressive state that enforced it to create a collectivist *mentalité*, one that allowed tsarist absolutism to reproduce itself.[84] "The principle of collective responsibility emerged as one of the key tools of authoritarian rule . . . Therein lay one of the keys to explaining how east and west came to diverge."[85] This perspective reflects a dominant narrative of Western development, where collective forms had to be overcome for a more "individualist" frame to emerge.[86]

Collective responsibility was indeed widely observed in Russia, as illuminated by the historians Horace Dewey and Ann Kleimola.[87] The practice of surety (*poruka*), of "persons who bore responsibility for the conduct of others," was an often dreaded but indispensable aspect of social life.[88] It made families or communities responsible for serious but also lesser crimes, such as murder or theft: the "surety" would have to pay reparations. Failure to comply with authorities resulted in collective fines.[89] The aforementioned *guba* system was itself a form of collective responsibility.[90] In tax collection, if one actor failed to pay taxes, the surety was obligated to pay them, upon severe penalty.[91] A large spectrum of tasks, judicial, administrative, military, fiscal, were thus performed through the pressure exercised by individuals from either the same family, kin group, or from some administrative unit.[92]

Similarly, collective responsibility remained more local and based on kinship groups throughout the Arabian Peninsula and Ottoman lands, where it prevailed as part of early Islamic custom. It ascribed responsibility to the tribe for actions of its members.[93] There was collective responsibility for murder or attempted murder. Blood money had to be paid by the murderer's solidarity group or by the community when the

---

[83] Kivelson 2002, 477.   [84] Dewey and Kleimola 1984, 190–91.
[85] Dewey and Kleimola 1982, 321. This Russian tradition of "collectivism" is affirmed even in contemporary textbooks; Barrington 2012, 84. However, historians have challenged it where records permit; Dennison 2011.
[86] Macfarlane 1978; Greif 2006a.
[87] Dewey 1970; 1988; Dewey and Kleimola 1982; 1984.   [88] Dewey 1970, 337.
[89] Dewey and Kleimola 1984, 185.   [90] Martin 2007, 385; Kivelson 1996, 143–46.
[91] Dewey 1970, 342–43.   [92] Shaw 2006, 305–306; Pipes 1974, 98–99.
[93] Crone 1986; Mallat 2003, 702–703; Kuran 2011, 106.

perpetrator was unknown.[94] Collective responsibility also applied to taxation; though records survive mostly from the seventeenth century, its use was long-standing. The *kharādj*, for instance, was "in general levied not directly upon individual properties but – outside the suburban areas of the cities – collectively upon the villages, according to the amount and state of the cultivated lands there. Hence the shortfall from an individual in no way reduced the obligations of the collectively responsible body."[95] Collective responsibility also assisted conflict resolution; however, it was not as effective.[96] Nonetheless, especially in provincial towns, "the principle of collective responsibility may have remained a viable tool of social control well until the end of the empire."[97]

At this local level, the similarities with medieval England were striking. Particularly in the period of institutional emergence for the English Parliament, i.e. before 1300, collective responsibility underlay social organization, for instance regarding the keeping of the peace and punishment of crime. It defined the frankpledge system, an Anglo-Saxon inheritance probably, that was reinvigorated by the laws of Henry I and Edward I.[98] "The members acted as mutual sureties that none of them would commit an offence and that they would produce any member who did."[99] From the thirteenth century, frankpledge bound mainly the unfree and the landless from the age of 12, in an association of usually ten householders (the tithing). Freeholders and especially lords and the nobility could pledge their land. The system was enforced by royal agents, mostly the sheriff.[100] Similarly, the hundred was ultimately responsible for the fines payable if anyone who was not English was murdered (the *murdrum* fine),[101] a measure intended to protect the outnumbered Normans.

All administrative units were subject to collective responsibility of some kind. As Pollock and Maitland wrote:

The county is amerced [i.e. fined] for false judgments, the hundred is fined for murders, the townships are compelled to attend the justices, men are forced into frankpledge, the burghers are jointly and severally liable for the *firma burgi*, the manorial lord treats his villeins as one responsible group. Men are drilled and

---

[94] Ottoman secondary sources seem to pick up on the theme from the 1600s; Canbakal 2011, 90–91, 88.

[95] Subhan 2012. The practice was also common in Byzantine provinces; Herrin 2013, 20–21.

[96] Kuran 2011, 105.   [97] Canbakal 2011, 92.   [98] Hudson 2012, 169–71, 391–95.

[99] Hudson 2012, 391–92.

[100] Hudson 2012, 391–93, 555, 717. See also Cam 1930, 125, 124–28, 185–87; Morris 1910; Pollock and Maitland 1898, 558–64, 568–69.

[101] Hudson 2012, 405–409.

regimented into communities in order that the state may be strong and the land may be at peace. Much of the communal life that we see is not spontaneous.[102]

In fact, representation itself was a form of collective responsibility in England, as we have seen: originally an obligation imposed by the king, it bound the community that sent the representative to accept whatever was agreed with the king, on which originally there was little input except from the high nobility. Without this system of obligation, representation would not have been so extensive or so binding. Collective responsibility per se therefore cannot be blamed for Russian or Ottoman outcomes; causes of variation have to be sought elsewhere. The question rather is why England switched to a different, apparently more individualist trajectory, why these practices had divergent institutional effects at the polity level. I argue that collective responsibility did not disappear in England; it was transformed through effective coordination by the state. The system worked effectively only to the degree that the crown could mobilize this system at the center. Collective responsibility was applied to the state-sustained supra-local administrative unit, the county, not (simply) local community attachments. The necessary condition for this outcome was the greater infrastructural capacity of the state to administer justice and compel all units to appear at the center.

Frankpledge itself, at least the surety element of it, slowly disappeared by the fourteenth century in England both because it was failing to deliver criminals and enforce the peace and because a better substitute emerged: the centralized system of justice we have sketched in Part I, predicated on crown strength.[103] Moreover, this does not mean that collective responsibility was itself eliminated; it remained on different types of common duty, from jury duty to the many other obligations that flowed from land ownership or other types of social bonds, but especially judicial liability and parliamentary representation. Responsibility did not decrease; it was just more effectively aggregated by and at the center.

Why was collective responsibility more state-constituted than kin-based in England? The reasons are complex and part of the broader societal transformation of that period. Economists see the trend, one that applied more broadly in Western Europe, as a response to economic forces and trade growth.[104] According to Greif, whose seminal work has done the most to introduce these concepts into economic analysis, collective responsibility helped secure contract enforcement under conditions of limited government; but it had increased market size so much it was unable to cater to increasing demand.[105] For North and Thomas,

---

[102] Pollock and Maitland 1898, 688.   [103] Morris 1910, 157, 151–67.
[104] Benson 1989; North 1991; Greif 2002.   [105] Greif 2002.

replacing it improved economic efficiency;[106] for others, it increased revenue for European states, by undermining spontaneous order institutions.[107] These explanations highlight important trends but share a functionalism that has been critiqued in Chapter 2.

The more fundamental reason was the state's role in restricting collective responsibility and clan and kinship structures more generally. It is not an accident that, as Greif notes, mercantile community responsibility for debt was ended in England in 1275 by the Statute of Westminster, i.e. in the context of the reaffirmation of royal power that led to Parliament. Similar efforts were not as successful in Italy or the Holy Roman Empire.[108] The "representatives from the urban commercial sector" in Parliament in the 1290s[109] did not suffice to secure this outcome, as we have seen; their power was still very restricted. Rather, community responsibility systems were replaced as the alternative royal system of adjudication that was polity-wide and effective created a stable framework of law.

Moreover, contemporaneously, as Greif and Fukuyama have highlighted, extended kinship (the usual basis of collective responsibility) gave way to the nucleated family in the medieval West.[110] But this process was also not spontaneous;[111] the state was crucial. Typically, following Max Weber, the explanation focuses on the Church.[112] Two sweeping anthropological interpretations explored this. Jack Goody showed how heirship rights were restricted to a smaller circle of relatives through Church legislation.[113] Alan Macfarlane argued that "individualism" rose and the family-based peasant unit declined in the period focused in this account, the thirteenth century.[114] One need not accept the strongly materialist hypothesis advanced by Goody – that the Church's goal was to increase its landholdings – to acknowledge the central insight, that family unit size was reduced and the Church was an important factor.[115] As marriage was regulated both by prohibiting close degrees of consanguinity and by requiring spouse consent (as opposed to clan elder decision), clan power declined and extended family ties weakened.[116] Macfarlane traced similar trends on peasant structures but he viewed them too as endogenous to clan decline.[117]

Clans were weakened in England (compared to, say, Scotland) from at least the twelfth century. Causality cannot be conclusively established,

---

[106] North and Thomas 1973.   [107] Benson 1989.   [108] Greif 2006b, 231–32.
[109] Greif 2006b, 232.   [110] Greif 2006a; Fukuyama 2011a, 229–41.
[111] See Sabean et al. 2007 for a more nuanced chronological account.
[112] Weber 1978, 1244; Hall 1985a, 130–33; Lynch 2003.
[113] Goody 1983; Goody et al. 1976.   [114] Macfarlane 1978.
[115] Davis 1985; Houlbrooke 1984.   [116] Hudson 2012, 436–38, 776–82.
[117] Macfarlane 1978, 34–61.

however. Maybe kin relations were weaker in England already or maybe the Church was more effective there. Evidence suggests clans were not negligible. English Church reformers in the late eleventh century had prohibited seven degrees of consanguinity in marriage, as opposed to the official four;[118] the higher the degree of prohibition, the more the clan weakened. This suggests clans were originally strong.

But without the state, Church rules can rarely acquire polity-wide application. Land inheritance was also enforced through secular courts; royal power ensured that some customs (e.g. primogeniture) prevailed polity-wide whilst others were overridden. Land was increasingly concentrated as heirs decreased in number, especially through the legal form of entails.[119] Such measures defined the family unit ever more restrictively. That the Church alone did not weaken clans is seen by the cases of Italy and Flanders: despite great Church strength, clans remained strong, whilst central powers were weaker.[120] Whether Church-inspired practices were enforced by strong secular authorities mattered. Yet even if we accord the Church a central role, this still produces a variant of the central theme pursued throughout this book: it was not a stronger demand for individual rights that distinguished England (or even the West more broadly), it was the more effective subjection of the population to a supra-local set of institutional restrictions, in this case, Church-derived and state-enforced, that accounts for the differences. The demand for rights was endogenous to that compellence.[121]

The same inverse relation between clan power and state capacity is observed in Russia. The most powerful elite, the princes and *boyars*, retained a strong clan structure that made them less amenable to tsarist control, as Kollmann's study showed.[122] In fact, "the only significant limitations on individual property in [pre-Petrine] Russia" admitted by Weickhardt in his reconsideration of property rights "were in favor of the clans rather than the state."[123] Similarly, the *mestnichestvo*, the system that protected the status of and order of precedence among the *boyars*, exacerbated natural kin-based rivalries without providing counterbalancing incentives to collaboration.[124] Although, as Kivelson notes, these relations were symbiotic with the tsarist regime and operational[125] (Russia was indeed becoming a formidable power), the capacity to

---

[118] Worby 2010; Hudson 2012, 436, 778.   [119] Biancalana 2001; Hudson 2012, 652.
[120] Heers 1974; 2008; d'Avray 2001, 189.   [121] Cf. Fukuyama 2011a, 231.
[122] Kollmann 1999.   [123] Weickhardt 1993, 665.
[124] Poe 2006, 439–42; Kleimola 1977, 25–26; Bogatyrev 2006, 254–55. But see Kollmann 1999, ch. 4.
[125] Kivelson 1996.

transcend communal structures (rather than just to mobilize them) was restricted in Russia as compared to England.

Tsars used collective responsibility to ensure political loyalty in these groups in the fifteenth and sixteenth centuries.[126] For historian Richard Hellie, this obligation explained the lack of resistance against the state.[127] However, the issue is not collective obligation per se, but that it depended more on pre-existing kin alliances[128] rather than state-imposed relations, as it did in England. The system inhibited collective action on a supra-local, bureaucratic level, as it reinforced kin obligations and ties at the family and local level;[129] it did not dilute them.

Where developments more closely resembled the English pattern was with the gentry, the lower servitor class, which we saw at the center of Russia's second-best constitutionalism. Among them, as Kivelson has argued, "clan played a rather insignificant role."[130] This group was also more dependent on the tsar. Gentry social relations revolved around the "much closer-knit immediate family,"[131] echoing English developments. Partible inheritance decreased family units making them more dependent on the state, although this system also served gentry interests.[132] As state control over the gentry rose, its structures of collective responsibility were also gradually extended beyond the family and onto administrative units, "in matters of public safety and criminal persecution, for fiscal dues, but also to deal with vagrant runaways in the seventeenth century."[133]

Nonetheless, collective responsibility was not as effectively harnessed by the Russian state at the polity level. Consequently, as noted by Dewey and Kleimola, "the net result of the decline of kinship there was not the emergence of individualism. On the contrary, collective responsibility was extended throughout the fabric of Russian life." In fact, this explains the paradox noted earlier, between the atomism observed by historians and the extensive collectivist practices: "Collective responsibility became the cement that held an atomized society together in a way that laid the basis for the ascendancy of the all-powerful authoritarian state." This result is typically attributed "partly to attitudes and values deeply rooted in Russia's past, partly to the conscious effort of the state, the landowners, and others in authority."[134]

However, this account suggests the deeper reason was not a polarity of collectivism versus individualism; it was the incapacity of the Russian state to centralize these structures at the supra-local level, across all social groups. Ascribing Russian autocratic outcomes to deeply rooted values

---

[126] Dewey 1987. The practice declined after Ivan IV.   [127] Hellie 2000, 18.
[128] Dewey and Kleimola 1982, 328–29.   [129] Kleimola 1977, 26.
[130] Kivelson 1996, 103.   [131] Kivelson 1994, 202, 200.   [132] Kivelson 1994.
[133] Dewey and Kleimola 1982, 330, 334.   [134] Dewey and Kleimola 1982, 335, 334.

assumes the validity of "revealed preferences": these often tell us only what actors *could* do, not necessarily what they wanted, despite ex post rationalizations.

13.3.2 Estates as Corporate Bodies and Corporations

The other major hypothesis that has shaped accounts of both East and West focuses on two other forms of collective organization as central to the Western trajectory: estates organized either as corporate bodies or as legally defined corporations, mostly in the economic realm. Neither of these forms emerged in the non-Western cases. I argue, however, that the stronger this corporative organization, the more representation was undermined. Only where the state was able to effectively regulate and contain it, as in England, did it support representative institutions. So, its absence or weakness elsewhere cannot explain representative divergence.

(a) *Estates as Corporate Bodies.* Europe is widely held to have diverged because monarchs "in England, France, the Germanies, Poland and Bohemia solved the problem [of co-opting social groups] by sharing sovereignty with parliaments and by giving privileges to corporate estates."[135] An estate is a group of people defined by similar legal status, "to which is attached a bundle of rights and duties, privileges and obligations, legal capacities and incapacities, which are publicly recognized."[136] Corporate estates were highlighted by Max Weber, who connected them to bureaucratic outcomes: the *Ständestaat*, the state composed of estates, explained the transition from feudalism to capitalism; but it also provided necessary structures for the emergence of constitutionalism.[137] Corporate estates more generally have long formed a central part in historical accounts of representative practice on the European Continent.[138] Corporations as a form of associative practice are also increasingly treated in theoretical accounts of political pluralism.[139]

Similarly, estates and corporate bodies with privilege and immunities are integrally connected, in such accounts, with the rise of towns as independent political actors,[140] separated from the feudal countryside and endowed with freedoms as well as legal personhood. Different immunities (of service, taxation, jurisdiction) were constitutive of the new, non-feudal order. Influential theories, as explored in earlier chapters, connected the immunities of urban social actors, sometimes allied with a monarchy intent on limiting the feudal aristocracy, with

---

[135] Kollmann 1987, 2; Berman 2018, 16–19.   [136] Marshall 1964, 193.
[137] Weber 1978, 1085–87; Poggi 1978, 36–59; Hall 1985a, 137.
[138] Lousse 1935; 1952; de Lagarde 1937.   [139] Muñiz-Fraticelli 2014; Levy 2014.
[140] Poggi 1978, 37; van Zanden et al. 2012, 12–13.

representative government, following nineteenth-century liberal historiography.[141] As Barrington Moore also argued for democracy, the "feudal" immunities of certain groups were central to the right of resistance based on a social contract[142] and to the concept of autonomy that are critical to some foundational statements in both state and regime emergence.[143]

However, urban immunities and autonomy had an inverse effect on representative emergence at the polity level, as I have argued in Chapter 8, echoing work that emphasizes how urban autonomy inhibits economic growth.[144] We need to separate the idea of autonomy from the empirical account of how it was effectively institutionalized in diverse societies. Urban growth was beneficial when the state regulatory framework was strong, as in England.

The role of privilege is also misunderstood. How *privileges* of estates lead to representation, democracy, even the state, is not sufficiently explained. In some accounts, it was noble privilege that was involved in undercutting absolutism and the old order.[145] The nobility actively sought office and service as privileges that increased their social power. Securing office was usually considered to be "in inverse proportion to the power of the Crown" and could be seen as one of the "rights of political participation," which again exemplifies the assumed genetic connection between privilege and right. Key of course was the "privilege" to attend Parliament as well as to elect deputies to the estates, which was typically tied to property ownership. From the Prussian Junkers to the French *noblesse de robe*, high office would appear to be the essence of corporative privilege.[146] Constitutionalism spread, in this logic, by extending these entrenched social privileges to broader groups. For Greif, for instance, "political assemblies were composed of individuals and corporate bodies with independent administrative capacity."[147]

In Poggi's classic sociological account, rights and prerogatives of both the ruler and the *Stände* were transformed during absolutism. Roman law codifications and bureaucratic "public law" connected the feudal order, the intermediary *Ständestaat*, and finally the constitutional nineteenth-century state.[148] However, that corporate estates developed where constitutional democracy later emerged (after many reversals), like France or Germany, does not mean that they caused those outcomes. In fact, where

---

[141] Guizot 1851; Spruyt 1994. French historiography now focuses on the nobility instead. See especially the work of John Major 1960b; 1964; 1994; Major and Holt 1991.
[142] Moore 1967, 415.   [143] Poggi 1978; Mann 1984; Hall 1994.
[144] Epstein 2000a; Ogilvie 2011; Stasavage 2014.   [145] Anderson 1974a; Bush 1983.
[146] Bush 1983, 86, 79–120, 121–205.   [147] Greif 2008, 31; Herb 2003.
[148] Poggi 1978, 56–62, 86–87.

corporate bodies possessed privileges, the modern representative state (and democratic practices) emerged precariously through either revolution and/or war, as again in France or Germany, precisely to shatter those privileges.[149] Further, would such a transformation have occurred if England did not already serve as a model (with its own, less radical revolution in the past)? Such accounts describe, but don't explain, this radical transformation. Rather than a genetic link between privileged estates and constitutionalism, the Continental cases suggest that the more entrenched corporate status and privilege was, the weaker the state, the more coercive the state expansion, and the likelier the absolutism.

What was "distinctively peculiar" to England, by contrast, was that its nobles and all social actors possessed so *few* corporate privileges. Office and representation were not privileges in the period of parliamentary emergence, but obligations. As Stubbs wrote, "the English law does not regard the man of most ancient and purest descent as entitled thereby to any right or privilege which is not shared by every freeman," a point examined in Chapter 3. English social classes were thus more open and porous than Continental ones, at least in the early period. The "great peculiarity of the baronial estate in England as compared with the continent, [was] the absence of the idea of caste": the baronage was not defined by blood.[150] There was "no closed or sworn order or fraternity of nobles, and even less of knights."[151] It was a nobility established by the royal summons to Parliament, to which no formal right existed; only custom consolidated the presence of some members of the nobility.[152]

The English nobility had fewer privileges, as this book has argued, crucially in its lack of fiscal immunity.[153] By being uniformly subjected to taxation, it was not as separated from the rest of society nor did it possess a set of juridically defined privileges (although exceptions existed of course).[154] By contrast, throughout Europe nobilities became increasingly exempt from the fourteenth century, either from all or usually from most direct taxes, as we have seen.[155] The greater the corporative privilege, the weaker the representative governance: no taxation of the rich, no polity-wide representative governance.

The positive institutional outcomes flowing from weak corporate groupness are not specific to Europe or to representation. In Africa, the

---

[149] Moore 1967; Koenigsberger 1971; Asch 2003; Skocpol 1979. See now the comprehensive overview of European developments in Berman 2018, 19–105.
[150] Stubbs 1896, 185.   [151] Cam 1970b, 266.
[152] Powell and Wallis 1968, 219–31; Stubbs 1896, 190–91. Only after Parliament emerged did some privileges accrue to the peerage; Bush 1983, 139; Asch 2003, 25–28.
[153] Bush 1983, 29, 49; Ormrod 2008.   [154] Willard 1934, 162.   [155] Bush 1983, 27–64.

weakness/absence of group associations, including ones that were neither kin- nor territory-based, meant that political centralization was also stronger, as Osafo and Robinson strikingly highlighted.[156] Reconsidering the European model allows us to reassess points of commonality with other regions. In any case, the absence of corporate estates does not suffice to explain the lack of representation in the non-Western cases.

(b) *Representation and Corporations.* Corporations are the other form of collective organization that was absent in the East but central to the West and seen as constitutive of the liberal political and economic order.[157] Might this be related to the absence of representation too? Corporations in fact effectively extended the principle of collective responsibility, which Russian scholars identified with absolutism, as seen. However, impersonal corporations are widely assumed to herald an apparently "individualist," "modern" political and economic form, so the connection with collective responsibility does not appear obvious, though it was noted by Greif.[158] An account of origins demonstrates how closely enmeshed corporations were with patterns of collective responsibility systematically enforced by the state. Once again, the prevalence of collective responsibility cannot suffice to explain the divergent Eastern path on this dimension. The question is rather why collective responsibility transformed into corporative structures in the West but not elsewhere. This cannot be fully answered, but some necessary conditions can be assessed.

Perhaps the main hypothesis ties "the evolution of the western corporation" "to the weakening of central authority following the demise of the western Roman Empire."[159] Though central authority indeed weakened on the Continent, the most effectively institutionalized version of the economic corporation occurred in England and Holland[160] where central (and taxing) powers were strongest, as we have seen. State power is particularly crucial for perhaps the original form of political corporations, the boroughs[161] – these are more relevant to an account of representative institutions. The incorporated English borough was built on state obligation, especially the collective responsibility to collect taxation due to the crown (the *firma burgi*, the borough tax farm).[162] This institutionalization proceeded from the right to self-taxation to possession of a seal, right to set by-laws, to own land, freedom of serfs, guild liberties, but also to send representatives to Parliament. All these gradually accumulated to provide a corporate legal status to some *royal* boroughs. But these rights were given by and dependent on the crown. "Every borough in England from

[156] Osafo-Kwaako and Robinson 2013.   [157] Ciepley 2013; Kuran 2005; Owen 1991, 3.
[158] Greif 2006b.   [159] Kuran 2005, 792–93.
[160] Kuran 2005, 807; and Chapters 3 and 7.   [161] Weinbaum 1937.   [162] Laski 1917.

the city of London downwards live[d] in daily peril of forfeiting its charters, of seeing its mercantile privileges annulled, of seeing its elected magistrates displaced and itself handed over to the mercies of some royal *custos* or *firmarius*."[163] It was the common subjection to a frame of royal coercion that institutionalized these practices on a systematic basis in England.

Corporations did not enhance representation originally. Borough representation *decreased* as Parliament consolidated, from an average of about 85 to about 75 between Edward I and III (out of over 500 boroughs).[164] The boroughs were selected typically by the sheriff and were summoned with the counties.[165] Given attendance had a high cost, which boroughs had to cover themselves, it was sometimes avoided.[166] Similar disincentives were posed by the higher rate of taxation imposed on boroughs compared to the counties: towns overall contributed "the largest proportion" of both direct and indirect taxation.[167] "Independence" was costly. Whether boroughs escaped representation at a significant level was a controversial topic among historians, but May McKisack "venture[d] to assert ... that towns which lay within great 'liberties' were more likely to escape representation than royal boroughs were."[168] Urban "independence" similarly originally meant the imposition of obligations on the wealthiest families by the Catalan crown.[169]

So, although boroughs developed as a form partly through their representative obligations, it is not also the case that boroughs as *corporate* units shaped representation originally. Their importance in later accounts of the constitutional structures of England[170] should not be projected to an account of origins. As we have seen, their numbers and status were greatly overshadowed by the knights.

Nor can we claim that corporative structures or guilds were unique to Europe, which might otherwise have explained representative divergence. Civic organization, especially of guilds, was also robust in the Ottoman Empire. As in the West, guild leaders were elected and their position had to be validated through court procedure, they could tax their members,

---

[163] Pollock and Maitland 1898, 678.   [164] McKisack 1962, 11, 27.
[165] Pollock and Maitland 1898, 641–42.   [166] Pollock and Maitland 1898, 641.
[167] Dodd 2007, 267–68; Willard 1933, 419–20.
[168] McKisack 1962, 21. As presence in Parliament became increasingly a privilege over time, boroughs started being invaded by landed gentry, causing protest; McKisack 1962, 100; Roskell 1954, 48–49. Recent data by economists suggest representation was higher in boroughs with royal farm grants; Angelucci et al. 2020. But it was not the "self-government" and "independence" generated by the farm grant that led to representation; it was their status as *royal* towns, with specific obligations towards the crown, that did so, a pattern we have found throughout Europe.
[169] Bensch 1995, 316 and ch. 8.6.   [170] Webb and Webb 1908, 261–404.

and could set prices and regulate practice.[171] Moreover, Islamic guilds, unlike European ones, seem to have been "a spontaneous development from below, created, not in response to a State need, but to the social requirements of the labouring masses themselves," and maintaining "either an open hostility to the State, or an attitude of sullen mistrust."[172] That only individuals could be sued suggests they adhered to a system of personal responsibility not the legal fiction of a corporation. But that is not why they never aggregated to a representative system. Rather, Western guilds, as the economic historian Sheilagh Ogilvie has argued, were highly dependent on state power.[173] In fact, for historian Patricia Crone, capitalism itself emerged in the West only when the state "drew the teeth of such semi-autonomous groups as exist[ed] within it";[174] the same may be said about representation. In any case, the building blocks of Western constitutional structures seem to be present elsewhere; it is their collective organization that differed.

13.4   Conclusion

The last three chapters have integrated two canonical non-Western cases in order to further refine the plausibility of the central contention in this book, namely that what truly distinguishes the English case as the most effective parliament-builder was stronger control especially over the most powerful actors. They have shown how these cases differed less in practice than commonly believed from Western ones, at least at the micro level, raising the bar in identifying the factors that truly account for differences. The non-Western cases did not lack demands for rights, limits to arbitrariness, or a concern with equality. To the contrary, they were distinguished often by being fair and institutionalizing practices the West did not adopt for centuries, like partible inheritance as opposed to primogeniture.[175] We observed bureaucratic principles where England applied patrimonialism. The Ottomans even prevented a nobility from forming, stemming the sharp social divisions this generated.

The culture of resistance to unjust authority was so engrained in "the Near Eastern concept of state" that some historians have seen it as a cause

---

[171] İnalcık 1986; Lewis 1937; Faroqhi 1984; 1986b; Yi 2004; Rafeq 1991; Baer 1970. Byzantine (and Roman) guilds had similar, and often rebellious, urban political activity, like Western guilds; Vryonis 1963; Horden 1986; Maniatis 2001.

[172] Lewis 1937, 35–36. Similarly, Gerber 1994, 113–26, 180. Cf. Greif 2006b, 235.

[173] Ogilvie 2019, 36–82; 2011, 160–91.   [174] Crone 1999, 260.

[175] As Kokkonen and Sundell 2014 have shown, primogeniture was even established in all European monarchies by 1801.

for the "decline" of the Ottoman Empire:[176] as Darling has argued, it "legitimized … the possibility of resistance to rulers and their policies."[177] Tax resistance shows, Darling noted, that commitment to the state was based "on the government's performance: no rewards for the elite and no justice for the populace meant no loyalty, no military support, and no taxes."[178] "Seditious" Ottoman coffee houses even preceded English ones.[179] When Janissaries assassinated sultans, they were acting in the name of the people and against sultanic arbitrariness, as Ottomanist Cemal Kafadar observed.[180] These traits help explain how the empire lasted so long.[181]

Yet beheading the English king in 1649 is considered a defense of liberty but executing Osman II in 1622 is deemed emblematic of a non-law-governed regime. Once again, this discrepancy reflects the impact of observing state–society interaction in England through a central Parliament.[182] Same action, different framework, different label.

Obligation was present in the non-Western cases; it elicited their despotic labeling after all. But it was mobilized mostly at the local level and often based on traditional social axes, such as kinship or village groups. English centralization was more pervasive and it integrated communities at the local level within a central structure. The more incentives for centralization were left to the pressures of war, which were intermittent and top-down, the more inadequate they were. England diverged not through greater individualism, but by more effectively deploying power to force individuals to act in common with others, from whom they would normally be divided, often at the expense of fairness – in short, by compellence, even violence – not by granting more rights. The demand for the latter was simply the response.

---

[176] Barkey 1994 and others have challenged the concept of decline, but social cohesion did decline after the 1600s.

[177] Darling 1996, 302; Faroqhi 1992.   [178] Darling 1996, 302.   [179] Barkey 1991, 205.

[180] Kafadar 2008; Tezcan 2010, 6–9.

[181] A similar insight underlies the revisionist account of Byzantine "imperialism" by Anthony Kaldellis, although, in the absence of representation, the ideological frame of popular participation and of mechanisms of accountability was provided by the concept of the republic; Kaldellis 2015.

[182] It also reflects the prejudice of "Orientalism"; Said 1978.

14 Conclusion

This book has aimed to show that justice rather than taxes was at the foundation of representative governance. If taxes mattered, they did so in an inverse way than that usually assumed: it was not the bargaining advantage of societal groups but the incapacity of elites to avoid taxation and royal justice that catalyzed representative institutions. This suggests that an important argument can be added to the debate on the desirability of "taxing the rich," a policy mainly adopted when arguments about fairness have prevailed, as strikingly shown by political scientists Scheve and Stasavage.[1] When elites are exempt, they lack the incentives to hold government accountable and therefore enough incentives to participate in public institutions. Other social groups lack the power to do so effectively, so representative governance falters. State power is fundamental in this dynamic, however, to keep elites in check. The bargaining model has instead been so influential in modern social science partly because it has been supported by one of the most dominant theories of democracy, the rational median voter theorem. This linked the extension of the franchise with the increase in the size of government via taxation.[2] Yet revisionist literature has cast doubt on this model,[3] especially by showing that state capacity, rather than fiscal pressures, was key in shaping institutional and political outcomes,[4] echoing the conclusions of this book.

Acknowledging the importance of state power, moreover, highlights the central role of obligation, successfully imposed, in establishing the representative order. This goes against a liberal predilection to focus on rights, even entitlements, especially the right to escape collective social frames that restrict individual liberty. What the modern constitutional order achieved, rather, was to supplant obligation imposed through a hierarchical system by an authority little bound by consent with

[1] Scheve and Stasavage 2016.
[2] Meltzer and Richard 1981; Boix 2003; Acemoglu and Robinson 2005.
[3] Aidt and Jensen 2009; Ansell and Samuels 2014; Mares and Queralt 2015.
[4] Soifer 2013; Slater et al. 2014.

obligation defined and derived from below.[5] Losing sight of how this system emerged through the successful imposition of supra-local obligation obscures a key point: the liberal constitutional order is predicated on the necessary step of forcing broad social groups to define their interests in collective ways.

This set of claims raises a number of insights and questions, only a few of which can be covered in these concluding remarks. First, our theories of emergence often draw from observed or preferred outcomes, which I have called the normative/empirical inversion. Second, highlighting the importance of state capacity and power begs the question of how such power was first constituted; I offer some observations on this difficult question. Finally, one may ask how we can reconcile this account of inversions with the early modern accounts of English weakness and French (and other) strength. The remaining pages will address these points.

14.1   The Normative/Empirical Inversion

The analysis has noted the intriguing paradox that the posited outcome of representative institutions (shift of sovereignty to social groups) was the inverse of the conditions of emergence (high concentration of central powers). In normative theory, separation of powers is assumed to be the ultimate desideratum; but some key representative regimes were distinguished by institutional fusion at the time of emergence. Many historical stereotypes actually stem from two common and related conceptual errors: either mistaking a consequent for a cause or mistaking a normative prescription for an empirical description. Popular sovereignty was articulated as a norm precisely because (and where) power was already effectively concentrated in the ruler's hands. Norms of rights and power limits became predominant because (and where) power had already fewer empirical limits than elsewhere. Norms, in other words, don't always reflect reality; they often seek to change it. I have called this the "normative/empirical inversion"; it can be discerned in practically every foundational premise of the different theoretical approaches to the topic treated in this book (Table 14.1).

For instance, although private property is touted as the cornerstone of Western development, the most robust representative regime developed where conditionality of property rights was most strongly articulated, England. Similarly, while rational bureaucracy is the hallmark of effective

[5] Klosko 2005.

304 Why Representation in the West

Table 14.1 *The normative/empirical inversion*

	Normative goal/posterior outcome	Empirical reality/antecedent condition
Institutional dimension	Rights to social groups	Concentration of powers
	Separation of powers	Institutional fusion
	Private property	Conditional rights to land
	Rational bureaucracy	Patrimonial networks
	Limits to central authority	Superior extractive capacity
	"Absolute" powers	Social fragmentation
	Individual rights	Collective responsibility
	Separation of church and state	Subordination of church to state
	Equitable distribution of land	Concentration of land rights in the state

state formation according to Weberian accounts, patrimonial, personal-istic networks built the most integrated infrastructure, as we saw in the comparison of England with the Ottoman Empire.[6] And while limits to central authority are thought to define representativeness of a regime, superior extractive capacity, especially over the most powerful actors, is what distinguished the most constitutional cases. Conversely, absolute powers are assumed to denote state strength, but they typically reflect a level of social fragmentation that required extreme measures to be overcome.

Further, the delineation of individual rights became sharper because (and where) collective responsibility was originally effectively and sys-tematically imposed; when large numbers of individuals were united by common responsibilities the incentive to demand greater individual rights became salient. Where central authority was strong, only collective action could effectively counteract it – atomized individuals lacked power. Conversely, where central authority had weak penetration into society, the burden felt by society was relatively weak, as were the incentives – and the ability – to organize collectively to counteract such authority. The claim here is not of a necessary connection between all these conditions; groups have obtained rights without the concentration of powers observed in England. It is about a path that is neglected but generated the most sustainable polity-wide institutions.

---

[6] I have already pointed out that Weber was careful to identify the distinctiveness of England.

This revision also impacts another common assumption in the literature, which has not been touched on so far: that the separation of church
and state was a crucial feature of the modern representative order. The
clear demarcation of a separate religious authority "accustomed rulers to
the idea that they were not the ultimate source of the law," unlike, for
instance, Chinese emperors. It also "pave[d] the way for the modern
secular state," as argued by Fukuyama.[7] Although a lack of separation is
typically identified in the modern period with Catholic states that had a
turbulent transition to democracy, such as Italy or Spain, many Northern
European cases with highly effective constitutional regimes either still
have no separation, such as the United Kingdom or Denmark, or only
instituted it in the 2000s, such as Sweden or Norway.[8] It was thus not
separation from but control of the church that was conducive to a constitutional order. The English crown's advantage over the Church long
preceded Henry VIII's break with Rome in 1534: when in 1170 the
Archbishop of Canterbury, Thomas Becket, tried to thwart the extension
of royal justice over ecclesiastical members under Henry II, Henry's
followers murdered him. The lack of church–state separation accordingly
cannot be blamed, for instance, for the obstacles to communal self-
governance under Islam.[9]

The separation of church and state is instead a modern, liberal desideratum, not a necessary historical component of state and regime
formation.[10] It is not simply that canon law remained widely important
in many critical areas, such as marriage, criminal law, testamentary law
and probate jurisdiction, in England at least until the seventeenth
century;[11] it is that Christian laws and practices established some key
conditions that structured state authority throughout Europe, especially
the rule of Roman law.[12] The Church was critical for the elaboration of
the principles of representation and conciliarism,[13] as well as the creation
of a common ideology and language and of networks of trust and
community.[14] It provided the norms that connected material or technological innovations to outcomes that transformed society, as the sociologist John Hall has argued.[15] Moreover, as argued here, in the very earliest
stages, the "Peace of God" was critical for the pacification of territory,

---

[7] Fukuyama 2011a, 273, 267.
[8] These are also monarchies with strong welfare states; McDonagh 2015.
[9] Kuran 2011, 107. The survival of clan culture, which Kuran rightly focuses on, is the real
underlying problem, though I suggest this is not an issue of theology but of state power.
[10] Even in some modern European countries with established churches, the fusion of
religion and politics had remarkable effects in building national states; Grzymala-Busse
2015.
[11] Helmholz 2003.   [12] Fukuyama 2011a, 262–75.   [13] Tierney 1995.
[14] Mann 1986, 379–83.   [15] Hall 1985b.

typically around a church, throughout Continental Europe. Gregorian chants in Romanesque churches quieted the warrior brain. This history sheds a different light on developing countries today that struggle to combine religion with effective democratic control and reinforces the need to highlight the normative/empirical inversion.

14.2   Whence State Power?

The common denominator behind most instances of the normative/ empirical inversion and of the main dynamics in this book was effective state power. If power was as important as the English case suggests, where did it originate? The question exceeds the bounds of this account and its complexity requires full-length treatment. What this account can offer, however, is two insights about the implications of this analysis on this long-standing question. We might refine, first, the classic distinction in social science made by Michael Mann between despotic and infrastructural power, and, second, the distinction between direct and indirect rule, which is revitalizing our understanding of governance and has regained currency in the analysis of failing or developing states, civil wars, and foreign intervention.

14.2.1   Despotism, Weakness, and Infrastructural Power

This account has emphatically affirmed the importance of ruler power in generating institutional outcomes widely assumed to respond to bottom-up demand. However, as sociologists Hechter and Kabiri have noted:

the idea that social order is produced in top-down fashion by resourceful central authorities leaves a fundamental question begging: Just how can this power ever manage to be concentrated in the first place? To this question, top-down theorists have little in the way of an answer, save for the (often valid) idea that it is imposed exogenously on fragmented territories by more powerful states.[16]

Conquest, indeed, appears as a powerful argument. The invasion of 1066 was a watershed event. However, as the Castilian, Hungarian, Ottoman and other cases have also shown, invasion alone cannot establish effective control: where rulers distributed lands with high levels of autonomy, future control was undermined. The fact that in England conquest had centralizing outcomes was *predicated* on royal strength. Conquest could just as much be used to justify strong separatist claims. We have seen how a thirteenth-century text claimed that English earls deserved privileges

---

[16] Hechter and Kabiri 2008, 47.

vis-à-vis the king because their "ancestors came with William the Bastard and conquered their lands with the sword," which meant they would "defend them with the sword against anyone who tries to usurp them."[17] English kings simply neutralized such claims.

Rather, at least three more factors were important in shaping English outcomes. First, the Anglo-Saxon heritage already displayed a degree of centralization, based on the county as administrative unit.[18] Political organization after the Norman Conquest was thus path-dependent. However, past organization does not sufficiently explain post-conquest outcomes either. Crucially, Normans also exterminated the Anglo-Saxon aristocracy[19] – had they not done so, they would have faced centrifugal forces.[20] However, despite a dynamic start, English extractive capacity saw fluctuations for almost a century, as discussed in Parts II and III. Critical to this process were the judicial reforms of Henry I and Henry II – and this is the third factor, foregrounded by this account: justice had a crucial role in establishing power throughout an extensive territory and population, just as has been observed in studies of modern civil wars and emerging polities.[21]

But the argument in this book, like these modern studies, mostly only describes how some actors wielded power more effectively than others; it does not explain such superior capacity. It is one thing to point out that the more effective actors monopolize judicial functions; it is quite another to explain why and how they succeed in doing so or how they establish control in the first place. This remains a thorny question. Perhaps the most promising hypothesis is the one advanced by historian Eleanor Searle, who argued that the Norman practice of selecting only one heir within strong kinship groups generated both strong leadership and relentless pressures to expand to accommodate the losers, resulting in "predatory kingship."[22] The unfairness of excluding siblings or competitors through primogeniture forced the ruler to expand his power: he protected himself from rivals by compensating them with spoils. This insight echoes the finding of political scientists Kokkonen and Sundell, who argued that primogeniture had formative effects on European monarchies, ensuring greater stability and survival.[23] Power can result from trying to compensate for unfairness. This is still not a final answer, of course, since many states adopted primogeniture but not all succeeded equally in deploying power. A comparison with the clan structures of polities, whether vertical

---

[17] Quoted in Spencer 2014, 73.   [18] Campbell 1995; 2000; Loyn 1984.
[19] Fleming 1991, 215–31.
[20] Normans also effectively centralized not only the English counties, but other regions which they controlled, from Normandy to Sicily; Crouch 2002; Norwich 1992.
[21] Mampilly 2011; Arjona 2016.   [22] Searle 1988.   [23] Kokkonen and Sundell 2014.

or horizontal, as well as the mobilization of ideas of community, might help refine the claim.

It is easier, however, to distinguish different forms of power. Michael Mann's distinction between despotic and infrastructural power is arguably one of the most important distinctions in the literature on the state aiming to parse the puzzle of power.[24] Despotic power is defined as "the range of actions which the elite is empowered to undertake without routine, institutionalized negotiation with civil society groups." Infrastructural power, on the other hand, is "the capacity to actually penetrate civil society, and to implement logistically political decisions throughout the realm."[25] The concept of infrastructural power, which has been used extensively in this book to describe the English case, captures the most important component of effective state power.

However, the definition of despotic power raises some questions, especially where such power is assumed to "have been virtually unlimited." For instance, the Chinese emperor "owned the whole of China and could do as he wished with any individual or group within his domain." Similarly, the Roman emperor or early modern kings claimed "unlimited," "absolute" powers;[26] so did Peter the Great, "probably the least constrained of European rulers"[27] and, later, the Soviet state/party elite. Despotic power, in other words, is the "Red Queen" type of power, unconstrained, unaccountable, and capricious.[28] The notion of despotic power as power held by the state (whether "above" society or within it) remains central to Mann's theory and the literature more widely.[29]

In the argument presented here, by contrast, despotism (or what is assumed to be its cognate, absolutism[30]) denotes a *deficit* of state infrastructural power. It is precisely when the most powerful social groups retained autonomous powers and were beyond the jurisdiction of the state that we observe "despotic" regimes or faltering constitutional ones. These were the nobles controlling *latifundia* in Castile, the Russian *boyars* vying with the tsars for authority, the French nobles exempt from taxation and holding seigneurial rights of jurisdiction, or the Hungarian and Polish nobles who could not be compelled to pay taxes or accept a majority decision.

Scholars of the developing world, of political economy, and of totalitarian regimes have long noted that arbitrariness "in part results from

---

[24] Mann 1984; 1986; Soifer and vom Hau 2008.   [25] Mann 1984, 188, 211, 189.
[26] Mann 1984, 188–89.   [27] Taylor 2003, 40.   [28] Mann 1984, 189.
[29] See the discussion of Mann 2008, 355–56. Also, Ekelund and Tollison 1997, 227; Acemoglu 2005. The burgeoning literature on authoritarian rule adopts a much more nuanced conception of despotic power; see Brownlee 2007; Slater 2010; Svolik 2012.
[30] Absolutism was never assumed to be arbitrary; the ruler was subject to laws, but not to any other human; Henshall 1992.

weakness," as John Hall noted.[31] Migdal explained how many observed pathologies in developing societies "stemmed from the ... resistance posed by chiefs, landlords, bosses, rich peasants, clan leaders ... (for convenience, 'strongmen'),"[32] as did scholars of Africa, for instance Zolberg, who noted that the "major problem is not too much authority, but too little."[33] Similarly, late developing countries adopted "intrusive economic policies," as political scientist Kiren Chaudhry observed, due to "failures to create acceptably functioning markets, signaling the administrative ineffectiveness of [their] regulatory and extractive institutions."[34] The same pathology underlies the current spread of authoritarian governance from Russia and Eastern Europe to Latin America and Southeast Asia. Even when, as in Russia, a ruler succeeds in placing some of the most powerful (the "oligarchs") under his control,[35] infrastructural power has remained weak,[36] requiring autocratic mechanisms to retain control.[37] Such weakness helps explain why collective action among the oligarchs has failed, inhibiting greater accountability.[38]

But the remedy, across different fields, is often believed to lie in greater "liberties," "restraints," or "pluralism," or in a "politically weak" state and a "consensually strong state equilibrium."[39] The emphasis here is to shift the focus and see all these elements as endogenous to a more effective centralization of power, conditional on an effective system of justice that delimits the more powerful social actors. Centralization is the critical missing step that cannot be taken for granted, as Acemoglu and Robinson's recent work also emphasizes.[40]

14.2.2 Direct Rule, Indirect Rule, and English Rule

Another implication about power and state- and institution-building that flows from this book's argument concerns the distinction between direct and indirect rule as alternative forms of power-building. These concepts have underlain both the theory and the practice of colonial rule, as well as the more recent literature on property rights regimes, intervention, and post-war governance.[41] They sprung from English colonial rule over

[31] John A. Hall 1986, 163. [32] Migdal 1988, 33. [33] Zolberg 1969, x.
[34] Chaudhry 1993, 252. [35] Milanovic 2019. [36] Markus 2015; Frye 2021.
[37] Treisman 2018.
[38] Markus 2017. That oligarchs have been compelled to provide services the state could not, to deal with the crisis of the 2020 pandemic, could trigger some form of collective action, my argument suggests; Troianovski 2020.
[39] John A. Hall 1986, 163–64; Acemoglu 2005, 1199; Acemoglu and Robinson 2017.
[40] Acemoglu and Robinson 2012, 80–81.
[41] Gerring et al. 2011; Hechter and Kabiri 2008; Boone 2014.

India and Africa,[42] itself influenced by the anthropological thinking of Henry Maine.[43] They are complex and controversial concepts,[44] and as political scientist Catherine Boone has shown, their implementation was in fact refracted through the bargaining powers of local elites and rural structures.[45] Only a generalized discussion is thus possible here. In theory, indirect rule meant that much of local governance devolved to rural elites,[46] while the colonial ruler retained sovereign powers on the use of force, especially for defense and taxation. In direct rule, on the other hand, officials were appointed by the ruling power at all levels of administration, with policy at the local level decided at the center. Despite a long and controversial record under colonial conditions, indirect rule is attracting attention not least due to its assumed affinities with the decentralized, federal approach to politics.[47] The approach seems to display a democratic support for local preferences with a non-coercive system of rule, thus offering the possibility of accommodation between typically incompatible dynamics, although as Boone emphasizes, it was neither democratic nor participatory in practice, but led by local elites.[48] But it certainly remains relevant to our understanding of governance structures in the developing world.[49]

Typically, indirect rule is seen as distinctly English.[50] It echoes the stereotypes about English governance that have been considered in this book: an assumed "weak" state and "amateur" officials, drawn from local power-holders and relying on custom. Direct rule, on the other hand, seems more congruent with a Continental, interventionist, and "statist" stereotype that echoes the dispatch of royal officials in the provinces, such as the *intendants* during French absolutist rule – a sign of a "strong," legislating state.

The analysis in this book has hopefully succeeded in showing that the "statist" assumption – which has, after all, been long debunked in the historical literature on European absolutism – relies on a misconception: outsiders dispatched to govern and inspect provinces appear as absolutist because weak infrastructural control prevented rulers from effectively penetrating localities.[51] Conversely, indirect governance is possible where local organization is both developed and amenable to

---

[42] Ashton 1947; Crowder 1964; Mamdani 1996b.   [43] Mantena 2010.
[44] Lange 2009, 1–44.
[45] Boone 2003. Boone develops a more nuanced breakdown of indirect and direct rule.
[46] Matthews 1937, 433; Boone 2003, 31.
[47] Ashton 1947; Gerring et al. 2011; Hechter and Kabiri 2008.   [48] Boone 2003, 32.
[49] Mamdani 1996a; Boone 2014.
[50] Matthews 1937, 433; Crowder 1964. The French used it too; Boone 2014, 30n22.
[51] This somewhat resembles what Boone calls "administrative occupation"; Boone 2003, 33.

Table 14.2 *Direct, indirect, English, and French rule*

	Direct rule	English rule	French rule	Indirect rule
State level	**State** officials	**State** officials	**State** officials	**State** officials
Local level	**State** officials	Local officials	**State** officials	Local officials
Policy	**State** policy	**State** policy	Local policy	Local policy

control. Similar patterns are also identified by Boone and others in colonial settings.[52]

But the additional insight presented here is that indirect rule differs from what the English state itself applied internally and that, accordingly, the distinction between direct and indirect rule is missing two alternatives, the original English and French ones. The English alternative was the most effective method of rule but also very difficult to achieve. It used local officials (the "amateur" freeholder, duty-bound to perform service to the state mostly on account of his landholdings) to channel local custom through *state* policies and laws (the "common law" – Table 14.2). This explains how the English state achieved such remarkable levels of jurisdictional uniformity and extractive capacity whilst maintaining the myth of a "weak state."[53] Moreover, the medieval French strategy of state expansion also differed from the modern understanding of direct rule. As Strayer explained, "Philip Augustus had hit on a formula which was followed by all his successors. When a province came under direct control of the king it preserved its customs and its institutions, but the customs were enforced and the institutions were staffed by men sent out from the royal court at Paris"[54] – i.e. state officials applied local laws.

The flipside, however, was that the area that was effectively controlled under the English formula was much smaller. "England failed in its attempt to annex Scotland, made only slight headway in Ireland and spent several centuries in gaining full control of so small a province as Wales. France, on the other hand, attached firmly to the crown territories as diverse as Normandy, Languedoc, Dauphine, and Brittany."[55] Ironically, English rule was closer to what we would today call direct rule than the French model. It was also harder to impose on heterogeneous populations; hence the adoption of indirect rule across much of the British Empire.

[52] Boone 2003. See also Gerring et al. 2011.
[53] The conventional contrast is concisely articulated in Badie and Birnbaum 1983, 103–34.
[54] Strayer 1969, 5.   [55] Strayer 1969, 5.

Although, as mentioned, this book cannot resolve the rather intractable problem of the origins of state power, it has offered some observations that may help clarify and deepen our understanding of the mechanics of power, whilst jettisoning commonplace assumptions that continue to permeate social scientific work and whilst confirming recent reassessments of the benefits of centralization. By reassessing the foundations of social power in medieval England, it suggests a more nuanced way of conceptualizing how central and local powers interact and the need to beware of the often-distorting optical effects of how power is distributed via institutions, especially representative ones.

14.3   Passages to Modernity

If, as argued, England was strong and France weak in the Middle Ages, how are we to reconcile this narrative with classic accounts of Continental absolutist strength and English weakness in the early modern period? And how was it that by the seventeenth century, Charles I (1625–49) could simply cease to call Parliament for eleven years when it proved too recalcitrant? Conversely, France had raised troops so large and waged war so effectively by the 1660s that Europe feared the spread of "universal monarchy."[56] By the time of the French Revolution, in Barrington Moore's memorable phrase, the nobility had become "a decorative appanage of the king."[57] If so, isn't this more recent period more relevant to a causal account of parliamentary emergence?

This book rests on the premise that the foundation for the institutional divergence of European polities can be traced back to the medieval period. This does not assume determinism or teleology, as modern outcomes depended on many crucial developments in the intervening centuries, tracing which exceeds the bounds of this book. But it does imply that much of the observed variation in the early modern period can be viewed as endogenous to this institutional heritage. Charles may have suspended Parliament arbitrarily, but resistance to the crown during the Civil War was channeled through centuries-old parliamentary structures, as were the later political conflicts between Tories and Whigs. Parliament also coordinated the effects of the economic changes that transformed politics after the seventeenth century. It was a long-standing, highly formed institution that was able to "credibly commit" to honor debt obligations.[58] Debt was not lacking in France or Spain nor was capital. Economic historians have shown that French private markets were highly developed and Spanish monarchs had regular access to credit, despite the

[56] Lisola 1667.   [57] Moore 1967, 40.   [58] North and Weingast 1989.

absence or weakness of constitutional constraints.[59] They differed rather in the locus of financial interactions: these were privatized or localized in the Continental cases, rather than subject to central public linkages institutionalized via Parliament as in England.

The privatization of power relations in France also helps explain why the nobility was gradually disempowered by the king in the 1600s. As it never developed a polity-wide frame of institutional cooperation, the nobility was unable to sustain a concerted institutional front vis-à-vis the king. Replicating a pattern found repeatedly in this book, early strength of a social group meant low initial incentives for collective action, resulting in weak institutional formation and collective rights in the long run.

Moreover, the drastic increase of power achieved by Louis XIV displays some key features identified in early English institution-building. The common narrative of French growth focuses on the "centralization" pursued through the *intendants*, officials dispatched from the center to circumvent the local power structures composed of governors and provincial nobilities and to raise taxation.[60] Indeed, the explosion of taxation noted by historians in this period owed much to this practice. But this was a similar strategy to that adopted by medieval English kings, as we have seen, based on itinerant officials that aimed to supplant local power structures (in the judicial realm). As in England, conditional relations with the crown shaped the *intendants'* effectiveness: they were originally revocable and not purchasable. Governors also became temporary, i.e. conditional, and their troops dependent on Louis.[61]

The difference with England lay not in the intrusiveness of French central institutions but in their lower effectiveness. French society, and especially the privileged orders, remained harder to control. However, as they had not resolved their collective action problem due to the earlier weakness of the crown, they did not respond to royal expansion in a unified way; resistance remained local. Although a revisionist approach has framed these interactions within a model of "social collaboration" with the king,[62] they still reflected royal weakness.[63] When the crown attempted to assert control after 1695 by imposing taxation on those privileged orders, they indeed acted collectively (as this book would predict) and developed the language of "liberty" and "citizenship" leading up to the French Revolution – a provocative finding by historian Michael Kwass.[64] However, the state was

---

[59] Hoffman et al. 2000; Drelichman and Voth 2014.
[60] Mousnier 1984, 502–51; Ertman 1997, 131–32; Downing 1992, 123–24.
[61] Lough 1961, 235–37; Finer 1975, 132.
[62] See the overview of this rich literature in Beik 2005.   [63] Mettam 1988.
[64] Kwass 2000.

not strong enough to prevail, as sociologist Theda Skocpol argued in her classic study, so this confrontation produced neither an effective state nor representative institutions, but social revolution.[65]

Nonetheless, England had deviated from the conditions described in this book already by the fifteenth century. By then, "a poor and weak crown was confronted by wealthy and arrogant magnates."[66] This condition was partly caused by the spread of "bastard" feudalism, a much-debated historical phenomenon.[67] As royal power grew,[68] local lords were forced to hire retainers, often assumed to have offered only military service.[69] However, administrative service was also prevalent from the 1200s;[70] lords especially needed judges to handle their legal cases.[71] Originally these relations were regulated through royal courts.[72] This trend of retainers grew after the fourteenth century, however, and much social power was privatized, a condition that under a weak crown enabled the Wars of the Roses (1455–85) between rival aristocratic factions. Despite fluctuations, the landed English nobility became increasingly powerful in later centuries. Even in the mid-nineteenth century, aristocratic landowners were not only the richest actors, they also dominated parliamentary politics and cabinet positions. From this perspective, "England represents an extreme instance of the continuity of aristocratic power in European history."[73]

From the standpoint of this book, however, it was precisely the shift "from tenure to contract"[74] from the fourteenth century, i.e. from a form of dependent organization to a more privatized and decentralized one, that eventually undermined social order and parliamentary politics. The Tudor reassertion of authority also failed to establish equivalent ties of enduring institutionalized conditionality within the framework of a changing, commercializing economy, resulting in weakness. For instance, land appropriated from the Dissolution of Monasteries was sold, leading to a one-off increase in the royal Treasury[75] and a decline in parliamentary exchange: during this time almost three quarters of royal revenue was non-parliamentary.[76] As O'Brien and Hunt noted, Tudor fiscal prowess was "temporary"; Stuart extractive capacity was quite weak.[77] Between 1550 and 1640 real per capita taxation was only 65 percent of that collected between 1330 and 1440 (the highpoint of medieval collection). Further, despite strident narratives of confiscatory taxation, between 1550 and 1640 overall taxation declined on average per year by

---

[65] Skocpol 1979.   [66] Elton 1955, 10.   [67] Bellamy 1989; Coss 1989.
[68] Coss 1989, 53–54.   [69] Coss 1989, 30–33.   [70] Waugh 1986, 812–15.
[71] Maddicott 1978b.   [72] Waugh 1986, 832–33.   [73] Dewald 1996, 4–5.
[74] McFarlane 1944.   [75] Batho 1967, 275; Hollis 1994.   [76] Braddick 1996, 11–12.
[77] O'Brien and Hunt 1993, 153, 147–68.

0.17 percent,[78] whilst it rose by 0.53 percent in the earlier period. In fact, taxes declined between 1550 and 1640 at a steeper rate than did the economy (which shrunk by an average by 0.05 percent in real per capita terms, whereas it rose by 0.3 percent annually between 1330 and 1440). Although feudal obligations did rise between 1541 and 1602, they were now out of sync with a commercializing economy and had lost their connection to service.[79]

Conditions settled only after the Glorious Revolution, when conditionality was reimposed on a new basis: debt and commercial growth now restructured political relations, vesting power-holders with incentives to monitor parliamentary politics.[80] Once again, a highly effective state (now an increasingly sovereign parliament) was necessary for this outcome, one that achieved the second highest rate of tax extraction after 1688 (after the Netherlands). If anything, the nobility's well-documented strength in the next two centuries might help explain why the extension of the franchise was so delayed in England. If the state had been able to compel it as effectively as in the early stages in this book, voting reform may have even happened earlier.

*

In conclusion, I will highlight some implications of this argument for three debates in current policy: the fiscal politics of state-building in developing countries, the political economy of redistribution, and the problem of political order. The revision offered in this book has relevance because the bargaining model has been influencing policy in international organizations such as the IMF and the OECD. Developing countries have turned to domestic resource mobilization especially after recent financial crises, so taxation is being used for institution-building.[81] "State-society bargaining around tax" is assumed to make "a unique contribution to building more effective, accountable states and public institutions." Even in such public policy scholarship, this mechanism is traced to European history, especially to the narrative of seventeenth-century England and Holland, where war pushed governments to negotiate with capital-holders.[82] The lesson is assumed to carry into the modern world. However, the relevance of the mechanism is moot in cases where social groups lack capital and bargaining power to demand concessions from the state, as often occurs in developing countries.

---

[78] It was the non-parliamentary indirect taxation that doubled after 1550; Braddick 1996, 10.
[79] Hurstfield 1955 and online Appendix A for all data.   [80] Stasavage 2003; Pincus 2009.
[81] Keen 2012, 3.   [82] OECD 2008, 7.

Once we reassess the historical record, three different implications for scholarship on the developing world emerge. First, social groups do not need to be strong or commercial before taxation is demanded; they are more likely to engage in collective action and demand rights when taxation is already successfully imposed. What matters is whether the tax is a burden that unites groups, not how much or what kind of wealth they have.[83] Second, states should not fear such collective action, as it typically is accompanied by enhanced extraction. This requires a background condition, however. Some state capacity must pre-exist any bargaining dynamic if the latter is to contribute to representation. Critical institutions have to precede the imposition of taxation if the latter is to provide incentives for the demand of greater accountability and good governance: as even ISIS understood, the provision of justice offers powerful incentives. Though compelling, "no taxation without representation" is a slogan, not a causal mechanism.

The second major implication of the argument concerns the political economy of redistribution. Inequality is one of the most important pathologies of the current political and economic orders.[84] In the developing world, inequality of land remains central. Despite long-standing efforts at reform in Latin America, for instance, only about half of all arable land has been either redistributed or expropriated between 1930 and 2008.[85] Crucially, this change has not had appreciable impact on levels of inequality;[86] results in Africa are similar.[87] The English case suggests that it may be helpful to rethink the necessity of land redistribution for political and economic development; at least, the implications of England's historical land regime have not been fully thought through.

After all, land inequality in Latin America was lower than that observed in Britain, either historically or even today: even half a century ago, 90 percent of the land in Latin America was controlled by 10 percent of the population, but in 1873 all land and homes in Britain were in the hands of 3.6 percent of the population.[88] Yet England led both the Agricultural and the Industrial Revolutions and was the most evolved constitutional regime, and the latter already before agriculture ceased to be the most important economic resource. The aristocracy remained dominant into the modern period not simply because of land distribution but because

---

[83] See also Weigel 2020 and the cases listed in Boucoyannis 2015b, 326n49.

[84] Hacker and Pierson 2010; Gilens 2012; Piketty 2014.   [85] Albertus 2015, 8–9.

[86] Most studies attribute the decline in inequality in the last decades to policies such as higher education spending, stronger foreign direct investment, or higher tax revenues; Tsounta and Osueke 2014, 4–5.

[87] World Bank 1975; Deininger and Binswanger 1999.

[88] Even today 0.6 percent of the population (members of the extended royal family mostly) holds about 70 percent of the land; Lapp 2004, 2; Cahill 2001.

the crown weakened as conditionality receded and the privatization of state–society relations suggested above grew, as argued above. What this account has shown instead is that a certain type of inequality is necessary for more efficient outcomes: only when power is skewed in favor of the state can actors be incentivized to support the creation of a representative institutional structure (with the economic effects that flow from this). Adam Smith famously noted that inequality in the acquisition of property made government necessary, a theme recently revived.[89] The claim here is that government power shapes the effects of this inequality.

Rather than the distribution of land, this account has highlighted the type of property rights as crucial, whether conditional or not. Neo-institutional theory has reoriented social science towards property rights but has focused on security as the trait that optimized outcomes instead. As noted earlier, historians have questioned any radical change in security after the posited watershed of 1688, but security remains an intuitively important concept.[90] This is enhanced by a widespread understanding of property rights as rights that "individuals appropriate over their own labor and the goods and services they possess."[91] The main threat, according to this view, both historically and empirically, has been state predation.[92]

This conception of "absolute" rights over things, however, goes against the standard legal definition of rights as relations between people, not people and things: "a thing cannot bring or defend a lawsuit."[93] The relational understanding suggests that rights over property imply distributional dynamics,[94] namely "bundles of rights" between individuals that have to be defined through some socially negotiated process.[95] The rights of one actor or group have to be protected from encroachment from other *actors* – the enforcing actor is thus crucial. When the English crown could limit its most powerful subjects from predating on their tenants in the early period, England's biggest constitutional gains transpired. The crown could do so because it could enforce its conditional relations with those power-holders. It was the *conditional insecurity* of property rights that had institutional consequences. When royal power to sustain this regime declined in the following centuries, Parliament's capacity to shape political outcomes backslided. The next stage of conditionality, after 1660, was predicated on commerce and debt as noted, as well as strong extractive powers. Today,

[89] Smith [1776] 1981b, V.i.b.2; Boix 2015.
[90] Acemoglu et al. 2005a, 394–95; Cox 2016.
[91] North 1990, 33. This misconception is common; see for instance Pipes 1999, xv–xvi and as noted by Grey 1980, 69.
[92] North 1990; Levi 1988.
[93] Donahue 1980, 30, citing Hohfeld 1964. Also, Sprankling 2017, §§1.01–1.04.
[94] Knight 1992.   [95] Grey 1980, 69.

conditionality, as applied by international organizations, is a controversial concept, but most critiques focus on the substance of the conditions rather than the principle of dependence per se.[96] This account supports its importance for conditions of emergence.

Finally, the argument may also illuminate the broader problem of political order. In a classic of political science, Samuel Huntington attributed political instability in modernizing societies to mass political participation under conditions of low institutionalization.[97] The implied but troubling solution was to restrict political participation and justify authoritarian governance to strengthen institutions.[98] The implication of this account is decidedly different: the problem is not disruptive political participation or low institutionalization per se. These are symptoms of inadequate control over the greatest power-holders – it is the latter that should be the prime target. The less power-holders can be compelled to serve the public good, the less efficient the institutionalization, and the more reason for political participation to be aimed against the regime, thus causing political instability – that is what the democratic contract entails. Liberal political order depends on compelling the powerful to comply with political obligation, especially relating to justice. Obligation – not rights nor cost–benefit calculations nor bargaining over taxation – first propelled the formation of representative institutions in the West, which then allowed rights to become institutionalized. And many of these rights were responses to institutionalized unfairness (as we have seen with regards to primogeniture, for instance).

The English philosopher Francis Bacon pointed out in 1617 that part of what made England's judicial system distinct was that the institution of Justices of the Peace "knits noblemen and gentlemen together, and in no place else but here in England are noblemen and gentlemen incorporated: for abroad in other countries noblemen meddle not with any parcel of justice but in martial affairs: matter of justice, that belongs to the gownmen; and this is it that makes those noblemen the more ignorant and the more oppressors: but here amongst us they are incorporated with those that execute justice, and so being warriors are likewise made instruments of peace; and that makes them truly noble."[99] Though realities were hardly as noble, the point here is that nobles had been *compelled* to such service in common with "lower" orders. This outcome was not a spontaneous one; it was the result of power "properly deployed," as was the liberal constitutional order it generated.[100]

---

[96] Babb and Carruthers 2008.   [97] Huntington 1968.
[98] As explained by Fukuyama 2011b.   [99] Bacon 1872, 303.   [100] Bates 2014, 50.

Bibliography

Abbasi, Muhammad Zubair. 2012. "The Classical Islamic Law of Waqf: A Concise Introduction." *Arab Law Quarterly* 26 (2): 121–53.

Abou-El-Haj, Rifa'at Ali. 1991. *Formation of the Modern State: The Ottoman Empire, Sixteenth to Eighteenth Centuries.* Albany: State University of New York Press.

Abramson, Scott, and Carles Boix. 2012. "The Roots of the Industrial Revolution: Political Institutions or (Socially Embedded) Know-How?" Unpublished manuscript, Princeton.

——— 2019. "Endogenous Parliaments: The Domestic and International Roots of Long-Term Economic Growth and Executive Constraints in Europe." *International Organization* 73 (4): 793–837.

Abu Zahra, Muhammad. 1955. "Family Law." In *Law in the Middle East*, ed. M. Khadduri and H. J. Liebesny, 132–78. Washington, DC: Middle East Institute.

Abulafia, David. 1995. "The Rise of Aragon-Catalonia." In *The New Cambridge Medieval History*, ed. D. Abulafia, 644–61. Cambridge: Cambridge University Press.

Acemoglu, Daron. 2005. "Politics and Economics in Weak and Strong States." *Journal of Monetary Economics* 52 (7): 1199–1226.

Acemoglu, Daron, Simon Johnson, and James A. Robinson. 2002. "Reversal of Fortune: Geography and Institutions in the Making of the Modern World Income Distribution." *The Quarterly Journal of Economics* 117 (4): 1231–94.

——— 2005a. "Institutions as a Fundamental Cause of Long-Run Growth." In *Handbook of Economic Growth*, ed. P. Aghion and S. N. Durlauf, 386–472. Amsterdam: Elsevier.

——— 2005b. "The Rise of Europe: Atlantic Trade, Institutional Change, and Economic Growth." *The American Economic Review* 95 (3): 546–79.

Acemoglu, Daron, and James Robinson. 2005. *Economic Origins of Dictatorship and Democracy: Economic and Political Origins.* Cambridge: Cambridge University Press.

——— 2012. *Why Nations Fail: The Origins of Power, Prosperity and Poverty.* New York: Crown Business.

——— 2017. "The Emergence of Weak, Despotic and Inclusive States." NBER Working Paper no. 23657. National Bureau of Economic Research, Cambridge, MA.

Acemoglu, Daron, James Robinson, and Thierry Verdier. 2004. "Alfred Marshall Lecture: Kleptocracy and Divide-and-Rule: A Model of Personal Rule." *Journal of the European Economic Association* 2 (2/3): 162–92.

Actes du Parlement de Paris. 1863. Vol. 1: *1254–1299*. Paris: H. Plon.

Adams, Julia. 1994. "Trading States, Trading Places: The Role of Patrimonialism in Early Modern Dutch Development." *Comparative Studies in Society and History* 36 (2): 319–55.

2005. *The Familial State: Ruling Families and Merchant Capitalism in Early Modern Europe*. Ithaca, NY: Cornell University Press.

Adanir, Fikret. 2006. "Semi-Autonomous Provincial Forces in the Balkans and Anatolia." In *The Cambridge History of Turkey, Volume 3: The Later Ottoman Empire, 1603–1839*, ed. S. Faroqhi, 157–85. New York: Cambridge University Press.

Ágoston, Gábor. 2005. *Guns for the Sultan: Military Power and the Weapons Industry in the Ottoman Empire*. New York: Cambridge University Press.

Aidt, Toke S., and Peter S. Jensen. 2009. "The Taxman Tools Up: An Event History Study of the Introduction of the Personal Income Tax." *Journal of Public Economics* 93 (1–2): 160–75.

Albert, Pere. 2002. *The Customs of Catalonia between Lords and Vassals*. Tempe: Arizona Center for Medieval and Renaissance Studies.

Albertus, Michael. 2015. *Autocracy and Redistribution: The Politics of Land Reform*. Cambridge: Cambridge University Press.

Alef, Gustave. 1983. "The Crisis of the Muscovite Aristocracy: A Factor in the Growth of Monarchical Power." In *Rulers and Nobles in Fifteenth-Century Muscovy*. London: Variorum Reprints.

Alfani, Guido, and Francesco Ammannati. 2017. "Long-Term Trends in Economic Inequality: The Case of the Florentine State, c. 1300–1800." *The Economic History Review* 70 (4): 1072–1102.

Allen, Robert C. 1992. *Enclosure and the Yeoman: The Agricultural Development of the South Midlands, 1450–1850*. Oxford: Clarendon Press.

n.d. *Laborers' Relative Wages*. University of California, Davis. Available at https://gpih.ucdavis.edu/Datafilelist.htm.

Álvarez-Nogal, Carlos, and Leandro Prados de La Escosura. 2007. "The Decline of Spain (1500–1850): Conjectural Estimates." *European Review of Economic History* 11 (03): 319–66.

2012. "The Rise and Fall of Spain (1270–1850)." *The Economic History Review* 66 (1): 1–37.

Anderson, Perry. 1974a. *Lineages of the Absolutist State*. London: New Left Books.

1974b. *Passages from Antiquity to Feudalism*. London: New Left Books.

Angelucci, Charles, Simone Meraglia, and Nico Voigtländer. 2020. "How Merchant Towns Shaped Parliaments: From the Norman Conquest of England to the Great Reform Act." NBER Working Paper no. 23606. National Bureau of Economic Research, Cambridge, MA.

Ansell, Ben W., and David Samuels. 2014. *Inequality and Democratization: An Elite-Competition Approach*. New York: Cambridge University Press.

Arendt, Hannah. 1970. *On Violence*. New York: Harcourt.

Arjona, Ana. 2016. *Rebelocracy: Social Order in the Colombian Civil War*. Cambridge: Cambridge University Press.

Armstrong, John Alexander. 1972. "Old-Regime Governors: Bureaucratic and Patrimonial Attributes." *Comparative Studies in Society and History* 14 (1): 2–29.

Arnold, Benjamin. 1991. *Princes and Territories in Medieval Germany*. Cambridge: Cambridge University Press.

Artonne, André. 1912. *Le Mouvement de 1314 et Les Chartes Provinciales de 1315*. Paris: F. Alcan.

Asch, Ronald G. 2003. *Nobilities in Transition, 1550–1700: Courtiers and Rebels in Britain and Europe*. London: Bloomsbury.

Ashton, E. H. 1947. "Democracy and Indirect Rule." *Africa: Journal of the International African Institute* 17 (4): 235–51.

Aston, T. H., and C. H. E Philpin. 1985. *The Brenner Debate: Agrarian Class Structure and Economic Development in Pre-Industrial Europe*. Cambridge: Cambridge University Press.

Atçıl, Abdurrahman. 2017. *Scholars and Sultans in the Early Modern Ottoman Empire*. Cambridge: Cambridge University Press.

Aubert, Félix. 1894. *Histoire du Parlement de Paris de L'origine à François Ier 1250–1515*. Genève: Mégariotis Reprints.

[1890] 1977. *Le Parlement de Paris, de Philippe Le Bel à Charles VII, 1314–1422: Sa Compétence, Ses Attributions*. Genève: Slatkine-Megariotis Reprints.

Autrand, Françoise, and Philippe Contamine. 1979. "La France et L'Angleterre Histoire Politique et Institutionnelle Onzième-Quinzième Siècles." *Revue Historique* 262 (1): 117–68.

Aylmer, G. E. 1961. *The King's Servants: The Civil Service of Charles I, 1625–1642*. New York: Columbia University Press.

Babb, Sarah L., and Bruce G. Carruthers. 2008. "Conditionality: Forms, Function, and History." *Annual Review of Law and Social Science* 4: 13–29.

Bacon, Francis. 1872. *The Letters and the Life of Francis Bacon*. London: Longmans, Green and Company.

Badie, Bertrand, and Pierre Birnbaum. 1983. *The Sociology of the State*. Chicago: University of Chicago Press.

Baer, Gabriel. 1970. *The Structure of Turkish Guilds and Its Significance for Ottoman Social History*. Jerusalem: Israel Academy of Sciences and Humanities.

Bailey, Mark. 2014. *The Decline of Serfdom in Late Medieval England: From Bondage to Freedom*. Woodbridge: Boydell Press.

2021. *After the Black Death: Economy, Society, and the Law in Fourteenth-Century England*. Oxford: Oxford University Press.

Bairoch, Paul, Jean Batou, and Pierre Chèvre. 1988. *The Population of European Cities, 800–1850: Data Bank and Short Summary of Results*. Geneva: Droz.

Bak, János M. 1990. "The Late Medieval Period, 1382–1526." In *A History of Hungary*, ed. P. F. Sugar, P. Hanák, and T. Frank, 54–82. Bloomington: Indiana University Press.

1999. *The Laws of the Medieval Kingdom of Hungary, Volume 1: 1000–1301*. Idyllwild, CA: C. Schlacks.

Baker, John H. 2002. *An Introduction to English Legal History*, 4th ed. London: Butterworths LexisNexis.

2003. *The Oxford History of the Laws of England, Volume 6: 1483–1558*. Oxford: Oxford University Press.

Baker, Robert L. 1961. "The English Customs Service, 1307–1343: A Study of Medieval Administration." *Transactions of the American Philosophical Society* 51 (6): 3–76.

Baldwin, James. 2012. "Petitioning the Sultan in Ottoman Egypt." *Bulletin of the School of Oriental and African Studies* 75 (3): 499–524.

Baldwin, John W. 1986. *The Government of Philip Augustus: Foundations of French Royal Power in the Middle Ages*. Berkeley: University of California Press.

Ball, Norman. 1995. "Representation in the English House of Commons: The New Boroughs, 1485–1640." *Parliaments, Estates and Representation* 15 (1): 117–24.

Balla, Eliana, and Noel D. Johnson. 2009. "Fiscal Crisis and Institutional Change in the Ottoman Empire and France." *The Journal of Economic History* 69 (3): 809–45.

Bardach, J. 1965. "Gouvernants et Gouvernés en Pologne Pendant le Moyen Âge et Temps Modernes." *Anciens Pays et Assemblées d'États* XXXVI: 268–85.

1977. "La Formation des Assemblées Polonaises au XVe Siècle et la Taxation." *Anciens Pays et Assemblées d'États* LXX: 249–96.

Barker, Ernest. 1913. *The Dominican Order and Convocation: A Study of the Growth of Representation in the Church During the Thirteenth Century*. Oxford: Clarendon Press.

Barkey, Karen. 1991. "The Use of Court Records in the Reconstruction of Village Networks: A Comparative Perspective." *International Journal of Comparative Sociology* 32: 195–216.

1994. *Bandits and Bureaucrats: The Ottoman Route to State Centralization*. Ithaca, NY: Cornell University Press.

2008. *Empire of Difference: The Ottomans in Comparative Perspective*. Cambridge: Cambridge University Press.

Barkey, Karen, and Ira Katznelson. 2011. "States, Regimes, and Decisions: Why Jews Were Expelled from Medieval England and France." *Theory and Society* 40 (5): 475–503.

Barratt, Nick. 1999a. "English Royal Revenue in the Early Thirteenth Century and Its Wider Context, 1130–1330." In *Crises, Revolutions and Self-Sustained Growth: Essays in European Fiscal History, 1130–1830*, ed. W. M. Ormrod, M. Bonney, and R. Bonney, 59–96. Stamford: Shaun Tyas.

1999b. "The Revenues of John and Philip Augusts Revisited." In *King John: New Interpretations*, ed. S. D. Church, 75–99. Woodbridge: Boydell Press.

Barrington, Lowell W. 2012. *Comparative Politics: Structures and Choices*. Boston: Cengage Learning.

Barrow, Julia. 1989. "Education and the Recruitment of Cathedral Canons in England and Germany, 1100–1225." *Viator* 20: 117–38.

Barta, István. 1975. *A History of Hungary*. London: Collet's.

Bartlett, Robert. 2000. *England under the Norman and Angevin Kings, 1075–1225*. Oxford: Oxford University Press.

Barzel, Yoram, and Edgar Kiser. 2002. "Taxation and Voting Rights in Medieval England and France." *Rationality and Society* 14 (4): 473–507.

Bates, Robert H. 1988. "Lessons from History, or the Perfidy of English Exceptionalism and the Significance of Historical France." *World Politics* 40 (4): 499–516.

2008. *When Things Fell Apart: State Failure in Late-Century Africa.* New York: Cambridge University Press.

2014. "The New Institutionalism: The Work of Douglas North." In *Institutions, Property Rights, and Economic Growth: The Legacy of Douglass North,* ed. S. N. Galiani and I. Sened, 50–65. Cambridge: Cambridge University Press.

Bates, Robert H., and Da-Hsiang Donald Lien. 1985. "A Note on Taxation, Development, and Representative Government." *Politics and Society* 14 (1): 53–70.

Batho, Gordon. 1967. "Landlords in England: The Crown." In *The Agrarian History of England and Wales,* ed. H. P. R. Finberg and J. Thirsk, 256–75. London: Cambridge University Press.

Bean, J. M. W. 1968. *The Decline of English Feudalism: 1215–1540.* Manchester: Manchester University Press.

1991. "Landlords." In *The Agrarian History of England and Wales, Volume 3: 1348–1500,* ed. E. Miller, 526–86. Cambridge: Cambridge University Press.

Beaumanoir, Philippe de. 1900. *Coutumes de Beauvaisis,* Volume 2. Paris: A. Picard et fils.

Becker, Marvin B. 1960. "Some Aspects of Oligarchical, Dictatorial and Popular Signorie in Florence, 1282–1382." *Comparative Studies in Society and History* 2 (4): 421–39.

Beier, A. L. 2008. "'A New Serfdom': Labor Laws, Vagrancy Statutes, and Labor Discipline in England, 1350–1800." In *Cast Out: Vagrancy and Homelessness in Global and Historical Perspective,* ed. A. L. Beier and P. Ocobock, 35–63. Columbis: Ohio University Press.

Beik, William. 1985. *Absolutism and Society in Seventeenth Century France: State Power and Provincial Aristocracy in Languedoc.* Cambridge: Cambridge University Press.

2005. "The Absolutism of Louis XIV as Social Collaboration." *Past & Present* 188: 195–224.

Bellamy, John G. 1970. *The Law of Treason in England in the Later Middle Ages.* Cambridge: Cambridge University Press.

1973. *Crime and Public Order in England in the Later Middle Ages.* London: Routledge & Kegan Paul.

1989. *Bastard Feudalism and the Law.* London: Routledge.

Bellomo, Manlio. 1995. *The Common Legal Past of Europe, 1000–1800.* Washington, DC: Catholic University of America Press.

Benito i Monclus, Pere. 2003. *Senyoria de la Terra i Tinença Pagesa al Comtat de Barcelona (Sègles XI–XIII),* Vol. 51. Barcelona: Consell superior d'investigaciones científiques.

Bennett, Judith M. 2010. "Compulsory Service in Late Medieval England." *Past & Present* 209: 7–51.

Bensch, Stephen P. 1995. *Barcelona and Its Rulers, 1096–1291*. Cambridge: Cambridge University Press.

Benson, Bruce L. 1989. "The Spontaneous Evolution of Commercial Law." *Southern Economic Journal* 55 (3): 644–61.

Benson, Robert Louis, Giles Constable, and Carol Dana Lanham. 1985. *Renaissance and Renewal in the Twelfth Century*. Oxford: Oxford University Press.

Beresford, M. W. 1967. *New Towns of the Middle Ages: Town Plantation in England, Wales, and Gascony*. New York: Praeger.

Berman, Harold Joseph. 1983. *Law and Revolution: The Formation of the Western Legal Tradition*. Cambridge, MA: Harvard University Press.

Berman, Sheri. 2018. *Democracy and Dictatorship in Europe: From the Ancien Régime to the Present Day*. New York: Oxford University Press.

Besley, Timothy, and Torsten Persson. 2009. "The Origins of State Capacity: Property Rights, Taxation, and Politics." *American Economic Review* 99 (4): 1218–44.

———. 2011. *Pillars of Prosperity: The Political Economics of Development Clusters*. Princeton, NJ: Princeton University Press.

Biancalana, Joseph. 2001. *The Fee Tail and the Common Recovery in Medieval England, 1176–1502*. Cambridge: Cambridge University Press.

Bisson, Thomas N. 1961. "An Early Provincial Assembly: The General Court of Agenais in the Thirteenth Century." *Speculum: A Journal of Medieval Studies* 36 (2): 254–81.

———. 1964. *Assemblies and Representation in Languedoc in the Thirteenth Century*. Princeton, NJ: Princeton University Press.

———. 1969. "Consultative Functions in the King's Parlements (1250–1314)." *Speculum: A Journal of Medieval Studies* 44 (3): 353–73.

———. 1972. "The General Assemblies of Philip the Fair: Their Character Reconsidered." *Studia Gratiana* 15: 538–64.

———. 1978. "The Problem of the Feudal Monarchy: Aragon, Catalonia, and France." *Speculum: A Journal of Medieval Studies* 53 (3): 460–78.

———. 1982. "Celebration and Persuasion: Reflections on the Cultural Evolution of Medieval Consultation." *Legislative Studies Quarterly* 7 (2): 181–204.

———. 1984. *Fiscal Accounts of Catalonia under the Early Count-Kings (1151–1213)*, Volume 1. Berkeley: University of California Press.

———. 1986. *Medieval Crown of Aragon: A Short History*. Oxford: Oxford University Press.

———. 1989. "Feudalism in Twelfth-Century Catalonia." In *Medieval France and Her Pyrenean Neighbours: Studies in Early Institutional History*, 153–78. London: Hambledon Press.

———. 1994. "The "Feudal Revolution." *Past & Present* 142: 6–42.

———. 1996. "The Origins of the Corts of Catalonia." *Parliaments, Estates and Representation* 16: 31–45.

———. 2003. "Cortes, Crown of Aragón." In *Medieval Iberia: An Encyclopedia*, ed. E. M. Gerli and S. G. Armistead, 264–66. New York: Routledge.

———. 2009. *The Crisis of the Twelfth Century: Power, Lordship, and the Origins of European Government*. Princeton: Princeton University Press.

Blaas, P. B. M. 1978. *Continuity and Anachronism: Parliamentary and Constitutional Development in Whig Historiography and in the Anti-Whig Reaction between 1890 and 1930*. The Hague: M. Nijhoff.

Black, Jane W. 1994. "Natura Feudi Haec Est: Lawyers and Feudatories in the Duchy of Milan." *The English Historical Review* 109 (434): 1150–73.

Blank, Meredith, Mark Dincecco, and Yuri Zhukov. 2017. "Political Regime Type and Warfare: Evidence from 600 Years of European History." Unpublished manuscript.

Blaufarb, Rafe. 2010. "The Survival of the Pays d'États: The Example of Provence." *Past & Present* 209 (1): 83–116.

Blaydes, Lisa, and Eric Chaney. 2013. "The Feudal Revolution and Europe's Rise: Political Divergence of the Christian West and the Muslim World before 1500 CE." *American Political Science Review* 107 (1): 16–34.

Blaydes, Lisa, and Christopher Paik. 2016. "The Impact of Holy Land Crusades on State Formation: War Mobilization, Trade Integration, and Political Development in Medieval Europe." *International Organization* 70 (3): 551–86.

Blickle, Peter. 1997a. *Obedient Germans? A Rebuttal: A New View of German History*. Charlottesville: University Press of Virginia.

1997b. *Resistance, Representation, and Community*. Oxford: Oxford University Press.

Bloch, Marc. 1953. *The Historian's Craft*. New York: Knopf.

1961. *Feudal Society*, two vols. in one. London: Routledge & Kegan Paul.

1965. *Feudal Society*, Volume 1. London: Routledge & Kegan Paul.

Blockmans, Willem Pieter. 1976. "Le Régime Réprentatif en Flandre dans le Cadre Européen au Bas Moyen Âge, Avec un Projet d'application des Ordinateurs." *Études présentées à la Commission internationale pour l'histoire des assemblées d'États* 56: 212–45.

1978. "A Typology of Representative Institutions in Late Medieval Europe." *Journal of Medieval History* 4: 189–215.

1989. "Voracious States and Obstructing Cities: An Aspect of State Formation in Preindustrial Europe." *Theory and Society* 18 (5): 733–55.

1998. "Representation (since the Thirteenth Century)." In *The New Cambridge Medieval History*, ed. C. T. Allmand, 29–64. Cambridge: Cambridge University Press.

Blockmans, Willem Pieter, and Walter Prevenier. 1999. *The Promised Lands: The Low Countries under Burgundian Rule, 1369–1530*. Philadelphia: University of Pennsylvania Press.

Blommaert, W. 1915. *Les Châtelains de Flandre; Étude d'histoire Constitutionnelle*. Gand: E. van Goethem & cie.

Blum, Jerome. 1961. *Lord and Peasant in Russia: From the Ninth to the Nineteenth Century*. Princeton, NJ: Princeton University Press.

Bodde, Derk. 1981. "Feudalism in China." In *Essays on Chinese Civilization*, 85–131. Princeton, NJ: Princeton University Press.

Bogatyrev, Sergei. 2000. *The Sovereign and His Counsellors: Ritualised Consultations in Muscovite Political Culture, 1350–1570s*. Helsinki: Academia Scientiarum Fennica.

2006. "Ivan IV (1533–1584)." In *The Cambridge History of Russia*, ed. M. Perrie, 240–63. Cambridge: Cambridge University Press.

Boix, Carles. 2003. *Democracy and Redistribution*. Cambridge: Cambridge University Press.

2015. *Political Order and Inequality: Their Foundations and Their Consequences for Human Welfare*. New York: Cambridge University Press.

Bolton, J. L. 1980. *The Medieval English Economy, 1150–1500*. London: J. M. Dent.

Bongert, Yvonne. 1949. *Recherches sur les Cours Laïques du Xe au XIIIe Siècle*. Paris: Picard.

Bónis, György. 1965. "The Hungarian Feudal Diet (13th–18th Centuries)." *Anciens Pays et Assemblées d'États* 36: 287–307.

Bonney, Richard. 2012. "The Rise of the Fiscal State in France, 1500–1914." In *The Rise of Fiscal States: A Global History, 1500–1914*, ed. B. Yun Casalilla and P. K. O'Brien, 93–110. New York: Cambridge University Press.

Boone, Catherine. 2003. *Political Topographies of the African State: Territorial Authority and Institutional Choice*. Cambridge: Cambridge University Press.

2014. *Property and Political Order in Africa: Land Rights and the Structure of Politics*. New York: Cambridge University Press.

Boone, Marc. 2010. "Le Comté de Flandre au XIVe Siècle: Les Enquêtes Administratives et Juridiques Comme Armes Politiques dans les Conflits Entre Villes et Prince." In *Quand Gouverner C'est Enquêter: Les Pratiques Politiques de L'enquête Princière (Occident, XIIIe–XIVe Siècles)*, ed. T. Pécout, 461–80. Paris: De Boccard.

Bosker, Maarten, Eltjo Buringh, and Jan L. van Zanden. 2013. "From Baghdad to London: Unraveling Urban Development in Europe and the Arab World 800–1800." *Review of Economics and Statistics* 95 (4): 1418–37.

Boucoyannis, Deborah. 2015a. "The Historiography of the Medieval English Parliament." Unpublished manuscript, Charlottesville, University of Virginia.

2015b. "No Taxation of Elites, No Representation: State Capacity and the Origins of Representation." *Politics & Society* 43: 303–32.

2017. "How Much Capital, How Much Coercion? War and the Formation of the State." Unpublished manuscript, University of Virginia.

Boutemy, André. 1943. *Recueil de Textes Historiques Latin du Moyen Âge*. Bruxelles: Lebegue.

Bracton, Henry de. 1977. *On the Laws and Customs of England*. Vol. 4. Cambridge, MA: Harvard University Press.

Braddick, M. J. 1996. *The Nerves of State: Taxation and the Financing of the English State, 1558–1714*. Manchester: Manchester University Press.

Bradford, Phil. 2007. "Parliament and Political Culture in Early Fourteenth Century England." Unpublished PhD thesis, University of York, UK.

2011. "A Silent Presence: The English King in Parliament in the Fourteenth Century." *Historical Research* 84 (224): 189–211.

Brand, Paul. 1992. *The Making of the Common Law*. London: Hambledon Press.

1997. "The Formation of the English Legal System." In *Legislation and Justice*, ed. A. Padoa Schioppa, 103–21. Oxford: Clarendon Press.

2003. *Kings, Barons and Justices: The Making and Enforcement of Legislation in Thirteenth-Century England*. Cambridge: Cambridge University Press.

2004. "Petitions and Parliament in the Reign of Edward I." *Parliamentary History* 23 (1): 14–38.

2007. "Henry II and the Creation of the English Common Law." In *Henry II: New Interpretations*, ed. C. Harper-Bill and N. Vincent, 215–41. Woodbridge: Boydell Press.

2009. "Understanding Early Petitions: An Analysis of the Content of Petitions to Parliament in the Reign of Edward I." In *Medieval Petitions: Grace and Grievance*, ed. W. M. Ormrod, G. Dodd, and A. Musson, 99–119. Woodbridge: York Medieval Press.

Braumoeller, Bear F., and Gary Goertz. 2000. "The Methodology of Necessary Conditions." *American Journal of Political Science* 44 (4): 844–58.

Bräutigam, Deborah, Odd-Helge Fjeldstad, and Mick Moore. 2008. *Taxation and State-Building in Developing Countries: Capacity and Consent*. Cambridge: Cambridge University Press.

Brennan, Geoffrey, and James M. Buchanan. 1980. *The Power to Tax: Analytical Foundations of a Fiscal Constitution*. Cambridge: Cambridge University Press.

Brenner, Robert. 1976. "Agrarian Class Structure and Economic Development in Pre-Industrial Europe." *Past & Present* 70: 30–75.

1993. *Merchants and Revolution: Commercial Change, Political Conflict, and London's Overseas Traders, 1550–1653*. Princeton, NJ: Princeton University Press.

Brewer, John. 1989. *The Sinews of Power: War, Money, and the English State, 1688–1783*. New York: Knopf.

Britnell, Richard H. 1978. "English Markets and Royal Administration before 1200." *Economic History Review* 31 (2): 183–96.

1981. "The Proliferation of Markets in England, 1200–1349." *Economic History Review* 34: 209–21.

Broadberry, Stephen, Bruce Campbell, Alexander Klein, Mark Overton, and Bas van Leeuwen. 2015. *British Economic Growth, 1270–1870*. Cambridge: Cambridge University Press.

Broadberry, Stephen, Bruce Campbell, and Bas van Leeuwen. 2010. "English Medieval Population: Reconciling Time Series and Cross Sectional Evidence." Unpublished manuscript, University of Warwick.

Brown, A. L. 1989. *The Governance of Late Medieval England 1272–1461*. London: Edward Arnold.

Brown, Elizabeth A. R. 1970. "Philip the Fair, Plena Potestas and the Aide Pur Fille Marier of 1308." In *Representative Institutions in Theory and Practice*, 3–27. Brussels: Les Éditions de la Librairie Encyclopédique.

1972a. "Cessante Causa and the Taxes of the Last Capetians: The Political Application of a Philosophical Maxim." *Studia Gratiana* 15: 567–87.

1972b. "Representation and Agency Law in the Later Middle Ages." *Viator: Medieval and Renaissance Studies* 3: 329–64.

1974. "The Tyranny of a Construct: Feudalism and Historians of Medieval Europe." *American Historical Review* 79 (4): 1063–88.

Brown, Peter B. 1983. "The Zemskii Sobor in Recent Soviet Historiography." *Russian History* 10 (1): 77–90.

Brown, Warren. 2011. *Violence and the Law in England.* New York: Longman.

Brownlee, Jason. 2007. *Authoritarianism in an Age of Democratization.* Cambridge: Cambridge University Press.

Brucker, Gene A. 1962. *Florentine Politics and Society, 1343–1378.* Princeton, NJ: Princeton University Press.

Bubenicek, Michelle, ed. Forthcoming. *Doléances. Approches Comparées de la Plainte Politique Comme Voie de Régulation Dynamique des Rapports Gouvernants-Gouvernés (Fin XIIIe–Premier XIXe S.).* Besançon: Cahiers de la MSHE Ledoux.

Bubenicek, Michelle, and Richard Partington. 2015. "Justice, Law and Lawyers." In *Government and Political Life in England and France, c.1300–c.1500,* ed. C. Fletcher, J.-P. Genêt, and J. Watts, 150–82. Cambridge: Cambridge University Press.

Buch, Henri. 1965. "Représentation et Députation en Belgique du XIIIe au XVIe Siècle." *Anciens Pays et Assemblées d'États* 37: 29–46.

Bulst, Neithard. 1992. *Die Französischen Generalstände von 1468 und 1484: Prosopographische Untersuchungen Zu Den Delegierten.* Sigmaringen: Thorbecke.

Burgers, Jan. 2009. "De Grafelijke Raad in Holland en Zeeland Ten Tijde Van Graaf Willem III (1304–1337)." *Jaarboek voor Middeleeuwse Geschiedenis* 12.
2011. "The Prince and His Subjects. The Administration of the County of Holland in the First Half of the Fourteenth Century: The Evidence from the Registers." In *Representative Assemblies, Territorial Autonomies, Political Cultures,* ed. A. Nieddu and F. Soddu, 107–16. Sassari: Editrice democratica sarda.

Burkhardt, Julia. 2015. "Procedure, Rules and Meaning of Political Assemblies in Late Medieval Central Europe." *Parliaments, Estates and Representation* 35 (2): 153–70.

Burt, Caroline. 2013. *Edward I and the Governance of England, 1272–1307.* Cambridge: Cambridge University Press.

Bush, M. L. 1983. *Noble Privilege.* New York: Holmes & Meier.

Buylaert, Frederik. 2015. "Lordship, Urbanization and Social Change in Late Medieval Flanders." *Past & Present* 227 (1): 31–75.

Cabrera, E. 1989. "The Medieval Origins of the Great Landed Estates of the Guadalquivir Valley." *Economic History Review* 42 (4): 465–83.

Cahen, Claude. 1970. "Y a-t-il Eu des Corporations Professionnelles dans le Monde Musulman Classique?" In *The Islamic City: A Colloquium* ed. A. Hourani and S. M. Stern, 51–63. Philadelphia: University of Pennsylvania Press.

Cahill, K. 2001. *Who Owns Britain?* Edinburgh: Canongate.

Calvert, Randall. 1995. "Rational Actors, Equilibrium, and Social Institutions." In *Explaining Social Institutions,* ed. J. Knight and I. Sened, 57–94. Ann Arbor: University of Michigan Press.

Cam, Helen Maud. 1930. *The Hundred and the Hundred Rolls: An Outline of Local Government in Medieval England.* London: Methuen.

1935. "Suitors and Scabini." *Speculum: A Journal of Medieval Studies* 10 (2): 189–200.

1963. "The Community of the Shire and the Payment of Its Representatives in Parliament." In *Liberties and Communities in Medieval England*, 236–47. New York: Barnes & Noble.

1970a. "The Legislators of Medieval England." In *Historical Studies of the English Parliament*, ed. E. B. Fryde and E. Miller, 168–94. Cambridge: Cambridge University Press.

1970b. "The Theory and Practice of Representation in Medieval England." In *Historical Studies of the English Parliament*, ed. E. B. Fryde and E. Miller, 262–78. Cambridge: Cambridge University Press.

Campbell, Bruce M. S. 2008. "Benchmarking Medieval Economic Development: England, Wales, Scotland, and Ireland, c.1290." *The Economic History Review* 61 (4): 896–945.

Campbell, James. 1995. "The Late Anglo-Saxon State: A Maximum View." *Proceedings of the British Academy* 87: 37–65.

2000. *The Anglo-Saxon State*. London: Hambledon Press.

Canbakal, Hülya. 2011. "Vows as Contract in Ottoman Public Life (17th–18th Centuries)." *Islamic Law and Society* 18 (1): 85–115.

Cannari, Luigi, and Giovanni D'Alessio. 2007. "Le Opinioni Degli Italiani Sull'evasione Fiscale." Working Paper No. 618, Banca d'Italia.

Capoccia, Giovanni, and R. Daniel Kelemen. 2007. "The Study of Critical Junctures: Theory, Narrative, and Counterfactuals in Historical Institutionalism." *World Politics* 59 (3): 341–69.

Capoccia, Giovanni, and Daniel Ziblatt. 2010. "The Historical Turn in Democratization Studies: A New Research Agenda for Europe and Beyond." *Comparative Political Studies* 43 (8–9): 931–68.

Capua, J. V. 1983. "Feudal and Royal Justice in Thirteenth-Century England: The Forms and the Impact of Royal Review." *The American Journal of Legal History* 27 (1): 54–84.

Carpenter, Christine. 1983. "Law, Justice and Landowners in Late Medieval England." *Law and History Review* 1 (2): 205–37.

1994. "Gentry and Community in Medieval England." *The Journal of British Studies* 33 (4): 340–80.

Carpenter, David A. 1995. "The Plantagenet Kings." In *The New Cambridge Medieval History*, ed. D. Abulafia, 314–57. Cambridge: Cambridge University Press.

1996. *The Reign of Henry III*. London: Hambledon Press.

2000. "The Second Century of English Feudalism." *Past & Present* 168: 30–71.

Carruthers, Bruce G. 1996. *City of Capital: Politics and Markets in the English Financial Revolution*. Princeton, NJ: Princeton University Press.

Carsten, F. L. 1954. *The Origins of Prussia*. Oxford: Clarendon Press.

1959. *Princes and Parliaments in Germany, from the Fifteenth to the Eighteenth Century*. Oxford: Clarendon Press.

Carus-Wilson, E. M., and Olive Coleman. 1963. *England's Export Trade, 1275–1547*. Oxford: Clarendon Press.

Cattan, Henry. 1955. "The Law of the Waqf." In *Law in the Middle East*, ed. M. Khadduri and H. J. Liebesny, 203–22. Washington, DC: Middle East Institute.

Cazelles, Raymond. 1962. "Les Mouvements Révolutionnaires du Milieu du XIVe Siècle et le Cycle de L'action Politique." *Revue Historique* 228 (2): 279–312.

Centeno, Miguel Angel. 2002. *Blood and Debt: War and the Nation-State in Latin America*. University Park, PA: Pennsylvania State University Press.

Chang, Ha-Joon. 2002. *Kicking Away the Ladder: Development Strategy in Historical Perspective*. London: Anthem.

Chaudhry, Kiren Aziz. 1993. "The Myths of the Market and the Common History of Late Developers." *Politics & Society* 21 (3): 245–74.

1997. *The Price of Wealth: Economies and Institutions in the Middle East*. Ithaca, NY: Cornell University Press.

Cheibub, José Antonio. 1998. "Political Regimes and the Extractive Capacity of Governments: Taxation in Democracies and Dictatorships." *World Politics* 50 (3): 349–76.

Cheyette, Fredric. 1962. "Procurations by Large-Scale Communities in Fourteenth-Century France." *Speculum: A Journal of Medieval Studies* 37 (1): 18–31.

Chrimes, S. B. 1966. *An Introduction to the Administrative History of Mediaeval England*, 3rd ed. New York: Barnes & Noble.

Christine de Pizan. 1994. *The Book of the Body Politic*. Cambridge: Cambridge University Press.

The Chronicle of James I, King of Aragon. 1883. London: Chapman & Hall.

Church, Clive, and Randolph Head. 2013. *A Concise History of Switzerland*. Cambridge: Cambridge University Press.

Ciepley, David. 2013. "Beyond Public and Private: Toward a Political Theory of the Corporation." *The American Political Science Review* 107 (1): 139–58.

Çirakman, Asli. 2001. "From Tyranny to Despotism: The Enlightenment's Unenlightened Image of the Turks." *International Journal of Middle East Studies* 33 (1): 49–68.

Clamageran, Jean Jules. 1867. *Histoire de L'impôt en France*. Vol. 1. Paris: Guillaumin et Cie.

Clanchy, M. T. 1974. "Law, Government, and Society in Medieval England." *History* 59 (195): 73–78.

Clark, Gregory. 2014. "Nominal and Real Wages, England, 1209–1869." http:// faculty.econ.ucdavis.edu/faculty/gclark/data.html.

Clarke, Maude Violet. 1936. *Medieval Representation and Consent: A Study of Early Parliaments in England and Ireland, with Special Reference to the Modus Tenendi Parliamentum*. London: Longmans.

Clemente Campos, María Belén. 1993. "La Adquisición del Privilegio del Voto por la 'Provincia' de Extremadura: Notas Para el Estudio de las Cortes de Castilla en la Edad Moderna." Unpublished manuscript, University of Extremadura.

Clodfelter, Micheal. 2008. *Warfare and Armed Conflicts: A Statistical Encyclopedia of Casualty and Other Figures, 1494–2007*, 3rd ed. Jefferson, NC: McFarland.

Coffman, D'Maris. 2017. "Fiscal States and Sovereign Debt Markets: A New Paradigm for Apprehending Historical Structural Change." In *The Political Economy of the Eurozone*, ed. I. Cardinale, D. M. Coffman, and R. Scazzieri, 37–59. Cambridge: Cambridge University Press.

Coffman, D'Maris, Leonard Adrian, and Larry Neal, eds. 2013. *Questioning Credible Commitment: Perspectives on the Rise of Financial Capitalism*. Cambridge: Cambridge University Press.

Cohen, Esther. 1993. *The Crossroads of Justice: Law and Culture in Late Medieval France*. Leiden: E. J. Brill.

Coleman, Edward. 2003. "Representative Assemblies in Communal Italy." In *Political Assemblies in the Earlier Middle Ages*, ed. P. S. Barnwell and M. Mostert, 193–210. Turnhout: Brepols.

2004. "Cities and Communes." In *Italy in the Central Middle Ages: 1000–1300*, ed. D. Abulafia, 27–57. Oxford: Oxford University Press.

Collins, James B. 1994. *Classes, Estates, and Order in Early Modern Brittany*. Cambridge: Cambridge University Press.

Conant, Kenneth John. 1973. *Carolingian and Romanesque Architecture, 800 to 1200*, 3rd ed. Harmondsworth: Penguin.

Congleton, Roger D. 2011. *Perfecting Parliament: Constitutional Reform, Liberalism, and the Rise of Western Democracy*. Cambridge: Cambridge University Press.

Contamine, Philippe. 1972. *Guerre, État et Société à la Fin du Moyen Âge. Études sur les Armées des Rois De France 1337–1494*. Paris: Mouton.

1976. "De la Puissance aux Privilèges: Doléances de la Noblesse Française Envers la Monarchie aux XIVe et XVe Siècles." In *La Noblesse au Moyen Âge XIe–XVe Siècles: Essais à la Mémoire de Robert Boutruche*, 236–57. Paris: Presses Universitaires de France.

1997. *La Noblesse au Royaume de France de Philippe Le Bel à Louis XII: Essai de Synthèse*. Paris: Presses Universitaires de France.

Cooke, Elizabeth. 2006. *Land Law*. Oxford: Oxford University Press.

Coolidge, Archibald Cary. 1910. "The Development of Hungarian Constitutional Liberty." *American Historical Review* 15 (2): 359–61.

Corbett, W. J. 1957. "The Development of the Duchy of Normandy and the Norman Conquest of England." In *The Cambridge Medieval History*, ed. J. R. Tanner, C. W. Previté-Orton, and Z. N. Brooke, 481–520. Cambridge: Cambridge University Press.

Cortes de los Antiguos Reinos de Aragón y de Valencia y Principado de Cataluña. 1896. Vol. 1. Madrid: Real Academia de la Historia.

Cortes de los Antiguos Reinos de León y de Castilla. 1861. Vol. 1. Madrid: Impr. y estereotipia de M. Rivadeneyra.

Cortes de los Antiguos Reinos de León y de Castilla. 1866. Vol. 4. Madrid: Impresores de la Casa Real.

Corvisier, André. 1992. *Histoire Militaire de la France*. Vol. 1: *Des origines à 1715*. Paris: Presses Universitaires de France.

Coss, Peter R. 1989. "Bastard Feudalism Revised." *Past & Present* 125: 27–64.

1995. "The Formation of the English Gentry." *Past & Present* 147: 38–64.

2003. *The Origins of the English Gentry*. Cambridge: Cambridge University Press.

Coulson, Noel J. 1971. *Succession in the Muslim Family*. Cambridge: Cambridge University Press.

Cox, Gary W. 2016. *Marketing Sovereign Promises: Monopoly Brokerage and the Growth of the English State*. New York: Cambridge University Press.

Croft, J. Pauline. 2003. *King James*. Basingstoke: Palgrave Macmillan.

Crone, Patricia. 1986. "The Tribe and the State." In *States in History*, ed. J. A. Hall, 48–77. Oxford: Blackwell.

1999. "Weber, Islamic Law, and the Rise of Capitalism." In *Max Weber & Islam*, ed. T. E. Huff and W. Schluchter, 247–72. New Brunswick, NJ: Transaction.

Crouch, David. 2002. *The Normans: The History of a Dynasty*. London: Hambledon Press.

Crowder, Michael. 1964. "Indirect Rule: French and British Style." *Africa: Journal of the International African Institute* 34 (3): 197–205.

Crummey, Robert O. 1983. *Aristocrats and Servitors: The Boyar Elite in Russia, 1613–1689*. Princeton, NJ: Princeton University Press.

1987. *The Formation of Muscovy, 1304–1613*. London: Longman.

Curtis, Daniel R., and Michele Campopiano. 2014. "Medieval Land Reclamation and the Creation of New Societies: Comparing Holland and the Po Valley, c.800–c.1500." *Journal of Historical Geography* 44: 93–108.

d'Avray, David. 2001. "Lay Kinship Solidarity and Papal Law." In *Law, Laity, and Solidarities: Essays in Honour of Susan Reynolds*, ed. P. Stafford, J. L. Nelson, and J. Martindale, 188–99. Manchester: Manchester University Press.

Dahl, Robert A. 1971. *Polyarchy: Participation and Opposition*. New Haven: Yale University Press.

Daileader, Philip. 1999. "The Vanishing Consulates of Catalonia." *Speculum: A Journal of Medieval Studies* 74 (1): 65–94.

Darling, Linda T. 1996. *Revenue-Raising and Legitimacy: Tax Collection and Finance Administration in the Ottoman Empire, 1560–1660*. Leiden: E. J. Brill.

2013. *A History of Social Justice and Political Power in the Middle East: The Circle of Justice from Mesopotamia to Globalization*. New York: Routledge.

Davies, Brian. 2006. "Local Government and Administration." In *The Cambridge History of Russia*, ed. M. Perrie, 464–85. Cambridge: Cambridge University Press.

Davies, Robert Rees. 1990. *Domination and Conquest: The Experience of Ireland, Scotland, and Wales, 1100–1300*. Cambridge: Cambridge University Press.

Davis, John P. 1905. *Corporations: A Study of the Origin and Development of Great Business Combinations and of Their Relation to the Authority of the State*. New York: Putnam.

Davis, Nancy J., and Robert V. Robinson. 2006. "The Egalitarian Face of Islamic Orthodoxy: Support for Islamic Law and Economic Justice in Seven Muslim-Majority Nations." *American Sociological Review* 71 (2): 167–90.

Davis, Natalie Zemon. 1985. "Review of *The Development of the Family and Marriage in Europe*, by Jack Goody." *American Ethnologist* 12 (1): 149–51.

Dawson, John Philip. 1940. "The Codification of the French Customs." *Michigan Law Review* 38 (6): 765–800.

1960. *A History of Lay Judges*. Cambridge: Harvard University Press.

1968. *The Oracles of the Law*. Ann Arbor: University of Michigan Law School.

de Carné, Louis Joseph Marie. 1875. *Les États de Bretagne et L'administration de Cette Province Jusqu'en 1789*. Paris: Didier.

de Lagarde, Georges. 1937. "Individualisme et Corporatisme au Moyen Âge." In *L'organisation Corporative du Moyen Âge à la Fin de l'Ancien Régime*. Louvain: Bibliothèque de l'Université.

de Roover, Raymond. 1965. "The Organization of Trade." In *The Cambridge Economic History of Europe*, ed. M. M. Postan, E. E. Rich, and E. Miller, 42–118. Cambridge: Cambridge University Press.

de Schepper, Hugo, and J.-M. Cauchies. 1997. "Legal Tools of the Public Power in the Netherlands, 1200–1600." In *Legislation and Justice*, ed. A. Padoa Schioppa, 229–68. Oxford: Clarendon Press.

de Soto, Hernando. 2000. *The Mystery of Capital: Why Capitalism Triumphs in the West and Fails Everywhere Else*. New York: Basic Books.

de Vries, Jan. 1984. *European Urbanization, 1500–1800*. Cambridge, MA: Harvard University Press.

2001. "The Transition to Capitalism in a Land without Feudalism." In *Peasants into Farmers? The Transformation of Rural Economy and Society in the Low Countries (Middle Ages–19th Century) in Light of the Brenner Debate*, ed. P. C. M. Hoppenbrouwers and J. L. van Zanden, 67–84. Turnhout: Brepols.

de Vries, Jan, and A. M. van der Woude. 1997. *The First Modern Economy: Success, Failure, and Perseverance of the Dutch Economy, 1500–1815*. Cambridge: Cambridge University Press.

Dean, Trevor. 2004. "The Rise of the Signori." In *Italy in the Central Middle Ages: 1000–1300*, ed. D. Abulafia, 104–24. Oxford: Oxford University Press.

2012. "Ferrara and Mantua." In *The Italian Renaissance State*, ed. A. Gamberini and I. Lazzarini, 112–31. Cambridge: Cambridge University Press.

Decoster, Caroline. 2002. "La Convocation à L'assemblée de 1302, Instrument Juridique au Service de la Propagande Royale." *Parliaments, Estates and Representation* 22 (1): 17–36.

Deininger, Klaus, and Hans Binswanger. 1999. "The Evolution of the World Bank's Land Policy: Principles, Experience, and Future Challenges." *The World Bank Research Observer* 14 (2): 247–76.

DeLong, J. Bradford. 2000. "Overstrong against Thyself: War, the State, and Growth in Europe on the Eve of the Industrial Revolution." In *A Not-So-Dismal Science: A Broader View of Economies and Societies*, ed. M. Olson and S. Kähkönen, 138–67. Oxford: Oxford University Press.

DeLong, J. Bradford, and Andrei Shleifer. 1993. "Princes and Merchants: European City Growth before the Industrial Revolution." *The Journal of Law & Economics* 36 (2): 671–702.

Demyttenaere, A. 2003. "Galbert of Bruges on Political Meeting Culture: Palavers and Fights in Flanders during the Years 1127 and 1128." In *Political Assemblies in the Earlier Middle Ages*, ed. P. S. Barnwell and M. Mostert, 151–92. Turnhout: Brepols.

Dennison, Tracy K. 2011. *The Institutional Framework of Russian Serfdom.* Cambridge: Cambridge University Press.

Denton, Jeffrey Howard. 1981. "The Clergy and Parliament in the Thirteenth and Fourteenth Centuries." In *The English Parliament in the Middle Ages*, ed. R. G. Davies and J. H. Denton, 88–108. Philadelphia: University of Pennsylvania Press.

Derville, Alain. 2002. *Les Villes de Flandre et D'artois (900–1500).* Villeneuve d'Ascq: Presses Universitaires du Septentrion.

Desjardins, Arthur. 1871. *États-Généraux (1355–1614): Leur Influence sur le Gouvernement et la Législation du Pays.* Paris: A. Durand et P. Lauriel.

Desportes, Pierre. 1989. "Les Pairs de France et la Couronne." *Revue Historique* 282: 305–40.

Dewald, Jonathan. 1996. *The European Nobility, 1400–1800.* New York: Cambridge University Press.

Dewey, Horace W. 1964. "Immunities in Old Russia." *Slavic Review* 23 (4): 643–59.

———. 1970. "Suretyship and Collective Responsibility in Pre-Petrine Russia." *Jahrbücher für Geschichte Osteuropas* 18 (3): 337–54.

———. 1971. "Muscovite Princes and Monasterial Privileges." *The Slavonic and East European Review* 49 (116): 453–57.

———. 1987. "Political Poruka`in Muscovite Rus'." *The Russian Review* 46 (2): 117–33.

———. 1988. "Russia's Debt to the Mongols in Suretyship and Collective Responsibility." *Comparative Studies in Society and History* 30 (2): 249–70.

Dewey, Horace W., and Ann M. Kleimola. 1982. "From the Kinship Group to Every Man His Brother's Keeper: Collective Responsibility in Pre-Petrine Russia." *Jahrbücher für Geschichte Osteuropas* 30 (3): 321–35.

———. 1984. "Russian Collective Consciousness: The Kievan Roots." *The Slavonic and East European Review* 62 (2): 180–91.

Dhondt, J. 1948. "Développement Urbain et Initiative Comtale en Flandre au XIe Siècle." *Revue du Nord* 30: 133–56.

———. 1950. "Les Origines des États de Flandre." *Anciens Pays et Assemblées d'États* I: 1–52.

Dickson, P. G. M. 1967. *The Financial Revolution in England: A Study in the Development of Public Credit, 1688–1756.* London: St. Martin's Press.

Dijkman, Jessica. 2011. *Shaping Medieval Markets: The Organisation of Commodity Markets in Holland, c. 1200–c. 1450.* Leiden: E. J. Brill.

DiMaggio, Paul J., and Walter W. Powell. 1983. "The Iron Cage Revisited: Institutional Isomorphism and Collective Rationality in Organizational Fields." *American Sociological Review* 48 (2): 147–60.

Dincecco, Mark. 2009. "Fiscal Centralization, Limited Government, and Public Revenues in Europe, 1650–1913." *The Journal of Economic History* 69 (1): 48–103.

———. 2011. *Political Transformations and Public Finances: Europe, 1650–1913.* Cambridge: Cambridge University Press.

———. 2017. *State Capacity and Economic Development: Present and Past.* Cambridge: Cambridge University Press.

Dincecco, Mark, and Yuhua Wang. 2018. "Violent Conflict and Political Development over the Long Run: China Versus Europe." *Annual Review of Political Science* 21: 341–58.

Dion, Douglas. 1998. "Evidence and Inference in the Comparative Case Study." *Comparative Politics* 30 (2): 127–46.

Dodd, Gwilym. 2001. "The Hidden Presence: Parliament and the Private Petition in the Fourteenth Century." In *Expectations of the Law in the Middle Ages*, ed. A. Musson, 135–49. Rochester, NY: Boydell Press.

2007. *Justice and Grace: Private Petitioning and the English Parliament in the Late Middle Ages*. Oxford: Oxford University Press.

2014. "Reason, Conscience and Equity: Bishops as the King's Judges in Later Medieval England." *History* 99 (335): 213–40.

Dodd, Gwilym, and A. K. McHardy, eds. 2010. *Petitions to the Crown from English Religious Houses, c.1272–c.1485*. Woodbridge: Boydell Press.

Domar, Evsey D. 1970. "The Causes of Slavery or Serfdom: A Hypothesis." *The Journal of Economic History* 30 (1): 18–32.

Donahue, Charles, Jr. 1980. "The Future of the Concept of Property Predicted from Its Past." In *Property*, ed. J. R. Pennock and J. W. Chapman, 28–68. New York: New York University Press.

Doucet, Roger. 1948. *Les Institutions de la France au XVIe Siècle*. Paris: Picard.

Downing, Brian M. 1992. *The Military Revolution and Political Change: Origins of Democracy and Autocracy in Early Modern Europe*. Princeton, NJ: Princeton University Press.

Doyle, William. 1996. *Venality: The Sale of Offices in Eighteenth-Century France*. Oxford: Clarendon Press.

Drelichman, Mauricio. 2007. "Sons of Something: Taxes, Lawsuits, and Local Political Control in Sixteenth-Century Castile." *The Journal of Economic History* 67 (3): 608–642.

2009. "License to Till: The Privileges of the Spanish Mesta as a Case of Second-Best Institutions." *Explorations in Economic History* 46 (2): 220–40.

Drelichman, Mauricio, and Hans-Joachim Voth. 2010. "The Sustainable Debts of Philip II: A Reconstruction of Castile's Fiscal Position, 1566–1596." *The Journal of Economic History* 70 (4): 813–42.

2014. *Lending to the Borrower from Hell: Debt, Taxes, and Default in the Age of Philip II*. Princeton, NJ: Princeton University Press.

Du Boulay, F. R. H. 1978. "Law Enforcement in Medieval Germany." *History* 63 (209): 345–55.

Du Mège, Alexandre. 1844. *Histoire des Institutions Religieuses, Politiques, Judiciares et Littéraires de la Ville de Toulouse*. Toulouse: Chapelle.

Ducoudray, Gustave. 1902. *Les Origines du Parlement de Paris et la Justice aux XIIIe et XIVe Siècles*. Paris: Hachette.

Duesberg, Jacques. 1932. *Les Juridictions Scabinales en Flandre et en Lotharingie au Moyen-Âge*. Louvain: Université de Louvain.

Dumolyn, Jan. 2000. "The Legal Repression of Revolts in Late Medieval Flanders." *The Legal History Review* 68 (4): 479–521.

2006. "Nobles, Patricians and Officers: The Making of a Regional Political Elite in Late Medieval Flanders." *Journal of Social History* 40 (2): 431–52.

2007. "The Political and Symbolic Economy of State Feudalism: The Case of Late-Medieval Flanders." *Historical Materialism* 15 (2): 105–31.

2015. "Les 'Plaintes' des Villes Flamandes à la Fin du XIIIe Siècle et les Discours et Pratiques Politiques de la Commune." *Le Moyen Âge: Revue d'histoire et de philologie* 121 (2): 383–407.

Dumolyn, Jan, and Jelle Haemers. 2015. "Reclaiming the Common Sphere of the City. The Revival of the Bruges Commune in the Late Thirteenth Century." In *La Légitimité Implicite au Moyen Âge*, ed. J.-P. Genêt, 161–88. Paris: Sorbonne.

Dumolyn, Jan, and Bart Lambert. 2014. "Cities of Commerce, Cities of Constraints: International Trade, Government Institutions and the Law of Commerce in Later Medieval Bruges and the Burgundian State." *Tijdschrift voor Sociale en Economische Geschiedenis* 11 (4): 89–102.

Dunning, Thad. 2008. *Crude Democracy: Natural Resource Wealth and Political Regimes*. Cambridge: Cambridge University Press.

Duus, Peter. 1976. *Feudalism in Japan*, 2nd ed. New York: Knopf.

Dyer, Christopher. 2002a. *Making a Living in the Middle Ages: The People of Britain 850–1520*. New Haven: Yale University Press.

2002b. "Small Places with Large Consequences: The Importance of Small Towns in England, 1000–1540." *Historical Research* 75 (187): 1–24.

Eckhart, F. 1939. "La Diète Corporative Hongroise." In *L'organisation Corporative du Moyen Âge à la Fin de L'ancien Régime*, 211–24. Louvain: Bibliothèque de l'Université.

Edwards, Jeremy, and Sheilagh Ogilvie. 2012. "What Lessons for Economic Development Can We Draw from the Champagne Fairs?" *Explorations in Economic History* 49 (2): 131–48.

Edwards, John Goronwy. 1925. "The Personnel of the Commons in Parliament under Edward I and Edward II." In *Essays in Medieval History Presented to Thomas Frederick Tout*, ed. A. G. Little and F. M. Powicke, 197–214. Manchester: Printed for the subscribers.

1926. "'Re-Election' and the Medieval Parliament." *History* 11 (43): 204–10.

1934. "The *Plena Potestas* of English Parliamentary Representatives." In *Oxford Essays in Medieval History Presented to Herbert Edward Salter*, 141–54. Oxford: Clarendon Press.

Ekelund, Robert B., and Robert D. Tollison. 1997. *Politicized Economies: Monarchy, Monopoly, and Mercantilism*. College Station: Texas A&M University Press.

Elliott, J. H. 1963. *The Revolt of the Catalans: A Study in the Decline of Spain (1598–1640)*. Cambridge: Cambridge University Press.

Elster, Jon. 2006. "Tocqueville on 1789: Preconditions, Precipitants, and Triggers." In *The Cambridge Companion to Tocqueville*, ed. C. B. Welch, 49–80. Cambridge: Cambridge University Press.

2009. *Alexis De Tocqueville: The First Social Scientist*. Cambridge: Cambridge University Press.

Elton, G. R. 1955. *England under the Tudors*. London: Putnam.

Emilsson, Erik Örjan. 2005. *Before 'the European Miracles': Four Essays on Swedish Preconditions for Conquest, Growth and Voice*. Gothenburg: University of Gothenburg.

Engel, Pál. 1990. "The Age of the Angevins, 1301–1382." In *A History of Hungary*, ed. P. F. Sugar, P. Hanák, and T. Frank, 34–53. Bloomington: Indiana University Press.

2001. *The Realm of St. Stephen: A History of Medieval Hungary, 895–1526.* London: St. Martin's Press.

Engel, Pál, Gyula Kristó, and András Kubinyi. 2008. *Histoire de la Hongrie Médiévale.* Vol. 2. Rennes: Presses Universitaires de Rennes.

English Constitutional Documents. 1894. Vol. 1: 6. Philadelphia: University of Pennsylvania Press.

Epstein, Mark A. 1982. "The Leadership of the Ottoman Jews in the Fifteenth and Sixteenth Centuries." In *Christians and Jews in the Ottoman Empire: The Functioning of a Plural Society*, ed. B. Braude and B. Lewis, 101–15. New York: Holmes & Meier.

Epstein, Stephan R. 1996a. "Taxation and Political Representation in Italian Territorial States." In *Finances Publiques et Finances Privées au Bas Moyen Âge*, ed. M. Boone and W. Prevenier, 101–15. Leuven: Garant.

1996b. *Genoa & the Genoese, 958–1528.* Chapel Hill: University of North Carolina Press.

2000a. *Freedom and Growth: The Rise of States and Markets in Europe, 1300–1750.* London: Routledge.

2000b. "The Rise and Fall of Italian City-States." In *A Comparative Study of Thirty City-State Cultures: An Investigation*, ed. M. H. Hansen, 277–94. Copenhagen: Kongelige Danske Videnskabernes Selskab.

Ertman, Thomas. 1997. *Birth of the Leviathan: Building States and Regimes in Medieval and Early Modern Europe.* Cambridge: Cambridge University Press.

Eszláry, Károly. 1959. *Histoire des Institutions Publiques Hongroises.* Vol. 1. Paris: M. Rivière.

1963. *Histoire des Institutions Publiques Hongroises.* Vol. 2. Paris: M. Rivière.

Fairbank, John King, and Merle Goldman. 1998. *China: A New History.* Cambridge, MA: Harvard University Press.

Faroqhi, Suraiya. 1984. *Towns and Townsmen of Ottoman Anatolia: Trade, Crafts and Food Production in an Urban Setting, 1520–1650.* Cambridge: Cambridge University Press.

1986a. "Political Initiatives "from the Bottom Up" in the Sixteenth- and Seventeenth-Century Ottoman Empire: Some Evidence for Their Existence." In *Osmanistische Studien Zur Wirtschafts- und Sozialgeschichte*, ed. H. G. Majer, 24–33. Wiesbaden: Harrassowitz.

1986b. "Town Officials, *Timar*-Holders, and Taxation in the Late Sixteenth-Century Crisis as Seen from Corum." *Turcica* 18: 52–82.

1992. "Political Activity among Ottoman Taxpayers and the Problem of Sultanic Legitimation (1570–1650)." *Journal of the Economic and Social History of the Orient* 35 (1): 1–39.

1994. "Crisis and Change, 1590–1699." In *An Economic and Social History of the Ottoman Empire, 1300–1914*, ed. H. İnalcık and D. Quataert, 411–626. New York: Cambridge University Press.

Farrow, Lee A. 2004. *Between Clan and Crown: The Struggle to Define Noble Property Rights in Imperial Russia.* Newark: University of Delaware Press.

Favier, Jean. 1974. *Paris au XVe Siècle, 1380–1500.* Paris: Hachette.

Fawtier, Robert. 1953. "Parlement d'Angleterre et États-Généraux de France au Moyen Âge." In *Comptes-rendus des séances de l'Académie des Inscriptions et Belles-Lettres,* 275–284. Paris: Académie des Inscriptions et Belles-Lettres.

Fayard, E. 1876. *Aperçu Historique sur le Parlement de Paris.* Vol. 1. Lyon: Scheuring.

Fedorowicz, J. K., Maria Bogucka, and Henryk Samsonowicz, eds. 1982. *A Republic of Nobles: Studies in Polish History to 1864.* Cambridge: Cambridge University Press.

Fenwick, Carolyn Christine. 1983. "The English Poll Taxes of 1377, 1379 and 1381: A Critical Examination of the Returns." Unpublished PhD thesis, University of London.

Filan, Kerima. 2007. "Women Founders of Pious Endowments in Ottoman Bosnia." In *Women in the Ottoman Balkans: Gender, Culture and History,* ed. A. Buturović and I. C. Schick, 99–126. London: I. B. Tauris.

Finer, Samuel E. 1975. "State and Nation-Building in Europe: The Role of the Military." In *The Formation of National States in Western Europe,* ed. C. Tilly, 84–163. Princeton, NJ: Princeton University Press.

———. 1997. *The History of Government from the Earliest Times.* Vol. II: *The Intermediate Ages.* Oxford: Oxford University Press.

Firnhaber-Baker, Justine. 2006. "From God's Peace to the King's Order: Late Medieval Limitations on Non-Royal Warfare." *Essays in Medieval Studies* 23: 19–30.

———. 2012. "Jura in Medio: The Settlement of Seigneurial Disputes in Later Medieval Languedoc." *French History* 26(4): 441–59.

Fleischer, Cornell H. 1986. *Bureaucrat and Intellectual in the Ottoman Empire: The Historian Mustafa Ali (1541–1600).* Princeton, NJ: Princeton University Press.

Fleming, Robin. 1991. *Kings and Lords in Conquest England.* Cambridge: Cambridge University Press.

Fligstein, Neil. 1996. "Markets as Politics: A Political-Cultural Approach to Market Institutions." *American Sociological Review* 61 (4): 656–73.

Floquet, Amable. 1840. *Essai Historique sur L'échiquier de Normandie.* Rouen: Édouard Frère.

Floria, B. 2000. "The Evolution of Immunity among Secular Landholders during the Formation of the Unified Polish and Russian States." *Russian Studies in History* 39 (3): 9–30.

Font Rius, José María. 1985. "Orígenes del Régimen Municipal de Cataluña." In *Estudis Sobre els Drets i Institucions Locals en la Catalunya Medieval,* 281–560. Barcelona: Publicacions i Edicions de la Universitat de Barcelona.

Fortescue, John. [c. 1470] 1997. *On the Laws and Governance of England.* Cambridge: Cambridge University Press.

Fratcher, William F. 1973. "Trust." *International Encyclopedia of Comparative Law.* Vol. 6.

Freedman, Paul H. 1991. *The Origins of Peasant Servitude in Medieval Catalonia.* Cambridge: Cambridge University Press.

Froianov, I. 1986. "On the Question of a Seigneurial System in Ancient Russia." *Russian Social Science Review* 27 (3): 30–54.

Frost, Robert I. 2015. *The Oxford History of Poland-Lithuania*. Vol. 1. Oxford: Oxford University Press.

Fryde, E. B. 1955. "Loans to the English Crown 1328–31." *English Historical Review* 70 (275): 198–211.

——— 1979. "The Financial Policies of the Royal Governments and Popular Resistance to Them in France and England, c. 1270–c.1420." *Revue Belge de philologie et d'histoire* 57: 824–60.

——— 1991. "Royal Fiscal Systems and State Formation in France from the 13th to the 16th Century, with Some English Comparisons." *Journal of Historical Sociology* 4 (3): 236–87.

——— 1992. "Magnate Debts to Edward I and Edward III: A Study of Common Problems and Contrasting Royal Reaction to Them." *National Library of Wales Journal* 27 (3): 249–87.

——— 1996. *Handbook of British Chronology*, 3rd ed. Cambridge: Cambridge University Press.

Frye, Timothy. 2021. *Weak Strongman: The Limits of Power in Putin's Russia*. Princeton, NJ: Princeton University Press.

Frymer, Paul. 2017. *Building an American Empire: The Era of Territorial and Political Expansion*. Princeton, Nj: Princeton University Press.

Fuchs, Ralf-Peter. 2003. "The Supreme Court of the Holy Roman Empire: The State of Research and the Outlook." *The Sixteenth Century Journal* 34 (1): 9–27.

Fügedi, Erik. 1986. *Castle and Society in Medieval Hungary (1000–1437)*. Budapest: Akadémiai Kiadó; Distributor, Kultura.

Fukuyama, Francis. 2004. *State-Building: Governance and World Order in the 21st Century*. Ithaca, NY: Cornell University Press.

——— 2011a. *The Origins of Political Order: From Prehuman Times to the French Revolution*. New York: Farrar, Straus & Giroux.

——— 2011b. "Samuel Huntington's Legacy." *Foreign Policy*, January 6.

Furgeot, Henri. 1920. *Actes du Parlement de Paris. 2 Série, De L'an 1328 à L'an 1350. Jugés*. Paris: Imprimairie nationale.

Gallia Regia; Ou, État des Officiers Royaux des Bailliages et des Sénéchaussées de 1328 à 1515. 1942. Paris: Imprimairie nationale.

Ganshof, François Louis. 1932. *Recherches sur les Tribunaux de Châtellenie en Flandre avant le Milieu du XIIIe Siècle*. Paris: Anvers.

——— 1939. "Les Transformations de L'organisation Judiciaire dans le Comté de Flandre Jusqu'à L'avènement de la Maison de Bourgogne." *Revue Belge de philologie et d'histoire* 18 (1): 43–61.

——— 1949. *La Flandre sous les Premiers Comtes*, 3rd ed. Bruxelles: La Renaissance du livre.

——— 1951. "Le Droit Urbain en Flandre au Début de la Première Phase de Son Histoire (1127)." *Tijdschrift voor Rechtsgeschiedenis* 19: 387–416.

——— 1964. *Feudalism*, 3rd ed. New York: Harper.

Garnett, George, and John Hudson. 2015. "Introduction." In *Magna Carta*, ed. J. C. Holt, 1–32. Cambridge: Cambridge University Press.

Gaudiosi, Monica M. 1988. "The Influence of the Islamic Law of Waqf on the Development of the Trust in England: The Case of Merton College." *University of Pennsylvania Law Review* 136 (4): 1231–61.

Gehlbach, Scott, and Edmund J. Malesky. 2014. "The Grand Experiment That Wasn't? New Institutional Economics and the Postcommunist Experience." In *Institutions, Property Rights, and Economic Growth: The Legacy of Douglass North*, ed. S. Galiani and I. Sened, 223–47. Cambridge: Cambridge University Press.

Gelderblom, Oscar. 2013. *Cities of Commerce: The Institutional Foundations of International Trade in the Low Countries, 1250–1650.* Princeton, NJ: Princeton University Press.

Genet, Jean-Philippe, and Michel Le Mené. 1987. *Genèse de L'état Moderne: Prélèvement et Redistribution.* Paris: Éditions du Centre national de la recherche scientifique.

Gennaioli, Nicola, and Hans-Joachim Voth. 2015. "State Capacity and Military Conflict." *The Review of Economic Studies* 82 (4): 1409–48.

George, Alexander L., and Andrew Bennett. 2005. *Case Studies and Theory Development in the Social Sciences.* Cambridge, MA: MIT Press.

Gerber, Haïm. 1981. "The Muslim Law of Partnerships in Ottoman Court Records." *Studia Islamica* 53: 109–19.

   1987. *The Social Origins of the Modern Middle East.* Boulder, CO: Lynne Rienner.

   1994. *State, Society, and Law in Islam: Ottoman Law in Comparative Perspective.* Albany: State University of New York Press.

Gerbet, Marie-Claude. 1977–79. "La Population Noble dans le Royaume de Castille Vers 1500. La Repartition Géographique De Ses Differéntes Composantes." *Annales de Historia antigua y medieval* 20: 78–99.

   1984. "Majorat, Stratégie Familiale et Pouvoir Royal en Castille D'après Quelques Exemples Pris en Estrémadure à la Fin du Moyen Âge." In *Les Espagnes Médiévales: Aspects Économiques et Sociaux: Mélanges Offerts à Jean Gautier Dalché.* Paris: Belles Lettres.

   1992. *L'Espagne au Moyen Âge: VIIIe–XVe Siècle.* Paris: A. Colin.

Gerring, John. 2004. "What Is a Case Study and What Is It Good For?" *The American Political Science Review* 98 (2): 341–54.

   2007. *Case Study Research: Principles and Practices.* New York: Cambridge University Press.

Gerring, John, Daniel Ziblatt, Johan Van Gorp, and Julián Arévalo. 2011. "An Institutional Theory of Direct and Indirect Rule." *World Politics* 63 (3): 377–433.

Gerschenkron, Alexander. 1962. *Economic Backwardness in Historical Perspective: A Book of Essays.* Cambridge, MA: Belknap Press of Harvard University Press.

Gieysztor, Aleksander. 1966. "L'impôt Foncier dans le Royaume de Pologne aux XIVe et XVe Siècles." In *L'impôt dans le Cadre de la Ville et de L'état*, 317–28. Brussels: Collection Histoire 13.

   1979. *History of Poland*, 2nd ed. Warsaw: PWN, Polish Scientific Publishers.

Gilens, Martin. 2012. *Affluence and Influence: Economic Inequality and Political Power in America.* Princeton, NJ: Princeton University Press.

Gilissen, John. 1954. "Les Villes en Belgique: Histoire des Institutions Administratives et Judicaires des Villes Belges." *Recueils de la Société Jean Bodin* 6: 531–604.

Giordanengo, Gérard. 1990. "État Droit Féodal Et France (XIIᵉ–XIVᵉ Siècles)." In *L'état Moderne: Le Droit, L'espace et les Formes de L'état*, ed. N. Coulet and J.-P. Genêt, 61–83. Paris: Éditions du CNRS.

Given-Wilson, Chris. 2000. "The Problem of Labour in the Context of English Government, c.1350–1450." In *The Problem of Labour in Fourteenth-Century England*, ed. J. Bothwell, P. J. P. Goldberg, and W. M. Ormrod, 85–100. Woodbridge: York Medieval Press.

Glaeser, Edward L., and Andrei Shleifer. 2002. "Legal Origins." *Quarterly Journal of Economics* 117: 1193–1229.

Glenn, H. Patrick. 2014. *Legal Traditions of the World: Sustainable Diversity in Law*, 5th ed. Oxford: Oxford University Press.

Goertz, Gary. 2003. "Cause, Correlation, and Necessary Conditions." In *Necessary Conditions: Theory, Methodology, and Applications*, ed. G. Goertz and H. Starr, 47–64. Lanham, MD: Rowman & Littlefield.

Goffman, Daniel. 2002. *The Ottoman Empire and Early Modern Europe*. Cambridge: Cambridge University Press.

Goldstone, Jack A. 1983. "Capitalist Origins of the English Revolution: Chasing a Chimera." *Theory and Society* 12 (2): 143–80.

Goody, Jack. 1983. *The Development of the Family and Marriage in Europe*. Cambridge: Cambridge University Press.

Goody, Jack, Joan Thirsk, and E. P. Thompson. 1976. *Family and Inheritance: Rural Society in Western Europe, 1200–1800*. Cambridge: Cambridge University Press.

Górski, Karol. 1966. "The Origins of the Polish Seym." *The Slavic and East European Journal* 44 (102): 122–38.

	1968. "Les Débuts de la Représentation de la "Communitas Nobilium" dans les Assemblées D'états de L'est Européen." *Anciens Pays et Assemblées d'États* 47: 39–55.

	1976. "Les Chartes de la Noblesse en Pologne aux XIVe et XVe Siècles." In *Album Elemér Mályusz*, ed. E. Mályusz, 247–71. Bruxelles: Éditions de la Librairie encyclopédique.

Gorski, Philip S. 2003. *The Disciplinary Revolution: Calvinism and the Rise of the State in Early Modern Europe*. Chicago: University of Chicago Press.

Grafe, Regina. 2012. *Distant Tyranny: Markets, Power, and Backwardness in Spain, 1650–1800*. Princeton, NJ: Princeton University Press.

Graham, Hugh F. 1987. "Pomest'e." *The Modern Encyclopedia of Russian and Soviet History*: 29–33.

Gras, Norman Scott Brien. 1918. *The Early English Customs System: A Documentary Study of the Institutional and Economic History of the Customs from the Thirteenth to the Sixteenth Century*. Vol. 18. Cambridge, MA: Harvard University Press.

Gray, Kevin J., and Susan Francis Gray. 2009. *Elements of Land Law*, 5th ed. Oxford: Oxford University Press.

Greif, Avner. 1994. "On the Political Foundations of the Late Medieval Commercial Revolution: Genoa during the Twelfth and Thirteenth Centuries." *The Journal of Economic History* 54 (2): 271–87.

	1998. "Self-Enforcing Political Systems and Economic Growth: Late Medieval Genoa." In *Analytic Narratives*, ed. R. H. Bates, A. Greif, M. Levi, and J.-L. Rosenthal, 25–64. Princeton, NJ: Princeton University Press.

2002. "Institutions and Impersonal Exchange: From Communal to Individual Responsibility." *Journal of Institutional and Theoretical Economics* 158 (1): 168–204.

2006a. "Family Structure, Institutions, and Growth: The Origins and Implications of Western Corporations." *The American Economic Review* 96 (2): 308–12.

2006b. "History Lessons: The Birth of Impersonal Exchange: The Community Responsibility System and Impartial Justice." *The Journal of Economic Perspectives* 20 (2): 221–36.

2008. "The Impact of Administrative Power on Political and Economic Developments." In *Institutions and Economic Performance*, ed. E. Helpman, 17–63. Cambridge, MA: Harvard University Press.

Greif, Avner, and David D. Laitin. 2004. "A Theory of Endogenous Institutional Change." *The American Political Science Review* 98 (4): 633–52.

Grey, Thomas C. 1980. "The Disintegration of Property." In *Property*, ed. J. R. Pennock and J. W. Chapman, 69–85. New York: New York University Press.

Grzymala-Busse, Anna Maria. 2015. *Nations under God: How Churches Use Moral Authority to Influence Policy*. Princeton, NJ: Princeton University Press.

Guenée, Bernard. 1968. "Espace et États dans la France du Bas Moyen Âge." *Annales. Économies, Sociétés, Civilisations* 23: 744–58.

Guilleré, Christian. 1997. "Les Élites Urbaines Catalanes à la Fin du Moyen Âge: L'example Géronais." In *Les Élites Urbaines au Moyen Âge*, 269–85. Paris: Publications de la Sorbonne.

Guiso, Luigi, Paola Sapienza, and Luigi Zingales. 2016. "Long-Term Persistence." *Journal of the European Economic Association* 14 (6): 1401–36.

Guizot, François. 1851. *Histoire des Origines du Gouvernement Représentatif en Europe*. Paris: Didier.

Gunlicks, Arthur B. 2003. "The Origins of the Länder." In *The Länder and German Federalism*, 7–52. Manchester: Manchester University Press.

Haber, Stephen H., Noel Maurer, and Armando Razo. 2003. *The Politics of Property Rights: Political Instability, Credible Commitments, and Economic Growth in Mexico, 1876–1929*. Cambridge: Cambridge University Press.

Haber, Stephen H., and Victor Menaldo. 2011. "Do Natural Resources Fuel Authoritarianism? A Reappraisal of the Resource Curse." *American Political Science Review* 105 (1): 1–26.

Haboush, JaHyun Kim. 2009. *Epistolary Korea: Letters in the Communicative Space of the Choson, 1392–1910*. New York: Columbia University Press.

Hacker, Jacob S., and Paul Pierson. 2010. *Winner-Take-All Politics: How Washington Made the Rich Richer – and Turned Its Back on the Middle Class*. New York: Simon & Schuster.

Hall, John A. 1985a. *Powers and Liberties: The Causes and Consequences of the Rise of the West*. Oxford: Blackwell.

1985b. "The Rise of Christian Europe." In *Powers and Liberties: The Causes and Consequences of the Rise of the West*, 111–44. Oxford: Blackwell.

1986. "States and Economic Development." In *States in History*, 154–76. Oxford: Blackwell.

1994. *Coercion and Consent: Studies on the Modern State.* Cambridge: Polity Press.

Hall, Peter A. 1986. *Governing the Economy: The Politics of State Intervention in Britain and France.* New York: Oxford University Press.

Hallam, Elizabeth M., and Judith Everard. 2001. *Capetian France, 987–1328.* London: Longman.

Hallam, Henry. 1869. "Of the Feudal System, Especially in France." In *View of the State of Europe During the Middle Ages*, 71–149. London: Alex Murray & Son.

Halliday, Paul D. 2010. *Habeas Corpus: From England to Empire.* Cambridge, MA: Harvard University Press.

Halperin, Charles J. 2002. "Muscovy as a Hypertrophic State: A Critique." *Kritika: Explorations in Russian and Eurasian History* 3 (3): 501–507.

Hanley, Sarah. 1983. *The Lit de Justice of the Kings of France: Constitutional Ideology in Legend, Ritual, and Discourse.* Princeton, NJ: Princeton University Press.

Harding, Alan. 1984. "The Revolt against the Justices." In *The English Rising of 1381*, ed. R. H. Hilton and T. H. Aston, 165–93. Cambridge: Cambridge University Press.

2002. *Medieval Law and the Foundations of the State.* Oxford: Oxford University Press.

Harriss, Gerald L. 1963a. "Aids, Loans and Benevolences." *Historical Journal* 6 (1): 1–19.

1963b. "The Commons' Petitions of 1340." *The English Historical Review* 78 (309): 625–54.

1975. *King, Parliament, and Public Finance in Medieval England to 1369.* Oxford: Clarendon Press.

1978. "Thomas Cromwell's 'New Principle' of Taxation." *The English Historical Review* 93 (369): 721–38.

1981. "The Formation of Parliament, 1272–1377." In *The English Parliament in the Middle Ages*, ed. R. G. Davies and J. H. Denton, 26–60. Philadelphia: University of Pennsylvania Press.

Hartshorne, Charles Henry. 1871. "An Itinerary of King Edward the First." *Collectanea Archaeologica* 2: 115–36, 311–41.

Haskins, Charles Homer. 1915. *The Normans in European History.* Boston: Houghton Mifflin.

Haskins, George L. 1938. "The Petitions of Representatives in the Parliaments of Edward I." *The English Historical Review* 53 (209): 1–20.

Hatcher, John. 1981. "English Serfdom and Villeinage: Towards a Reassessment." *Past & Present* 90: 3–39.

Hayek, Friedrich A. von. 1960. *The Constitution of Liberty.* Chicago: University of Chicago Press.

1973. *Law, Legislation, and Liberty.* Vol. 1. Chicago: University of Chicago Press.

Head, Thomas, and Richard Allen Landes. 1992. *The Peace of God: Social Violence and Religious Response in France around the Year 1000.* Ithaca, NY: Cornell University Press.

Hébert, Michel. 2014. *Parlementer: Assemblées Représentatives et Échange Politique en Europe Occidentale á la Fin du Moyen Âge.* Paris: Éditions de Boccard.

Hechter, Michael, and William Brustein. 1980. "Regional Modes of Production and Patterns of State Formation in Western Europe." *American Journal of Sociology* 85 (5): 1061–94.

Hechter, Michael, and Nika Kabiri. 2008. "Attaining Social Order in Iraq." In *Order, Conflict, and Violence*, ed. S. N. Kalyvas, I. Shapiro, and T. E. Masoud, 43–74. Cambridge: Cambridge University Press.

Heerma van Voss, Lex. 2001. *Petitions in Social History*. Cambridge: Cambridge University Press.

Heers, Jacques. 1974. *Le Clan Familial au Moyen Âge; Étude sur les Structures Politiques et Sociales des Milieux Urbains*. Paris: Presses Universitaires de France.

2008. *Le Clan des Médicis: Comment Florence Perdit ses Libertés (1200–1500)*. Paris: Perrin.

Heirbaut, Dirk. 2001. "Flanders: A Pioneer of State-Orientated Feudalism? Feudalism as an Instrument of Comital Power in Flanders During the Middle Ages (1000–1300)." In *Expectations of the Law in the Middle Ages*, ed. A. Musson, 23–34. Rochester, NY: Boydell Press.

Helle, Knut. 2003. "Towards Nationally Organised Systems of Government: Introductory Survey." In *The Cambridge History of Scandinavia*, ed. K. Helle, 345–52. Cambridge: Cambridge University Press.

Hellie, Richard. 1971. *Enserfment and Military Change in Muscovy*: Chicago: University of Chicago Press.

1987. "Zemskii Sobor." In *The Modern Encyclopedia of Russian and Soviet History*, vol. 45, 226–34. Gulf Breeze, FL: Academic International Press.

1998. "Why Did the Muscovite Elite Not Rebel ?" *Russian History* 25 (1): 155–62.

2000. "Thoughts on the Absence of Elite Resistance in Muscovy." *Kritika: Explorations in Russian and Eurasian History* 1 (1): 5–20.

2006a. "The Law." In *The Cambridge History of Russia*, ed. M. Perrie, 360–86. Cambridge: Cambridge University Press.

2006b. "The Peasantry." In *The Cambridge History of Russia*, ed. M. Perrie, 286–97. Cambridge: Cambridge University Press.

Helmholz, R. H. 1990. "Continental Law and Common Law: Historical Strangers or Companions?" *Duke Law Journal* 6: 1207–28.

1999. "Magna Carta and the Ius Commune." *The University of Chicago Law Review* 66 (2): 297–371.

2003. *The Oxford History of the Laws of England*. Vol. I: *The Canon Law and Ecclesiastical Jurisdiction from 597 to the 1640s*. Oxford: Oxford University Press.

Hendrix, Cullen S. 2010. "Measuring State Capacity: Theoretical and Empirical Implications for the Study of Civil Conflict." *Journal of Peace Research* 47 (3): 273–85.

Henneman, John Bell. 1970. "The French Estates General and Reference Back to Local Constituents, 1343–1355." In *Representative Institutions in Theory and Practice* 31–52. Brussels: Les Éditions de la Librairie Encyclopédique.

1971. *Royal Taxation in Fourteenth Century France: The Development of War Financing 1322–1356*. Princeton, NJ: Princeton University Press.

1976. *Royal Taxation in Fourteenth-Century France: The Captivity and Ransom of John II, 1356–1370*. Philadelphia: American Philosophical Society.

1978. "The Military Class and the French Monarchy in the Late Middle Ages." *American Historical Review* 83: 946–65.

1983. "Nobility, Privilege and Fiscal Politics in Late Medieval France." *French Historical Studies* 13 (1): 1–17.

1989. "Taxation, French." In *Dictionary of the Middle Ages*, ed. J. R. Strayer, 618–25. New York: Charles Scribner's Sons.

1999. "France in the Middle Ages." In *The Rise of the Fiscal State in Europe, c. 1200–1815*, ed. R. Bonney, 101–22. New York: Oxford University Press.

Hennigan, Peter C. 2004. *The Birth of a Legal Institution: The Formation of the Waqf in Third-Century A.H. Hanafi Legal Discourse*. Leiden: Brill.

Henshall, Nicholas. 1992. *The Myth of Absolutism: Change and Continuity in Early Modern European Monarchy*. London: Longman.

Herb, Michael. 2003. "Taxation and Representation." *Studies in Comparative International Development* 38 (3): 3–31.

2005. "No Representation without Taxation? Rents, Development, and Democracy." *Comparative Politics* 37 (3): 297–316.

Herrin, Judith. 2013. *Margins and Metropolis: Authority across the Byzantine Empire*. Princeton, NJ: Princeton University Press.

Hervieu, Henri. 1879. *Recherches sur les Premiers États Généraux et les Assemblées Représentatives Pendant la Première Moitié du Quatorizième Siècle*. Paris: Thorin.

Heydemann, Steven. 2000. *War, Institutions, and Social Change in the Middle East*. Berkeley: University of California Press.

Heyneman, Stephen P. 2004. *Islam and Social Policy*. Nashville: Vanderbilt University Press.

Hilaire, Jean. 2011. *La Construction de L'état de Droit dans les Archives Judiciaires de la Cour de France au XIIIe Siècle*. Paris: Dalloz.

Hildesheimer, Françoise, and Monique Morgat-Bonnet. 2011. *État Méthodique des Archives du Parlement de Paris*. Paris: Archives Nationales de France.

Hillgarth, J. N. 1978. *The Spanish Kingdoms, 1250–1516*. Vol. II: *1410–1516: Castilian Hegemony*. Oxford: Clarendon Press.

Hilton, R. H. 1969. *The Decline of Serfdom in Medieval England*. London: Macmillan.

Hilton, R. H., and Jacques Le Goff. 1980. "Féodalité and Seigneurie in France and England." In *Britain and France, Ten Centuries*, ed. D. Johnson, F. Crouzet, and F. Bédarida, 39–64. London: Dawson.

Hintze, Otto. 1970. "Typologie der Standischen Verfassungen des Abendlandes." In *Staat und Verfassung. Gesammelte Abhandlungen zur Allgemeinen Verfassungsgeschichte*, 120–39. Göttingen: Vandenhoeck & Ruprecht.

1975a. "The Formation of States and Constitutional Development: A Study in History and Politics." In *The Historical Essays of Otto Hintze*, ed. F. Gilbert, 155–77. New York: Oxford University Press.

1975b. *The Historical Essays of Otto Hintze*, ed. F. Gilbert. New York: Oxford University Press.

1975c. "Military Organization and the Organization of the State." In *The Historical Essays of Otto Hintze*, ed. F. Gilbert, 180–215. New York: Oxford University Press.

1975d. "The Preconditions of Representative Government in the Context of World History." In *The Historical Essays of Otto Hintze*, ed. F. Gilbert, 305–53. New York: Oxford University Press.

Hirschman, Albert O. 1970. *Exit, Voice, and Loyalty: Responses to Decline in Firms, Organizations, and States*. Cambridge, MA: Harvard University Press.

Hoffman, Philip T. 1994. "Early Modern France, 1450–1700." In *The Making of Modern Freedom*, ed. P. T. Hoffman and K. Norberg, 226–52. Stanford, CA: Stanford University Press.

2015. *Why Did Europe Conquer the World?* Princeton, NJ: Princeton University Press.

Hoffman, Philip T., and Kathryn Norberg, eds. 1994. *Fiscal Crises, Liberty, and Representative Government, 1450–1789*. Stanford, CA: Stanford University Press.

Hoffman, Philip T., Gilles Postel-Vinay, and Jean-Laurent Rosenthal. 2000. *Priceless Markets: The Political Economy of Credit in Paris, 1660–1870*. Chicago: University of Chicago Press.

Hoffman, Philip T., and Jean-Laurent Rosenthal. 1997. "The Political Economy of Warfare and Taxation in Early Modern Europe: Historical Lessons for Economic Development." In *The Frontiers of the New Institutional Economics*, ed. J. N. Drobak and J. V. C. Nye, 31–55. San Diego: Academic Press.

Hohfeld, Wesley Newcomb. 1964. *Fundamental Legal Conceptions, as Applied in Judicial Reasoning*. New Haven: Yale University Press.

Holden, Alice M. 1930. "The Imperative Mandate in the Spanish Cortes of the Middle Ages." *The American Political Science Review* 24 (4): 886–912.

Holdsworth, William Searle. 1922. *A History of English Law*, 3rd ed. Vol. I. London: Methuen & Co.

1923a. *A History of English Law*, 3rd ed. Vol. II. London: Methuen & Co.

1923b. *A History of English Law*, 3rd ed. Vol. III. London: Methuen & Co.

Hollis, Daniel W., III. 1994. "The Crown Lands and the Financial Dilemma in Stuart England." *Albion: A Quarterly Journal Concerned with British Studies* 26 (3): 419–42.

Hollister, C. Warren. 1976. *The Making of England, 55 B.C. to 1399*, 3rd ed. Lexington, MA: Heath.

Holt, James Clarke. 1972. "Politics and Property in Early Medieval England." *Past & Present* 57: 3–52.

1981. "The Prehistory of Parliament." In *The English Parliament in the Middle Ages*, ed. R. G. Davies and J. H. Denton, 1–28. Philadelphia: University of Pennsylvania Press.

1982. "Feudal Society and the Family in Early Medieval England: I. The Revolution of 1066." *Transactions of the Royal Historical Society*, 5th ser. 32: 193–212.

2015. *Magna Carta*, 3rd ed. Cambridge: Cambridge University Press.

Holt, Mark P. 1988. "The King in Parliament: The Problem of the Lit de Justice in Sixteenth-Century France." *The Historical Journal* 31 (3): 507–23.

Holton, R. J. 1985. *The Transition from Feudalism to Capitalism*. New York: St. Martin's Press.

Holub, Joseph. 1958. "La Représentation Politique en Hongrie au Moyen Âge." *Xe Congrès international des sciences historiques: Études présentées à la Commission internationale pour l'histoire des assemblées d'états* XVIII: 77–121.

Homans, George Caspar. 1950. *The Human Group*. New York: Harcourt.

Hopcroft, Rosemary L. 1999. "Maintaining the Balance of Power: Taxation and Democracy in England and France, 1340–1688." *Sociological Perspectives* 42 (1): 69–95.

Hørby, Kai. 1997. "Church and State in Medieval and Early Modern Denmark: The Legal Issue." In *Legislation and Justice*, ed. A. Padoa Schioppa, 197–209. Oxford: Clarendon Press.

Horden, Peregrine. 1986. "The Confraternities of Byzantium." *Studies in Church History* 23: 25–45.

Hosking, Geoffrey. 2000. "Patronage and the Russian State." *The Slavonic and East European Review* 78 (2): 301–20.

     2001. *Russia and the Russians: A History*. Cambridge, MA: Harvard University Press.

Hough, Jerry F., and Robin M. Grier. 2015. *The Long Process of Development: Building Markets and States in Pre-Industrial England, Spain, and Their Colonies*. New York: Cambridge University Press.

Houlbrooke, R. A. 1984. "Review of 'The Development of the Family and Marriage in Europe', by Jack Goody." *The English Historical Review* 99 (393): 816–18.

Hoyt, Robert S. 1961. "Representation in the Administrative Practice of Anglo-Norman England." In *Album Helen Maud Cam*, 15–26. Louvain: Publications Universitaires de Louvain.

Huang, Ray. 1998. "The Ming Fiscal Administration." In *The Cambridge History of China*, ed. D. Twitchett and F. W. Mote, 106–71. Cambridge: Cambridge University Press.

Hudson, John. 1994. *Land, Law, and Lordship in Anglo-Norman England*. Oxford: Oxford University Press.

     1996a. *The Formation of the English Common Law: Law and Society in England from the Norman Conquest to Magna Carta*. New York: Longman.

     ed. 1996b. *The History of English Law: Centenary Essays on "Pollock and Maitland."* Oxford: Oxford University Press.

     2012. *The Oxford History of the Laws of England, Volume 2: 900–1216*. Oxford: Oxford University Press.

Hui, Victoria Tin-bor. 2005. *War and State Formation in Ancient China and Early Modern Europe*. New York: Cambridge University Press.

Humphries, Jane, and Jacob Weisdorf. 2019. "Unreal Wages? Real Income and Economic Growth in England, 1260–1850." *The Economic Journal* 129 (623): 2867–87.

Hung, Ho-fung. 2011. *Protest with Chinese Characteristics: Demonstrations, Riots, and Petitions in the Mid-Qing Dynasty*. New York: Columbia University Press.

Huntington, Samuel P. 1968. *Political Order in Changing Societies*. New Haven: Yale University Press.

Hurstfield, J. 1955. "The Profits of Fiscal Feudalism, 1541–1602." *The Economic History Review* 8 (1): 53–61.

Huscroft, Richard. 2009. *The Norman Conquest: A New Introduction.* Harlow: Longman.

Hyams, Paul R. 1980. *King, Lords and Peasants in Medieval England: The Common Law of Villeinage in the Twelfth and Thirteenth Centuries.* Oxford: Clarendon Press.

Ibbetson, D. J. 2001. *Common Law and Ius Commune.* London: Selden Society.

Ibn Rušd, Muḥammad b Aḥmad. 1996. *The Distinguished Jurist's Primer: A Translation of Bidāyat Al-Mujtahid.* Doha, Qatar: Centre for Muslim Contribution to Civilization.

Illsley, J. S. 1976. "Parliamentary Elections in the Reign of Edward I." *Bulletin of the Institute of Historical Research* 44: 24–40.

Imber, Colin. 1997. *Ebu's-Suùd: The Islamic Legal Tradition.* Edinburgh: Edinburgh University Press.

   2006. "Government, Administration and Law." In *The Ottoman Empire as a World Power, 1453–1603,* ed. S. Faroqhi, 205–40. New York: Cambridge University Press.

   2010. "The Ottoman Empire (Tenth/Sixteenth Century)." In *The New Cambridge History of Islam,* ed. M. Fierro, 332–65. Cambridge: Cambridge University Press.

   2011. "The Law of the Land." In *The Ottoman World,* ed. C. Woodhead. New York: Routledge.

   2019. *The Ottoman Empire, 1300–1650: The Structure of Power.* New York: Macmillan.

İnalcık, Halil. 1973. *The Ottoman Empire: The Classical Age, 1300–1600.* London: Weidenfeld & Nicolson.

   1986. "Appointment Procedure of a Guild Warden (Kethudd)." *Wiener Zeitschrift für die Kunde des Morgenlandes*: 135–42.

   1992. "Comments on 'Sultanism': Max Weber's Typification of the Ottoman Polity." *Princeton Papers in Near Eastern Studies*: 49–72.

   1994. "The Ottoman State: Economy and Society, 1300–1600." In *An Economic and Social History of the Ottoman Empire, 1300–1916,* ed. H. İnalcık and D. Quataert, 9–409. New York: Cambridge University Press.

Isenmann, Eberhard. 1999. "The Holy Roman Empire in the Middle Ages." In *The Rise of the Fiscal State in Europe, c. 1200–1815,* ed. R. Bonney, 243–80. New York: Oxford University Press.

Itzkowitz, Norman. 1980. *Ottoman Empire and Islamic Tradition.* Chicago: University of Chicago Press.

Jago, Charles. 1981. "Habsburg Absolutism and the Cortes of Castile." *The American Historical Review* 86 (2): 307–26.

   1992. "Review Essay: Crown and Cortes in Early-Modern Spain." *Parliaments, Estates and Representation* 12 (2): 177–92.

Jennings, Ronald C. 1975. "The Office of Vekil (Wakil) in 17th Century Ottoman Sharia Courts." *Studia Islamica* 42: 147–69.

Joinville, Jean. 1821–27. "Histoire de Saint-Louis." In *Collection Complete des Mémoires Relatifs à L'histoire de France Depuis le Règne de Philippe Auguste, Jusqu'au Commencement du Dix-Septième Siècle,* ed. C. B. Petitot, 52 vols. Paris.

Jones, N. G. 1998. "Trusts in England after the Statute of Uses: A View from the Long 16th Century." In *Itinera Fiduciae: Trust and Treuhand in Historical Perspective*, ed. R. H. Helmholz and R. Zimmermann, 173–205. Berlin: Duncker & Humblot.

Jones, Philip James. 1965. "Communes and Despots: The City State in Late-Medieval Italy." *Transactions of the Royal Historical Society* 15: 71–96.

1997. *The Italian City-State: From Commune to Signoria*. Oxford: Clarendon Press.

2010. "Communes and Despots: The City State in Late-Medieval Italy." In *Communes and Despots in Medieval and Renaissance Italy*, ed. B. Paton and J. E. Law, 3–26. Farnham: Ashgate.

Jones, W. R. 1966. "Bishops, Politics, and the Two Laws: The Gravamina of the English Clergy, 1237–1399." *Speculum: A Journal of Medieval Studies* 41 (2): 209–45.

Jusselin, Maurice. 1912. "Comment la France se Préparait à la Guerre de Cent Ans." *Bibliothèque de l'École des chartes* 73: 209–36.

Kaeuper, Richard W. 1988. *War, Justice, and Public Order: England and France in the Later Middle Ages*. Oxford: Clarendon Press.

Kafadar, Cemal. 1995. *Between Two Worlds: The Construction of the Ottoman State*. Berkeley: University of California Press.

2008. "Janissaries and Other Riff-Raff of Ottoman Instabul: Rebels without a Cause?" In *Identity and Identity Formation in the Ottoman World: A Volume of Essays in Honor of Norman Itzkowitz*, ed. B. Tezcan and K. K. Barbir, 113–34: Madison, WI: University of Wisconsin Press.

Kagay, Donald J. 1981. "The Development of the Cortes in the Crown of Aragon, 1064–1327." Unpublished PhD thesis, Fordham University.

1988. "Structures of Baronial Dissent and Revolt under James I (1213–76)." *Mediaevistik* 1: 61–85.

1999. "Princeps Namque: Defense of the Crown and the Birth of the Catalan State." *Mediterranean Studies* 8: 55–87.

Kaiser, Daniel H. 1980. *The Growth of the Law in Medieval Russia*. Princeton, NJ: Princeton University Press.

1992. *The Laws of Rus': Ten to Fifteenth Centuries*. Salt Lake City, UT: C. Schlacks.

Kaldellis, Anthony. 2015. *The Byzantine Republic: People and Power in New Rome*. Cambridge, MA: Harvard University Press.

Kamali, Elizabeth Papp, and Thomas A. Green. 2018. "The Assumptions Underlying England's Adoption of Trial by Jury for Crime." In *Law and Society in Later Medieval England and Ireland: Essays in Honour of Paul Brand*, ed. T. R. Baker, 51–81. New York: Routledge.

Kamen, Henry. 2014. *Spain 1469–1714: A Society in Conflict*, 4th ed. London: Longman.

Karaman, K. Kıvanç. 2009. "Decentralized Coercion and Self-Restraint in Provincial Taxation: The Ottoman Empire, 15th–16th Centuries." *Journal of Economic Behavior & Organization* 71 (3): 690–703.

Karaman, K. Kıvanç, and Şevket Pamuk. 2010. "Ottoman State Finances in European Perspective, 1500–1914." *The Journal of Economic History* 70 (3): 593–629.

2013. "Different Paths to the Modern State in Europe: The Interaction between Warfare, Economic Structure, and Political Regime." *American Political Science Review* 107 (3): 603–26.

Karaman, K. Kıvanç, Şevket Pamuk, and Seçil Yıldırım-Karaman. 2019. "Money and Monetary Stability in Europe, 1300–1914." *Journal of Monetary Economics*.

Karpf, David. 2016. *Analytic Activism: Digital Listening and the New Political Strategy*. New York: Oxford University Press.

Kashtanov, S. M. 1971. "The Centralised State and Feudal Immunities in Russia." *The Slavonic and East European Review* 49 (115): 235–54.

Keen, Maurice. 2003. *England in the Later Middle Ages: A Political History*, 2nd ed. London: Routledge.

Keen, Michael. 2012. "Taxation and Development—Again." IMF Working Paper. Washington, DC: IMF.

Keenan, Edward L. 1986. "Muscovite Political Folkways." *Russian Review* 45 (2): 115–81.

Keep, J. L. H. 1957. "The Decline of the Zemsky Sobor." *The Slavonic and East European Review* 36 (86): 100–22.

Keep, John. 1970. "The Muscovite Élite and the Approach to Pluralism." *The Slavonic and East European Review* 48 (111): 201–31.

Keirstead, Thomas. 1990. "The Theater of Protest: Petitions, Oaths, and Rebellion in the Shoen." *Journal of Japanese Studies* 16 (2): 357–88.

Kelemen, R. Daniel. 2016. "Constructing the European Judiciary." Paper presented to Council for European Studies, Philadelphia.

Kermeli, Eugenia. 2008. "Central Administration Versus Provincial Arbitrary Governance: Patmos and Mount Athos Monasteries in the 16th Century." *Byzantine and Modern Greek Studies* 32 (2): 189–202.

Kettering, S. 1989. "Patronage and Kinship in Early Modern France." *French Historical Studies* 16: 408–35.

Kibler, William W., and Grover A. Zinn. 1995. *Medieval France: An Encyclopedia*. New York: Garland.

Kitschelt, Herbert, and Steven Wilkinson. 2007. *Patrons, Clients, and Policies: Patterns of Democratic Accountability and Political Competition*. Cambridge: Cambridge University Press.

Kivelson, Valerie A. 1994. "The Effects of Partible Inheritance: Gentry Families and the State in Muscovy." *Russian Review* 53 (2): 197–212.

1996. *Autocracy in the Provinces: The Muscovite Gentry and Political Culture in the Seventeenth Century*. Stanford, CA: Stanford University Press.

1997. "Merciful Father, Impersonal State: Russian Autocracy in Comparative Perspective." *Modern Asian Studies* 31 (3): 635–63.

2002. "Muscovite 'Citizenship': Rights without Freedom." *The Journal of Modern History* 74 (3): 465–89.

Kleimola, Ann M. 1975. "Justice in Medieval Russia: Muscovite Judgment Charters (Pravye Gramoty) of the Fifteenth and Sixteenth Centuries." *Transactions of the American Philosophical Society* 65 (6): 1–93.

1977. "Muscovy Redux." *Russian History* 4 (1): 23–30.

Klein, Julius. 1920. *The Mesta: A Study in Spanish Economic History, 1273–1836.* Cambridge, MA: Harvard University Press.

Klosko, George. 2005. *Political Obligations.* Oxford: Oxford University Press.

Knight, Jack. 1992. *Institutions and Social Conflict.* Cambridge: Cambridge University Press.

1995. "Models, Interpretations and Theories: Constructing Explanations of Institutional Emergence and Change." In *Explaining Social Institutions,* ed. J. Knight and I. Sened, 95–120. Ann Arbor: University of Michigan Press.

Knoll, Paul W. 1968. "Casimir the Great and the University of Cracow." *Jahrbücher für Geschichte Osteuropas* 16 (2): 232–49.

1972. *The Rise of the Polish Monarchy: Piast Poland in East Central Europe, 1320–1370.* Chicago: University of Chicago Press.

Koenigsberger, Helmuth G. 1971. *Estates and Revolutions: Essays in Early Modern European History.* Ithaca, NY: Cornell University Press.

1978. "Monarchies and Parliaments in Early Modern Europe: Dominium Regale or Dominium Politicum et Regale." *Theory and Society* 5 (2): 191–217.

1988. "The Beginnings of the States General of the Netherlands." *Parliaments, Estates and Representation* 8 (2): 101–14.

Kokken, H. 1991. "Steden en Staten: Dagvaarten Van Steden en Staten Van Holland Onder Maria Van Bourgondièe en Het Eerste Regentschap Van Maximiliaan Van Oostenrijk (1477–1494)." Leiden dissertation, The Hague.

Kokkonen, Andrej, and Anders Sundell. 2014. "Delivering Stability: Primogeniture and Autocratic Survival in European Monarchies 1000–1800." *The American Political Science Review* 108 (2): 438–53.

Kollmann, Nancy Shields. 1987. *Kinship and Politics: The Making of the Muscovite Political System, 1345–1547.* Stanford, CA: Stanford University Press.

1999. *By Honor Bound: State and Society in Early Modern Russia.* Ithaca, NY: Cornell University Press.

2012. *Crime and Punishment in Early Modern Russia.* Cambridge: Cambridge University Press.

Körner, Martin. 1999. "The Swiss Confederation." In *The Rise of the Fiscal State in Europe, c. 1200–1815,* ed. R. Bonney, 327–58. New York: Oxford University Press.

Kosto, Adam J. 2001a. "The Liber Feudorum Maior of the Counts of Barcelona: The Cartulary as an Expression of Power." *Journal of Medieval History* 27 (1): 1–22.

2001b. "The Limited Impact of the *Usatges de Barcelona* in Twelfth-Century Barcelona." *Traditio* 56: 53–88.

2012. *Hostages in the Middle Ages.* Oxford: Oxford University Press.

Koziol, Geoffrey. 1987. "Monks, Feuds, and the Making of Peace in Eleventh-Century Flanders." *Historical Reflections* 14: 531–49.

Kümin, Beat, and Andreas Würgler. 1997. "Petitions, Gravamina and the Early Modern State: Local Influence on Central Legislation in England and Germany (Hesse)." *Parliaments, Estates and Representation* 17 (1): 39–60.

Kunt, İ Metin. 1983. *The Sultan's Servants: The Transformation of Ottoman Provincial Government, 1550–1650.* New York: Columbia University Press.

Kunt, İ Metin, and Christine Woodhead. 1995. *Süleyman the Magnificent and His Age: The Ottoman Empire in the Early Modern World.* London: Longman.

Kuran, Timur. 2001. "The Provision of Public Goods under Islamic Law: Origins, Impact, and Limitations of the Waqf System." *Law & Society Review* 35 (4): 841–98.

———. 2005. "The Absence of the Corporation in Islamic Law: Origins and Persistence." *The American Journal of Comparative Law* 53 (4): 785–834.

———. 2011. *The Long Divergence: How Islamic Law Held Back the Middle East.* Princeton, NJ: Princeton University Press.

———. 2014. "Institutional Roots of Authoritarian Rule in the Middle East: Civic Legacies of the Islamic Waqf." Unpublished Manuscript. http://ssrn.com/abstract=2449569.

Kwass, Michael. 2000. *Privilege and the Politics of Taxation in Eighteenth-Century France: Liberté, Égalité, Fiscalité.* Cambridge: Cambridge University Press.

Lachmann, Richard. 1985. "Feudal Elite Conflict and the Origins of English Capitalism." *Politics & Society* 14 (3): 349–78.

Ladero Quesada, Miguel Angel. 1973. *La Hacienda Real De Castilla en el Siglo XV.* La Laguna: Santa Cruz de Tenerife.

———. 1984. "Les Cortès de Castille et la Politique Financière de la Monarchie 1252–1369." *Parliaments, Estates and Representation* 4 (2): 107–24.

———. 1999. "Castile in the Middle Ages." In *The Rise of the Fiscal State in Europe, c. 1200–1815,* ed. R. Bonney, 177–99. New York: Oxford University Press.

Lalinde Abadia, J. 1966. *La Jurisdicción Real Inferior en Cataluña ("Corts, Veguers, Batlles").* Barcelona: Museo de Historia de la Ciudad.

Landemore, Hélène. 2012. "Deliberation, Cognitive Diversity, and Democratic Inclusiveness: An Epistemic Argument for the Random Selection of Representatives." *Synthese* 190 (7): 1209–31.

Lane, Frederic Chapin. 1966. *Venice and History.* Baltimore, MD: Johns Hopkins University Press.

———. 1973. *Venice, a Maritime Republic.* Baltimore, MD: Johns Hopkins University Press.

Lane, Frederic Chapin, and Reinhold C. Mueller. 1997. *Money and Banking in Medieval and Renaissance Venice: Coins and Moneys of Account.* Baltimore, MD: Johns Hopkins University Press.

Lange, Matthew. 2009. *Lineages of Despotism and Development: British Colonialism and State Power.* Chicago: University of Chicago Press.

Langlois, Charles Victor. 1890. "Les Origines du Parlement de Paris." *Revue Historique* 42: 74–114.

———. 1909. "Doléances Recueillies par les Enquêteurs de Saint Louis et des Derniers Capétiens Directs." *Revue Historique* 100 (1): 63–95.

Langmuir, Gavin I. 1961. "Concilia and Capetian Assemblies, 1179–1230." In *Album Helen Maud Cam,* 27–63. Louvain: Publications Universitaires de Louvain.

Lansing, Carol. 2010. "Magnate Violence Revisited." In *Communes and Despots in Medieval and Renaissance Italy*, ed. J. E. Law and B. Paton, 35–48. Farnham: Ashgate.

Lapp, Nancy Diane. 2004. *Landing Votes: Representation and Land Reform in Latin America*. New York: Palgrave Macmillan.

Lapsley, Gaillard Thomas. [1914] 1925. "Introduction." In *An Essay on the Origins of the House of Commons, by Désiré Pasquet*. Cambridge: Cambridge University Press.

———. 1951a. "The Interpretation of the Statute of York." In *Crown, Community, and Parliament in the Later Middle Ages: Studies in English Constitutional History*, 153–230. Oxford: Blackwell.

———. 1951b. "Knights of the Shire in the Parliaments of Edward II." In *Crown, Community, and Parliament in the Later Middle Ages*, 111–52. Oxford: Blackwell.

Laski, Harold J. 1917. "The Early History of the Corporation in England." *Harvard Law Review* 30 (6): 561–88.

Lassalmonie, Jean-François. 2000. "Un Discours à Trois Voix sur le Pouvoir: Le Roi et les États Généraux de 1484." In *Penser le Pouvoir au Moyen Âge (VIIIe–XVe Siècle)*, ed. F. Autrand, D. Boutet, and J. Verger, 127–55. Paris: Éditions Rue d'Ulm.

Law, John E., and Bernadette Paton, eds. 2010. *Communes and Despots in Medieval and Renaissance Italy*. Farnham: Ashgate.

Le Mené, Michel. 2000. "'Tenir en Fief' à la Fin du Moyen Âge." In *Guerre, Pouvoir et Noblesse au Moyen Âge: Mélanges en L'honneur de Philippe Contamine*, ed. P. Contamine, J. Paviot, and J. Verger, 439–51. Paris: Presses de l'Université de Paris-Sorbonne.

Lee, Alexander. 2018. *Humanism and Empire: The Imperial Ideal in Fourteenth-Century Italy*. Oxford: Oxford University Press.

Lee, Daniel. 2008. "Private Law Models for Public Law Concepts: The Roman Law Theory of Dominium in the Monarchomach Doctrine of Popular Sovereignty." *The Review of Politics* 70 (3): 370–99.

Leges Henrici Primi. 1972. Oxford: Clarendon Press.

Lemarignier, Jean François. 1970. *La France Médiévale: Institutions & Société*. Paris: A. Colin.

Les Grandes Chroniques de France. 1837. Vol. V. Paris: Librairie Techener.

Les Olim ou Registres des Arrêts Rendus par la Cour du Roi, 1254–1318. 1842. Vol. 2. Paris: Imprimerie royale.

Les Sûretés Personnelles: Civilisations Archaïques, Antiques et Orientales. 1974. Vol. 28.

Les Sûretés Personnelles: Moyen Âge et Temps Modernes. 1971. Vol. 29.

Levi, Margaret. 1988. *Of Rule and Revenue*. Berkeley: University of California Press.

Levitsky, Steven, and Daniel Ziblatt. 2018. *How Democracies Die*. New York: Crown.

Levy, Jacob T. 2014. *Rationalism, Pluralism, and Freedom*. New York: Oxford University Press.

Lewis, Bernard. 1937. "The Islamic Guilds." *The Economic History Review* 8 (1): 20–37.

Lewis, Peter Shervey. 1962. "The Failure of the French Medieval Estates." *Past & Present* 23: 3–24.

Liber Legis Langobardorum. 1896. Göttingen.

Lindkvist, Thomas. 1997. "Law and the Making of the State in Medieval Sweden." In *Legislation and Justice*, ed. A. Padoa Schioppa, 211–28. Oxford: Clarendon Press.

———. 2003. "Kings and Provinces in Sweden." In *The Cambridge History of Scandinavia*, ed. K. Helle, 221–36. Cambridge: Cambridge University Press.

Lisola, François Baron de. 1667. *The Buckler of State and Justice against the Design Manifestly Discovered of the Universal Monarchy*. London.

Lloyd, T. H. 1977. *The English Wool Trade in the Middle Ages*. Cambridge: Cambridge University Press.

Lönnroth, Erik. 1955. "Representative Assemblies in Medieval Sweden." *Xe Congrès international des sciences historiques: Études présentées à la Commission internationale pour l'histoire des assemblées d'états*.

Lord, R. H. 1930. "The Parliaments of the Middle Ages and the Early Modern Period." *Catholic Historical Review* 16 (2): 125–44.

Lot, Ferdinand. 1904. *Fidèles ou Vassaux? Essai sur la Nature Juridique du Lien Qui Unissait les Grands Vassaux à la Royauté Depuis le Milieu du IXème Jusqu'à la Fin du XIIème Siècle*. Paris: E. Bouillon.

Lot, Ferdinand, and Robert Fawtier. 1958. *Histoire des Institutions Françaises au Moyen Âge*. Vol. 2: *Institutions Royales*. Paris: Presses Universitaires de France.

Lot, Ferdinand, Robert Fawtier, and Michel de Boüard. 1957. *Histoire des Institutions Françaises au Moyen Âge*. Vol. 1: *Institutions seigneuriales*. Paris: Presses Universitaires de France.

Lott, John R., and Lawrence Kenny. 1999. "Did Women's Suffrage Change the Size and Scope of Government?" *Journal of Political Economy* 107 (6): 1163–98.

Lough, J. 1961. "France under Louis XIV." In *The New Cambridge Modern History, Volume 5: The Ascendancy of France, 1648–88*, ed. F. L. Carsten, 222–47. Cambridge: Cambridge University Press.

Lousse, Émile. 1935. "Parlementarisme ou Corporatisme? Les Origines des Assemblées D'états." *Revue Historique de Droit Français et Étranger* 14 (4): 683–706.

———. 1952. *La Société d'ancien Régime: Organisation et Représentation Corporatives*. Louvain: Éditions Universitas.

Lovett, A. W. 1987. "The Vote of the Millones (1590)." *The Historical Journal* 30 (1): 1–20.

Loyn, H. R. 1984. *The Governance of Anglo-Saxon England 500–1087*. London: E. Arnold.

Loyseau, Charles. 1678. *Les Œuvres de Maistre Charles Loyseau: Traité des Seigneuries*. Paris.

Luchaire, Achille. 1892. *Manuel des Institutions Françaises, Période des Capétiens Directs*. Paris: Hachette.

Lukowski, Jerzy, and W. H. Zawadzki. 2006. *A Concise History of Poland*, 2nd ed. Cambridge: Cambridge University Press.

Lynch, Katherine A. 2003. *Individuals, Families, and Communities in Europe, 1200–1800: The Urban Foundations of Western Society*. Cambridge: Cambridge University Press.

Lyon, Bryce Dale. 1978. "Medieval Constitutionalism: A Balance of Power." In *Studies of West European Medieval Institutions*. London: Variorum Reprints.

Lyon, Bryce Dale, and Adriaan E. Verhulst. 1967. *Medieval Finance. A Comparison of Financial Institutions in Northwestern Europe*. Brugge: De Tempel.

Macfarlane, Alan. 1978. *The Origins of English Individualism: The Family, Property and Social Transition*. Oxford: Blackwell.

Machiavelli, Niccolò. 1965. *The Art of War*. Indianapolis: Bobbs-Merrill.

1970. *The Discourses*. Harmondsworth: Penguin Books.

MacKay, Angus. 1977. *Spain in the Middle Ages: From Frontier to Empire, 1000–1500*. London: Macmillan.

Macmillan, Donald. 1906. *George Buchanan: A Biography*. Edinburgh: G. A. Morton.

Maddicott, John Robert. 1978a. "The County Community and the Making of Public Opinion in Fourteenth-Century England." *Transactions of the Royal Historical Society* 28: 27–43.

1978b. *Law and Lordship: Royal Justices as Retainers in Thirteenth and Fourteenth-Century England*. Oxford: Past and Present Society.

1981. "Parliament and the Constituencies, 1272–1377." In *The English Parliament in the Middle Ages*, ed. R. G. Davies and J. H. Denton, 61–87. Manchester: Manchester University Press.

1984. "Magna Carta and the Local Community 1215–1259." *Past & Present* 102: 25–65.

1993. "Review of *The Image of Aristocracy in Britain, 1000–1300* by David Crouch." *The English Historical Review* 108 (428): 672–74.

1994. *Simon de Montfort*. Cambridge: Cambridge University Press.

2004. "Montfort, Simon de, Eighth Earl of Leicester (c.1208–1265)." *Oxford Dictionary of National Biography*. Oxford University Press. www.oxforddnb.com /view/article/8505.

2010. *The Origins of the English Parliament, 924–1327*. Oxford: Oxford University Press.

2016. "Parliament and the People in Medieval England." *Parliamentary History* 35 (3): 336–51.

Maddison, Angus. 2003. *The World Economy: Historical Statistics*. Paris: Development Centre of the Organisation for Economic Co-operation and Development.

Madison, James, Alexander Hamilton, and John Jay, eds. 1987. *The Federalist Papers*. Harmondsworth: Penguin.

Magni, Cesare. 1937. *Il Tramonto Del Feudo Lombardo*. Milan: A. Giuffrè.

Magnou-Nortier, Elizabeth. 1996. "La Féodalité en Crise. Propos sur 'Fiefs and Vassals' de Susan Reynolds." *Revue Historique* 296 (2): 253–348.

Mahdavy, Hussein. 1970. "The Patterns and Problems of Economic Development in Rentier States: The Case of Iran." In *Studies in the Economic History of the Middle East*, ed. M. A. Cook, 428–67. Oxford: Oxford University Press.

Mahmasani, Subhi. 1955. "Transactions in the Shari'a." In *Law in the Middle East*, ed. M. Khadduri and H. J. Liebesny, 179–202. Washington, DC: Middle East Institute.

Mahoney, James. 2000a. "Path Dependence in Historical Sociology." *Theory and Society* 29 (4): 507–48.

2000b. "Strategies of Causal Inference in Small-N Analysis." *Sociological Methods & Research* 28 (4): 387–424.

2010. *Colonialism and Postcolonial Development: Spanish America in Comparative Perspective*. New York: Cambridge University Press.

Mahoney, James, and Kathleen Thelen. 2010. "A Theory of Gradual Institutional Change." In *Explaining Institutional Change: Ambiguity, Agency, and Power*, ed. J. Mahoney and K. A. Thelen, 1–37. Cambridge: Cambridge University Press.

Maine, Henry Sumner. 1906. *Ancient Law, Its Connection with the Early History of Society and Its Relation to Modern Ideas*. London: J. Murray.

Maitland, Frederic W. 1893. *Records of the Parliament Holden at Westminster (A.D. 1305)*. London: Rolls Series.

Major, J. Russell. 1951. *The Estates General of 1560*. Princeton, NJ: Princeton University Press.

1955. "The Payment of the Deputies to the French National Assemblies, 1484–1627." *The Journal of Modern History* 27 (3): 217–29.

1960a. *The Deputies to the Estates General in Renaissance France*. Madison, WI: University of Wisconsin Press.

1960b. *Representative Institutions in Renaissance France, 1421–1559*. Madison, WI: University of Wisconsin Press.

1964. "The Crown and the Aristocracy in Renaissance France." *American Historical Review* 69: 631–45.

1980. *Representative Government in Early Modern France*. New Haven: Yale University Press.

1994. *From Renaissance Monarchy to Absolute Monarchy: French Kings, Nobles, & Estates*. Baltimore, MD: Johns Hopkins University Press.

Major, J. Russell, and Mack P. Holt. 1991. *Society and Institutions in Early Modern France*. Athens: University of Georgia Press.

Makkai, László. 1990a. "The Foundation of the Hungarian Christian State, 950–1196." In *A History of Hungary*, ed. P. F. Sugar, P. Hanák, and T. Frank, 15–22. Bloomington: Indiana University Press.

1990b. "Transformation into a Western-Type State, 1196–1301." In *A History of Hungary*, ed. P. F. Sugar, P. Hanák, and T. Frank, 23–33. Bloomington: Indiana University Press.

Mallat, Chibli. 2003. "From Islamic to Middle Eastern Law: A Restatement of the Field (Part I)." *The American Journal of Comparative Law* 51 (4): 699–750.

Mamdani, Mahmood. 1996a. *Citizen and Subject: Contemporary Africa and the Legacy of Late Colonialism*. Princeton, NJ: Princeton University Press.

1996b. "Indirect Rule, Civil Society, and Ethnicity: The African Dilemma." *Social Justice* 23: 145–50.

Mampilly, Zachariah Cherian. 2011. *Rebel Rulers: Insurgent Governance and Civilian Life During War*. Ithaca, NY: Cornell University Press.

Mandaville, Jon E. 1979. "Usurious Piety: The Cash Waqf Controversy in the Ottoman Empire." *International Journal of Middle East Studies* 10 (3): 289–308.

Maniatis, George C. 2001. "The Domain of Private Guilds in the Byzantine Economy, Tenth to Fifteenth Centuries." *Dumbarton Oaks Papers* 55: 339–69.

Manin, Bernard. 1997. *The Principles of Representative Government.* Cambridge: Cambridge University Press.

Mann, Michael. 1984. "The Autonomous Power of the State." *Archives Européennes de Sociologie* 25 (2): 185–213.

   1986. *The Sources of Social Power.* Vol. I: *A History of Power from the Beginning to A.D. 1760.* Cambridge: Cambridge University Press.

   1988. "State and Society, 1130–1815: An Analysis of English State Finances." In *States, War, and Capitalism: Studies in Political Sociology,* 73–123. Oxford: Blackwell.

   2008. "Infrastructural Power Revisited." *Studies in Comparative International Development* 43 (3–4): 355–65.

Mantena, Karuna. 2010. *Alibis of Empire: Henry Maine and the Ends of Liberal Imperialism.* Princeton, NJ: Princeton University Press.

Mares, Isabela, and Didac Queralt. 2015. "The Non-Democratic Origins of Income Taxation." *Comparative Political Studies* 48 (14): 1974–2009.

Markus, Stanislav. 2015. *Property, Predation, and Protection: Piranha Capitalism in Russia and Ukraine.* New York: Cambridge University Press.

   2017. "The Atlas That Has Not Shrugged: Why Russia's Oligarchs Are an Unlikely Force for Change." *Daedalus* (Spring): 101–12.

Marlow, Louise. 1997. *Hierarchy and Egalitarianism in Islamic Thought.* New York: Cambridge University Press.

Marongiu, Antonio. 1968. *Medieval Parliaments: A Comparative Study.* London: Eyre & Spottiswoode.

Marsh, Robert M. 1962. "The Venality of Provincial Office in China and in Comparative Perspective." *Comparative Studies in Society and History* 4 (4): 454–66.

Marshall, T. H. 1964. *Class, Citizenship, and Social Development.* Garden City, NY: Doubleday.

Martin, Isaac William, Ajay K. Mehrotra, and Monica Prasad. 2009a. "The Thunder of History: The Origins and Development of the New Fiscal Sociology." In *The New Fiscal Sociology: Taxation in Comparative and Historical Perspective,* ed. I. W. Martin, A. K. Mehrotra, and M. Prasad, 1–28. Cambridge: Cambridge University Press.

   eds. 2009b. *The New Fiscal Sociology: Taxation in Comparative and Historical Perspective.* Cambridge: Cambridge University Press.

Martin, Janet. 1986. *Treasure of the Land of Darkness: The Fur Trade and Its Significance for Medieval Russia.* Cambridge: Cambridge University Press.

   2007. *Medieval Russia: 980–1584,* 2nd ed. Cambridge: Cambridge University Press.

Martin, John Jeffries, and Dennis Romano, eds. 2000. *Venice Reconsidered: The History and Civilization of an Italian City-State, 1297–1797.* Baltimore, MD: Johns Hopkins University Press.

Martín Martín, José Luis. 1984. "Sur les Origines et les Modalités de la Grande Propriété du Bas Moyen Âge en Estrémadure et dans la Transierra de Léon." In *Les Espagnes Médiévales: Aspects Économiques et Sociaux: Mélanges Offerts à Jean Gautier Dalché*, 81–91. Paris: Belles Lettres.

Marx, Karl. 1973. *Grundrisse: Foundations of the Critique of Political Economy*. Harmondsworth: Penguin Books.

1981. *Capital: A Critique of Political Economy*. Vol. 1. London: Penguin.

Masschaele, James. 2008. *Jury, State, and Society in Medieval England*. New York: Palgrave Macmillan.

Masselin, Jehan. 1835. *Journal des États Généraux de France Tenus à Tours en 1484 Sous le Règne de Charles VIII*. Paris: Imprimerie royale.

Mathias, Peter, and Patrick O'Brien. 1976. "Taxation in Britain and France, 1715–1810: A Comparison of the Social and Economic Incidence of Taxes Collected for the Central Governments." *Journal of European Economic History* 5: 601–50.

Matthews, Z. K. 1937. "An African View of Indirect Rule in Africa." *Journal of the Royal African Society* 36 (145): 433–37.

Mayhew, Nicholas. 1992. "From Regional to Central Minting, 1158–1464." In *A New History of the Royal Mint*, ed. C. E. Challis, 83–178. Cambridge: Cambridge University Press.

1995. "Modelling Medieval Monetisation." In *A Commercialising Economy: England 1086 to c. 1300*, ed. R. H. Britnell and B. M. S. Campbell, 55–77. Manchester: Manchester University Press.

McDonagh, Eileen. 2015. "Ripples from the First Wave: The Monarchical Origins of the Welfare State." *Perspectives on Politics* 13 (4): 992–1016.

McEvedy, Colin, and Richard Jones. 1978. *Atlas of World Population History*. New York: Penguin.

McFarlane, K. B. 1944. "Parliament and 'Bastard Feudalism'." *Transactions of the Royal Historical Society* 26: 53–79.

1947. "Loans to the Lancastrian Kings: The Problem of Inducement." *Cambridge Historical Journal* 9 (1): 51–68.

1962. "England and the Hundred Years War." *Past & Present* 22: 3–18.

1965. "Had Edward I a 'Policy' Towards the Earls?" *History* 1: 145–59.

McGowan, Bruce. 1981. *Economic Life in Ottoman Europe: Taxation, Trade, and the Struggle for Land, 1600–1800*. Cambridge: Cambridge University Press.

1994. "The Age of the Ayans." In *An Economic and Social History of the Ottoman Empire, 1300–1914*, ed. H. İnalcık and D. Quataert, 637–758. New York: Cambridge University Press.

McIlwain, Charles Howard. 1910. *The High Court of Parliament and Its Supremacy; an Historical Essay on the Boundaries between Legislation and Adjudication in England*. New Haven: Yale University Press.

1932. "Medieval Estates." In *The Cambridge Medieval History*, ed. J. B. Bury, ch. 23. New York: Macmillan.

McKisack, May. 1962. *The Parliamentary Representation of the English Boroughs during the Middle Ages*. New York: Barnes & Noble.

McNeill, William Hardy. 1986. *Venice: The Hinge of Europe, 1081–1797*. Chicago: University of Chicago Press.

Megarry, Robert, and William Wade. 2012. *The Law of Real Property*. London: Sweet & Maxwell.

Meltzer, Allan H., and Scott F. Richard. 1981. "A Rational Theory of the Size of Government." *Journal of Political Economy* 89 (5): 914–27.

Ménard, Claude, and Mary M. Shirley. 2014. "The Contribution of Douglass North to New Institutional Economics." In *Institutions, Property Rights, and Economic Growth: The Legacy of Douglass North*, ed. S. Galiani and I. Sened, 11–29. Cambridge: Cambridge University Press.

Menes, Valérie. 2010. "Les Premiers Acteurs de la Vie Parlementaire en France: Les Légistes du Parlement de Paris (1254–1278)." In *Assemblées Parlementaires dans le Monde, du Moyen Âge à Nos Jours*, ed. J. Garrigues et al., 155–67. Paris: Assemblée Nationale.

Merriman, Roger Bigelow. 1911. "The Cortes of the Spanish Kingdoms in the Later Middle Ages." *The American Historical Review* 16 (3): 476–95.

[1918] 1962. *The Rise of the Spanish Empire in the Old World and in the New*. Vol. 1: *The Middle Ages*. New York: Cooper Square Publishers.

Merryman, John Henry, and Rogelio Pérez-Perdomo. 2007. *The Civil Law Tradition: An Introduction to the Legal Systems of Europe and Latin America*, 3rd ed. Stanford, CA: Stanford University Press.

Mettam, Roger. 1988. *Power and Faction in Louis XIV's France*. Oxford: Blackwell.

Migdal, Joel S. 1988. *Strong Societies and Weak States: State-Society Relations and State Capabilities in the Third World*. Princeton, NJ: Princeton University Press.

Milanovic, Branko. 2019. "Putin's Oligarchs and Yeltsin's Oligarchs: All the Same?" *The Globalist*, November 13.

Millar, Fergus. 1992. *The Emperor in the Roman World (31 BC–AD 337)*. Ithaca, NY: Cornell University Press.

Miller, Edward. 1970. "Introduction." In *Historical Studies of the English Parliament*, ed. E. B. Fryde and E. Miller, 1–30. Cambridge: Cambridge University Press.

1975. "War, Taxation and the English Economy in the Late Thirteenth and Early Fourteenth Centuries." In *War and Economic Development: Essays in Memory of David Joslin*, ed. J. M. Winter, 11–31. Cambridge: Cambridge University Press.

Miller, James. 1983. "The Polish Nobility and the Renaissance Monarchy: The 'Execution of the Laws' Movement: Part One." *Parliaments, Estates and Representation* 3 (2): 65–87.

Millet, Hélène. 2003. *Suppliques et Requêtes: Le Gouvernement par la Grâce en Occident (XIIe–XVe Siècle)*. Rome: École française de Rome.

Milsom, S. F. C. 1976. *The Legal Framework of English Feudalism*. Cambridge: Cambridge University Press.

1981. *Historical Foundations of the Common Law*, 2nd ed. London: Butterworths.

1985. *Studies in the History of the Common Law*. London: Hambledon Press.

The Mirror of Justices. 1895. London: B. Quaritch.

Mitchell, Sydney Knox. 1951. *Taxation in Medieval England*. New Haven: Yale University Press.

Moe, Terry M. 2005. "Power and Political Institutions." *Perspectives on Politics* 3 (2): 215–33.

Molho, Anthony. 1971. *Florentine Public Finances in the Early Renaissance, 1400–1433*. Cambridge, MA: Harvard University Press.

Møller, Jørgen. 2017. "The Birth of Representative Institutions: The Case of the Crown of Aragon." *Social Science History* 41 (2): 175–200.

    2018. "The Ecclesiastical Roots of Representation and Consent." *Perspectives on Politics* 16 (4): 1075–84.

Molnár, Miklós. 2001. *A Concise History of Hungary*. New York: Cambridge University Press.

Monahan, Arthur P. 1987. *Consent, Coercion, and Limit: The Medieval Origins of Parliamentary Democracy*. Kingston: McGill-Queen's University Press.

Montesquieu, Charles de Secondat. [1748] 1989. *The Spirit of the Laws*. Cambridge: Cambridge University Press.

Moore, Barrington. 1967. *Social Origins of Dictatorship and Democracy: Lord and Peasant in the Making of the Modern World*. Boston: Beacon Press.

Moore, Mick. 2004. "Revenues, State Formation, and the Quality of Governance in Developing Countries." *International Political Science Review* 25 (3): 297–319.

    2008. "Between Coercion and Contract: Competing Narratives on Taxation and Governance." In *Taxation and State-Building in Developing Countries: Capacity and Consent*, ed. D. Brautigam, O.-H. Fjeldstad, and M. Moore, 34–63. Cambridge: Cambridge University Press.

Morgan, Shepard Ashman. 1911. *The History of Parliamentary Taxation in England*. New York: Moffat, Yard and Co.

Morris, William Alfred. 1910. *The Frankpledge System*. New York: Longmans, Green, and Co.

    1926. *The Early English County Court: An Historical Treatise with Illustrative Documents*. Berkeley: University of California Press.

Morris, William Alfred, and Joseph Reese Strayer, eds. 1940. *The English Government at Work, 1327–1336*. Vol. II: *Fiscal Administration*. Cambridge: The Medieval Academy of America.

Mousnier, Roland. 1984. *The Institutions of France under the Absolute Monarchy 1598–1789*. Vol. II: *The Organs of State and Society*. Chicago: University of Chicago Press.

Mueller, Reinhold C., and Frederic Chapin Lane. 1997. *The Venetian Money Market: Banks, Panics, and the Public Debt, 1200–1500*. Baltimore, MD: Johns Hopkins University Press.

Mundy, John Hine. 1954. *Liberty and Political Power in Toulouse, 1050–1230*. New York: Columbia University Press.

Muñiz-Fraticelli, Victor. 2014. *The Structure of Pluralism: On the Authority of Associations*. Oxford: Oxford University Press.

Munro, John H. 2003. "The Medieval Origins of the Financial Revolution: Usury, Rentes, and Negotiability." *International History Review* 25 (3): 505–62.

    2012. "The Late Medieval Decline of English Demesne Agriculture: Demographic, Monetary and Political-Fiscal Factors." In *Town and*

Countryside in the Age of the Black Death: Essays in Honour of John Hatche, ed. M. Bailey and S. Rigby, 299–348. Turnhout: Brepols.

Murphey, Rhoads. 1999. *Ottoman Warfare 1500–1700*. New Brunswick, NJ: Rutgers University Press.

Musson, Anthony. 1997. "Twelve Good Men and True? The Character of Early Fourteenth-Century Juries." *Law and History Review* 15 (1): 115–44.

———. 2000. "New Labour Laws, New Remedies? Legal Reaction to the Black Death 'Crisis'." In *Fourteenth Century England*, ed. C. Given-Wilson, W. M. Ormrod, and N. Saul, 73–88. Woodbridge: Boydell Press.

———. 2001. *Medieval Law in Context: The Growth of Legal Consciousness from Magna Carta to the Peasants' Revolt*. Manchester: Manchester University Press.

Musson, Anthony, and W. M. Ormrod. 1999. *The Evolution of English Justice: Law, Politics, and Society in the Fourteenth Century*. Basingstoke: Macmillan.

Myers, A. R. 1981. "Parliament, c. 1422–1509." In *The English Parliament in the Middle Ages*, ed. R. G. Davies and J. H. Denton, 141–84. Manchester: Manchester University Press.

Myśliwski, Grzegorz. 2008. "From Feudal Rents Towards a Tax System in Central Europe (the Thirteenth to the Fifteenth Century)." In *La Fiscalità Nell'economia Europea Secc. XII–XVIII*, 271–78. Firenze: Firenze University Press.

Nader, Helen. 1990. *Liberty in Absolutist Spain: The Habsburg Sale of Towns, 1516–1700*. Baltimore, MD: Johns Hopkins University Press.

Najemy, John M. 1982. *Corporatism and Consensus in Florentine Electoral Politics, 1280–1400*. Chapel Hill, NC: University of North Carolina Press.

Naseemullah, Adnan, and Paul Staniland. 2016. "Indirect Rule and Varieties of Governance." *Governance* 29 (1): 13–30.

Neeson, J. M. 1993. *Commoners, Common Right, Enclosure and Social Change in England, 1700–1820*. Cambridge: Cambridge University Press.

Neu, Tim. 2015. "'Little Tools of State Formation': The Admission of Nobles to Imperial and Territorial Diets in Early Modern Germany." *Parliaments, Estates and Representation* 35 (2): 186–204.

Neveux, François, and Claire Ruelle. 2005. *La Normandie Royale: Des Capétiens aux Valois, XIIIe–XIVe Siècle*. Rennes: Ouest-France.

Nicholas, David. 1991. "Of Poverty and Primacy: Demand, Liquidity, and the Flemish Economic Miracle, 1050–1200." *The American Historical Review* 96 (1): 17–41.

———. 1992. *Medieval Flanders*. London: Longman.

Nightingale, Pamela. 2004. "The Lay Subsidies and the Distribution of Wealth in Medieval England, 1275–1334." *The Economic History Review* 57 (1): 1–32.

Nijenhuis, I. D. A., J. A. N. Burgers, E. E. F. Dijkhof, Karin Van Leeuwen, and Marijke Van Faassen. 2009. "Representation and Governance in the Netherlands, 1250–1983: Materials for a Comprehensive History of Politics." *Parliaments, Estates and Representation* 29 (1): 2–15.

Nilsson, Klas. 2017. *The Money of Monarchs: The Importance of Non-Tax Revenue for Autocratic Rule in Early Modern Sweden*. Lund: University of Lund.

North, Douglass C. 1981. *Structure and Change in Economic History*. New York: Norton.

1990. *Institutions, Institutional Change, and Economic Performance.* Cambridge: Cambridge University Press.

1991. "Institutions." *The Journal of Economic Perspectives* 5 (1): 97–112.

North, Douglass C., and Robert Paul Thomas. 1971. "The Rise and Fall of the Manorial System: A Theoretical Model." *The Journal of Economic History* 31 (4): 777–803.

1973. *The Rise of the Western World: A New Economic History.* Cambridge: Cambridge University Press.

North, Douglass C., John J. Wallis, and Barry R. Weingast. 2009. *Violence and Social Orders: A Conceptual Framework for Interpreting Recorded Human History.* Cambridge: Cambridge University Press.

North, Douglass C., and Barry R. Weingast. 1989. "Constitutions and Commitment: The Evolution of Institutional Governing Public Choice in Seventeenth-Century England." *The Journal of Economic History* 49 (4): 803–32.

Norwich, John Julius. 1992. *The Normans in Sicily: The Normans in the South 1016–1130 and the Kingdom in the Sun 1130–1194.* London: Penguin.

Nugent, Jeffrey B., and Nicholas Sanchez. 1989. "The Efficiency of the Mesta: A Parable." *Explorations in Economic History* 26: 261–84.

Nüssli, Christos, and Marc-Antoine Nüssli. 2008. "Euratlas: Georeferenced Historical Vector Data." Yverdon-les-Bains, Switzerland: Euratlas-Nüssli.

O'Brien, Patrick Karl. 1993. "Total Revenue to English Crown, 1485–1815." European State Finance Database. www.le.ac.uk/hi/bon/ESFDB/OBRIEN/engm008.txt.

O'Brien, Patrick Karl, and Philip A. Hunt. 1993. "The Rise of a Fiscal State in England, 1485–1815." *Historical Research* 66 (160): 129–76.

1999. "England 1485–1815." In *The Rise of the Fiscal State in Europe, c. 1200–1815,* ed. R. Bonney, 53–100. New York: Oxford University Press.

O'Callaghan, Joseph F. 1975. *A History of Medieval Spain.* Ithaca, NY: Cornell University Press.

1989. *The Cortes of Castile-León, 1188–1350.* Philadelphia: University of Pennsylvania Press.

2003. "Administration, Territorial." In *Medieval Iberia: An Encyclopedia,* ed. E. M. Gerli, 28–32. New York: Routledge.

O'Gorman, Frank. 1993. "The Electorate before and after 1832." *Parliamentary History* 12 (2): 171–83.

Oakley, Francis. 1983. "Legitimation by Consent: The Question of the Medieval Roots." *Viator* 14: 303–35.

OECD. 2008. "Governance, Taxation and Accountability." DAC Guidelines and Reference Series. Paris: OECD.

Ogilvie, Sheilagh. 2011. *Institutions and European Trade: Merchant Guilds, 1000–1800.* Cambridge: Cambridge University Press.

2019. *The European Guilds: An Economic Analysis.* Princeton, NJ: Princeton University Press.

Olson, Mancur. 1965. *The Logic of Collective Action: Public Goods and the Theory of Groups.* Cambridge, MA: Harvard University Press.

1993. "Dictatorship, Democracy, and Development." *American Political Science Review* 87 (3): 567–576.

2000. *Power and Prosperity: Outgrowing Communist and Capitalist Dictatorships.* New York: Basic Books.

"Ordinances of 1311." 1975. In *English Historical Documents III, 1189–1327*, ed. H. Rothwell, 527–39. London: Eyre & Spottiswoode.

Ormrod, W. M. 1987. "The English Crown and the Customs, 1349–63." *The Economic History Review* 40 (1): 27–40.

1990a. "Agenda for Legislation, 1322–c.1340." *The English Historical Review* 105 (414): 1–33.

1990b. *The Reign of Edward III: Crown and Political Society in England, 1327–1377.* New Haven: Yale University Press.

1991. "The Crown and the English Economy, 1290–1348." In *Before the Black Death: Studies in 'Crisis' of the Early Fourteenth Century*, ed. B. M. S. Campbell, 149–83. Manchester: Manchester University Press.

1992. "Total French Treasury Receipts and Notional Total English Revenue, 1322–45 (Expressed in Metric Tonnes of Fine Silver)." European State Finance Database.

1994. "Total Notional Revenue of the English Crown, 1462–1485." European State Finance Database.

1995. *Political Life in Medieval England, 1300–1450.* New York: St. Martin's Press.

1999. "England in the Middle Ages." In *The Rise of the Fiscal State in Europe, c. 1200–1815*, ed. R. Bonney, 19–52. New York: Oxford University Press.

2008. "Poverty and Privilege: The Fiscal Burden in England (XIIIth–XVth Centuries)." In *La Fiscalità Nell'economia Europea Secc. XII–XVIII*, 637–56. Firenze: Firenze University Press.

2009. "Introduction: Medieval Petitions in Context." In *Medieval Petitions: Grace and Grievance*, ed. W. M. Ormrod, G. Dodd, and A. Musson, 1–11. Woodbridge: York Medieval Press.

2011. "Government Records: Fiscality, Archives and the Economic Historian." In *Dove Va la Storia Economica? Metodi e Prospettive, Secc. XIII–XVIII*, ed. F. Ammannati, 197–224. Firenze: Firenze University Press.

2013. "Henry V and the English Taxpayer." In *Henry V: New Interpretations*, ed. G. Dodd, 187–216. Woodbridge: York Medieval Press.

Ormrod, W. M., and Janos Barta. 1995. "The Feudal Structure and the Beginnings of State Finance." In *Economic Systems and State Finance*, ed. R. Bonney, 53–79. Oxford: Oxford University Press.

Ormrod, W. M., Gwilym Dodd, and Anthony Musson, eds. 2009. *Medieval Petitions: Grace and Grievance.* Woodbridge: York Medieval Press.

Ormrod, W. M., Helen Killick, and Phil Bradford. 2017. *Early Common Petitions in the English Parliament, c. 1290–c. 1420.* Cambridge: Cambridge University Press.

Orrman, Eljas. 2003. "The Condition of the Rural Population." In *The Cambridge History of Scandinavia*, ed. K. Helle, 581–610. Cambridge: Cambridge University Press.

Ortí Gost, Pere. 2000. *Renda i Fiscalitat en Una Ciutat Medieval: Barcelona, Segles XII–XIV.* Barcelona: Consejo Superior de Investigaciones Científicas Institución Milá y Fontanals.

Orwin, C. S. 1967. *The Open Fields*, 3rd ed. Oxford: Clarendon Press.

Osafo-Kwaako, Philip, and James A. Robinson. 2013. "Political Centralization in Pre-Colonial Africa." *Journal of Comparative Economics* 41 (1): 6–21.

Ostrowski, Donald. 2002. "The Façade of Legitimacy: Exchange of Power and Authority in Early Modern Russia." *Comparative Studies in Society and History* 44 (3): 534–63.

    2004. "The Assembly of the Land (Zemskii Sobor) as a Representative Institution." In *Modernizing Muscovy: Reform and Social Change in Seventeenth-Century Russia*, ed. J. Kotilaine and M. Poe, 111–36. London: Routledge.

    2006. "The Growth of Muscovy (1462–1533)." In *The Cambridge History of Russia*, ed. M. Perrie, 213–39. Cambridge: Cambridge University Press.

Owen, Thomas C. 1991. *The Corporation under Russian Law, 1800–1917: A Study in Tsarist Economic Policy*. Cambridge: Cambridge University Press.

Özel, Oktay. 1999. "Limits of the Almighty: Mehmed II's 'Land Reform' Revisited." *Journal of the Economic and Social History of the Orient* 42 (2): 226–46.

Padgett, John Frederick, and Walter W. Powell. 2012. *The Emergence of Organizations and Markets*. Princeton, NJ: Princeton University Press.

Padoa Schioppa, Antonio, ed. 1997. *Legislation and Justice*. Oxford: Clarendon Press.

Palgrave, Francis, ed. 1827. *The Parliamentary Writs and Writs of Military Summons*. Vol. I. London: Eyre & Spottiswoode.

Palliser, D. M. 2000. "Towns and the English State, 1066–1500." In *The Medieval State: Essays Presented to James Campbell*, ed. J. R. Maddicott, D. M. Palliser, and J. Campbell, 126–45. London: Hambledon Press.

Palmer, Robert C. 1982. *The County Courts of Medieval England, 1150–1350*. Princeton, NJ: Princeton University Press.

    1985. "The Origins of Property in England." *Law and History Review* 3 (1): 1–50.

    1993. *English Law in the Age of the Black Death, 1348–1381: A Transformation of Governance and Law*. Chapel Hill, NC: University of North Carolina Press.

Paris, Matthew 1852. *English History from the Year 1235 to 1273*. Vol. 1. London: Henry G. Bohn.

    1853. *English History from the Year 1235 to 1273*. Vol. 2. London: Henry G. Bohn.

Parker, David. 1996. *Class and State in Ancien Regime France: The Road to Modernity?* London: Routledge.

Parker, Geoffrey. 1976. "The Military Revolution 1560–1660: A Myth?" *Journal of Modern History* 48 (2): 195–214.

    1996. *The Military Revolution: Military Innovation and the Rise of the West, 1500–1800*, 2nd ed. Cambridge: Cambridge University Press.

Parsons, John Carmi. 1994. *Eleanor of Castile: Queen and Society in Thirteenth-Century England*. Basingstoke: Macmillan.

Parthasarathi, Prasannan. 2011. *Why Europe Grew Rich and Asia Did Not: Global Economic Divergence, 1600–1850*. Cambridge: Cambridge University Press.

Payling, S. J. 1999. "County Parliamentary Elections in Fifteenth-Century England." *Parliamentary History* 18 (3): 237–59.

Pécout, Thierry. 2010. *Quand Gouverner c'est Enquêter: Les Pratiques Politiques de L'enquête Princière, Occident, XIIIe–XIVe Siècles*. Paris: De Boccard.

Pennington, D. H. 1981. "A Seventeenth-Century Perspective." In *The English Parliament in the Middle Ages*, ed. R. G. Davies and J. H. Denton, 185–200. Philadelphia: University of Pennsylvania Press.

Pepinsky, Thomas B. 2017. "Regions of Exception." *Perspectives on Politics* 15 (4): 1034–52.

Perrens, F. T. 1860. *Étienne Marcel et le Gouvernement de la Bourgeoisie au Quatorzième Siècle (1356–1358)*. Paris: L. Hachette.

——— 1873. *La Démocratie en France au Moyen Âge: Histoire des Tendances Démocratiques dans les Populations Urbaines et XIVe au XVe Siècle*. Paris: Didier.

Perroy, Édouard. 1943–45. "Feudalism or Principalities in 15th Century France." *Bulletin of the Institute of Historical Research (BIHR)* 20.

Phelps Brown, E. H., and Sheila V. Hopkins. 1962. "Seven Centuries of the Prices of Consumables, Compared with Builders' Wage-Rates." In *Essays in Economic History*, ed. E. M. Carus-Wilson, 179–96. New York: St. Martin's Press.

Phillips, Carla Rahn, and William D. Phillips. 1997. *Spain's Golden Fleece: Wool Production and the Wool Trade from the Middle Ages to the Nineteenth Century*. Baltimore, MD: Johns Hopkins University Press.

Picot, Georges. 1874. "Les Élections aux États-Généraux dans les Provinces de 1302 à 1614." *Séances et travaux de l'Académie des sciences morales et politiques* 2: 209–21.

——— 1901. *Documents Relatifs aux Etats Généraux et Assemblées Réunis Sous Philippe Le Bel*. Paris.

Pierson, Paul. 2000. "Increasing Returns, Path Dependence, and the Study of Politics." *The American Political Science Review* 94 (2): 251–67.

——— 2004. *Politics in Time: History, Institutions, and Social Analysis*. Princeton, NJ: Princeton University Press.

Piketty, Thomas. 2014. *Capital in the Twenty-First Century*. Cambridge, MA: The Belknap Press of Harvard University Press.

Pincus, Steven. 2009. *1688: The First Modern Revolution*. New Haven: Yale University Press.

Pincus, Steven, and James Robinson. 2011. "What Really Happened During the Glorious Revolution?" Unpublished manuscript.

Pipes, Richard. 1974. *Russia under the Old Regime*. London: Weidenfeld & Nicolson.

——— 1994. "Was There Private Property in Muscovite Russia?" *Slavic Review* 53 (2): 524–30.

——— 1999. *Property and Freedom*. New York: Alfred A. Knopf.

Pirenne, Henri. 1925. *Medieval Cities: Their Origins and the Revival of Trade*. Princeton, NJ: Princeton University Press.

Pitkin, Hanna Fenichel. 2004. "Representation and Democracy: Uneasy Alliance." *Scandinavian Political Studies* 27 (3): 335–42.

Plucknett, T. F. T. 1940. "Parliament." In *The English Government at Work, 1327–1336*, ed. J. F. Willard and W. A. Morris, 82–128. Cambridge, MA: The Medieval Academy of America.

1956. *A Concise History of the Common Law*, 5th ed. London: Butterworth.

Plutarch. 1914. *Plutarch's Lives*. Vol. 8. London: W. Heinemann.

Poe, Marshall. 1998. "What Did Russians Mean When They Called Themselves 'Slaves of the Tsar'?" *Slavic Review* 57 (3): 585–608.

2002. "The Truth About Muscovy." *Kritika: Explorations in Russian and Eurasian History* 3 (3): 473–86.

2006. "The Central Government and Its Institutions." In *The Cambridge History of Russia*, ed. M. Perrie, 435–63. Cambridge: Cambridge University Press.

Poggi, Gianfranco. 1978. *The Development of the Modern State: A Sociological Introduction*. Stanford, CA: Stanford University Press.

1990. *The State: Its Nature, Development, and Prospects*. Cambridge: Polity Press.

Polanyi, Karl. 1944. *The Great Transformation*. New York: Farrar & Rinehart.

Pollard, A. F. 1920. *The Evolution of Parliament*. New York: Longmans.

1942. "Receivers of Petitions and Clerks of Parliament." *The English Historical Review* 57 (226): 202–26.

Pollock, Frederick, and Frederic William Maitland. 1898. *The History of English Law before the Time of Edward I*, 2nd ed. Vol. I. Cambridge: The University Press.

1899. *The History of English Law before the Time of Edward I*, 2nd ed. Vol. II. Cambridge: The University Press.

Pomeranz, Kenneth. 2000. *The Great Divergence: Europe, China, and the Making of the Modern World Economy*. Princeton, NJ: Princeton University Press.

2011. "Ten Years After: Responses and Reconsiderations." *Historically Speaking* 12 (4): 20–25.

Poole, Austin Lane. 1946. *Obligations of Society in the XII and XIII Centuries*. Oxford: Clarendon Press.

Poos, L. R. 1983. "The Social Context of Statute of Labourers Enforcement." *Law and History Review* 1 (1): 27–52.

Porta, Rafael La, Florencio Lopez-de-Silanes, and Andrei Shleifer. 2008. "The Economic Consequences of Legal Origins." *Journal of Economic Literature* 46 (2): 285–332.

Porter, James. 1771. *Observations on the Religion, Law, Government, and Manners of the Turks. The Second Edition, Corrected and Enlarged by the Author. To Which Is Added, the State of the Turkey Trade, from Its Origin to the Present Time*. London: J. Nourse.

Post, Gaines. 1943a. "Plena Potestas and Consent in Medieval Assemblies: A Study in Romano-Canonical Procedure and the Rise of Representation, 1150–1325." *Traditio* 1: 355–408.

1943b. "Roman Law and Early Representation in Spain and Italy, 1150–1250." *Speculum: A Journal of Medieval Studies* 18 (2): 211–32.

1946. "A Romano-Canonical Maxim, 'Quod Omnes Tangit,' in Bracton." *Traditio* 4: 197–251.

Potter, Mark, and Jean-Laurent Rosenthal. 1997. "Politics and Public Finance in France: The Estates of Burgundy, 1660–1790." *Journal of Interdisciplinary History* 27 (4): 577–612.

2002. "The Development of Intermediation in French Credit Markets: Evidence from the Estates of Burgundy." *The Journal of Economic History* 62 (4): 1024–49.

Powell, J. Enoch, and Keith Wallis. 1968. *The House of Lords in the Middle Ages: A History of the English House of Lords to 1540.* London: Weidenfeld & Nicolson.

Power, Eileen Edna. 1942. *The Wool Trade in English Medieval History.* London: Oxford University Press.

Powers, David S. 1999. "Islamic Family Endowment (Waqf)." *Vanderbilt Journal of Transnational Law* 32: 1167–90.

Prestwich, Michael. 1972. *War, Politics and Finance under Edward I.* London: Faber.

1980. *Documents Illustrating the Crisis of 1297–98 in England.* London: Royal Historical Society.

1985. "Magnate Summonses in England in the Later Years of Edward I." *Parliaments, Estates and Representation* 5 (2): 97–101.

1988. *Edward I.* Berkeley: University of California Press.

1990. *English Politics in the Thirteenth Century.* New York: St. Martin's Press.

1996. *Armies and Warfare in the Middle Ages: The English Experience.* New Haven: Yale University Press.

2003. *The Three Edwards: War and State in England, 1272–1377,* 2nd ed. New York: Routledge.

2004. "Bigod, Roger (IV), Fifth Earl of Norfolk (c.1245–1306)." *Oxford Dictionary of National Biography.* Oxford University Press. www.oxforddnb.com/view/art icle/8505.

2005. *Plantagenet England, 1225–1360.* Oxford: Clarendon Press.

2006. "The Enterprise of War." In *A Social History of England, 1200–1500,* ed. R. Horrox and W. M. Ormrod, 74–90. Cambridge: Cambridge University Press.

Procter, Evelyn S. 1936. "The Development of the Catalan *Corts* in the Thirteenth Century." In *Homenaje a Antoni Rubió I Lluch,* 525–46. Barcelona: la Casa de caritat.

1959. "The Towns of Leon and Castille as Suitors before the King's Court in the Thirteenth Century." *English Historical Review* 74 (290): 1–22.

1980. *Curia and Cortes in León and Castile, 1072–1295.* Cambridge: Cambridge University Press.

Przeworski, Adam. 2009. "Conquered or Granted? A History of Suffrage Extensions." *British Journal of Political Science* 39 (2): 291–321.

Puga, Diego, and Daniel Trefler. 2014. "International Trade and Institutional Change: Medieval Venice's Response to Globalization." *The Quarterly Journal of Economics* 129 (2): 753–821.

Putnam, Bertha Haven. 1906. "The Justices of Labourers in the Fourteenth Century." *The English Historical Review* 21 (83): 517–38.

1908. *The Enforcement of the Statutes of Labourers during the First Decade after the Black Death, 1349–1359.* New York: Longmans, Green & Co.

1929. "The Transformation of the Keepers of the Peace into the Justices of the Peace 1327–1380." *Transactions of the Royal Historical Society* 12: 19–48.

Putnam, Robert D., Robert Leonardi, and Raffaella Nanetti. 1993. *Making Democracy Work: Civic Traditions in Modern Italy*. Princeton, NJ: Princeton University Press.

Queller, Donald E. 1986. *The Venetian Patriciate: Reality Versus Myth*. Urbana: University of Illinois Press.

Raban, Sandra. 2000. *England under Edward I and Edward II, 1259–1327*. Oxford: Blackwell.

Raccagni, Gianluca. 2013. "The Appellate Jurisdiction, the Emperor and the City-Republics in Early 13th-Century Northern Italy." In *Law and Disputing in the Middle Ages*, 181–200. Copenhagen: DJØF Publishing.

Rady, Martyn. 1999. "Erik Fügedi and the Elefánthy Kindred." *The Slavonic and East European Review* 77 (2): 295–308.

  2000. *Nobility, Land, and Service in Medieval Hungary*. Basingstoke: Palgrave Macmillan.

  2001. "The 'Title of New Donation' in Medieval Hungarian Law." *The Slavonic and East European Review* 79 (4): 638–52.

  2005. "Rethinking Jagiełło Hungary (1490–1526)." *Central European History* 3 (1): 3–18.

  2014. "Hungary and the Golden Bull of 1222." *Storie Instituţională Şi Administrativă* 24 (2): 87–108.

  2015. *Customary Law in Hungary: Courts, Texts, and the Tripartitum*. New York: Oxford University Press.

Rafeq, Abdul-Karim. 1991. "Craft Organization, Work Ethics, and the Strains of Change in Ottoman Syria." *Journal of the American Oriental Society* 111 (3): 495–511.

Raftis, J. A. 1997. *Peasant Economic Development within the English Manorial System*. Stroud: Sutton.

Ramsay, James Henry. 1925a. *A History of the Revenues of the Kings of England, 1066–1399*. Vol. 1. Oxford: Clarendon Press.

  1925b. *A History of the Revenues of the Kings of England, 1066–1399*. Vol. 2. Oxford: Clarendon Press.

Ravina, Mark. 1999. *Land and Lordship in Early Modern Japan*. Stanford, CA: Stanford University Press.

Rayner, Doris. 1941a. "The Forms and Machinery of the 'Commune Petition' in the Fourteenth Century. Part I." *The English Historical Review* 56 (222): 198–233.

  1941b. "The Forms and Machinery of the 'Commune Petition' in the Fourteenth Century. Part II (Continued)." *The English Historical Review* 56 (224): 549–70.

Reuter, Timothy. 2006. "The Medieval German *Sonderweg*? The Empire and Its Rulers in the High Middle Ages." In *Medieval Polities and Modern Mentalities*, ed. J. L. Nelson, 388–412. Cambridge: Cambridge University Press.

Revkin, Mara. 2016. "The Legal Foundations of the Islamic State." Washington, DC: Brookings Institution.

Reynolds, Susan. 1994. *Fiefs and Vassals: The Medieval Evidence Reinterpreted*. Oxford: Oxford University Press.

  1997. *Kingdoms and Communities in Western Europe, 900–1300*, 2nd ed. Oxford: Clarendon Press.

Richardson, H. G., and G. O. Sayles. 1931. "The King's Ministers in Parliament, 1272–1307." *English Historical Review* 46: 529–50.

1932. "The King's Ministers in Parliament, 1272–1377 (Continued)." *English Historical Review* 47 (187): 377–97.

1981. *The English Parliament in the Middle Ages.* London: Hambledon Press.

Rigaudière, Albert. 1988. "Législation Royale et Construction de L'état dans la France du XIIIe Siècle." In *Renaissance du Pouvoir Législatif et Genèse de L'état,* ed. A. Gouron and A. Rigaudière, 203–36. Montpellier: Société d'histoire du droit et des institutions des anciens pays de droit écrit.

1994. *Pouvoirs et Institutions dans la France Médiévale.* Vol. 2. Paris: A. Colin.

2003. *Penser et Construire L'état dans la France du Moyen Âge: XIIIe–XVe Siècle.* Paris: Comité pour l'histoire économique et financière de la France.

Roberts, Michael. 1956. *The Military Revolution.* Belfast: M. Boyd.

1967. "The Military Revolution, 1560–1660." In *Essays in Swedish History.* London: Weidenfeld & Nicolson.

Robinson, James, and Ragnar Torvik. 2013. "Institutional Comparative Statics." In *Advances in Economics and Econometrics: Tenth World Congress,* ed. D. Acemoglu, M. Arellano, and E. Dekel, 97–134. New York: Cambridge University Press.

Rodrik, Dani. 2003. *In Search of Prosperity: Analytic Narratives on Economic Growth.* Princeton, NJ: Princeton University Press.

Rosenthal, Jean-Laurent, and Roy Bin Wong. 2011. *Before and Beyond Divergence: The Politics of Economic Change in China and Europe.* Cambridge, MA: Harvard University Press.

Roskell, John Smith. 1954. *The Commons in the Parliament of 1422: English Society and Parliamentary Representation under the Lancastrians.* Manchester: Manchester University Press.

1956. "The Problem of the Attendance of the Lords in Medieval Parliaments." *Historical Research* 29 (80): 153–204.

Ross, Michael L. 2001. "Does Oil Hinder Democracy?" *World Politics* 53 (3): 325–61.

2004. "Does Taxation Lead to Representation?" *British Journal of Political Science* 34 (2): 229–49.

2012. *The Oil Curse: How Petroleum Wealth Shapes the Development of Nations.* Princeton, NJ: Princeton University Press.

Rotuli Parliamentorum. 1783. Vol. I. London.

Rowen, Herbert H. 1988. *The Princes of Orange: The Stadholders in the Dutch Republic.* Cambridge: Cambridge University Press.

Rowland, Daniel. 1990. "Did Muscovite Literary Ideology Place Any Limits on the Power of the Tsar?" *Russian Review* 49 (2): 125–55.

Rozen, Minna. 2010. *A History of the Jewish Community in Istanbul: The Formative Years, 1453–1566.* Leiden: Brill.

Rubin, Avi. 2012. "From Legal Representation to Advocacy: Attorneys and Clients in the Ottoman Nizamiye Courts." *International Journal of Middle East Studies* 44 (1): 111–27.

Rubinat, M. T. 2002. "Dépenses, Administration Financière et Origines du Conseil Municipal en Catalogne (XIIe–XIIIe Siècles)." In *La Fiscalité des Villes au Moyen Âge,* ed. D. Menjot and M. S. Martinez. Toulouse: Privat.

Rucquoi, Adeline. 1986. "Le Roi, Les Villes, Les Nobles en Castille (1300–1450)." In *Pouvoirs et Sociétés Politiques dans les Royaumes Ibériques au Bas Moyen Âge*, 57–75. Nice: Université de Nice.

———. 1987. "Pouvoir Royal et Oligarchies Urbaines D'Alfonso X à Fernando IV." In *Genèse Médiévale de L'état Moderne. La Castille et la Navarre (1250–1370)*, 173–82. Valladolid: Ámbito.

———. 1993. *Histoire Médiévale de la Péninsule Ibérique*. Paris: Éditions du Seuil.

Rudolph, Lloyd I., and Susanne Hoeber Rudolph. 1979. "Authority and Power in Bureaucratic and Patrimonial Administration: A Revisionist Interpretation of Weber on Bureaucracy." *World Politics* 31 (2): 195–227.

Ruggiero, Guido. 1979. "Modernization and the Mythic State in Early Renaissance Venice: The Serrata Revisited." *Viator* 10: 245–56.

Ruiz, Teofilo F. 1977. "The Transformation of the Castilian Municipalities: The Case of Burgos 1248–1350." *Past & Present* 77: 3–32.

———. 1982. "Oligarchy and Royal Power: The Castilian Cortes and the Castilian Crisis 1248–1350." *Parliaments, Estates and Representation* 2 (2): 95–101.

Ruiz Martín, Felipe, and Angel García Sanz. 1998. *Mesta, Trashumancia y Lana en la España Moderna*. Madrid: Fundación Duques de Soria.

Runciman, Walter G. 1993. "The Origins of the Modern State in Europe and as a Topic in the Theory of Social Selection." In *Visions sur le Développement des États Européens: Théories et Historiographies de L'état Moderne: Actes du Colloque*, ed. W. P. Blockmans and J.-P. Genêt, 45–60. Rome: Ecole française de Rome.

Russocki, Stanislaw. 1976. "The High Court of Colloquium Generale." In *Questiones Medii Aevi*. University of Warsaw.

Sabaté i Curull, Flocel. 1997. *El Territori de la Catalunya Medieval: Percepció de L'espai i Divisió Territorial al Llarg de L'edat Mitjana*. Barcelona: Fundació Salvador Vives i Casajuana.

Sabean, David Warren, Simon Teuscher, and Jon Mathieu. 2007. *Kinship in Europe: Approaches to Long-Term Developments (1300–1900)*. New York: Berghahn Books.

Sablonier, Roger. 1998. "The Swiss Confederation." In *The New Cambridge Medieval History*, ed. C. Allmand, 645–70. Cambridge: Cambridge University Press.

Sacks, David Harris. 1994. "The Paradox of Taxation: Fiscal Crises, Parliament, and Liberty in England, 1450–1640." In *Fiscal Crises, Liberty, and Representative Government, 1450–1789*, ed. P. T. Hoffman and K. Norberg, 7–66. Stanford, CA: Stanford University Press.

Şahin, Kaya. 2013. *Empire and Power in the Reign of Süleyman: Narrating the Sixteenth-Century Ottoman World*. Cambridge: Cambridge University Press.

Said, Edward W. 1978. *Orientalism*. New York: Pantheon Books.

Salmon, J. H. M. 1967. "Venality of Office and Popular Sedition in Seventeenth-Century France: A Review of a Controversy." *Past & Present* 37: 21–43.

Salrach, Josep M. 1987. *Història de Catalunya*. Vol. 2: *El procés de feudalització*. Barcelona: Edicions 62.

Sambanis, Nicholas. 2004. "Using Case Studies to Expand Economic Models of Civil War." *Perspectives on Politics* 2 (2): 259–79.

Sánchez-Albornoz, Claudio. 1991. *España, Un Enigma Histórico.* Vol. II. Barcelona: Edhasa.

Sánchez Martínez, Manuel. 1995. *El Naixement de la Fiscalitat D'estat a Catalunya: Segles XII–XIV.* Vic, Spain: Eumo.

Sánchez Martínez, Manuel, and Pere Ortí Gost. 1997. *Corts, Parlaments i Fiscalitat a Catalunya: Els Capítols del Donatiu (1288–1384).* Barcelona: Generalitat de Catalunya Departament de Justícia.

Sanders, I. J. 1960. *English Baronies: A Study of Their Origin and Descent, 1086–1327.* Oxford: Clarendon Press.

Sautel-Boulet, Marguerite. 1955. "Le Rôle Jurisdictionnel de la Cour des Pairs aux XIIIe et XIVe Siècles." In *Recueil de Travaux Offert à M. Clovis Brunel,* 507–20. Paris: Société de l'École des chartes.

Sayles, G. O. 1950. *The Medieval Foundations of England.* London: Methuen & Co.

——— 1974. *The King's Parliament of England.* New York: Norton.

——— 1988. *The Functions of the Medieval Parliament of England.* London: Hambledon Press.

Sayles, G. O., and H. G. Richardson, eds. and trans. 1955. *Fleta.* London: B. Quaritch.

Schacht, Joseph. 1964. *An Introduction to Islamic Law.* Oxford: Clarendon Press.

Schelling, Thomas C. 1966. *Arms and Influence.* New Haven: Yale University Press.

Scheve, Kenneth, and David Stasavage. 2012. "Democracy, War, and Wealth: Evidence of Two Centuries of Inheritance Taxation." *American Political Science Review* 106 (1): 81–102.

——— 2016. *Taxing the Rich: A History of Fiscal Fairness in the United States and Europe.* Princeton, Nj: Princeton University Press.

Schickler, Eric. 2001. *Disjointed Pluralism: Institutional Innovation and the Development of the U.S. Congress.* Princeton, NJ: Princeton University Press.

Schneider, Irene. 2006. *The Petitioning System in Iran: State, Society and Power Relations in the Late 19th Century.* Wiesbaden: Harrassowitz.

Schoenblum, Jeffrey A. 1999. "The Role of Legal Doctrine in the Decline of the Islamic Waqf: A Comparison with the Trust." *Vanderbilt Journal of Transnational Law* 32 (4): 1191–1227.

Schück, Herman. 1987. "Sweden's Early Parliamentary Institutions from the Thirteenth Century to 1611." In *The Riksdag: A History of the Swedish Parliament,* ed. M. F. Metcalf and H. Schück, 5–60. New York: St. Martin's Press.

——— 2003a. "The Political System (1319–1520)." In *The Norwegian Kingdom: Succession Disputes and Consolidation,* ed. K. Helle, 679–709. Cambridge: Cambridge University Press.

——— 2003b. "Sweden under the Dynasty of the Folkungs." In *The Norwegian Kingdom: Succession Disputes and Consolidation,* ed. K. Helle, 392–410. Cambridge: Cambridge University Press.

Schulze, Winfried. 1986. "Majority Decision in the Imperial Diets of the Sixteenth and Seventeenth Centuries." *The Journal of Modern History* 58: S46–S63.

Schumpeter, Joseph Alois. [1918]1991. "The Crisis of the Tax State." In *The Economics and Sociology of Capitalism*, ed. R. Swedberg, 99–140. Princeton, NJ: Princeton University Press.

Scott, James C. 1985. *Weapons of the Weak: Everyday Forms of Peasant Resistance.* New Haven: Yale University Press.

    1998. *Seeing Like a State: How Certain Schemes to Improve the Human Condition Have Failed.* New Haven: Yale University Press.

Scott, Tom. 2012. *The City-State in Europe, 1000–1600: Hinterland, Territory, Region.* Oxford: Oxford University Press.

Searle, Eleanor. 1988. *Predatory Kinship and the Creation of Norman Power, 840–1066.* Berkeley: University of California Press.

Seawright, Jason. 2002. "Testing for Necessary and/or Sufficient Causation: Which Cases Are Relevant?" *Political Analysis* 10 (2): 178–93.

Shatzmiller, Maya. 2001. "Islamic Institutions and Property Rights: The Case of the 'Public Good' Waqf." *Journal of the Economic and Social History of the Orient* 44 (1): 44–74.

Shaw, Denis J. B. 2006. "Towns and Commerce." In *The Cambridge History of Russia*, ed. M. Perrie, 298–316. Cambridge: Cambridge University Press.

Shennan, J. H. 1998. *The Parlement of Paris*, 2nd ed. Phoenix Mill: Sutton.

Shepsle, Kenneth A. 1989. "Studying Institutions: Some Lessons from the Rational Choice Approach." *Journal of Theoretical Politics* 1 (2): 131–47.

Shneidman, J. Lee. 1970. *The Rise of the Aragonese-Catalan Empire, 1200–1350.* Vol. 1. New York: New York University Press.

Simpson, A. W. B. 1986. *A History of the Land Law*, 2nd ed. Oxford: Clarendon Press.

Skinner, Quentin. 1978. *The Foundations of Modern Political Thought.* Vol. II: *The Age of Reformation.* Cambridge: Cambridge University Press.

Skocpol, Theda. 1979. *States and Social Revolutions: A Comparative Analysis of France, Russia, and China.* Cambridge: Cambridge University Press.

    1992. *Protecting Soldiers and Mothers: The Political Origins of Social Policy in the United States.* Cambridge, MA: Belknap Press of Harvard University Press.

Skocpol, Theda, and Vanessa Williamson. 2016. *The Tea Party and the Remaking of Republican Conservatism.* New York: Oxford University Press.

Skovgaard-Petersen, Inge. 2003. "The Danish Kingdom: Consolidation and Disintegration." In *The Cambridge History of Scandinavia*, ed. K. Helle, 353–68. Cambridge: Cambridge University Press.

Skwarczyński, P. 1956. "The Problem of Feudalism in Poland up to the Beginning of the 16th Century." *The Slavonic and East European Review* 34 (83): 292–310.

Slater, Dan. 2010. *Ordering Power: Contentious Politics and Authoritarian Leviathans in Southeast Asia.* Cambridge: Cambridge University Press.

Slater, Dan, and Erica Simmons. 2010. "Informative Regress: Critical Antecedents in Comparative Politics." *Comparative Political Studies* 43 (9): 886–917.

Slater, Dan, Benjamin Smith, and Gautam Nair. 2014. "Economic Origins of Democratic Breakdown? The Redistributive Model and the Postcolonial State." *Perspectives on Politics* 12 (2): 353–74.

Small, C. M. 1977. "Appeals from the Duchy of Burgundy to the Parlement of Paris in the Early 14th Century." *Mediaeval Studies* 39: 350–68.

Small, Graeme. 2009. *Late Medieval France*. Basingstoke: Palgrave Macmillan.

Smith, Adam. [1776] 1981a. *An Inquiry into the Nature and Causes of the Wealth of Nations*. Vol. I. Indianapolis: Liberty Classics.

[1776] 1981b. *An Inquiry into the Nature and Causes of the Wealth of Nations*. Vol. II. Indianapolis: Liberty Classics.

Smith, Joshua Toulmin. 1850. *Parallels between the Constitution and Constitutional History of England and Hungary*, 2nd ed. Boston: Ticknor Reed and Fields.

Snow, Vernon F. 1963. "The Evolution of Proctorial Representation in Medieval England." *The American Journal of Legal History* 7 (4): 319–39.

Sobroqués, Santiago. 1957. *Historia Social y Economica de España y América*. Vol. 2: *Patriciado Urbano; Reyes Catolicos; Descubrimiento de America*. Barcelona: Editorial Teide.

Soifer, Hillel. 2013. "State Power and the Economic Origins of Democracy." *Studies in Comparative International Development* 48 (1): 1–22.

Soifer, Hillel, and Matthias vom Hau. 2008. "Unpacking the Strength of the State: The Utility of State Infrastructural Power." *Studies in Comparative International Development* 43 (3): 219–30.

Somers, Margaret R. 1993. "Citizenship and the Place of the Public Sphere: Law, Community, and Political Culture in the Transition to Democracy." *American Sociological Review* 58 (5): 587–620.

Soule, Claude. 1968. *Les États Généraux de France (1302–1789): Étude Historique, Comparative et Doctrinale*. Heule.

Southern, R. W. 1970. *Medieval Humanism and Other Studies*. Oxford: Blackwell.

Spencer, Andrew M. 2008. "Royal Patronage and the Earls in the Reign of Edward I." *History* 93 (1): 20–46.

2014. *Nobility and Kingship in Medieval England: The Earls and Edward I, 1272–1307*. Cambridge: Cambridge University Press.

Sprankling, John G. 2017. *Understanding Property Law*. Durham, NC: Carolina Academic Press.

Spruyt, Hendrik. 1994. *The Sovereign State and Its Competitors: An Analysis of Systems Change*. Princeton, NJ: Princeton University Press.

Spufford, Peter. 1988. *Money and Its Use in Medieval Europe*. Cambridge: Cambridge University Press.

1996. "Currency Exchanges, Medieval and Early Modern Data Bank." www2 .scc.rutgers.edu/memdb/search_form_spuf.php.

Stacey, Robert C. 1995. "Jewish Lending and the Medieval English Economy." In *A Commercialising Economy: England 1086 to c. 1300*, ed. R. H. Britnell and B. M. S. Campbell, 78–101. Manchester: Manchester University Press.

1997. "Parliamentary Negotiation and the Expulsion of the Jews from England." *Thirteenth Century England* 6: 77–101.

Stasavage, David. 2003. *Public Debt and the Birth of the Democratic State: France and Great Britain, 1688–1789*. Cambridge: Cambridge University Press.

2007a. "Cities, Constitutions, and Sovereign Borrowing in Europe, 1274–1785." *International Organization* 61 (3): 489–525.

2007b. "Partisan Politics and Public Debt: The Importance of the 'Whig Supremacy' for Britain's Financial Revolution." *European Review of Economic History* 11 (1): 123–53.

2010. "When Distance Mattered: Geographic Scale and the Development of European Representative Assemblies." *American Political Science Review* 104 (4): 625–43.

2011. *States of Credit: Size, Power, and the Development of European Polities.* Princeton, NJ: Princeton University Press.

2014. "Was Weber Right? The Role of Urban Autonomy in Europe's Rise." *American Political Science Review* 108 (2): 337–54.

The Statutes of the Realm. 1810. Vol. I. London: Record Commission.

Steel, Anthony Bedford. 1954. *The Receipt of the Exchequer, 1377–1485.* Cambridge: The University Press.

Steinberg, Marc W. 2016. *England's Great Transformation: Law, Labor, and the Industrial Revolution.* Chicago: University of Chicago Press.

Stevenson, E. R. 1940. "The Escheator." In *The English Government at Work, 1327–1336,* ed. W. A. Morris and J. R. Strayer, 109–67. Cambridge, MA: The Medieval Academy of America.

Stokes, H. P. 1915. "The Relationship between the Jews and the Royal Family of England in the Thirteenth Century." *Transactions of the Jewish Historical Society of England* 8: 153–70.

Stone Sweet, Alec. 2000. *Governing with Judges: Constitutional Politics in Europe.* Oxford: Oxford University Press.

Strayer, Joseph Reese. 1969. "Normandy and Languedoc." *Speculum: A Journal of Medieval Studies* 44 (1): 1–12.

1970a. *Les Gens de Justice du Languedoc Sous Philippe Le Bel.* Toulouse: Association Marc Bloch.

1970b. *On the Medieval Origins of the Modern State.* Princeton, NJ: Princeton University Press.

1980. *The Reign of Philip the Fair.* Princeton, NJ: Princeton University Press.

Strayer, Joseph Reese, and Charles Holt Taylor. 1939. *Studies in Early French Taxation.* Cambridge, MA: Harvard University Press.

Stubbs, William. 1878. *The Constitutional History of England in Its Origin and Development.* Vol. III. Oxford: Clarendon Press.

1880. *The Constitutional History of England in Its Origin and Development,* 3rd ed. Vol. II. Oxford: Clarendon Press.

1896. *The Constitutional History of England in Its Origin and Development,* 4th ed. Vol. II. Oxford: Clarendon Press.

1913. *Select Charters and Other Illustrations of English Constitutional History, from the Earliest Times to the Reign of Edward the First,* 9th ed. Oxford: Clarendon Press.

Subhan, Abdus. 2012. *Kharādj.* Brill Online. http://referenceworks.brillonline.com /entries/encyclopaedia-of-islam-2.

Summerhill, William R. 2008. "Fiscal Bargains, Political Institutions, and Economic Performance." *Hispanic American Historical Review* 88 (2): 219–33.

Sussman, Nathan. 1992. "Mints and Debasements: Monetary Policy in France During the Second Phase of the Hundred Years War: 1400–1425." *The Journal of Economic History* 52 (2): 452–54.

Svolik, Milan W. 2012. *The Politics of Authoritarian Rule*. Cambridge: Cambridge University Press.

Tabacco, Giovanni. 1989. *The Struggle for Power in Medieval Italy: Structures of Political Rule*. Cambridge: Cambridge University Press.

Tait, James. 1914. "Review of *Essai sur les Origines de la Chambre des Communes* by D. Pasquet." *English Historical Review* 29 (116): 750–54.

Takeuchi, Hiroki. 2014. *Tax Reform in Rural China: Revenue, Resistance, and Authoritarian Rule*. New York: Cambridge University Press.

Taylor, Brian D. 2003. *Politics and the Russian Army: Civil–Military Relations, 1689–2000*. Cambridge: Cambridge University Press.

Taylor, Charles Holt. 1938. "An Assembly of French Towns in March 1318." *Speculum: A Journal of Medieval Studies* 13 (3): 295–303.

1939. "Assemblies of Towns and War Subsidy, 1318–1319." In *Studies in Early French Taxation*, 109–200. Cambridge, MA: Harvard University Press.

1954. "The Composition of Baronial Assemblies in France, 1315–1320." *Speculum: A Journal of Medieval Studies* 29 (2): 433–59.

1968. "French Assemblies and Subsidy in 1321." *Speculum: A Journal of Medieval Studies* 43 (2): 217–44.

TeBrake, William H. 2002. "Taming the Waterwolf: Hydraulic Engineering and Water Management in the Netherlands During the Middle Ages." *Technology and Culture* 43 (3): 475–99.

Teele, Dawn Langan. 2014. "Ordinary Democratization: The Electoral Strategy That Won British Women the Vote." *Politics & Society* 42 (4): 537–61.

Teschke, Benno. 2003. *The Myth of 1648: Class, Geopolitics and the Making of Modern International Relations*. London: Verso.

Texier, Ernest. 1905. *Etude sur la Cour Ducale et les Origines du Parlament de Bretagne*. Rennes: Librairie J. Plihon & L. Hommay.

Tezcan, Baki. 2010. *The Second Ottoman Empire: Political and Social Transformation in the Early Modern World*. Cambridge: Cambridge University Press.

Thelen, Kathleen. 2003. "How Institutions Evolve: Insights from Comparative-Historical Analysis." In *Comparative Historical Analysis in the Social Sciences*, ed. J. Mahoney and D. Rueschemeyer, 208–40. Cambridge: Cambridge University Press.

Thierry, Augustin. 1853. *Essai sur L'histoire de la Formation et des Progrès du Tiers État*. Paris: Furne.

Thomas, Hugh M. 2014. *The Secular Clergy in England, 1066–1216*. Oxford: Oxford University Press.

Thompson, Guy Llewelyn. 1991. *Paris and Its People under English Rule: The Anglo-Burgundian Regime, 1420–1436*. Oxford: Clarendon Press.

Thompson, I. A. A. 1976. *War and Government in Habsburg Spain, 1560–1620*. London: Athlone Press.

Tierney, Brian. 1983. "The Idea of Representation in the Medieval Councils of the West." *Concilium* 19: 25–30.

1995. "Freedom and the Medieval Church." In *The Origins of Modern Freedom in the West*, ed. R. W. Davis, 64–100. Stanford, CA: Stanford University Press.

Tilly, Charles, ed. 1975. *The Formation of National States in Western Europe.* Princeton, NJ: Princeton University Press.

   1990. *Coercion, Capital, and European States, AD 990–1990.* Cambridge: Blackwell.

   2009. "Extraction and Democracy." In *The New Fiscal Sociology: Taxation in Comparative and Historical Perspective,* ed. I. W. Martin, A. K. Mehrotra, and M. Prasad, 173–82. Cambridge: Cambridge University Press.

Timmons, Jeffrey F. 2005. "The Fiscal Contract: States, Taxes, and Public Services." *World Politics* 57 (4): 530–67.

   2010. "Taxation and Representation in Recent History." *The Journal of Politics* 72 (1): 191–208.

Tocqueville, Alexis de. 2011. *De Tocqueville: The Ancien Régime and the French Revolution.* Cambridge: Cambridge University Press.

Tout, T. F. 1920. *Chapters in the Administrative History of Medieval England.* Vol. 2. Manchester: Manchester University Press.

Tracy, James D. 1990. *Holland under Habsburg Rule, 1506–1566: The Formation of a Body Politic.* Berkeley: University of California Press.

Treisman, Daniel. 2007. *The Architecture of Government: Rethinking Political Decentralization.* Cambridge: Cambridge University Press.

   2018. *The New Autocracy: Information, Politics, and Policy in Putin's Russia.* Washington, DC: Brookings Institution.

Troianovski, Anton. 2020. "As Local Health Systems Buckle, Russia's Oligarchs Take Charge." *New York Times,* May 7.

Tsounta, Evridiki, and Anayochukwu I. Osueke. 2014. "What Is Behind Latin America's Declining Income Inequality?" Working Paper 14/124. Washington, DC: International Monetary Fund.

Turner, Ralph V. 1968. "The Origins of the Medieval English Jury: Frankish, English, or Scandinavian?" *Journal of British Studies* 7 (2): 1–10.

   1977. "The Origins of Common Pleas and King's Bench." *The American Journal of Legal History* 21 (3): 238–54.

   1985. *The English Judiciary in the Age of Glanvill and Bracton, c. 1176–1239.* Cambridge: Cambridge University Press.

   2003. *Magna Carta: Through the Ages.* Harlow: Pearson.

Tyan, Emile. 1955. "Judicial Organization." In *Law in the Middle East,* ed. M. Khadduri and H. J. Liebesny, 236–78. Washington, DC: Middle East Institute.

Ulph, Owen. 1951. "The Mandate System and Representation to the Estates General under the Old Regime." *The Journal of Modern History* 23 (3): 225–31.

Unwin, George. 1918a. "The Estate of Merchants, 1336–65." In *Finance and Trade under Edward III,* 179–255. Manchester: Manchester University Press.

   1918b. *Finance and Trade under Edward III.* Manchester: Manchester University Press.

Uruszczak, Wacław. 1997. "Constitutional Devices Implementing State Power in Poland, 1300–1700." In *Legislation and Justice,* ed. A. Padoa Schioppa, 175–96. Oxford: Clarendon Press.

Vahtola, Jouko. 2003. "Population and Settlement." In *The Cambridge History of Scandinavia*, ed. K. Helle, 559–80. Cambridge: Cambridge University Press.

Vale, M. G. A. 2001. *The Princely Court: Medieval Courts and Culture in North-West Europe, 1270–1380*. Oxford: Oxford University Press.

Vallerani, Massimo, and Sarah Rubin Blanshei. 2012. *Medieval Public Justice*. Washington, DC: Catholic University of America Press.

van Bavel, Bas J. P. 2008. "The Organization and Rise of Land and Lease Markets in Northwestern Europe and Italy, c. 1000–1800." *Continuity and Change* 23 (Special Issue): 13–53.

2010. "The Medieval Origins of Capitalism in the Netherlands." *Bijdragen en Mededelingen voor de Geschiedenis der Nederlanden* 125: 45–80.

2016. *The Invisible Hand? How Market Economies Have Emerged and Declined since AD 500*. Oxford: Oxford University Press.

van Bavel, Bas J. P., Jessica Dijkman, Erika Kuijpers, and Jaco Zuijderduijn. 2012. "The Organisation of Markets as a Key Factor in the Rise of Holland from the Fourteenth to the Sixteenth Century: A Test Case for an Institutional Approach." *Continuity and Change* 27 (3): 347–78.

van Bavel, Bas J. P., and Phillipp R. Schofield. 2008. *The Development of Leasehold in Northwestern Europe, c. 1200–1600*. Turnhout: Brepols.

van Bochove, Christiaan, Heidi Deneweth, and Jaco Zuijderduijn. 2015. "Real Estate and Mortgage Finance in England and the Low Countries, 1300–1800." *Continuity and Change* 30 (1): 9–38.

van Caenegem, R. C. ed. 1966. *Les Arrêts et Jugés du Parlement de Paris Sur Appels Flamands: Conservés dans les Registres du Parlement*. Bruxelles: S.C.T.

1988. *The Birth of the English Common Law*, 2nd ed. Cambridge: Cambridge University Press.

van Werveke, H. 1965. "The Rise of Towns." In *The Cambridge Economic History of Europe*, ed. M. M. Postan, E. E. Rich, and E. Miller, 3–41. Cambridge: Cambridge University Press.

van Zanden, Jan Luiten. 2002. "The 'Revolt of the Early Modernists' and the 'First Modern Economy': An Assessment." *The Economic History Review* 55 (4): 619–41.

van Zanden, Jan Luiten, Eltjo Buringh, and Maarten Bosker. 2012. "The Rise and Decline of European Parliaments, 1188–1789." *The Economic History Review* 65 (3): 835–61.

Vassberg, D. E. 1984. *Land and Society in Golden Age Castile*. Cambridge: Cambridge University Press.

Verbruggen, J. F. 1997. *The Art of Warfare in Western Europe during the Middle Ages: From the Eighth Century to 1340*, 2nd ed. Woodbridge: Boydell Press.

Verhulst, Adriaan. 1999. *The Rise of Cities in North-West Europe*. Cambridge: Cambridge University Press.

Vicens Vives, Jaime. 1969. *An Economic History of Spain*. Princeton, NJ: Princeton University Press.

Vikør, Knut S. 2005. *Between God and the Sultan: A History of Islamic Law*. Oxford: Oxford University Press.

Vile, M. J. C. 1967. *Constitutionalism and the Separation of Powers*. Oxford: Clarendon Press.

Villers, Robert. 1984. "Réflexions sur les Premiers États Generaux de France au Début du XIVe Siècle." *Parliaments, Estates and Representation* 4 (2): 93–97.

Vincent, Nicholas. 2004a. "Edmund of Almain, Second Earl of Cornwall (1249–1300)." *Oxford Dictionary of National Biography.* Oxford University Press. www.oxforddnb.com/view/article/8505.

2004b. "Richard, First Earl of Cornwall and King of Germany (1209–1272)." *Oxford Dictionary of National Biography.* Oxford University Press. www .oxforddnb.com/view/article/8505.

Viollet, Paul. 1866. "Élections des Députés aux États-Généraux Réunis à Tours en 1464 et 1484." *Bibliothèque de l'école des chartes* 6 (2): 22–58.

von Oer, Rudolfine Freiin. 1983. "Quod Omnes Tangit as Legal and Political Argument: Germany, Late Sixteenth Century." *Parliaments, Estates and Representation* 3 (1): 1–6.

Vryonis, Speros, Jr. 1963. "Byzantine Δημοκρατία and the Guilds in the Eleventh Century." *Dumbarton Oaks Papers* 17: 287–314.

Waley, Daniel Philip. 2010. "The Use of Sortition in Appointments in the Italian Communes." In *Communes and Despots in Medieval and Renaissance Italy,* ed. J. E. Law and B. Paton, 27–33. Farnham: Ashgate.

Waley, Daniel Philip, and Trevor Dean. 2010. *The Italian City-Republics,* 4th ed. London: Longman.

Walker, J. T. 2010. "National Income in Domesday England." Unpublished manuscript, University of Reading.

Ward, J. P. 2001. "The Cities and States of Holland (1506–1515): A Participative System of Government under Strain." Unpublished PhD thesis, University of Leiden.

Warren, W. L. 1987. *The Governance of Norman and Angevin England 1086–1272.* Stanford, CA: Stanford University Press.

Waterbury, John. 1994. "Democracy without Democrats? The Potential for Political Liberalization in the Middle East." In *Democracy without Democrats? The Renewal of Politics in the Muslim World,* ed. G. Salame, 23–47. New York: I. B. Tauris.

Waugh, Scott L. 1983. "Reluctant Knights and Jurors: Respites, Exemptions, and Public Obligations in the Reign of Henry III." *Speculum: A Journal of Medieval Studies* 58 (4): 937–86.

1986. "Tenure to Contract: Lordship and Clientage in Thirteenth-Century England." *The English Historical Review* 101 (401): 811–39.

1988. *The Lordship of England: Royal Wardships and Marriages in English Society and Politics, 1217–1327.* Princeton, NJ: Princeton University Press.

Webb, Sidney, and Beatrice Webb. 1906. *English Local Government from the Revolution to the Municipal Corporations Act: The Parish and the County.* Vol. 1. London: Longmans, Green and Co.

1908. *English Local Government from the Revolution to the Municipal Corporations Act: The Manor and the Borough.* Vol. 2. London: Longmans, Green and Co.

Weber, Max. 1946. "The Social Psychology of World Religions." In *From Max Weber: Essays in Sociology,* ed. H. H. Gerth and C. W. Mills, 267–301. New York: Oxford University Press.

1947. *The Theory of Social and Economic Organization.* Glencoe, IL: Free Press.

1958. *The City*. Glencoe, IL: Free Press.

1978. *Economy and Society*, ed. G. Roth and C, Wittich. Berkeley: University of California Press.

Weickhardt, George G. 1992. "Due Process and Equal Justice in the Muscovite Codes." *Russian Review* 51 (4): 463–80.

1993. "The Pre-Petrine Law of Property." *Slavic Review* 52 (4): 663–79.

1994. "Was There Private Property in Muscovite Russia?" *Slavic Review* 53 (2): 531–38.

Weigel, Jonathan L. 2020. "The Participation Dividend of Taxation: How Citizens in Congo Engage More with the State When It Tries to Tax Them." *The Quarterly Journal of Economics* 135 (4): 1849–1903.

Weinbaum, Martin. 1937. *The Incorporation of Boroughs*. Manchester: Manchester University Press.

Weingast, Barry R. 1995. "The Economic Role of Political Institutions: Market-Preserving Federalism and Economic Development." *Journal of Law, Economics, & Organization* 11 (1): 1–31.

White, Albert Beebe. 1933. *Self-Government at the King's Command*. Minneapolis: University of Minnesota Press.

Wickham, Chris. 1997. "Justice in the Kingdom of Italy in the Eleventh Century." *Settimane di studio* 44: 179–255.

2003. *Courts and Conflict in Twelfth-Century Tuscany*. Oxford: Oxford University Press.

2014. "The 'Feudal Revolution' and the Origins of Italian City Communes." *Transactions of the Royal Historical Society (Sixth Series)* 24: 29–55.

2015. *Sleepwalking into a New World: The Emergence of Italian City Communes in the Twelfth Century*. Princeton, NJ: Princeton University Press.

Wilkinson, Bertie. 1937. *Studies in the Constitutional History of the Thirteenth and Fourteenth Centuries*. Manchester: Manchester University Press.

1977. *The Later Middle Ages in England, 1216–1485*. London: Longman.

Willard, James Field. 1933. "Taxation Boroughs and Parliamentary Boroughs, 1294–1336." In *Historical Essays in Honour of James Tait*, ed. J. G. Edwards, V. H. Galbraith, and E. F. Jacob, 417–35. London: Butler & Tanner.

1934. *Parliamentary Taxes on Personal Property, 1290 to 1334: A Study in Mediaeval English Financial Administration*. Cambridge, MA: Mediaeval Academy of America.

Willard, James Field, and William Alfred Morris, eds. 1940. *The English Government at Work, 1327–1336*. Vol. I: *Central and Prerogative Administration*. Cambridge, MA: The Medieval Academy of America.

Willard, James Field, William Alfred Morris, and William H. Dunham, eds. 1940. *The English Government at Work, 1327–1336*. Vol. III: *Local Administration and Justice*. Cambridge, MA: The Medieval Academy of America.

Willard, James Field, and Joseph R. Strayer, eds. 1947. *The English Government at Work, 1327–1336*. Vol. II: *Fiscal Administration*. Cambridge, MA: The Medieval Academy of America.

Williamson, Oliver E. 1985. *The Economic Institutions of Capitalism: Firms, Markets, Relational Contracting*. New York: Free Press.

Witt, Ronald G. 2012. *The Two Latin Cultures and the Foundation of Renaissance Humanism in Medieval Italy*. Cambridge: Cambridge University Press.

Wolfe, Martin. 1972. *The Fiscal System of Renaissance France*. New Haven: Yale University Press.

Wolffe, Bertram Percy. 1971. *The Royal Demesne in English History: The Crown Estate in the Governance of the Realm from the Conquest to 1509*. London: George Allen & Unwin.

Wong, Roy Bin. 1997. *China Transformed: Historical Change and the Limits of European Experience*. Ithaca, NY: Cornell University Press.

Wood, Ellen Meiksins. 2002. *The Origin of Capitalism: A Longer View*. London: Verso.

Wood, Gordon S. 1969. *The Creation of the American Republic, 1776–1787*. Chapel Hill, NC: University of North Carolina Press.

Worby, Sam. 2010. *Law and Kinship in Thirteenth-Century England*. Woodbridge: Boydell & Brewer.

World Bank. 1975. *Land Reform Sector Policy Paper*. Washington, DC: World Bank.

Wrigley, E. A., R. S. Davies, J. E. Oeppen, and R. S. Schofield. 1997. *English Population History from Family Reconstitution, 1580–1837*. Cambridge: Cambridge University Press.

Würgler, Andreas. 2008. "'The League of the Discordant Members' or How the Old Swiss Confederation Operated and How It Managed to Survive for So Long." In *The Republican Alternative*, ed. A. Holenstein, T. Maissen, and M. Prak, 29–50. Amsterdam: Amsterdam University Press.

   2014. "Diète Fédérale." In *Dictionnaire Historique de la Suisse*: https://hls-dhs-dss.ch/fr/articles/010076/2014-09-25/.

Wyczański, Andrzej. 1982. "The Problem of Authority in Sixteenth Century Poland: An Essay in Reinterpretation." In *A Republic of Nobles: Studies in Polish History to 1864*, ed. J. K. Fedorowicz, M. Bogucka, and H. Samsonowicz, 91–108. Cambridge: Cambridge University Press.

Yi, Eunjeong. 2004. *Guild Dynamics in Seventeenth-Century Istanbul: Fluidity and Leverage*. Leiden: Brill.

Youings, Joyce A. 1971. *The Dissolution of the Monasteries*. London: Allen & Unwin.

Zaret, David. 2000. *Origins of Democratic Culture: Printing, Petitions, and the Public Sphere in Early-Modern England*. Princeton, NJ: Princeton University Press.

Zlotnik, Marc D. 1979. "Muscovite Fiscal Policy: 1462–1584." *Russian History* 6 (1): 243–58.

Zolberg, Aristide R. 1969. *One-Party Government in the Ivory Coast*. Princeton, NJ: Princeton University Press.

   1980. "Strategic Interactions and the Formation of Modern States: France and England." *International Social Science Journal* 32 (4): 687–716.

Zuijderduijn, Jaco. 2010. "The Emergence of Provincial Debt in the County of Holland (Thirteenth–Sixteenth Centuries)." *European Review of Economic History* 14 (3): 335–59.

   2014. "On the Home Court Advantage: Participation of Locals and Non-Residents in a Village Law Court in Sixteenth-Century Holland." *Continuity and change* 29 (1): 19–48.

Index

Made in United States
North Haven, CT
19 October 2023

42938684R00220